lonely planet

VOLUNTEER

A TRAVELLER'S GUIDE TO MAKING A DIFFERENCE AROUND THE WORLD

MELBOURNE | OAKLAND | LONDON

CONTENTS

AUTHORS

CHARLOTTE HINDLE

Charlotte Hindle was coordinating author for this book, and also wrote the following chapters: 'International Volunteering – An Overview', 'Choosing Your Volunteer Experience', 'The Practicalities' and 'Coming Home'.

During her gap year Charlotte travelled overland from England to Australia. In Melbourne, she temped as a foot courier before landing a job at Lonely Planet (LP). She worked at LP's Head Office for three years. In 1991 she returned to England to set up LP's UK office which she ran until June 2002. She then took a mini-career break to spend the summer with her growing family and to consider more flexible, child-friendly work options. Lonely Planet then approached her to contribute to the following books: *The Gap Year Book; The Career Break Book;* and *The Travel Writing Book.* When Charlotte helped update the first edition of *The Gap Year Book* she re-wrote the 'Volunteering & Conservation' chapter. Since then, Charlotte has been fascinated by this sector and has written newspaper and travel articles on it and organised debates and talks on the subject. Charlotte is waiting for her two young daughters to be old enough to volunteer with her: they plan to work with street children in Latin America.

Charlotte is a freelance travel journalist and photographer. Over the years she has written for the following LP guides: *Australia, Mediterranean Europe, Walking in Britain, England* and *Britain* and her photographs appear in many others. She also writes for *Wanderlust* magazine and the *Independent* newspaper.

RACHEL COLLINSON

Rachel Collinson wrote the 'Do-it-Yourself Volunteer Placements' chapter.

While studying at university, Rachel taught English in Vienna, worked as a counsellor on a children's summer camp in the USA and volunteered on outdoor residentials. So, when she embarked on a career break after seven years in international marketing, it was a natural choice for her to spend a period doing volunteer work with children. In Ecuador she took on various roles in a home for street children and looked after special-needs babies in an orphanage. Other volunteering stints included visiting foreign nationals imprisoned for drug trafficking and writing a marketing plan for the director of a remote national park in Bolivia. Rachel's sideline in travel writing began in Australia during her career break.

MIKE RICHARD

Mike Richard wrote the sections of all chapters containing information for American volunteers.

Born and raised in the wilds of northern New England, Mike scribed his way through two university history departments before succumbing to global wanderlust. He has worked and played in Honolulu, studied Japanese in Hakodate, and taught English in Shanghai. Most recently, he served as a TEFL Volunteer with the US Peace Corps in Romania. When he's not writing for Lonely Planet or toiling away in a Federal Government cubicle, he can be found sampling the culture of Washington, DC.

NATE CAVALIERI

Nate Cavalieri wrote the 'Organised Volunteer Programmes' chapter.

Nate's entrée into the world of international volunteering happened in 2002 when he was a student at the Pop Wuj School in Quezaltenango, Guatemala and he volunteered crack data entry skills to assist the deployment of American Red Cross volunteers to the Gulf Coast in 2005. Nate has volunteered and travelled extensively throughout Europe, Central and North America, sometimes working as a musician and correspondent to various publications including the *Village Voice*, *Metro Times* and *Spin*. This is his first title with Lonely Planet. He currently resides in Sacramento, California, where he works as a freelance writer.

KORINA MILLER

Korina wrote 'Structured & Self-Funding Volunteer Programmes', 'Religious Organisations' and 'Start Your Own Charitable Project'.

Korina grew up on Vancouver Island. She packed her bags at 18 and hasn't quite unpacked since. En route she volunteered in India, in rural Uttar Pradesh and with remote tribal communities in Jharkhand. She also worked with minorities in southwest China on a sustainable tourism development project; ran an Asian arts charity in Vancouver; and managed an intercultural arts charity in London. These days she's back in Vancouver, working as a children's writing coach with a local charity. Korina studied intercultural communications and →

← development at Vancouver's Simon Fraser University and has an MA in migration studies from Sussex University. She's been an author with Lonely Planet since 1999, writing on everything from bears in the Canadian Rockies to street snacks in Beijing.

SARAH WINTLE

Sarah Wintle wrote the 'Tying Up Loose Ends' chapter and the sections of all chapters containing information for Australasian volunteers.

Sarah traded her backpack for a suitcase marked 'Bangkok' as an Australian Youth Ambassador for Development (AYAD) in 2005 and returned one year later loaded with memories. She can take or leave the title, but the programme gave her the chance to spread her wings in Asia while she worked for a regional conservation organisation. When she wasn't putting together a brochure, writing communication strategies or editing in Laos, she was chasing the best *khâo nĭaw má-mûang* (mango and sticky rice) in town, or travelling. She says her time away gave her a sense of *ìm jai* (full heart). Sarah has been writing for Lonely Planet since 2004 and has contributed to *Australia & New Zealand on a Shoestring* and *South East Asia on a Shoestring* among other titles.

EXPERT ADVISORS

KATHERINE TUBB

Katherine is the founder of 2Way Development (www.2waydev elopment.com), an international volunteer agency that places individual volunteers into development NGOs in Africa, Latin America and Asia. Katherine was a volunteer herself with VSO in Nepal where she worked for an environmental NGO. Katherine started her career working in the tourism industry, primarily as a researcher, and published work relating to ecotourism and sustainable tourism. She has a masters in development studies from the London School of Economics.

PAUL GOODYER

Paul Goodyer, CEO of Nomad Travel Stores and Travel Clinics (www .nomadtravel.co.uk), started travelling when he was 17. Following a few bouts of ill health and disasters with dodgy travel equipment, he set up Nomad in 1990. With five outlets combining travel clinics with travel gear shops, Paul and his wife, Cathy, his brother, Professor Larry Goodyer, and his staff, work hard to prepare people for travel. In 2002 Paul and Cathy set up a charitable project called Karmi Farm (http://www.nomadtravel.co.uk/t-karmifarmcharityproject.aspx) – a medical clinic for the local hill farmers of Darjeeling and Sikkim province (see p254 for a full case study). Paul advised on the 'What To Take' and 'Health & Hygiene' sections of this book.

ANTHONY LUNCH

 Anthony taught in The Gambia as a volunteer with VSO in the 1960s. He went to Oxford University and then joined Unilever, where he worked as a marketing manager in Belgium and UK.

Later he became MD of the French multinational, Phildar UK, and then held senior positions in corporate finance and international trade development.

He was appointed to the VSO Executive Council for seven years and in 1990 visited Nepal, where his son was doing a gap year. He became deeply involved with the village of Sermathang, helping build a larger school and starting a volunteer programme. In 2001, he set up MondoChallenge (www.mondochallenge.org), focussing on career breakers and older volunteers, and expanding into countries throughout Asia, Africa and South America.

DR KATE SIMPSON

 Dr Kate Simpson has spent over six years researching and working in the international volunteering industry. She has written extensively about gap years and international volunteering and has completed a PhD on these subjects at the University of Newcastle upon Tyne. Currently, she works with volunteers and the international volunteering industry to improve practices within this sector. For more information about the ethics of international volunteering, visit www.ethicalvolunteering.org.

Monitoring cheetahs in the
Namibian savannah with
Biosphere Expeditions

01 International Volunteering: an Overview

'Time is money.' How often have you heard that said? Perhaps it came to mind as you spent yet another late night in the office trying to meet a deadline; or perhaps you work in a profession where your time is billed in blocks of 15 minutes. Maybe you've just retired, having worked hard for years in return for an annual salary. Unless you're a professional parent, the chances are you're used to being paid for the work you do. And, whatever your circumstances, you probably consider your time a precious commodity.

So, why give your time for free? Or, as is the case with the majority of international volunteering opportunities, why pay for the privilege of working for nothing? This chapter offers a broad cross-section of answers to these questions.

'Think globally, act locally' was a phrase coined in 1972 by René Dubos, an adviser to the UN Conference on the Human Environment. Although the phrase initially referred to looking after our environment, it touched a global nerve and came to mean acting locally in any worthwhile capacity. Then, 12 years later, Bob Geldof and Midge Ure formed Band Aid and challenged the world not only to 'think' globally but 'act' globally as well, and raised money for famine relief in Ethiopia. Whatever you think of this campaign (and subsequent ones such as Make Poverty History), the actions of Geldof and Ure ignited high-level debate about world inequality. The ongoing efforts of many ensure that such imbalances are kept in the global media spotlight.

Buying white wristbands and donating money from the comfort of your lounge room to send abroad is one thing. Actually giving up your time and going to a poorer part of the world to contribute your knowledge, skills or labour is quite another. But this is exactly what an increasing number of people around the globe are choosing to do with their holidays, during gap years, on career breaks or upon retirement.

However, the more popular international volunteering becomes, the more difficult it is to pinpoint where to go, what to do and which organisation you want to volunteer with. For starters, the sheer number of volunteering opportunities today can be overwhelming. Then there's the problem that not all volunteering is good volunteering. There are plenty of volunteer organisations that are not meeting or responding to local needs, not working in proper partnership with host communities and certainly not working towards sustainable solutions. And, let's face it, no-one wants to become that volunteer who has just built a bridge where no bridge was needed.

Volunteering abroad should be the best thing you've ever done, but the onus is on you to act responsibly, do the research and find a volunteer programme that works both for you and for the host community. This book aims to equip you with all the tools to do just that.

One volunteer, Linda Walsh, who worked with street children in Rio de Janeiro for Task Brasil (p170), urges:

Go and volunteer. Love the experience, even when there are times when you feel unappreciated, tired, fed up or lost with the language. No matter what, if you throw yourself wholeheartedly into it you will love it and it will do more for you than you could ever imagine.

As Clodagh O'Brien, who volunteered in Borneo with the Orangutan Foundation UK (p175), succinctly puts it:

Every insect bite, cut, argument and awful bus journey was well worth it.

Why Volunteer?

This is a good question and one you need to think very carefully about. The most common reason to volunteer is the desire to 'give something back'. Vikki Cole, who volunteered on an environmental project with Trekforce (p115) in Borneo, explains:

Without sounding clichéd, I really wanted to be able to look back on my life and to have done something of substance that didn't directly benefit just me.

Jacqueline Hill, who volunteered with Voluntary Service Overseas (VSO, p94) building management capacity with local NGOs in Bangladesh, had similar feelings:

It had been a long-term dream. I had a vague plan that I'd spend the first 20 years of my career earning for myself and the next 20 giving something back.

Wanting to help others, wishing to do good and hoping to make a difference are all important reasons to volunteer. But nine times out of ten, they're not enough to make you to feel that your time was well spent: there need to be other reasons. And, as you can imagine, there are plenty to choose from. Mike Laird, who travelled with the Scientific Exploration Society (p136) to work on scientific, archaeological and community-aid projects in Bolivia, lists a well-balanced mix of altruistic and personal motivations for volunteering:

To see the delight on people's faces when they realise they now have a clean and safe water supply or better school facilities. To know that they will benefit from these for years to come. The personal benefits are almost too many to mention: being exposed to new cultures; seeing new places and sharing in great experiences; making new and lasting friendships and discovering a bit more about myself. That apart, I also got fitter, lost weight and felt terrific when I came home.

Mike picks up on a key point for travellers – volunteering is an excellent way to get under the skin of a country and come to grips with a different culture. The cultural-exchange

Is International Volunteering the New Colonialism?

The question of whether volunteering is the new colonialism gets asked a lot, and the short answers are: 'yes', 'no', 'sometimes' and 'maybe'. International volunteering is part of a long tradition of people from the West setting off to help or change the countries of the Global South (aka the developing world) and have adventures while they do it. Where once these people were missionaries and soldiers, colonialists and explorers, teachers and entrepreneurs – now they are international volunteers.

If volunteers travel in the belief that they have little to learn and a lot to give, then they do risk being little more than 'New Age colonialists'. No-one becomes an international volunteer for purely altruistic reasons: they also do it because it is exciting, because they might learn something, because they want to meet new people who live differently and because, just maybe, they might have something to offer. By acknowledging why you volunteer, you are telling our hosts that they are people you can learn from and with, not that they should be the grateful recipients of your altruism. You ask them to be your teachers, instead of forcing them to be your students.

So, whether international volunteering is the new colonialism or not is, in large part, down to the attitudes of you, the volunteer, and the organisation you go with. If you don't want to be a 21st-century colonialist, rule out organisations that suggest you'll be 'saving the world' or give a patronising image of the developing world. Then question yourself. Be open about why you want to be an international volunteer and what you have to learn from those you visit. Avoiding being patronising will take some effort and research, and will require getting rid of many of the usual preconceptions about the developing world.

For more information, look at the Volunteer Charter at www.volunteeringoptions.org.

Dr Kate Simpson

element of international volunteering is a key part of what both you and your hosts will get out of the whole experience. Plus, you can build volunteering into almost any segment of your travels, whether you decide to arrange it formally or just turn up and find a placement yourself (see p215).

The educational aspect of volunteering is equally crucial. In almost every placement you'll have the opportunity to learn a foreign language or to brush up on one. And many of the new skills you'll acquire or develop can be used back home in your profession. Recognising the that transferable skills can be gained while volunteering, the global management consulting group Accenture was one of the first companies to sign up to VSO's Business Partnership Scheme. Accenture spokesperson Gib Bulloch elaborates:

Volunteering with VSO allows staff to hone their leadership and communication skills. Often working in environments where they need to coach or influence people, they also develop key listening and understanding skills. Plus, volunteering abroad means that staff can add 'overseas work experience' to their CV – so crucial these days if you want to progress within an organisation.

Ben Keedwell, who volunteered with Kathmandu Environmental Education Project (KEEP, p158) developing a visitor and community centre in a national park, agrees wholeheartedly and goes even further:

International volunteering helps to increase understanding of development issues, consolidate practical skills, and gain first-hand experience of working in the field. Volunteers can develop self-confidence, focus their career objectives and show adaptability, self-motivation and dedication. All of these benefits can kick-start a career and can sometimes be more valuable than undergraduate (or even postgraduate) education.

Many volunteers have found that international volunteering has either helped their career or given them the necessary experience to change careers. For instance, Ann Noon wanted to switch from working in tourism to the charity sector. She volunteered as a press and marketing manager for the Inka Porter Project (no longer running), and says:

If I'd not gone to Peru, I almost certainly wouldn't have got the job I have today with Sightsavers International, a charity that works to combat blindness in developing countries. I am convinced that I did the right thing, even though it all seemed like a leap into the unknown at the time.

Similarly, Amanda Allen-Toland, an Australian Youth Ambassador for Development (AYAD, p112) with the Thailand Business Coalition on AIDS in Bangkok, could not have predicted the positive impact her volunteering experience would have on her career. She is now working as a programme manager for the Asia Pacific Business Coalition on HIV/AIDS in Melbourne, Australia. She explains:

It's paid dividends for me. I'm in an area I want to be in with a higher level of responsibility, excellent pay and job satisfaction. It's the icing on the cake. My experience working with TBCA and living in Thailand was so fantastic that even if my next role had been making fruit shakes, I'd do it all over again.

Kinds of International Volunteering

There are thousands of volunteer opportunities around the world and a number of different approaches to getting involved. The rest of this chapter offers an overview of what's out there. Detailed listings of recommended volunteer organisations are provided in Chapters 5 to 8, according to what they offer. If you're after something completely different, read Chapter 10 on how to set up your own grassroots charity.

Areas of Work

What tasks you perform as an international volunteer depends both on what you want to do, and on what is needed by the community or environment where you're going.

Within this framework you've got a number of broad choices, shown in the diagram on p12. The first choice is whether you want to work with people (usually called 'development volunteering') or with the environment and animals (referred to as 'conservation and wildlife volunteering').

Once you've made that basic choice, decide whether you consider yourself a skilled or unskilled volunteer. This is not as straightforward as it sounds. Skilled volunteers are often people such as teachers, accountants, civil engineers or nurses who work in their professions abroad. However, everyone has skills to offer: a parent might be skilled in conflict resolution, or a university graduate in acting and drama. In the final analysis, being skilled or unskilled will not necessarily dictate what area you work in, but it will impact on the level of responsibility you're given.

Whatever you decide, it's wise to be prepared for your role to change or develop. You might apply to do something, then find that something rather different is required of you once you reach your placement.

Development Volunteering

There are nine main areas within the development volunteering sector:

~ **Emergency and relief** An option for highly skilled and experienced volunteers only, this is where doctors, nurses, midwives, psychologists and so on, respond to humanitarian crises, conflicts, wars and natural diasters abroad (see p142). Some volunteers are on 72-hour standby to go anywhere in the world. Many of the organisations working in this sector have longer-term volunteer opportunities for skilled non-medical staff, such as logisticians or administrators.

~ **Working with children** Typically, work in this area might include volunteering as a sports coach, working in an orphanage or with street children. Rachel Oxberry arranged

Kinds of Volunteer Work

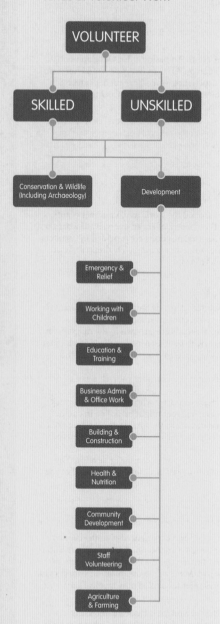

her own placements (for information on how to do this, see Chapter 8) in two orphanages in Ecuador and remembers:

I worked in a home looking after 20 children who were either abandoned or orphaned. I thought I was going there to help out generally and teach English but I actually took on the role of 'mother' too, trying to teach routine and discipline as well as doing the cleaning and laundry. I also coached sports, taught drawing and played games with the kids. I volunteered in an orphanage for children with special needs as well. I looked after babies under the age of one, preparing their food, feeding them, changing nappies and doing baby massage.

~ **Education and training** Most volunteer placements in this category are teaching English (with or without qualifications) in preschools and primary or secondary schools, although teaching adults is also common. Depending on your talents or qualifications, however, you could end up teaching almost anything. Sarah Turton volunteered with the Junior Art Club (p182) in Ghana and taught English along with art and photography. This is how she describes her time there:

Sometimes I had over 40 students crammed into a classroom designed for much less. Some of them would stroll in half an hour before the end of class or not turn up for weeks at a time and then expect to pick up where they left off. This was the way it had to be for students where farming and helping sell came first, and I had to develop a flexible teaching style. It was very tough at first and exhausted me but I loved every single second of my time there.

~ **Business administration and office work** Depending on your experience, you might work for a local Non-Governmental Organisation (NGO) writing fundraising proposals, managing a project or volunteering in their marketing, PR or finance departments. The aim of these placements is usually to train local people in the skills you possess so that they can become self-sufficient (such work is referred to as capacity-building).

~ **Building and construction** Good old-fashioned manual labour often plays a big part in volunteering overseas. You are usually sent as part of a team to help build schools, community centres, houses, bridges, dams or latrines. There is also a need for skilled volunteers in this area to work as civil or structural engineers and construction or site supervisors. Emma Campbell went with VentureCo Worldwide (p115) to Ecuador and quite literally volunteered with her bare hands:

We built a house on the coast of Ecuador, near a national park, so that future volunteers could base themselves there. We had no power tools so everything was done by hand! We were supported by a very friendly and hard-working bunch of locals that VentureCo were paying.

~ **Health and nutrition** Health professionals are required in this area, but you don't have to be a fully trained nurse, doctor, speech therapist, nutritionist or physiotherapist to contribute. Non-medical volunteers can often help in other areas, like the promotion of health and hygiene issues in a local community. Kate Sturgeon volunteered with Médecins Sans Frontières (MSF, Doctors Without Borders, p144) in Zimbabwe and explains:

I was the project nurse for an HIV/anti-retroviral programme working alongside the Ministry of Health to provide free anti-retroviral drugs in one of the first HIV/opportunistic infections clinics in the country. I ran 'follow-up' clinics, seeing all patients who had started on these drugs either weekly, monthly or quarterly to monitor their progress and any side effects.

~ **Community development** This covers a wide variety of community and social programmes. You might help women's groups set up income-generating schemes (eg selling handicrafts), work with a local village on empowerment issues or help establish a system for disposing of rubbish in a village or region.

~ **Staff volunteering** Some volunteer organisations, particularly those aimed at the youth market, need in-country volunteer staff to help manage and run their overseas programmes (see p125). You might be a medic on an expedition, an interpreter at a field base or a project manager working with a group of 17- to 24-year-olds. Michelle Hawkins volunteered with Raleigh International (p125) in Ghana, Costa Rica and Nicaragua and describes the roles she filled:

On the first expedition I was a public relations officer in Ghana. On the second I was project manager on a construction site in an Indian village in the rainforest. My role was to ensure that everything happened on time and under budget. I was also responsible for motivating the Venturers, briefing each one to be a 'Day Leader' and then assessing and reviewing what they had done well and what could be improved.

~ **Agriculture and farming** This one is almost exclusively for skilled volunteers. Communities often need horticulturalists, foresters, agronomists and agriculturalists.

One further option, if you have extensive travel plans and only want to spend a day or two doing something for others, is to get in touch with the organisation in your country that arranges prison visits abroad. In the UK, contact the UK charity **Prisoners Abroad** (☎ +44 (0)20-7561 6820; fax +44 (0)20-7561 6821; info@prisonersabroad.org.uk; www.prisonersabroad.org.uk; 89-93 Fontill Rd, Finsbury Park, London N4 3JH, UK). Their CEO, Pauline Crowe, reminds us:

Visiting a British prisoner detained overseas can be a really positive experience if you approach it with the right motivation and sensitivity. It's important for people detained in faraway places to know they are not forgotten. In some places it's reasonably easy to arrange a visit – particularly in South America and Southeast Asia. Visit the local British consulate and they will give you information about how to arrange it, what you can take in etc.

Australians who want to visit prisoners abroad can contact either the **New South Wales Council for Civil Liberties** (☎ +61 2 9286 3767; www.nswccl.org.au) which has an Australian Prisoners Abroad Subcommittee, or their nearest Australian embassy.

Conservation & Wildlife Volunteering

The words 'conservation' and 'wildlife' sum up most of the options for volunteering in this area. The majority of opportunities involve short-term stints working on long-term projects alongside scientists or other experts. Sometimes you're based in one location but often you join an expedition through a particular region.

Conservation Volunteering

Volunteering in conservation could involve clearing or constructing trails in African national parks, studying flora and fauna in a cloud-forest reserve in Ecuador or monitoring climate change in the Arctic. There are countless, wide-ranging options available.

For instance, Karen Hedges went to Madagascar with Azafady (p132) and worked on a variety of projects:

We planted trees with various communities and held workshops for the local people to teach them the importance of replanting in a country that has lost so much of its natural habitat. We also did a forest survey to measure how quickly forests in St Luce were diminishing through local use.

Archaeology and palaeontology also come under the conservation banner and are two fields that rely heavily on international volunteers (see opposite). Robert Driver travelled to Belize with Trekforce and worked in the jungle:

Our project involved clearing and 3D-mapping the most prominent ancient Mayan ruined city in northern Belize, called Kakantulix. The area of jungle around it had been subject to logging by the local community, who were reliant on the trees as a source of income. We had to clear the site of low-level vegetation and then map each ruin to gain an accurate image of what the site once looked like. The maps were forwarded to the Institute of Archaeology and Wildtracks (our project partner) and the area has since received protected status, is attracting sustainable tourism and is, in turn, generating an income for the local community.

Wildlife Volunteering

If you choose to work with animals you might do anything from helping monitor sea turtle populations in Costa Rica to analysing the migration of grey whales in Canada to working in a home for neglected or orphaned wild animals in Namibia.

Samantha Elson has participated in five programmes in Sri Lanka, Azores, the Altai Republic, Namibia and Peru with Biosphere Expeditions (p174). She describes her broad range of experiences:

I've worked with extremely enthusiastic scientists and have always felt part of the team. Volunteers are not just given the donkey work. It is really rewarding and I have learnt so much. I have no zoological training but have had the chance to do everything from photographing whale flukes for identification, measuring snow-leopard footprints in the snow, to releasing a cheetah from a humane trap.

Elaine Massie and Richard Lawson (see p65 for their Top Ten Tips from Two Volunteers) have undertaken 15 projects with Earthwatch (p171) and recount one of their best moments from the sea turtle programme in Costa Rica:

With a population on the verge of extinction every hatchling counts, so volunteers check each nest, count the number of hatchlings and put them in a bucket. They are then walked along the beach, released and allowed to crawl to the ocean escorted by volunteers, to ensure that none are eaten by crabs on the way. This is a wonderful job. Picking the wiggly hatchlings out of the sand at the nest site and seeing them scamper down the beach into the ocean is brilliant. Elaine wished the first couple of hatchlings, 'Goodbye, good luck and be careful,' not realising that she'd be releasing hundreds of hatchlings. Then it seemed unlucky not to wish them all the same. So, almost a thousand were wished 'Goodbye, good luck and be careful,' as they were safely seen to the ocean. Turtle hatchlings may well be the cutest baby animal ever and deserve all the protection and luck they can get.

Marine Conservation

Marine conservation straddles both the conservation and wildlife camps. Tasks for volunteers may include underwater surveys of coral reefs in the Philippines, diving with whale sharks in Honduras or helping with dolphin conservation in Florida.

Where in the World?

The short answer is 'anywhere'. Volunteering opportunities exist on every continent except Antarctica (although, who knows, by the time this book goes to press a conservation or wildlife expedition there might just be on the cards). However, the majority of volunteer placements are in Africa, Asia and Latin America, although a varying number of countries within these areas can be off-limits to volunteers for security reasons (see p37 for more information on this issue).

You can also volunteer in almost any geographical environment. There's lots of work in cities and towns as well as in rural areas and small villages, and in jungles, rainforests, deserts or on underwater (marine conservation) projects.

Archaeology

If you fancy yourself as the next Indiana Jones or Lara Croft, archaeology is probably not for you – volunteers are more likely to be digging out fire pits than unearthing buried treasure. You don't have to be a scientist or historian to take part, but you do need to be patient and committed. Real-life archaeology can be painstakingly slow and laborious, and you must log and record every find, no matter how insignificant.

This said, archaeology does have its glamorous side and there are opportunities to excavate burial chambers, temples and ancient shipwrecks.

Volunteers typically cover all their own expenses and camp or stay on site or in local guesthouses. You can work for just a few weeks or for a whole season and there are usually a few free days a week to do some exploring. However, you should be prepared for back-breaking, dusty days spent hunched over in the sun – bring a wide-brimmed hat and a big tube of sun screen!

The **Council for British Archaeology** (☎ +44 (0)1904 671417; http://new.archaeologyuk.org; St Mary's House, 66 Bootham, York YO30 7BZ, UK) and the **Archaeological Institute of America** (☎ +1 617-353 9361; aia@aia.bu.edu; www.archaeological.org; 656 Beacon St, Boston, MA 02215, USA) both publish annual lists of fieldwork opportunities around the world. The website www.archaeologyfieldwork.com also has field-work listings for the USA and worldwide. Some of the mainstream volunteering organisations also place volunteers on archaeological digs (see Scientific Exploration Society p136, Condordia p187).

If you fancy helping out on a marine excavation, the **Nautical Archaeology Society** (☎ +44(0)23-9281 8419; www.nauticalarchaeologysociety.org; Fort Cumberland, Fort Cumberland Rd, Portsmouth PO4 9LD, UK) offers specialist courses in Foreshore and Underwater Archaeology for aspiring marine archaeologists who have a PADI Open Water or equivalent diving certification.

There was rarely a dull moment during my six months – apart from the winter evenings. I ended up being interviewed by a TV crew about why I had come to teach Tibetan children; I was taken out to dinner by the local police, who took it in turns to stand up and make speeches thanking me for coming to do voluntary work, and who also serenaded me in turn (I then had to sing a song for them). I was propositioned by a man dressed as a monk; I visited various reincarnated holy men and had an important empowerment from one; I visited a nomadic family in their tent and bravely ate a home-made sausage which was dripping with blood. I visited a 'sky burial' site and saw some tufts of hair and bits of bone; I saw a frozen lake against a backdrop of black and snow-white mountains and a turquoise dawn sky. I saw the biggest plains in the world; I sat on the grasslands in summer and marvelled at the beauty of enormous flower-filled meadows surrounded by velvet hills that reminded me strangely of Ireland. I met the sweetest children in the world, who bring themselves and each other up, wash their own clothes in freezing water, walk from the classroom to your flat so that they can hold your hand and make the average Western child look like a spoilt, demanding brat.

My advice to people reading this book is: 'Go for it!'

Sharon Baxter

Sharon Baxter volunteered with Rokpa UK Overseas Projects (see p183) in Yushu, Tibet, for six months. She taught English as a foreign language to three classes of children ranging from five-year-olds to 19-year-olds at a boarding school. The children had all lost either one or both parents and generally came from very poor families.

Package Placement or DIY?

Once you know what you might want to do and where you might want to go, there are two things you need to consider. The first is what sort of volunteering experience you want, and the second is how to find the right volunteer opportunity for you. All the organisations offering volunteer opportunities are different and it is really important to find the one that best fits what you are looking for.

Local charities or NGOs in search of volunteers often don't have the time or resources to recruit directly (although some volunteer placements are organised this way). Instead, the most common practice is that they work with partners in Europe, the USA, Canada, Australia and New Zealand who match the right placement with the right volunteer. Throughout this process the emphasis should always be on meeting the needs of the host programme abroad, rather than on your individual requirements as a volunteer. (To avoid signing up with an organisation that does not operate this way, see p25 for a discussion of ethical volunteering.)

In these cases, partners can be limited companies, not-for-profit organisations or registered charities, although the latter often recruit and run their own volunteer programmes. Regardless of their status, all three are normally referred to as 'sending agencies'. Within this framework there are three main types of experiences that you can choose from: organised programmes, structured and self-funding programmes, and do-it-yourself placements.

Organised Volunteer Programmes

This category is comprised of organisations that offer all-inclusive, highly organised volunteer experiences. Almost everything is arranged for you: your volunteer placement; international flights; board and lodging; travel insurance; visas; orientation courses; in-country support and transport. Volunteers can work on either development or conservation and wildlife projects. They often work in teams, but individual placements are also common. The cost of volunteering through one of these organisations can seem high, although their 'all-inclusive' nature means that everything is covered in the cost (bar pocket money).

Organisations that recruit skilled volunteers like VSO, Australian Volunteers International (AVI, p129), Volunteer Service Abroad (VSA, p130) or Skillshare International (p139) also fall into this bracket due to the organised nature of their placements. This is also the case for organisations providing emergency and relief services, like MSF or Doctors of the World (Médecins du Monde, p144). However, this is where any similarities with other organisations in this category end. For full details, see the relevant sections in Chapter 5.

Organised volunteer programmes can be divided into three types:

~ **Options for the under 30s** Organised volunteer programmes catering specifically to the youth market, including gap-year students.

~ **Volunteering plus** These are organised volunteer programmes that offer a 'sandwich' or combined volunteering experience, combining a volunteer placement with other travel-related experiences. For instance, you could learn a language for one month, volunteer for one month, then undertake some adventurous group travel for a further month or two.

~ **Volunteering holidays** A good proportion of conservation and wildlife programmes fall into this subset because of their short time frames (often one to three weeks; see p29 for more information on the time frames involved). Otherwise, some organisations cater more to the holiday-maker who wants to do a spot of volunteering rather than to the serious and committed international volunteer. The increase in the number of this type of organisation has created a new term: voluntourism.

For details on organised volunteer programmes, see Chapter 5.

Structured & Self-funding Volunteer Programmes

Some charities and sending agencies offer a structured volunteer programme but might require you to find your own accommodation or book your own flights. Basically, not everything is organised for you, and this is reflected in the fee. There is support from your agency but much less hand-holding than with an organised volunteer programme – both in your home country prior to departure and once you're abroad.

In terms of independence, the next rung on the ladder is self-funding volunteering programmes. An agency will match you with an overseas placement but you're pretty much on your own from then on. You pay all your own costs, organise all the practical details (eg flights, visas and accommodation) and receive very little additional support.

For a detailed look at structured and self-funding volunteer programmes, see Chapter 6.

A Note on Religious Organisations

Religious organisations can operate both organised volunteer programmes and structured and self-funding volunteer programmes. The main difference is that much of the work is faith based. In addition, many of the placements are for periods of one year upwards. And, as you'd expect, religious organisations mostly conduct development rather than conservation and wildlife programmes.

For details of volunteering with religious organisations, see Chapter 7.

Do-It-Yourself Volunteer Placements

If you don't fancy any of these options, you can cut out the middle man and tee up a volunteer placement directly with a grassroots NGO or locally run programme. There are two main ways of doing this: you can either organise a placement using one of the many online databases of worldwide volunteering opportunities, or arrange a volunteer placement once you arrive in a country.

For details on do-it-yourself volunteer placements, see Chapter 8.

Who Can Go?

Almost anyone can volunteer: if you're aged between 18 and 75 you should be able to find a placement. New Zealand's largest provider of overseas volunteers, Volunteer Service Abroad (VSA), has an upper age limit of 75 years, for instance. If you're over 75, talk to your sending agency (and your travel insurance company) and you might be able to come to some arrangement. Catherine Raynor, Press Officer for VSO, remembers:

We had one volunteer working as an engineer in Mongolia and he had his 70th birthday while there. He became something of a local celebrity because the standard life expectancy in Mongolia is significantly lower. Various parties were held for him around the country and, at one point, he was even paraded through the town where he worked.

Interestingly, volunteering has been part of the international scene for long enough to allow some people to use it as a kind of lifelong education. In such cases, people usually find that what they learnt and what they had to offer were very different at different stages of their life.

Among southern hemisphere types, volunteering is particularly on the rise among the over 60s. In Australia, a government study found that Australians are world leaders in volunteering within their local communities once they are retired. A census in New Zealand, conducted in 2001, revealed that over one million people participated in volunteering in that country. On the international front, Australians and New Zealanders have taken to incorporating self-funding volunteering stints, such as assisting with a whale conservation project, into their travel itineraries and a record number of volunteer places are being offered on skilled volunteer programmes like Australian Youth Ambassador for Development (AYAD).

Volunteering attracts people from all round the world. Whether you go abroad alone or with a group of compatriots, you will meet and mix with volunteers of all nationalities and creeds. International volunteering is also drawing an increasingly diverse spectrum of candidates from within individual countries. In North America, for example, since the inception of President Kennedy's Peace Corps (p96) in the 1960s, volunteering overseas has often been stereotyped as a vehicle for relatively well-off – and generally white – twentysomethings to go out and 'save the world' by digging wells and teaching English in the developing world. However, recent world events have made volunteering an attractive option to Americans, for example, of African, Asian and Hispanic descent, of both liberal and conservative political stripes, and from a variety of faiths and backgrounds. Many more people have come to appreciate the benefits of international volunteering – including the forming of rewarding relationships, the gaining of linguistic and technical skills and the creativity and cultural awareness that flow from the experience.

In addition, there is a growing number of organisations that cater for volunteers with a disability. Anthony Lunch, Managing Director of MondoChallenge, says:

We are happy to welcome volunteers with a disability as long as their GP feels they are able to undertake the project. We always alert our country managers to the situation and they take all necessary steps or precautions. One of our volunteer teachers in Nepal suffered from multiple sclerosis and we are currently in negotiation with another volunteer in her 50s who has a stoma bag that needs to be changed regularly by medical staff. Obviously, everyone travels at their own risk, but we will always do our best to give volunteers any extra in-country support they may need.

See the listings in Chapters 5 to 8 to find out which organisations can cater for volunteers with a disability.

Finding the Time

A volunteer placement can last from a couple of days to two years or more. This means that volunteering can be fitted into your life at any time. If you're in full-time employment and want to spend one or two weeks of your annual leave volunteering, you can.

Robin Glegg, who has been on three wildlife projects with Biosphere Expeditions, explains:

Each expedition 'slot' lasts 12 days, although you can sign up for multiple slots. I signed up for one slot. As some of the locations are fairly remote, this gives you two days' travelling time if you are taking a two-week break from work. This works in well with my holiday schedule. Twelve days can be a little short in the field, but it is a practical time frame and a reasonable commitment for most working people.

However, many people want to volunteer for longer and choose to do it at a stage of their lives when they have more time. This means that your first encounter with volunteering might come in the year between school and higher education, or between university and before starting full-time employment. David Grassham, who helped upgrade facilities in a village school in India with VentureCo, says:

I had just finished university and wanted to have a year doing something completely different from the norm, and something that I may not have time to do once I eventually do start working.

Organisations for Asian Volunteers

The leading organised volunteer bodies in Asia are skills-based and include programmes such as **Japan Overseas Cooperation Volunteers (JOCV)** (☎ +81 3 5226 6660; www.jica.go.jp) and **Korea International Cooperation Agency** (☎ +82 31 7400 114; www.koica.go.kr). Much like Australia's AVI programme (p129), JOCV are placed in over 50 developing countries (with most going to Africa and Asia) and work in as many as 70 skilled fields including agriculture, forestry and electronics. Between 1965 and 2007, over 30,000 JOCV were sent to enhance 'bilateral friendly relations at the grassroots level.' The competition for JOCV volunteer positions is fierce, but the training and services that enable the two-year assignments are exemplary. The Korean equivalent, KOV, has been operating for 18 years and has sent skilled Korean volunteers to 27 countries. Its volunteers assist in many hands-on projects, from abalone farming to brick making and animal husbandry.

There's plenty of scope for Asian volunteers with other organisations operating both domestically and further afield. For further information, try:

~ **Yayasan Salam Malaysia** (www.salam.org.my) A referral service that organises volunteer opportunities for Malaysians at home and overseas, focusing particularly on education, health and community development. It also offers various relevant training courses.

.~ **Hong Kong Agency for Volunteer Service (AVS)** (☎ +852 2527 3825; www.avs.org.hk) A referral service that 'mobilises and organises volunteer services' and should be of particular interest to any aspiring volunteers living in Hong Kong. The website is available in Chinese and English.

~ **National Volunteer & Philanthropy Centre** (www.nvpc.org.sg) Singapore's leading volunteering agency brings together charities and not-for-profits with anyone interested in volunteering in Singapore. Non-residents are welcome to apply.

~ **Volunteering India** (www.volunteeringinindia.org) Run by the Society for Promotion of Environment and Sustainable Development, this organisation is based in Jaipur and runs a range of activities and programmes.

~ **Thai Volunteer Service** (☎ +66 (0)2 691 0437/9; volunteerservice@gmail.com; http://thaivolunteer.org/myweb) Focused on promoting volunteering among Thai university students, this outfit supports NGOs in the Mekong River region by linking up grassroots organisations to face the impacts of globalisation in a united way.

Sarah Wintle

Of course, plenty of people in the workforce take extended breaks or have gaps when changing jobs or careers. Jackie Bowles, for instance, worked with children and adolescents in Rio de Janeiro through Task Brasil:

I was dissatisfied with my job and really wanted to change my career. I didn't have any family responsibilities so I felt this was the perfect time to volunteer.

Kate Sturgeon, who volunteered in Zimbabwe, says:

I had three years of nursing on an HIV/infectious diseases unit at the Royal Free Hospital in London and I'd completed a Tropical Nursing Diploma and Advanced Diploma in Infectious Diseases. I felt I had enough experience to confidently work abroad. I then negotiated a career break from the Royal Free Hospital and they held my post open for me.

When you, the employee, decide you want to take a career break, that's great, but all too frequently it's your employer that makes the decision. This is what happened to Peter Bennett, who taught English in Sudan for seven months with the Sudan Volunteer Programme (p170):

Development-speak

Your bags are packed and you're off to volunteer, but where are you going? Is it the 'Third World'? The 'developing world'? A 'less-developed country'? Or are you travelling from the 'Minority' to the 'Majority World'? There are a lot of different terms, all with quite different meanings. Here are a few explanations.

~ **Third World** This term came out of the Cold War era and was used to denote countries that neither supported the West nor the Soviet bloc. Now it is used for countries that are seen as 'poor'. The implied hierarchy in the terms 'First' and 'Third' World, and the sense that these worlds are somehow separate from one another, means this term, though still used, is increasingly being rejected.

~ **Developing world** Probably the most popular term – and one that suggests that change is possible. However, it implies that much of the world is 'growing up' and that the only route to success is to be more like the countries deemed 'developed' or 'grown up'.

~ **Less-developed countries (LDCs)** This term was a favourite of school geography syllabuses, and is now seriously out of vogue. It sounds like the put-down that it is!

~ **Majority & Minority Worlds** These terms get away from the idea that the only way to categorise the world is according to a scale of greater or lesser development. Instead, they recognise that the majority of the world's population lives in developing countries, and that the majority of the world's countries are 'developing'. Hence, this is the Majority World. These terms are particularly popular with people looking for alternative forms of development, and those who question whether the world even has enough resources to allow everyone, everywhere to achieve 'Western-style' development. The only drawback is that most people don't have a clue what, or where, you are talking about when you use these terms.

~ **The Global South** This was an attempt to define development geographically – but it doesn't really work (just ask Australians or New Zealanders!). Now used as a political, rather than a geographical, category it has fewer hierarchical implications than the term 'developing' and, unlike the term 'Majority World', most people will know, more or less, what you are on about.

In reality, all these terms are problematic, as they try and lump everyone and everywhere into just two big categories, and the world is a lot more complex than that. Use them, but use them with caution, and be aware that there is an ideology lurking behind every label. In this book, we've used 'developing world', as it's the most widely understood.

Dr Kate Simpson

In financially depressed times, the bank I was working for made significant redundancies. As a senior manager I had been involved in deciding who we could do without – only to discover on the day that my name was on the list too. To be honest, I had also been thinking that I didn't want to spend all my working life absorbed in some fascinating but ultimately meaningless occupation, only to find that when retirement day finally arrived I didn't have the energy or enthusiasm or the good health to enjoy it.

If you find yourself in this situation, it could be the perfect springboard into volunteering. What better way to spend your redundancy cheque?

In recent years, international volunteering has become increasingly popular with retirees, who have a lifetime of skills to offer, as well as savings, maturity and a bit more time. In particular, North Americans with a few more years under their belts – and a few more dollars in their bank accounts – are applying for international volunteer placements in greater numbers than ever before. Some of these folk witnessed, or participated in, the early years of the Peace Corps and are eagerly (re)living their volunteer dream in retirement. Others have never found the time to venture abroad amid career and family responsibilities and are taking advantage of their new-found personal freedom to work overseas. Oliver Walker is 63 and taught English in Sri Lanka with MondoChallenge. He feels:

… there is a need for older volunteers who have seen a lot of life. They have time on their hands and are often young at heart, looking for adventure and a worthwhile experience. Volunteering is so rewarding.

Deborah Jordan and David Spinney were both retired head teachers when they went to Ethiopia to work in education with VSO (p94). Julie Jones, a grandmother, went to Kenya with Inspired Breaks (p126) to work in an orphan outreach programme:

My family and friends were a great support and gave me encouragement. My nine-year-old granddaughter thought it was 'cool' to have a granny doing something a bit unusual. What I did at Omwabini cannot be described as 'work'. Together with other volunteers, I visited far-flung communities, went out with a mobile clinic and spent time in a primary school where most of the children had lost at least one parent to AIDS.

Timing

Some things to take into consideration before deciding when to volunteer include the climate, the timing of your volunteer project, and, if you plan to combine volunteering with a holiday, at what point during your travels to do your volunteering stint.

The climate and the seasons will impact on how comfortable you feel when you are abroad. If you can't stand extreme heat or extreme cold, plan your volunteering to avoid these. Also, in some parts of the world hurricane or monsoon seasons can drastically affect your in-country experiences.

It may seem obvious, but some volunteer projects run only at certain times of the year. If you want to teach in a school or university, for instance, you can't turn up during the holidays (unless a summer school has been arranged). If you want to help protect baby sea turtles, like Elaine Massie and Richard Lawson (see p14), then obviously you need to volunteer during the nesting season.

If you plan to volunteer as part of an extended period of travel (eg during a gap year or career break) then it can fit almost anywhere in your itinerary. However, most gappers and career-breakers choose to volunteer at the beginning of their trip, as it's a good way to meet people to travel with afterward.

Useful Websites

Most volunteer organisations have detailed websites where you can learn a lot more about them and about volunteering in general. The websites of individual organisations are given in the listings sections of Chapters 5 to 8, but over the page is a list of more general websites:

~ **Australian Council for International Development (ACFID)** (www.acfid.asn.au) Broad-based volunteering information for Australians.

~ **DevJobs Australia** (www.devjobs.net.au/cms) International volunteering links plus the latest development research and jobs.

~ **Council for International Development (CID)** (www.cid.org.nz) A New Zealand site representing the non-government aid and development sector.

~ **Global Focus Aotearoa** (www.globalfocus.org.nz) A New Zealand site covering development issues in the region, with a directory of 1200 agencies and organisations working in the Pacific.

~ **Guide to Development Speak** (www.bbc.co.uk/worldservice/specials/916_dev_speak/index.shtml) Some jargon-busting from the BBC.

~ **InterVol** (www.intervol.org.uk) Offering free registration, this site has lots of information on international volunteering. You can search for opportunities and there's also an 'Ask the Expert' section.

~ **OneWorld UK** (www.oneworld.net) News, views, campaigns and information from an international network of people interested in global justice.

~ **Serve Your World** (www.serveyourworld.com) This well-organised guide to international volunteering addresses a variety of relevant topics, from the philosophical to the practical.

~ **Transitions Abroad** (www.transitionsabroad.com) An excellent general resource on living, working and volunteering abroad, with lots of articles and links.

~ **Volunteering Australia** (www.volunteeringaustralia.org) The site of Australia's governing body on volunteering, with links to not-for-profit organisations.

~ **Volunteering New Zealand** (www.volunteeringnz.org.nz) The New Zealand volunteering world's resource centre.

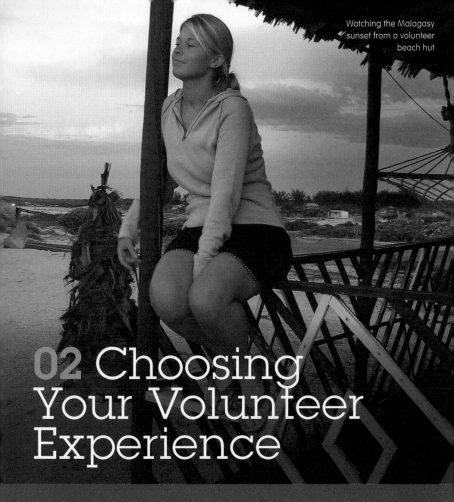

Watching the Malagasy sunset from a volunteer beach hut

02 Choosing Your Volunteer Experience

Arranging a Worthwhile Placement

The majority of volunteer placements are organised through an intermediary called a 'sending agency' (see p16 and Chapters 5 to 7 for more details). This means that it's crucial to choose an agency that operates in a way you feel comfortable with and that does its best to place volunteers on projects that are genuinely sustainable and responding to local needs. Even if you choose not to go through a sending agency, but contact an NGO or programme directly, you still need to take the same things into consideration.

There are hundreds of sending agencies based all over the world. And it's all too easy to make the wrong choice. Ian Flood is a 48-year-old mechanical engineer with 16 years' experience with Rolls-Royce. He did a language course in Ecuador and his language school organised for him to volunteer in a day centre for street children. His experience turned out to be a disappointing one:

The organisation that fixed my placement was not willing to look at my background and skills (even though they had my CV) and match what I had to offer to the volunteer programme. Instead, I felt like I was given 'any old' placement and it was only when I turned up that the people there really asked about my history and tried to use my skills and experience. By this stage it was too late. Any 18-year-old with good Spanish could have worked very usefully in the day centre. I felt my skills were underutilised.

On the other hand, when Jackie Bowles was looking for her placement with street children in Rio de Janeiro she was choosy right from the start:

I looked at several different projects but chose Task Brasil, as they have such a well-established volunteer programme. Some others I had researched were in great need of volunteers, but didn't really have the network to support them. In other words, I felt that a volunteer could build up relationships with the children and then suddenly leave the children on their own. With Task Brasil there is a healthy balance between the volunteers that help and the educator, so the children don't suffer when the volunteers leave. I volunteered for five months then returned for a further three months on a part-time basis because I missed it so much!

The key message here is that all organisations are different and work to varying standards. Many are excellent but some, like Ian Flood's, will dish out 'any old' placement with little consideration for you or your host programme. It's crucial to do your homework and check the credentials of any organisation you're considering volunteering with. Good credentials are what attracted Kate Sturgeon to Médecins Sans Frontières (MSF, Doctors Without Borders, p144). She remembers:

I primarily chose MSF because it's got such a good reputation. I liked its charter – that it is independent and not affiliated with any religion, culture or government and that it receives most of its money from donations. I liked the fact that they work where the most vulnerable people are and that they're often the first NGO in and the last out.

As well as checking out credentials, you need to feel that you share the philosophy and ethos that drives the sending agency you ultimately choose. This is what initially attracted Deborah Jordan and David Spinney to work with Voluntary Service Overseas (VSO, p94):

We knew about VSO and how it works in partnership with governments and NGOs in developing countries. We looked forward to living in a local community at a similar level to our colleagues, and working with them to achieve shared targets. We liked their approach of 'sharing skills' rather than giving out money or things. Their approach was not that of the 'do-gooder' with poor people overseas, but a much more professional commitment to working with skilled individuals in their context to bring about sustainable change.

But there are many other factors that may influence your choice of agency or programme. Emma Campbell who volunteered with VentureCo (p115) in South America says:

I searched under 'responsible travel' on the Web. I was looking for a company that was carbon neutral and that included Spanish lessons. I also wanted to be part of a group with mixed ages and backgrounds.

As volunteering can often seem expensive (see p30), the cost of a particular programme or placement is also a deciding factor. Ann Noon went to Peru and volunteered with the Inka Porter Project:

I spent a long time looking for the right project, as I wasn't keen on the idea of paying a lot of money, particularly as I am suspicious about what proportion of the (often substantial) fees organisations charge actually trickles down to the host project.

Sarah Turton, who volunteered with the Junior Art Club (p182) in Ghana, was also influenced by price as well as her interests and the environment in which she would be placed:

I searched the internet long and hard. I was influenced by cost and what was on offer. My main interest was Africa and art but I was also keen to go somewhere very remote and not be surrounded by Westerners and live as the Ghanaians live.

And, weighing in with the final word, Robert Driver who volunteered in the jungles of Belize, chose to volunteer with Trekforce (p115) for two different reasons:

They are a registered charity and, for me, this had two benefits. Firstly, being a charity they would have a real focus on preserving the environment as opposed to being partly focused on profits. Secondly, it meant I could fundraise to contribute towards the cost of going on the expedition. The number of people who took an interest in what I was doing and supported it was really encouraging.

All in all, there's a lot to be taken into account. This chapter examines many of the issues raised here in more depth and looks at other key deciding factors in choosing a sending agency or liaising directly with a local NGO or charity.

Ethical Volunteering

The ethics of international volunteering are complex, particularly with development work. On the surface it sounds like a match made in fairy tales: you help local people to help themselves; you benefit; they benefit and you all live happily ever after.

Of course, the reality may not be quite so 'charming'. The more you find out about international volunteering, the more aware you become of some key ethical issues. When this happens you start to ask yourself more questions and, hopefully, ask more questions of the organisations you are researching. This is a healthy process, as getting answers to some key questions is exactly what is required to ensure that everyone benefits for the long term from your volunteering experience.

Below are some basic questions you might have swirling around in your head. Responses follow, although they are often more 'grey' than 'black' or 'white' (reflecting the complexity of some of the issues involved).

Q1: How do I know if the host community or country will really benefit from my volunteering?
That's a crucial question. There should only ever be one reason for a volunteer programme to exist, and that is to meet the needs of a local community. Just as importantly, all volunteer programmes should do this in a sustainable way.

For instance, there's little point in a one-off placement where you're parachuted into a school, orphanage, community centre etc to work for a month or two and then leave. What happens to the work you were doing? How is it continued? Has your departure created a vacuum that no-one can fill, and your work therefore been more of a hindrance than a help?

Of course, there are exceptions to this rule. Perhaps you had a specific aim to achieve and you trained a local person to take over from you. That would be useful and classified as a sustainable volunteer project. However, you are more likely to find sustainable projects with sending agencies that have a long-term relationship with their partner programmes.

So, the bottom line is this: if you volunteer on a properly run programme (whether you apply through a sending agency or go direct) you will make a contribution that should be of benefit to those you wish to help.

Q2: If I only have a short amount of time to give, will I be able to 'make a difference'?
This is a tricky one and is discussed in more detail on p29. The answer very much depends on the aims and objectives of your project. The shorter the time you have, the more specific your project needs to be. For instance, volunteers with the faith-based charity Habitat for Humanity (p199) go overseas for two weeks and help build a house for a low-income family in great need of shelter. At the end of the two weeks they have achieved something tangible and worthwhile.

Q3: Am I actually doing more good by volunteering than just donating my money?
The two short answers to this question are 'yes' and 'no'. All organisations working overseas need money to implement their programmes. But sending yourself, as opposed to sending your money, means you are making a very special contribution.

Get the Most, Give the Most

People who volunteer generally hope to do something that they will find interesting, something they will learn from and something that will help other people. However, choosing between all the possible projects and organisations is more complex than just signing up with the first one to show you exciting pictures and an interesting blurb.

To get the most out of international volunteering you need to put effort into choosing who you go with and what you do. For while there are some fantastic projects to take part in, there are also some that are poorly organised and exploit both hosts' and travellers' expectations.

These seven questions are designed to help you learn as much as possible about the quality and value of the projects or placements an organisation offers BEFORE you arrive in the country with your newly packed backpack and a whole bundle of expectations.

Q1: What work will I be doing? Can the organisation provide you with a brief job description?
An organisation with a good volunteer programme should be able to tell you what you will be doing, including how many hours a day, how many days a week and what sort of work it will be. For example, if an organisation offers a placement in a school, this may or may not be teaching. Likewise, a placement may involve 50 hours a week or, and this does happen, a mere four hours. The greatest source of dissatisfaction for volunteers is usually not doing what they planned (and paid) to do.

Q2: Does the organisation work with a local partner organisation?
If a volunteer programme is to be of value to a local community it should work with, rather than be imposed on, that community. Good programmes will have been built in collaboration with a local partner organisation. Find out who that partner is and find out about the relationship. Key things to look for are: whether someone from the local organisation is involved in the day-to-day management of your project; what sort of consultation with the partners took place to to build that project and why the project is of value.

Q3: Does the organisation make any financial contributions to its volunteer programmes? If so, exactly how much is this?
Many volunteer organisations charge a lot of money, but where does it all go? Volunteer programmes need funds as well as labour; indeed, in much of the world, unskilled labour is often one thing of which there is little shortage. The most important thing is that your organisation is upfront about how your money is spent. So ask where your pennies are going, and be persistent about getting a clear figure, not a percentage of profits. Also, be aware that payments for your food and lodging often do not assist your volunteer programme.

Q4: Does the organisation have policies on ecotourism and ethical tourism? If so, how are they implemented?
Running volunteer programmes is ethically complex. If you really want to make a valuable contribution to the community you work with, then you have a responsibility to ensure that the organisation with which you travel has proper ecological and ethical policies. Look for organisations that have a long-term commitment to a community, employ local staff and have some mechanism for local consultation and decision making. Otherwise, how will you know that the clinic you built is really needed, or that an adult literacy programme is more relevant than a new bridge? How will you know that when you leave there will be the funds and commitment to maintain the project you have worked on?

Q5: What time frame is the volunteer programme run on?
A well-structured volunteer programme should have a clear time frame, and organisations should know from one year to the next whether a programme will continue. One-off

programmes, and especially placements, can be problematic. For example, if you are acting as an English teaching assistant for a month or two, what happens the rest of the school year? Are other volunteers sent or is the placement simply ended? It may be very disruptive for a class, a school or an orphanage to have a constantly changing number of staff. Establishing the level of commitment an organisation has to a given project or placement is vital in establishing the quality, and therefore value, of that volunteer programme.

Q6: Can the organisation give you precise contact details for your chosen programme?

Organisations tend to work in one of two ways. The better ones build a relationship with a host organisation, identify local needs, arrange placements and projects and then fill vacancies. A less positive approach is to wait for travellers to sign up and pay up, and then find relevant placements. A good organisation with well-run programmes should be able to let you know several months before you travel where you will be going and what exactly you will be doing. If they cannot (or will not) give you these details be very wary of the quality of the programme. Hastily arranged programmes can be disorganised, leaving both volunteers and local hosts with unclear expectations.

Q7: What support & training will you receive?

Organisations offer vastly different levels of training and support. Look for an organisation that offers not only pre-departure training but also in-country training and support. As a volunteer you want to be as much use as possible, learn as much as possible and have as good a time as possible. Training in both the practicalities of your volunteer job and the culture of where you are travelling to will help you get and give the most. Local support is also important. The type of programme you are on affects the amount of support required, but make sure you know what to expect before you go. If there is a local representative, how 'local' are they? Are they just down the road or several hours away by bus? Make sure there is somebody in the country with direct responsibility for you. All projects require problem solving at some point and you will need someone on hand to help you with this.

This guide is a publication by Gap Year Research; for more information visit
www.ethicalvolunteering.org.

Dr Kate Simpson

Photo: Paul Plota

A Pakistani man brings his granddaughter to Australian Aid International volunteers for treatment following the devastating 2005 earthquake

How valuable your contribution is depends on the effectiveness of the volunteer programme and feeds into the response given to the first question in this section. To some extent it also depends on what work you are doing. If you are passing on your skills to local people so they can do your job when you leave, if you are training the trainer or helping to build international understanding through cultural exchange then, obviously, this is invaluable work and much more important than money.

In addition, many sending agencies donate a proportion of the fees they charge to the overseas project you're working with. For a more detailed discussion of this, check out the response to question three in the Ethical Volunteering Guide written by Dr Kate Simpson, on p25.

Q4: Will my volunteering take a paid job away from a local person?

It is crucial that it doesn't, and you need to ask this question of your sending agency or local organisation (if you are finding your own placement) before you sign up. Again, there's no chance of this if your volunteer agency is reputable and well run but there is if it isn't.

Q5: Some sending agencies place thousands of volunteers annually, while others place relatively few. Is this an indication of how good they are?

Not at all. In fact, in the world of international volunteering small is often beautiful. Instead of looking at the number of volunteers, find out how many partner programmes an organisation works with abroad. The relationship between a sending agency and its partners is key. There needs to be mutual trust, frequent correspondence and visits, and long-term commitment if the relationship is to thrive.

So, beware the agencies that appear to offer every international volunteering option under the sun. You can't work with everyone everywhere. In fact, an abundance of choice usually means that host programme partnerships are weak, that not all projects are properly vetted and that quality control is poor.

In addition, check out how an organisation matches its placements to its volunteers, particularly if you plan to work in development. Some organisations spend hours interviewing volunteers, talking through the possibilities and really searching for the perfect match, while others either do this by telephone or not all (you simply apply online).

Q6: Is there a difference between volunteering with a registered charity, a not-for-profit organisation and a limited company?

Volunteer programmes are run by all three types of organisation. In the Listings section of Chapters 5 to 8 the status of organisations is given. However, it is questionable whether these distinctions make any real difference to your volunteer experience or the worth of a volunteer programme. Having said that, registered charities are normally regulated by national bodies and, from an ethical point of view, have an extra layer of responsibility to act in a genuinely charitable way. Of course, nothing is black and white. From time to time, charities are criticised for how they use their money, while certain limited companies within this sector choose to operate like not-for-profit organisations. Some sending agencies are set up as limited companies because decision making can sometimes be easier and quicker (no board of trustees to involve). Certainly, no-one wants to find out that a limited company is making vast profits from international volunteering.

The bottom line is this: all types of organisation should be transparent about how they spend your money.

Q7: As standards vary so much, are there any best-practice guidelines that organisations sign up to?

Interestingly, there is no governing body that regulates this growing, and sometimes profitable, sector. However, **Comhlámh** (☎ +353 (0)1-4783490; fax +353 (0)1-4783738; info@comhlamh .org; www.comhlamh.org; Ballast House, Aston Quay, Dublin 2, Ireland) – the Irish Association of Development Workers – has put together a Volunteer Charter and a Sending Agencies Code of Good Practice. It is hoped that both documents will be adopted by similar organisations in

Scotland, England and Wales. There is clearly a need for such self-regulation. Volunteers from outside the UK and Ireland should check whether organisations in their countries of origin follow similar regulatory guidelines.

At this stage, you might be thinking this is all getting rather too difficult. Take heart, it isn't. If you are asking the right questions of yourself, you'll ask the right questions of everybody else. And in this instance, 'everybody else' includes returned volunteers. It is particularly important to talk to volunteers who have recently returned from a placement with the sending agency or local NGO that you're thinking of volunteering with. This is one of the best ways of finding out what a project is really like on the ground.

Of course, you also need to ask questions of your sending agency or local NGO as well. To help you pick an ethical international volunteering organisation, seven key questions to ask are given in the box on p26. They have been put together by Dr Kate Simpson, who has spent over six years researching and working in the international volunteering industry and has also written extensively about gap years and international volunteering. She has completed a PhD on these subjects at the University of Newcastle upon Tyne.

How Long?

In the world of international volunteering there are short-term, medium-term and long-term placements. However, there's no real consensus on the length of time each category refers to. For the purposes of this book, short-term volunteering comprises one week to two months, medium-term is three months to 11 months and long-term is one year or more. Outside these time frames, some volunteering holidays will let you volunteer for less than a week (sometimes just a day or two) and, at the other end of the spectrum, some skills-based or faith-based charities expect a volunteering commitment of two years or more.

How long you volunteer for depends on how much time you have. Elaine Massie and Richard Lawson have volunteered on a variety of wildlife projects lasting from two to 14 days. They explain:

The length of the projects suits us very well, as we both work and so need to be able to fit the volunteering into our annual holidays.

Volunteering for such short amounts of time can work, particularly with conservation or wildlife projects where the financial contribution that volunteers make to sustainable research projects overseas is invaluable. (See the following section and Chapters 5 and 6 for more details on this.)

However, as a general rule of thumb, the shorter the volunteer placement, the more specific the project needs to be. Also, it is the accepted view that the longer the volunteer placement, the better it is for both you and the host programme. This makes total sense if you think about your volunteer placement as a new job (which, to all intents and purposes, it is). How useful are you in the first few months of starting a new job? Doesn't it take time to learn the ropes, to get to know everyone and to become familiar with new systems? Sarah Turton, who spent one month teaching in Ghana, confesses:

One month – that was too short. It takes a long time to adjust to somewhere that is so different to your own culture and I felt that I had just started to fit in properly and make good friends when I had to go home again.

This view is endorsed by Julie Jones, who worked on an orphan outreach programme in Kenya:

I came home after only four weeks and felt that I was leaving prematurely. I had only just got into the swing of things and felt there was more I could do.

Poonam Sattee volunteered for a year with Casa Alianza in Guatemala, where she worked with the street children. She says:

Just under a year – it worked out perfectly. As an organisation, they try and set up volunteer placements that are for a minimum of six months. This provides stability for the children and the volunteers are also able to get the most out of their time there.

Some skills-based and faith-based volunteer organisations require volunteers to sign up for a minimum of two years. Deborah Jordan and David Spinney went to Ethiopia, where they worked in education. For them to achieve the goals of their project, they found that two years was not sufficient:

We volunteered for a two-year placement and we were happy to do so. We recognised that it does take time to integrate into a new community and a different way of life and to earn the confidence and respect of new colleagues. We extended our contract by six months to enable us to complete the second phase (second academic year) of the programme and ensure a smooth handover to another volunteer and local colleagues.

This is not to say that only long-term volunteering is a valuable use of your time, money and limited resources. Nevertheless, the length of your volunteer placement will usually have a direct impact on how much you can achieve.

It is important to understand this link because it will help manage your expectations. Bottom line: you won't be able to do a great deal in a short amount of time and this can be frustrating. However, as was the case with Deborah Jordan and David Spinney, you can often extend a volunteer placement (visa regulations allowing).

You can also do the converse: curtail your placement. Ann Noon, who volunteered in Peru, describes finishing her placement early:

I volunteered for a year but returned home after 10 months – partly for financial reasons (too many pisco sours) and partly because I had problems with the tenants in my flat that needed resolving.

Obviously, breaking your volunteer commitment in this way should not be done lightly. Just as with a regular contract job, you have agreed to volunteer for a certain period of time and you should fulfil that obligation. However, being away from home for longish periods of time does come with its own set of potential problems. To minimise these (such as problems with tenants), see Chapter 4 Tying up Loose Ends.

Costs

It often comes as a surprise to would-be volunteers that giving up their time isn't enough. In the majority of cases, you also need to pay to volunteer. There are a number of reasons for this:

~ There are significant administrative costs involved in maintaining a well-managed volunteer programme and in finding you a volunteer placement. As such, it is normal for a fee to be charged (note: charities call this fee 'fundraising').

~ The host programme incurs costs by using volunteers. Volunteers have to be looked after, possibly trained and certainly supervised. Then there's the question of who is going to pay for board and lodging, in-country transport and any other ancilliary costs.

~ Hosting volunteers is often a way for local projects to earn an additional source of income. In many cases, a proportion of your fee (whether charged by a sending agency or a local NGO) will go towards helping fund the project you're working on.

The cost of volunteering varies considerably. It usually depends on the volunteering experience you want and how long you're going for. If you want an all-inclusive, bells-and-whistles organised volunteer programme, you might pay between US$3500 and US$4500 (£2200 and £2800; A$3300 and A$4300; NZ$4200 to NZ$5500) for a three-month placement. However, almost everything is paid upfront and all you'll have to take with you is spending money. For more detailed information on the costs of organised and structured volunteer programmes, see Chapters 5 to 7.

(As mentioned above, plenty of charities run organised volunteer programmes but their fees are referred to as 'fundraising'. See p48 for more details on this point.)

At the other extreme, you may sign up with a charity, NGO or sending agency that charges you a placement fee but then expects you to be completely self-funding. In the UK or US, if this is the case, you might be charged £850 (US$1350) in fees and have to pay all other costs, such as international flights, accommodation and food. In Australia, a prospective volunteer may pay between A$250 and A$400 (NZ$320 and NZ$510) in partially refundable fees, or as a deposit to reserve a place on a programme. Incidentally, these self-funding volunteer programme fees cannot be claimed as a tax deduction in Australia because they are not an expense incurred while earning assessable income. Check with the Australian Taxation Office's Volunteers and Tax guide for more details (www.ato.gov.au/nonprofit). For more details on self-funding volunteer placements, see Chapters 6 and 7. There is some good news for your wallet if you're a US or Canadian citizen: certain programme fees paid to charitable and religious sending organisations based in the Americas may be income tax deductible. Most of these organisations will advertise this fact on their websites.

Of course, you may think all this sounds much too expensive and decide to cut out the intermediaries and find your own placement. If you find one while you're travelling you'll have to pay only what the local NGO or charity charges (if anything). If you tee up a placement before you travel, you'll incur the small cost of registering with an online database of volunteer opportunities and all the travel- and living-related costs of volunteering. Although this is the cheapest option, it does come with far more risks. For a discussion of the pros and cons, see Chapter 8. For a detailed breakdown of how to budget for a self-funding volunteer placement, see p48.

Organisations running conservation and wildlife projects usually offer only organised or structured volunteer programmes and, more often than not, conservation and wildlife volunteering is more expensive than development volunteering. This is because many projects are expensive to run, take place in remote, inaccessible parts of the world and require lots of expensive equipment. It's also because volunteer fees are one of the main ways that a sustainable research project is funded. For more information see Chapters 5 and 6.

Whatever you pay your sending agency, it is important to understand where your money is going and who pays for what. Ask for a breakdown of costs if one isn't readily available; in many cases, you will find one on the organisation's website.

Having said all this, some volunteers don't pay anything. In fact, not only are their costs covered but they are also paid a small monthly stipend. (In most regions accepting international volunteers, stipends are in the range of US$100 to US$300 – enough to cover meals, local transportation, phone and internet usage, and other in-country incidental expenses.) This is the case with many of the skilled volunteer placements with organisations like VSO (p94), Skillshare International (p139), Doctors of the World (Médecins du Monde, p142), IESC Geekcorps (p140) or the Peace Corps (p96), to name but a few.

The Australian Government's volunteering programmes (including Australian Youth Ambassadors for Development (AYAD, p112) and Volunteering for International Development from Australia (VIDA, p130) include monthly allowances intended to cover the costs associated with living a modest life while undertaking an assignment. These allowances are anywhere

Photo: Azafady

Working hard digging a well in Madagascar

between A\$1000 and A\$1700 a month, depending on the destination. Airfares and travel insurance are also included. With the AYAD programme a variable establishment allowance is provided to cover visas and settling-in costs (like purchasing a local SIM card, or a kettle for that matter). A support allowance of A\$350 is provided to cover any equipment costs needed to complete assignment aims or help the volunteer with continuing language classes. A resettlement allowance of A\$600 is a welcome contribution to costs associated with returning to Australia. Volunteers in this programme are effectively tax exempt for the duration of their overseas assignment because they are not earning assessable income.

Local Culture

It is widely recognised that cultural exchange is one of the great benefits of international volunteering. However, living 24/7 in a foreign culture for several months or years has its challenges. Depending on where you go and what you do, you may encounter racism, sexism or homophobia. Female volunteers working in male-dominated societies have to overcome very specific gender issues and it is sometimes hard to be understanding of these and sensitive in dealing with them.

You may also have to deal with local people reacting to you based upon your government's foreign policies. International volunteers from the United States, for example, often face unique challenges. In the light of recent world events, the word 'American' may trigger intense reactions in many parts of the world, both positive and negative. Prepare yourself for this eventuality, and try to keep a low profile in public places. Loud exclamations in your native English while striding through the marketplace, for instance, may make you a target for pickpockets or cause an unexpected disturbance.

Australian and New Zealand volunteers are generally well received, particularly in the Asia-Pacific region, as governments from these two nations have made concerted efforts to build stability and prosperity in the region through their respective aid agencies. However, it's important to consider that certain political alliances the Australian Government has forged in recent years may not have a loyal fan base in parts of the Middle East and Indonesia.

In addition to political concerns, volunteers also have to come to terms with stereotypical notions local people might have about their nationality or culture. Perceptions about volunteers from the United States might be mixed, for instance. As the homeland of Hollywood, Microsoft and more global cultural icons than you can shake a Kentucky Fried Chicken drumstick at, many people believe they have a pretty good grasp of what an American is. On the one hand, folks from the US are generally considered outgoing, optimistic and independent; on the other, Americans are frequently thought of as rich, brash and arrogant.

On a more general note, like any traveller in a foreign culture you may be viewed as something of a novelty and become the focus of a lot of attention. Unlike a traveller however you can't just move on should it become overwhelming. This is exactly what Sarah Turton initially found in Ghana. She confides:

The first weekend in Ghana I spent in the village. I wanted to settle in. It was very strange as I didn't know what I was supposed to do. No-one was particularly responsible for me and I had this sense of apprehension about stepping out on my own. I mean, I stuck out like a very, very sore thumb. It has confirmed to me that I would HATE to be famous. I never realised how much I valued fitting in and being 'one of the crowd'. I didn't feel confident going out alone and I got so pestered. I was the only *obruni* (white person) for miles around.

To begin with, Jacqueline Hill, who volunteered in Bangladesh also felt a bit lost and stressed in her new environment:

I did my own shopping in the market, gradually working out what all the strange-looking vegetables were. I found cooking for myself difficult, as shopping was quite stressful. I generated a lot of attention, could not recognise much of what was on offer and had to haggle for everything.

And then, of course, there's the language barrier. Some sending agencies or local NGOs insist you speak the language of the country before you are accepted onto a programme. This is particularly the case in Latin America. If you think about it, this requirement makes perfect sense: as a volunteer you are ten times more useful if you can communicate with everyone.

So, part and parcel of choosing where to volunteer is thinking carefully about the culture and language of the country you wish to live in.

Living Conditions

What will the accommodation and food be like? How will you entertain yourself when you're not volunteering? These are important questions and it is wise to research the answers before you go abroad. Many volunteer organisations find accommodation for you, but if you are a self-funding volunteer it will be up to you to find your own accommodation.

Helen Tirebuck, Operations Manager at Challenges Worldwide (p139), says:

The country in which you are placed influences where you will stay. But, on the whole, our volunteers live with local hosts. This might be a young family who is interested in hosting a foreigner or it might be a colleague from the volunteer's host organisation who has a spare room. Living with a local host means there is instant support and local knowledge for the volunteer on their arrival in country. There is also no better way to integrate into a culture and learn about a new environment than from the locals themselves.

As Helen explains, homestays are common for international volunteers and have their advantages. However, not everyone wants to live as part of someone else's family for a sustained period of time and sometimes privacy can be an issue. Obviously, homestay experiences can also vary enormously, as Ian Flood found out when he volunteered in Bolivia:

I stayed with a large, very well-off family who employed four maids and lived in a big house. The father was a medical professor at the local university. I had a top-floor room with a large terrace, my own bathroom and great views over the city. This was an exception and subsequent families were less well off, but I still had my own room and good meals. I did not cook or wash up and they also did my laundry once a week.

Living in a shared flat or house with other volunteers is another popular option. Kate Sturgeon, who volunteered in Zimbabwe with Médecins Sans Frontières (p144), says:

I lived in a house with five other people. We had a big garden and a small swimming pool, so it was very nice. We had a lady who cooked our dinner during the week and did our washing and cleaning so we were terribly spoilt.

Sharon Baxter, who volunteered with Rokpa UK Overseas Projects (p183), lived in a shared flat when she volunteered in Tibet and tells a less luxurious story:

Inside the school compound there was a flat reserved for the English teachers. It had an indoor 'long drop' toilet. There were electric lights but no running water. As the flat was on the first floor it was hard work getting water, as it had to be carried up the stairs in aluminium buckets. Due to the altitude, any physical exertion made you breathless. The cooker in the flat regularly broke down, and I learnt how to purchase and replace the wire element. I washed my clothes by hand in a basin on the table. Clothes tended to dry very quickly even when the weather was cold, as the air is extremely dry.

Sharing your accommodation with a few flatmates is one thing, but sharing your kitchen with a totally different species is another, as Jacqueline Hill discovered when she volunteered in Bangladesh:

I had a fridge but it only had a small freezer compartment which needed constant defrosting. The ants got into everything, especially as they were able to chew through plastic. The smaller cockroaches also managed to get into the fridge. Cooking was difficult, particularly in the 40-degree heat and 98 per cent humidity of summer, and my diet became mainly mangoes. I did not get brave enough to buy live chickens but had a cooked meal every day at the office. I ate lots and lots and lots of rice, but on the whole a good, balanced diet of fish, meat and vegetables.

Where you live and how you adapt to domestic arrangements are important parts of your volunteer experience. As well as flats, rooms and houses (either shared or not), you will also find volunteers living in guesthouses, hostels and cheap hotels.

Who you live with is also a consideration. Sometimes it is refreshing to have the company of other volunteers, especially in the evenings. But, as Kate Sturgeon points out, it can be stressful:

There were six of us in the house and it was an intense way to live. If the team is good and the dynamics are healthy, it becomes your family and you make excellent friends. Trying to get privacy was not always easy but the hardest aspect for me was everyone knowing what you were doing all the time in or out of work.

Living on your own or with a friend or partner may be the best arrangement for some – see p39 for more details on volunteering with others.

Volunteering on a conservation and wildlife project is often another kettle of fish. Vikki Cole volunteered in the jungles of Borneo with Trekforce (p115) and this is how she describes her living conditions:

Mud. That pretty much sums up the part of the jungle we were living in. It was knee-deep clay mud, which also got deeper and gloopier the more it rained and the more we walked in it. Every day we washed in a little waterfall 200 metres below us, which sounds beautiful except for the leeches which, trust me, get everywhere. We also used this to wash our clothes in biodegradable soap. Our meals, which consisted every day of noodles or rice, were cooked by live-in locals who were camped with us. We slept in hammocks, which is a very interesting experience indeed. Trying to get into them while up to your knees in mud is definitely an acquired skill and was very funny after a few mess-mug-fulls of the rice wine that was passed around the camp at night! The jungle is definitely not the place for the squeamish: every bug and insect was on steroids and had tattoos. And everything bites or stings. But the wildlife and scenery is breathtaking.

Don't be put off by Vikki's experiences: it doesn't always have to be like that. Compared to Vikki, Robin Glegg, who volunteered with Biosphere Expeditions (p174), was positively pampered on one of his wildlife expeditions in the Altai (Siberia):

Accommodation consisted of tents. The toilet facilities were known as 'long drop'. Yes, a deep hole in the ground, surrounded by a toilet tent. But the meals were superb considering we were well away from civilisation; plenty of soups and stews with loads of vegetables and fruit. Having been in the field every day until 5 or 6pm, we would bowl into the large mess tent and be greeted by an evening meal prepared by a hired cook and helpers. We really were fed like kings. Washing ourselves was interesting. There were two or three shower tents, where the water was supposed to be heated by solar showers. However, the helpers started to boil water before we returned from the field, so that a warmish shower actually became a reality.

Finally, there's the issue of what you do with yourself when you're not volunteering. How do you spend your evenings?

Sometimes you're so shattered you just crawl thankfully into bed. Otherwise, volunteers make their own entertainment (this is where living with, or nearby, other volunteers can help). Of course, if you are working in a city or large town you'll have the usual night-time attractions (as long as you can afford them). Linda Walsh, who volunteered in Brazil, says:

Entertainment whilst living in Rio was endless. The volunteers were all really friendly and we had a very active social scene outside work.

Jacqueline Hill's experience in Bangladesh was different but rather closer to what a lot of international volunteers find themselves doing when they are not working:

Entertainment consisted mainly of reading (I got through the entire VSO library and had books sent from home), writing an internet diary, writing emails, letters and visiting local friends. I listened to the BBC World Service a lot and talking books. There really wasn't much else a single female could do.

Kerry Davies, who volunteered in Cambodia with VSO, agrees:

Evenings were quiet and the Cambodian people would often lock up their houses at 8pm. I spent my evenings reading books, watching DVDs bought locally and I also studied with the Open University, although I had to go to the capital, Phnom Penh, for an internet connection.

On the other hand, as many conservation and wildlife projects are group-based, the team spirit often continues long into the night. Clodagh O'Brien's experience in Borneo is typical:

We had a wonderful time. Many of the guys who worked at the reserve played guitar so we sang together pretty much every night, had bonfires, learned *poi* and, when the tropical rain set in, watched a DVD or two. Put it this way, I was rarely bored.

Robin Glegg, who has volunteered on many wildlife expeditions, remembers this about his last trip to Namibia:

After helping to clear the dishes (helpers were on hand to wash them) we all gathered around the campfire telling tales and generally discussing where the cheetahs were hiding and recapping the day's activities. We generally went to bed on the wrong side of midnight, with some of the group staying up until the last embers of the campfire had died.

The Working Week

As Dr Kate Simpson advises in her *Ethical Volunteering Guide* on p25, try to obtain a rough estimate of how many hours a week you will work before you go overseas. Also try to clarify what happens work-wise on weekends.

On most volunteer programmes you are expected to work full-time five days a week, with weekends off. Sometimes, though, you may work a six-day week. At times, the hours might be longer. Rachel Oxberry, who worked in an orphanage in Ecuador, says:

I generally worked six days a week from 7.30am to 9.00pm. Every so often I took a weekend off.

Sometimes you may need to work shifts. Jackie Bowles, who also worked in an orphanage, but in Brazil, says:

Volunteers had various timetables according to what suited the children and the educators. Your shift could either be 9am to 5pm with weekends off, or 7am to 7pm with every second day off.

Or your time might be a little more flexible, as with Peter Bennett, who was a volunteer teacher in Sudan:

At the university we were contracted to teach for 15 hours a week. In theory, we were expected to use the same time again for lesson planning and preparation. In addition, our host organisation expected us to get involved with other local voluntary initiatives. Time off was strongly discouraged and hard to negotiate.

Some volunteers, of course, don't wish to work full-time and opportunities do exist within well-managed volunteer programmes for part-time work. Jackie Bowles even did this after a period of full-time volunteering. She explains:

I volunteered for five months, then returned for a further three months on a part-time basis as I missed it so much!

What you want to avoid at all costs is any misunderstanding about the hours you'll be expected to work. There is nothing more discouraging than thinking you'll be volunteering full-time then finding that you're only needed for a couple of hours a day or less. Sometimes, this can happen mid-placement rather than at the start. Sharon Baxter, who taught in Tibet, comments:

When I first arrived we taught 15 classes a week. That was nice and easy and even with preparation and marking meant we still had plenty of free time. However, about half way through the six months, the school employed a Tibetan English teacher and cut our classes to only nine per week. There wasn't really enough to do after that and at times I felt a bit redundant.

If you are volunteering on a short-term or medium-term basis, the issue of holidays or extra time off might not be relevant. Poonam Sattee, who worked with street children in Guatemala, admits:

I was told I could have time off but I chose not to take it as I genuinely enjoyed my work and wanted to be there. I also knew I would be having a long holiday at the end of my time with Casa Alianza and so was prepared to wait.

Even on short-term or medium-term assignments, you can usually negotiate time off with your host organisation or you'll be given a certain amount of leave commensurate with the time you have worked. Whatever your arrangements for free time are, it is important to have a responsible and professional attitude towards arranging it.

However, if you are volunteering long term you will expect (and need) proper and pre-arranged vacation times. Many charities or sending agencies that arrange these types of placements have standard terms. For instance, Kerry Davies, who volunteered for two years in Cambodia, explains:

I had the choice of either the VSO holidays (four weeks plus all the public holidays – totalling 25 days) or UNICEF holidays (30 days plus seven UNICEF standard public holidays). I chose the latter as it was more flexible and I was working with other UNICEF staff.

Depending on how long you volunteer for, weekends off and holidays are an important part of your volunteer experience. Many international volunteers choose to travel at weekends to see more of the country in which they are living and many manage to visit neighbouring countries too. Oliver Walker taught in Sri Lanka and explains:

An Azafady Pioneer camp in a Madagascan village

At the weekends I stayed at a guest house in Kandy which is owned by the charity's representative. I became friendly with another volunteer and we travelled around the country together on Saturdays and Sundays.

Health, Safety & In-country Support

Volunteering in a foreign country miles away from home is not without its risks. If there's a medical or security emergency you need to know that the organisation you're volunteering with has up-to-date plans and procedures for dealing with the situation.

Before you travel overseas it is important that you feel fully briefed and prepared. In some cases there will be further briefings or training once you arrive in the country. For instance, Andrew Sansom, who volunteered with Biosphere Expeditions (p174) on wildlife projects in Slovakia and Sri Lanka, remembers:

At the start of the expedition, our leader took us through the Risk Register, which related to everything from wild animals to heatstroke. She then pointed out that we had already survived the biggest risk of all: Sri Lankan drivers.

When Robert Driver volunteered in of Belize with Trekforce (p115), he says:

We had intensive jungle training and an acclimatisation period, so when we went to the jungle for the first time we felt confident we could live there for eight weeks. Medics were also on the project site at all times.

One of the key ways to ensure that volunteers remain safe and well overseas is through in-country support. This means that your sending agency either has one or more local staff members whose job it is to help you and advise you, as well as deal with any emergencies. When choosing a volunteer organisation it is always wise to ask about in-country support and find out how 'local' the local support really is. Are they talking about a person just down the road or someone a hundred miles away looking after dozens of volunteers?

Rachel Guise, who volunteered in health and sanitation, sustainable livelihoods and conservation in Madagascar with Azafady (p132), says:

The charity ensured there was always a night guard at our campsite and there was always a local guide on site with us. We could go into town by ourselves if we chose, but the guides were always happy to come with us and offered advice and assistance. There were also other representatives of the charity in Madagascar who were easy to contact.

So much for predictable risks; however, what happens if the country you're volunteering in becomes politically unstable? In this case, not only do you need good in-country support, but well-planned security procedures. Sue Towler, Transform Programme Manager at the charity Tearfund (p208), had a difficult security issue to handle in early 2006 but the organisation was well prepared to assist staff in the field:

We had a Transform team in Bangalore, India, for four months, working with Tearfund's partner, Oasis. As with all teams, we had conducted a thorough risk assessment before departure and considered it safe for the team to travel. But a month into their stay, a leading Indian actor died, triggering major riots in the city. As news of the unrest reached us, the team was immediately advised to return to its accommodation on the outskirts of the city and to remain there until further notice. Events were unfolding quickly so we had a decision to make: was it safe for the team to stay or should we evacuate? We were particularly concerned when we learned that the unrest had prompted the British consulate in the city to close. We were in twice-daily phone contact with the team and our partner, Oasis, as well as in regular contact with Tearfund's Security Adviser and the Foreign and Commonwealth Office. Thankfully, the situation soon calmed and the consulate reopened, enabling us to avoid initiating our evacuation plan.

First-class support and emergency planning was also a feature of Jacqueline Hill's volunteer placement in Bangladesh:

Hmmm. Going to a Muslim country at the beginning of the Iraq war does not make for a restful placement. VSO were great at contacting us every day during the most difficult times to update us on the security situation and to explain their escalation procedure, ranging from recalling us all back to Dhaka through to full-scale evacuation. I'm happy to say we never got anywhere near that level, but we did stay indoors on Fridays for a few months, as that is the main day for prayers and things could get heated as people came out of the mosques. Apart from those exceptional circumstances, safety and security issues in Bangladesh were a feature of our in-country training.

Tried and tested procedures are also essential for medical emergencies. Michelle Hawkins, who volunteered as a staff member for Raleigh International (p125), was a project manager with the Bri Bri Indian community in a village in the Talamancan Indian Reserve of Costa Rica. She remembers:

Health and safety were paramount, as the village was only accessible by canoe and had no roads, electricity or phones. The nearest hospital was five hours away by river. I ran 'casualty-evacuation' drills to ensure we all knew what to do in the event of someone falling off the suspension bridge or getting bitten by a snake. End result: everyone fine.

Health, safety and in-country support are important elements of keeping safe when you volunteer. Smaller organisations, though, may have fewer resources: your pre-departure briefing may come in the form of a handbook and your emergency support may simply be a telephone number in your home country. Even this is likely to be more than you get if you arrange a placement yourself with a local charity or NGO, and this is something you should take into consideration. See p70 for the Top Ten Safety Tips for Female Volunteers and p67 for details on health and hygiene while volunteering.

Long-term Volunteering with Your Partner

We volunteered with VSO for two years in Ethiopia. We worked for the Ministry of Education, setting up a postgraduate qualification for teacher educators. We researched and wrote the Higher Diploma Programme with support and advice from colleagues in colleges and universities.

Because we had spent a year travelling through India prior to doing VSO, I think we had already recognised and adjusted to some of the challenges of living and travelling together in sometimes difficult circumstances.

For us, there were far more advantages than disadvantages to being a couple. It was reassuring to have one aspect of our lives familiar as we set off into the unknown and we were able to be mutually supportive. There were difficult and distressing times but we found that when one of us was 'down' the other was able to be 'up' and so we got through these periods. Sharing our problems helped us find solutions to them and we were able to be supportive of others, too. It added a new dimension to our relationship as we had different experiences to share.

The only disadvantage related to the fact that we were doing the same job. This meant that we were together almost ALL the time! We did have some professional disagreements, which inevitably spilled over into our personal lives. However, most of the time we worked together creatively and by the second year we had identified distinct roles for ourselves within the project. In our opinion, the ideal form of volunteering with a partner would be to have different jobs in the same place.

As an aside, we knew some couples where only one member had a placement while the other was an 'accompanying partner'. It was often difficult for the partner to find a role for themselves in a context where there were limited social opportunities.

Deborah Jordan & David Spinney

Who to Go With

You can volunteer on your own, with a friend or family member, or on team-based projects with people you either do or do not know. Sometimes the choice is down to you but sometimes it is up to your sending agency. Some organisations prefer to place you either on your own or in pairs.

Rachel Oxberry volunteered in Ecuador on her own and is a strong advocate of going solo:

I went alone which I feel helped me get the most out of my experience. I had to immerse myself fully in the culture and language and work out how to deal with very challenging situations. I was often out of my comfort zone which made me much stronger as a person.

Poonam Sattee, who volunteered in Guatemala, agrees:

I went by myself and that worked out fine. Initially, until I made friends, it was an isolating experience, but after the first two months I felt very settled. The pros of going by yourself are that you are much more independent and your Spanish will really take off. It helps you take more initiative and I think you are more likely to make local friends as opposed to relying on your group or partner. The cons: the initial stages of settling in can be quite tough, but apart from this my experience worked out well.

If you choose to volunteer alone, you will usually make friends pretty quickly when you arrive at your placement. But if your placement is an isolated one then your options may be limited. This is what Sharon Baxter experienced when she taught in Tibet:

I got a bit depressed and lonely towards the end. I spent the last two months on my own and by that time the weather was very cold and it got dark early. There didn't seem to be as many people around as in the summer. The children studied in the classrooms from 7pm until bedtime, so most nights I didn't see another human being after 7pm. Sitting on your own in a freezing flat with no radio or TV does eventually get a bit wearing. Very few people spoke any English and even though I made a few friends who could speak some English, it is difficult to get really close when there are language difficulties. By the end I was desperate to have an easy conversation with someone, without having to talk in pidgin English and wave my arms around.

The thought of volunteering with a friend can give you more confidence, particularly before you leave home and just after you arrive. But in some cases, it can mean that making other friends is not as easy as it would be if you were on your own. In Linda Walsh's experience it didn't make much difference to her stay in Brazil:

I went with a friend but we did different work. There were obvious advantages in this – we supported each other, especially when we were living out at the farm with no-one else around. When we were back in Rio with lots of other volunteers it didn't really make any difference as we worked different hours and had different friends. Overall, it was good to have a friend along, but not necessary.

Volunteering with a partner is a popular option for long-term volunteers and has it own set of advantages and disadvantages (see the boxed text opposite written by Deborah Jordan and David Spinney on volunteering with your partner). Sometimes you can volunteer with children, too. It's uncommon at this stage but is a growing trend. Jo Morgan volunteered with MondoChallenge and taught in the Indian Himalayas with her seven-year-old son, Liam. She admits:

On the first day he was embarrassed about the colour of his white skin and I began to wonder why I'd put him through this. But by the second day he'd made friends with his classmates, was 'one of the gang' and started to realise that children all over the world are basically the same and have similar needs and desires. He learned that some children have only one set of clothes, eat only rice and can't afford to be fussy. One of his friends had a birthday yet it was unmarked – no presents, cards or a party. Liam was initially incredulous but is now beginning to understand that these things are not to be taken for granted.

Of course, you may decide to set off on your own but join a team-based volunteer project in the field. These are more common on conservation and wildlife programmes than on development programmes. On many group-based volunteer programmes where everyone arrives and departs at the same time, you can ask to be put in touch with other team members prior to travelling overseas. This can help the team to bond, although evidence suggests that some groups need little help with this. On Robin Glegg's expedition to the Altai (Siberia) he remembers:

I went by myself and knew nobody who was going. There was slight trepidation at spending 12 days in the very close company of 12 or so individuals from various countries whom I'd never met. In reality it was a great way to meet a diverse group of people from different walks of life. We all jelled incredibly well and some close friendships were made. This certainly heightened the enjoyment of the expedition. When I did the Oman expedition it was a reunion with six of the 12 from the Altai trip.

But sometimes you're not so lucky. David Grassham volunteered in the Indian Himalaya and says with regret:

Unfortunately, our group did eventually split. Three girls tended to spend time only with each other, which was a shame. Even through I did get on with everyone, if you volunteer with a group it is possible that you may not like some of the other members. In our group, one particular person did seem to be disliked by quite a few others.

Meet the Organisation

As part of your research, try to meet representatives from the various charities or sending agencies that have volunteer programmes you're interested in. Many of these organisations hold regular information or briefing evenings, which are publicised on their websites, and many also attend the travel shows.

For UK residents, a special recruitment and volunteering event for the not-for-profit sector called Forum 3 (www.forum3.co.uk) ran for several years in London. The future of the event is uncertain, but if it goes ahead it usually takes place in October, and is a good place to meet many of the European and international volunteering organisations mentioned in this book. Unfortunately, there is no such organised event in the US or Australasia.

Summary of Questions

To recap, here are the key questions to ask all the organisations you may be interested in volunteering with. Depending on their answers, you can then make your choice:

~ **Organisation** What are your aims and objectives? Are you a charity, not-for-profit organisation or limited company? How long have you been established? What are your policies on ecotourism and ethical tourism and how are they implemented?

~ **Selection process** What are your selection criteria and processes? Will the interview be in person? What is the average age of volunteers? If I am working with children or vulnerable adults, will I need to have a criminal records clearance?

~ **The programmes** Do you work with local partner programmes? If so, how many partner programmes do you currently work with? How many of these partner programmes have you worked with for more than three years? How do I know I'll be working on a worthwhile, sustainable project that is needed by a local community? How will my work be continued after I leave? How many volunteers do you place annually? What job will I be doing and can you give me a brief job description? How do I know that my volunteering won't take a paid job away from a local person? What is the time frame of the volunteer project I'll be working on? What hours will I work? Will I need to speak the local language? What will the accommodation be like? Can I volunteer with another person? Can I talk to some returned volunteers?

~ **Costs** What exactly is included in the costs? Do you make a financial contribution to your volunteer programmes and, if so, exactly how much is this? Can I see a breakdown of where my money goes? Do you help with fundraising? (Only ask this if you're volunteering with a charity.)

~ **Pre-departure** What briefings, training and/or cultural orientation sessions are there?

~ **Health and safety** What health and safety and emergency procedures do you have in place? Are there staff members on site or do you have local representatives? If so, how far will they be from where I am volunteering? What medical care is available?

~ **Debriefing** Is there any support and debriefing procedure when I get home? How can I stay in touch with the organisation?

Do You Have What it Takes?

So, what qualities or skills make a good volunteer? Let's ask the experts – those that have 'been there, done that' and have heaps of advice and learning to pass on.

Poonam Sattee, who volunteered in Guatemala with street kids, suggests these are the qualities you need:

A good sense of humour. Lots of patience. An open mind – particularly to new ways of working, cultural norms, values and traditions. An ability to speak the language – if you are learning the language as you go along, it can be frustrating for you and the people you work with if you spend more time trying to understand what has been said than getting stuck into work. Also important are enthusiasm, initiative and dependability (the more you show the more responsibility you will be given).

Patience is a quality that comes up time and time again. Jacqueline Hill, who volunteered in Bangladesh, had to find plenty of patience, along with some other key qualities:

Flexibility and adaptability are key. These are the qualities that I developed hugely while I was away. Also important are appropriate self-confidence, the ability to work with others and not only accept, but make the most of, differences in approaches and ways of working. You need to build relationships too, often without the help of a common language. I found I had to 'switch off' quite a lot to generate the patience needed to get everyday things done. Everything took so much longer and was so much more complicated and difficult than at home – particularly anything to do with officialdom. Another thing I learned in Bangladesh was to ask for help. The ability to listen and think are much more important than telling other people what to do or rushing in and doing things.

Keeping an open mind was important for Poonam Sattee and was also key for Kerry Davies, who volunteered in Cambodia:

A good volunteer should approach their placement with an open mind. Cambodian logic is not generally the same as that of UK people. It is important to remember that your colleagues are all highly intelligent and have survived many atrocities in their life. They don't need anyone patronising them or thinking they are superior because they have had the luxury of an education. Cambodians have a great sense of humour and a smile speaks a thousand words. It takes a long time to fit in and gain their trust, but when you do the rewards are well worth the wait.

A New Zealander, John Gordon, worked as an agricultural tutor in Bougainville for the Volunteer Service Abroad (VSA, p123). He agrees that patience and respect are important:

You sow seeds, plant cuttings and graft on new ideas but whether they 'take' or not is part of someone else's future.

The Ills and Cures of Volunteering

This section on how to combat some of the common problems encountered by volunteers is aimed primarily at long-term volunteers working in developing countries. It is written by Katherine Tubb, director of 2Way Development, and is based upon her experiences of running a not-for-profit sending agency.

Homesickness

Some of you will feel this common condition of travelling overseas, some of you won't. One thing I have witnessed on many occasions with homesickness, especially with younger long-term volunteers, is that their placement seems like an eternity when they first get overseas. The temptation to go home, back to normality, predictability and safety, is very high.

~ **Cure** Keep time in perspective. Sure, 'there's no place like home'… but home is always there. The time you have will go very quickly! Short, well-timed trips home and people visiting you may prevent you missing home so much. Try to join social groups for support outside your workplace. One thing I always recommend is contacting your embassy for advice about these. Also, introduce familiar activities into your daily routine. Joining a local health club (if there is one) is good because it gives you an element of familiarity in your daily life which can be helpful.

Communication Shock

Volunteering is all about different cultures, both personally and professionally. There are elements of a culture that you may not be able to explain or understand – this is where communication comes in. Language barriers and a different way of communicating could be potential obstacles to your happiness when volunteering overseas. Volunteers can react negatively to new ways of communicating by isolating themselves from their surroundings and misinterpreting the behaviour of colleagues and friends.

~ **Cure** Allow yourself time to get used to your new home and work environment. Make allowances and give people the benefit of the doubt until you are accustomed to your surroundings. Be proactive in communicating – ask for information and assistance and for people to translate.

Privacy & Independence

Your host organisation may feel responsible for your welfare and may want to 'look after' you in a way you are not used to back home (particularly if you are a younger female volunteer). This is especially relevant to volunteers who are provided with accommodation by their host organisation. For instance, your host organisation may be concerned about you going out unaccompanied late at night. In addition, your accommodation may have little privacy, with people entering your bedroom without permission: something that may upset you but is perfectly normal to the people you're living with.

~ **Cure** Again, proactive, patient communication can go a long way towards resolving these situations. Patience and an understanding of different points of view and ways of life are important too.

Your Host Organisation

You may find certain elements of your workplace very frustrating when volunteering. The structure of the organisation with which you are volunteering may have apparent failures (from your perspective). Some of the problems that volunteers have mentioned to me are: poor management; badly spent funds; overstaffing; time-wasting; lack of transparency; poor strategic planning; and hierarchical staff relations.

~ **Cure** What is different may not necessarily be bad. If it clearly is, your role is to SLOWLY suggest ways that the organisation can improve. Please don't suggest a radical change in the running of your host organisation on day three (I know people who have done this), save this till week seven!

Your Role

You will see your time volunteering as helping. But how you want to help and what is needed may not be the same things. A great deal of your time may be devoted to fundraising, for instance, as a way of improving the capacity of your host organisation. You may be given a lot of office work instead of field work, which could conflict with your objectives for your volunteering experience. Initially you may not be given huge responsibilities and may not feel you are achieving what you set out to do.

~ **Cure 1** To start with (generally the first six weeks), you should not rely on the fact that you are committing your time and have paid a lot of money to get to the country to guarantee your integration and acceptance into your host organisation – this will take time. Work closely with your host organisation in negotiating a role for yourself that both you and they are happy with. Trust-building is really important in this process.

~ **Cure 2** 'Doing by learning' not 'learning by doing' is a good mantra here. Don't expect to change the world in your first six weeks. And when you do start 'doing', see your achievements for what they are. I have worked with volunteers who achieve a lot in their placement, even after the initial settling-in period, but still insist that they aren't doing enough. Write down your achievements, however small, and think carefully about the time you have and what you should realistically expect to achieve.

Support

The level of support you receive from the organisation you are volunteering with depends upon the nature of your placement. For individual volunteers working directly with local charities, orientation, advice and support might not be freely available. You might enter a situation where human resources are in short supply, and therefore you may not be assigned a member of staff to act as your supervisor and may not have the opportunity to 'job shadow'.

~ **Cure** It is important that individual volunteers take steps to support themselves, such as asking for adequate support from colleagues and being explicit about what they need.

General cures…

~ **The six-week rule** The first six weeks of overseas volunteering is a critical stage in adapting to new surroundings. When you are living and working in a new country as a long-term volunteer, you will have to adapt to a very different professional and home environment.

~ **Slow down** You probably will not operate as fast as you would in your home country when volunteering. This is fine! Take small steps to achieve what you want from your volunteering experience.

~ **Knowledge is power** Research the country you are volunteering in and the organisation you are volunteering with before leaving your home country. Also, it can be positive to establish communication with your colleagues in your host organisation before you depart. Expose yourself to as much information as possible about the country you are going to, such as images, documentaries, films and books, and try and talk to people who have been there.

Katherine Tubb
Director
2Way Development
www.2way.org.uk

Sandra Sinclair was also with VSA and worked as a midwife in Bougainville. She says a bit of realism is necessary:

You do have to accept that, as a foreign health professional, you can't change the world or do anything quickly. But I made small changes which I am confident are continuing.

Respect and understanding for the local people you work alongside are also crucial qualities, in Phil Sydor's eyes. He volunteered with Hands Around the World in Zambia, where he helped build a teaching centre and says it's important:

Not to assume you know it all! We worked with the local people, not as managers to tell them what to do, but as labourers. They had appointed a site manager and we made sure we deferred to her and asked her what we should be doing. The local people were surprised at this.

The ability to relate to all sorts of different people is what Elaine Massie and Richard Lawson believe is important. They have volunteered many times on short-term environmental projects and say:

You have to be able to get on with all sorts of people. Earthwatch volunteers range from 16 to 80 years of age and you may have this wide age range in your group. Also, you generally live in close quarters with everyone and there is often very little opportunity for you to have your 'own space'.

But for a comprehensive summary of what qualities you need to have as a volunteer on conservation and wildlife projects, let's turn to the words of Robin Glegg (a veteran of three expeditions):

You need to be open-minded, team-spirited and tolerant but enquiring. Do not expect to be 'nannied' and be prepared for some tough times, such as adverse weather, hard physical activity or basic living conditions. Be prepared to mix with people you have never met before and be prepared to experience a very different lifestyle to the one at home. Remember that the more you put in, the more you get out of these expeditions. Oh yes, I nearly forgot, do not necessarily expect to see lots of wildlife. The tragedy is that in many parts of the world, much of the wildlife has been poached, driven away or become extinct. Many Biosphere expeditions have been set up in order just to ascertain the presence of a species. Do not build up your hopes and you will not be disappointed.

Robin makes an extremely valuable point here. Part of 'having what it takes' to be an international volunteer, whether you work in development or conservation and wildlife, is to have realistic expectations of your placement. Nine times out of ten if a placement doesn't work out the reason is that the expectations of the volunteer didn't match the reality of the experience.

There are things you can do to ensure that you approach your placement in the right spirit of respect and tolerance. Research your chosen destination and leave cultural norms and expectations behind. Be mindful of how your arrival on the scene might impact on the locals you're working with. Successful volunteers are like sponges soaking up as much as possible about the circumstances they find themselves in and taking their cues from how the local people interact. For instance, casual clothing may be the norm in your country of origin but if you're working for an NGO or government agency in Laos, you'll be expected to wear modest traditional dress. If you're receiving a monthly allowance from your government, you may find yourself earning more than the locals you're working alongside, so be discreet. And remember that volunteers are subject to the laws of the local country. In Western democracies it's acceptable to be an anti-royalist, but in Thailand, speak out against the monarchy and not only do you cause great offence you could also become familiar with the interior of a local police station.

More Information

Publications
~ **Volunteer Work Overseas for Australians and New Zealanders** by Peter Hodge (Global Exchange, 2004). Tells how to find and prepare for a volunteer position from childcare to plumbing, with workplace issues to ponder and accounts from returned volunteers.

Useful Websites
~ **British Overseas NGOs for Development (BOND)** (www.bond.org.uk) A site which aims to improve the UK's contribution to international development through the exchange of ideas, experience and information.

~ **Center for Responsible Travel (CREST)** (www.responsibletravel.org) The website of this research institution is packed with quick tips on responsible travelling and has useful publications for download.

~ **Comhlámh** (www.comhlamh.org) A membership organisation that supports returned development workers and campaigns on global development issues. It is the Irish equivalent of BOND, NIDOS and WCIA (listed here).

~ **The Telegraph Adventure Travel Show** (www.adventureshow.co.uk)
A chance to make contact with some of the UK's international voluntary organisations.

~ **Destinations: The Holiday & Travel Show** (www.destinationsshow.com) One opportunity to meet some of the UK's international voluntary organisations.

~ **Ethical Volunteering** (www.ethicalvolunteering.org) Dr Kate Simpson's site on the topic of ethical volunteering.

~ **Network of International Development Organisations in Scotland (NIDOS)** (www.nidos.org.uk) A network of 55 Scottish-based associations with similar goals to BOND, WCIA and Comhlámh.

~ **ServiceLeader.org** (www.serviceleader.org) General articles on issues faced by North American volunteers, with links and information focusing on international service positions.

~ **Travelers' Philanthropy** (www.travelersphilanthropy.org) Run by CREST, this portal helps travellers make a difference at their destinations by learning about and donating to development projects.

~ **University of Michigan International Center** (http://internationalcenter.umich.edu) This US page offers scads of practical advice on choosing an international work or volunteer opportunity.

~ **University of Minnesota Learning Abroad Center** (www.umabroad.umn.edu) Although some resources are tailored to students, this website has plenty of tips for any US citizens considering international volunteering.

~ **Volunteering Options** (www.volunteeringoptions.org) Put together by Comhlámh, this site has lots of online information about international volunteering.

~ **Welsh Centre for International Affairs (WCIA)** (www.wcia.org.uk) This site is the Welsh equivalent of BOND, NIDOS and Comhlámh.

~ **World Service Enquiry** (www.wse.org.uk) Lots of information on international volunteering and working in development, including one-to-one advice and a newsletter called *Opportunities Abroad*.

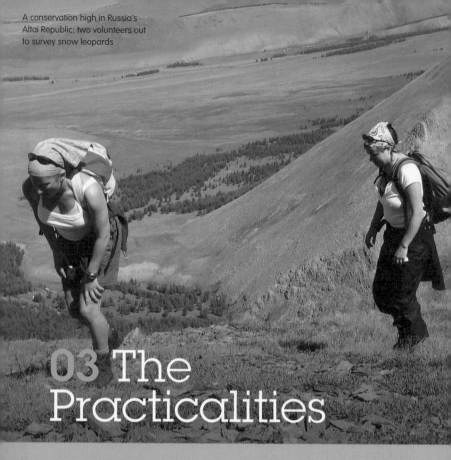

A conservation high in Russia's Altai Republic: two volunteers out to survey snow leopards

03 The Practicalities

This is where the fun really begins. You've done your research, you have an idea of what you'd like to do, where you might like to go and you've set aside the time. All you have to do now is make it happen…

Application & Selection

Most international volunteers apply to sending agencies eight to 12 months before they wish to volunteer. This time frame works well for three reasons: it gives you and your organisation enough time to find the right volunteer project; it allows you sufficient time to save the money; and it means you've got months in which to organise your life at home so you can go abroad (see Chapter 4 for more details on this).

If you are not as organised as this or have decided to volunteer at the last minute, don't worry. Most sending agencies will still work with you to find a placement with only a month or two's notice. However, places on the most popular conservation and wildlife expeditions can fill up a year in advance, and many of the organisations placing skilled volunteers need at least four months' notice.

In Australia and New Zealand, some sending agencies specialise in short-term placements and place volunteers without a great deal of experience or tertiary qualifications.

Placements such as these are usually for self-funding volunteers. Long-term placements, however, mostly require a commitment of at least a full year and people must have a minimum of a couple of years' experience in their area of expertise in order to meet the specific needs of the host organisation. Such programmes generally attract volunteers in their mid-twenties up. The application process is fairly rigorous and isn't unlike applying for a job, with specific selection criteria needing to be addressed, written references provided and the possibly of a phone interview. Personal qualities and attributes like cultural awareness, self-assurance, flexibility and good communication and interpersonal skills are viewed as equally important as professional experience, since these placements require living and working in a developing country.

The majority of sending agencies ask you to download an application form from their website. This usually asks for your personal details, including your education, qualifications, skills, medical history and any criminal convictions. It may also ask you a few questions, like: 'Why do you want to volunteer overseas?' 'What experiences have you had that show you are adaptable?' 'What are your strengths and weaknesses?' Usually, you then post this off with your CV, two references (one personal and one professional) and two passport-sized photos.

Some organisations prefer you to apply by sending in your CV with a covering letter. If this is the case, make sure that your covering letter tells the organisation why you want to volunteer and what you can offer. Eoghan Mackie, CEO of Challenges Worldwide (CWW, p139) tells us what he is looking for in a covering letter and at interview:

Each particular host organisation has its own culture which we will assess the applicant against. The applicant must also have the relevant professional experience our host partner is looking for. However, there are generic qualities that a person must show in their application (and later at interview) before we will seriously consider them for selection as a CWW volunteer. These include independence, adaptability, flexibility, communication skills, determination and a sense of humour. Perhaps the most important quality of all is the ability to be objective.

After you have sent in your application, you wait for the organisation to contact you. They will usually do this by phone to either arrange a personal interview or ask you to attend one of their selection or assessment days. These events are fascinating and usually involve problem-solving tasks and programmes designed to test how you work in a team. Jacqueline Hill, who volunteered in Bangladesh, remembers her assessment day with VSO:

It was well organised and a lot of fun. The day consisted of some group exercises and an individual interview. The interview goes into more depth, particularly about personal circumstances, than an ordinary job interview, but it was sensitively handled and we could see the reasons why it was important to make sure we were ready for the huge commitment we were signing up to. My advice to anyone going for the assessment day? Be yourself and enjoy it.

Sometimes the selection process takes place over a weekend, as it does if you apply to become a Raleigh International staff member. Duncan Purvis, training manager for Raleigh International (p108), explains:

Successful applicants will be invited to attend a Staff Assessment Weekend (SAW). This is an intensive two-day programme designed to recreate programme life and gives you a taste of what staff roles entail, as well as allowing us to assess your suitability. Depending upon your performance during the weekend, we will either offer you a post on a programme which makes best use of your particular skills and qualifications or suggest further action for you to take in order to reapply in the future.

If you are the type of volunteer the organisation is looking for, UK and US organisations will request a deposit from you (naturally this applies only to fee-based programmes). This could be anything from £50 to £500 (US$80 to US$800), and is usually non-refundable. Australasian organisations generally don't require a deposit. You will also need to read the organisation's terms & conditions document and sign it (very standard stuff). Some organisations also ask you to fill out a detailed medical history questionnaire and, if it throws up any potential problems, to visit a health expert nominated by them.

Over the subsequent weeks or months the organisation will work with you to find a suitable placement. As this is dependent on local demand, it is good to remain flexible about where you go (there may not be a demand for your skills in your country of first choice). Programme fees, or 'fundraising targets' as they're also called (see the next section for more), must usually be paid in instalments, with the final payment made three to six weeks before departure.

Of course, every organisation has a slightly different process. Conservation and wildlife programmes often have less stringent selection processes, because working with animals or the environment is quite different to working closely with local people in a development capacity. And if you arrange your own placement directly, some, none or all of this process may occur.

Raising the Money

Whether you volunteer through a sending agency in your own country or fix up a placement directly, costs will be involved. Even if you go with one of the organisations that covers your costs and pays you a small stipend (eg VSO, Médecins Sans Frontières, SkillShare International, Australian Volunteers International), you will still want extra money for weekends away, holidays and possibly independent travel after your placement has ended.

However much your volunteer placement costs, it is a good idea to start saving (or fundraising) as soon as you can. It can take volunteers up to a year to get the money together.

Paying vs Fundraising

If you volunteer with a charity, the money you pay for your placement is always referred to as the money you need to 'fundraise'. Effectively it is payment (you won't be able to go if you don't meet your fundraising target). However, charities don't like to call it that because the nature of how you saved the money is supposed to be different. One motivation for approaching the money issue in this way is that self-promotion is important to charities. It makes sense for them to encourage you to use their name to run special events to raise funds and to collect donations from friends, family and members of the public. In addition, for younger volunteers, in particular, fundraising is supposed to be part of your overall experience and integral to the self-development aspect of your volunteering experience.

Of course, if you're an older volunteer, or don't have time to fundraise and just want to pay out of your own pocket, this is allowed, though slightly frowned upon.

Your Budget

Regardless of what is (and is not) included in the overall fee or donation you pay your sending agency, it is a useful exercise to work out a detailed budget of all likely costs. Bear in mind while you're doing this that fluctuating exchange rates can affect that all-important account balance. It also pays to do some investigation into the cost of living at your destination. You may be surprised to learn, for instance, that Lagos and Hanoi were found to be more expensive than San Francisco in a 2006 worldwide cost-of-living survey.

You can break your budget into three main cost areas: pre-departure; in-country; and coming home.

On top of the world: Azafady volunteers reach the summit of Pic St Louis, Madagascar

Pre-departure Costs

Costs that apply here may include:

~ **Placement fee/donation** If you have arranged your placement directly with a grassroots NGO there may not be a fee (although you may be asked for a donation towards the project). Otherwise you may pay anything from £850 to £4000 (US$1350 to US$6350), depending on how long you're going for, where you're going, what you're doing and what is included in this cost. In Australia or New Zealand fees might range from A$650 to A$5000 (NZ$830 to NZ$6400). For more detailed information on the cost of specific volunteer programmes, see Chapters 5 to 8.

~ **Interviews and briefing events** Remember to budget for expenses (eg travel, accommodation) related to face-to-face interviews with your sending agency and also any follow-up briefing or training events.

~ **Research material** You may want to buy a couple of maps, guidebooks or language-learning CDs.

~ **Putting your life on hold** This is a big one, with potentially significant costs. So big, in fact, that the whole of Chapter 4 is devoted to everything you need to think about and organise at home before you leave. For instance, will you need to put your personal belongings into storage? Will you continue to pay rent? And what about the cost of redirecting your mail?

~ **International flights** Regardless of where you're going, flights will be a big part of your pre-departure budget. For more information on airline tickets and travel, see p54.

~ **Visas** For a discussion about whether you should obtain a tourist visa or a volunteering visa, see p57. Most tourist visas range in price between £11 (US$17) and £53 (US$84). Tourist visas for Asia are often quoted in US dollars and start from around US$30.

~ **Travel insurance** This could cost anything from around £400 (US$635) upwards for 12-month worldwide cover. You could certainly obtain travel insurance for less but you don't want to skimp when you're an international volunteer. Read the section on travel insurance on p58.

~ **Immunisations and medication** In the UK and US, most vaccinations cost between £20 to £64 (US$30 to US$100). Depending on your plans, a trip to the travel clinic could easily set you back £200 (US$315), including antimalarial medicines. In Australia, a standard consultation at a travel clinic will cost around A$60 plus any required vaccines, which range from A$5.50 to around A$130 for a rabies or typhoid vaccination. See p64 for more information on health-related matters.

~ **Medical kit** A decent medical kit in the US or UK will cost between £30 to £50 (US$50 to US$80). In Australia it's a similar investment – between A$105 to A$200 (excluding antimalarials). See p66 for suggestions on what your medical kit might contain.

~ **Equipment** The majority of volunteer organisations send you a kit list prior to departure (see p60 for our suggestions and ideas from returned volunteers on what to pack). What you spend on equipment depends on where you are going and what you are doing. The kit you need for marine conservation, for instance, can sometimes be more costly than for other projects. On a musical note, if you don't have one already you might want to invest in an MP3 player or put your music on a smartphone.

~ **Travel to airport** Something to add into your spreadsheet.

In-Country Costs

These costs may be more difficult to judge, as you're estimating from afar. However, the organisation you're volunteering with will be able to give you guidance; you can obtain an indication of costs from many guidebooks, too. It is also crucial to talk to returned volunteers.

Here are the main spending areas that you will need to consider:

~ **Travel to and from airport and placement** It's important to think about this from a safety perspective. In some cases a representative from your organisation will pick you up or drop you off, but you may have to pay for this. Otherwise, you'll need money for public transport or a taxi.

~ **Living expenses** This includes accommodation, food and drink, laundry and entertainment expenses, and spending money. How much you should budget for depends on the cost of living in the country and whether you are city based or in more rural surroundings. To a certain extent it also depends on your own standards and what you can afford. For reasons of cultural sensitivity though, regardless of what they can afford, volunteers rarely splurge on their accommodation. Rachel Oxberry volunteered in Ecuador and lived simply:

> I had my own room which was very basic with just a bed. I had a cold shower with hot water about once a week. My meals were pretty simple and I either hand washed or took my laundry to a Laundromat in town. I rarely left the home at night: I tended to read and go to bed. I was spending approximately US$40 a week.

~ **Keeping in touch** This is not a costly business these days, unless you use your mobile phone unwisely (presuming you do get network coverage). For a discussion of all the options for keeping in touch, see p73.

~ **Travel at weekends** Chances are you'll want to see a bit of the country you're in, get away for a short while to relieve any job-related stress or pop over the border to renew your visa. Weekend breaks are often a volunteer's lifeline, so you need to budget for them.

~ **Post-volunteer travel** Many international volunteers take the opportunity of being abroad to travel after their placement. You could choose to travel home slowly overland (as far as possible) or spend more time exploring the region where you are based. Whatever you choose, you may like to allow for this eventuality in your budgeting.

~ **Sundry expenses** You may want to buy a few presents for the folks back home or the people you have met while volunteering, or get some souvenirs for yourself. There are a hundred other reasons why you may need a little extra money floating around in your budget.

~ **Departure tax** Sometimes this is included in the cost of your ticket, sometimes it isn't. If it's not, don't forget to keep sufficient local currency so you can pay for it at the airport.

Coming Home

Coming home can be a costly business, too. If you don't have a job to return to, you may need enough money to cover several months of living expenses while you look for one. Of course, it all depends on your circumstances. Will you be able to stay with friends or family while you find work, or will you move straight back into your house and have to cover the mortgage? Will you need to find several months' rent plus a deposit on a flat or house? Realistically, it is a good idea to budget for between £2000 to £5000 (US$3170 to US$7940) as a decent coming-home fund. For more information on coming home, see Chapter 9.

Saving

If you are not volunteering for a charity, you won't have the opportunity to fundraise officially (although, of course, friends and family may still want to help you on your way, because you are planning to work for a good cause for free).

Many volunteers work hard for the privilege of volunteering. Maggie Wild has been a volunteer leader for TCV (The Conservation Volunteers, p133) for around 18 months on a variety of international projects. She says:

I worked for three years in a graduate job and saved from the moment I started with this in mind. Half of my wage every month went into a savings account and this has been my safety net for the past two years.

Sixty-nine-year-old David Daniels, who has undertaken two expeditions with the Scientific Exploration Society to the Amazon and Mongolia, funded his trip in the following way:

I'm spending the kids' inheritance.

Emma Campbell, who volunteered in Ecuador with VentureCo (p115), explains:

I used my redundancy money and I sold loads of my stuff on eBay.

If you do start early, there are heaps of ways you can save or raise money in everyday life. For instance, you could get a second job, sell your car, use public transport instead of taxis, eat out less often, cancel the cleaner or jog around the park rather than pay for an expensive gym membership.

Fundraising

If there's one thing that almost all volunteers say about fundraising, it's that it takes up lots of time. With this in mind, it's a good idea to focus on events or schemes that will give you the maximum return (although this can be hard to judge at the outset).

When fundraising, most volunteers start with friends and family. At the time we spoke to him, Michael Tuckwell was fundraising to volunteer with Task Brasil (p170) in Brazil. He explains:

I have a lifetime of connections and a full address book. I am also riding in the Bristol Biggest Bike Ride and have written to 78 people asking them to sponsor me for Task Brasil. To date, I have received £1200 from friends and family, some of whom have been extremely generous.

Vikki Cole, who volunteered in Borneo with Trekforce (p115), was also blessed with good personal contacts:

Fundraising is the best part. I began bullying people I knew to donate directly to the website I set up. My sister and I (she came with me) also held a Valentine's ball and curry nights. Needless to say, more men came to the curry nights than the ball. Writing to large corporations to ask for donations is tough and you have to prepare for a lot of rejections. But walking door-to-door on a high street can yield some great raffle prize donations.

Talking of big events that will bring the money in, this is Judith Stephen's experience of running two fundraising events for Doctors of the World (Médecins du Monde, p142):

We did: 1) a quiz night plus supper – this raised £1500 after deducting our expenses; and 2) a concert plus supper – this raised nearly £1000 after expenses. The venue for both was a local church crypt with good kitchen facilities, so making a two-course supper for 75 each time was manageable. We charged £25 per ticket for each event and managed to create a nice dinner of mince-based casserole, couscous and salad followed by strawberries and cream for less than £1.50 per head (including a free glass of wine). As with most things, the planning was crucial. We had a team of about eight friends managing specific tasks like serving the wine, keeping a tally of quiz scores etc. With the quiz questions you need to be careful – the questions must not be so hard that people feel stupid. Both events went very smoothly but required a lot of work.

If you are fundraising on behalf of a charity, the organisation itself will give you lots of help and pointers. Mark Jacobs, managing director of Azafady (p132), explains:

Fundraising resources include a full fundraising manual, fundraising documentation such as sponsorship forms, events to join in with and resources such as collection boxes, raffle tickets, posters and Christmas cards.

In Australia, trivia nights are a great way to gather people in the interests of a good cause. At around A$10 a head, it's a case of the more the merrier. Also, in a country known for its love of sport, it's no coincidence that events such as 24-hour marathons and cycling odysseys (only the fit need apply) are popular ways of convincing your nearest and dearest to empty their pockets of loose change to get you volunteering overseas.

Some organisations offer general advice on volunteer programme fundraising. **CrossCultural Solution's Fundraising Guide** (www.crossculturalsolutions.org) is one excellent resource for American and British volunteers. There's also an entire website devoted to fundraising ideas, resources and links – click over to www.fund-raising.com.

Creative Fundraising

I used my old sixth form to do a lot of fundraising. One of my ideas proved really successful. Having gone to an all-girls' school, I approached three of the male teachers and asked them if they were willing to get their legs waxed for charity. After three weeks' of persuasion they agreed. I hyped the event, produced 'wanted' posters of the teachers around the school and ran an assembly saying that it would be up to the school which teachers got their legs done. I then charged people to vote for the teacher they most wanted to see get their legs waxed. I ran the voting over one week. The results showed a tie between two particular teachers so I ran the event again, just between the two. Again, I charged for people to vote. After the voting was over, I charged people to come and see the event, sold popcorn, drinks etc, and if people wanted to wax the teacher's legs themselves, I charged them per wax strip. It was a simple event and with lots of friends I managed to raise £600.

Poonam Sattee

Poonam Sattee volunteered with Casa Alianza in Guatemala for a year, working with street children.

Preparation

Many of the larger sending agencies run pre-departure briefing and training events. Subjects covered usually include: managing your expectations; cultural awareness and integration; what life could be like on your placement; and what to do if something goes wrong. In the case of Maggie Wild, a volunteer leader for TCV (The Conservation Volunteers, p133), training sessions were tailored to her role:

As a leader, my training was different to that of the other volunteers. I took the following courses: Residential Leadership Training; International Leader Training; First Aid at Work; and Wilderness First Aid.

Even though this is specialist training, it is wise to consider what courses you could do independently to equip yourself for your placement. It is certainly a good idea to think about a first-aid and travel-safety course (for more information on both, see p66 and p71).

If you have a placement teaching English, you may want to obtain a teaching certificate. There are two main training systems: TEFL (Teacher of English as a Foreign Language) is most popular in Europe; and TESOL (Teachers of English to Speakers of Other Languages) is the main system in the USA. Before Sharon Baxter volunteered to teach in Tibet she says:

I took a course in Teaching English as a Foreign Language. I also tried to learn some Tibetan, but it is not easy, as different dialects are spoken in different regions.

Most volunteers prepare for their time overseas by learning the local language or reviving their dormant language skills. Poonam Sattee, who volunteered in Guatemala, says:

I really immersed myself in the language before I left – I spoke Spanish to everyone I could find. I found out as much as I could about Guatemala so it wouldn't be such a culture shock when I arrived. And I did research on the issues surrounding street children there.

Jacqueline Hill, who volunteered in Bangladesh, also tried to find out as much as possible about where she was going:

I attended the VSO training agreed with my placement adviser. I talked to friends and relatives from Pakistan and Bangladesh. I read the Lonely Planet guidebook – the only guidebook to Bangladesh available at the time. I was also able to talk to returned volunteers, as I was provided with a list. I had already travelled in Pakistan, so mistakenly thought I was prepared for the living conditions.

Talking to returned volunteers is very important. Also, if you are volunteering on a team-based project, your organisation will usually circulate contact details for everyone prior to departure. This means you can do a little preparation together, forward information of interest and pass on any tips. If you want to take this one step further, Karen Hedges, who volunteered in Madagascar, remembers:

I read some books on Madagascar and helped in the charity office for a few days before I went, to help understand more about the organisation I was going to work for.

Volunteers who expect their placement to be physically challenging also address this prior to departure. Ann Noon, who volunteered in Peru, advises:

I tried to do more sport in the run-up to leaving, to be better equipped to deal with living at altitude.

In the months before you leave, your sending agency will also be in regular contact, forwarding you information packs, detailed handbooks and generally keeping you informed about what's happening, what you should be doing and when you need to do it by.

Useful Documents

Your sending agency will let you know of any documentation you may need to take with you. However, a few bits of paper you might like to add to this list are given here.

~ **International driving permit** These need to be taken in addition to your normal driving licence and are valid for one year only. In the UK, you can apply for one through the **AA** (www.theaa.com), **RAC** (www.rac.co.uk) or some post offices. In the US, **AAA** (www.aaa.com) and **NAC** (+1 800 622 2136; http://www.thenac.com) are the only entities federally authorised to distribute permits; AAA's online application form is the most convenient way to get one. In Canada, **CAA** (http://www.caa.ca/travel-documents) is the way to go. In Australia, members of the **Australian Automobile Association** (www.aaa.asn.au) can issue these.

~ **Itinerary print-out** Of course, you're likely to want to take this for your own purposes anyway, but in addition you may be required to show it as evidence of onward travel at border crossings or airports.

~ **Criminal record clearance** If you are working with children or vulnerable adults, your sending agency will probably arrange for one of these as part of their checking and selection process. If they don't, it is something you should arrange. In the UK, log onto the **Disclosure & Barring Service (DBS)** (http://www.homeoffice.gov.uk/agencies-public-bodies/dbs) for a list of umbrella organisations that can arrange one for you. In the States, either your local police department or the FBI's **Criminal Justice Information Services** (CJIS) (www.fbi.gov/hq/cjisd/fprequest.htm) can supply you with a document indicating you have no criminal record. Canadians must visit their local police station for fingerprinting and a criminal record check application. Australians should contact the Criminal Records Section of their relevant state or territory police department.

~ **Curriculum vitae** Your CV may be required by your host organisation, especially if your work history is impressive.

~ **Birth certificate** There's no harm in taking a photocopy of this along with you.

~ **Passport photos** A few wide-eyed shots may be handy when applying for tourist visas.

~ **Photo ID** Always useful to have on you. A driving licence should fit the bill.

Airline Tickets

If you are a self-funding volunteer or going through a sending agency that requires you arrange your own flights, here's a quick reminder of how to get the best deals.

Seasonal Limits

Think carefully about your departure date, because the price of your ticket will depend on this. Try to avoid departing during school and major national holidays, as all airline fares are at their peak during these times.

When to Purchase

Ideally, you should start looking for bargain fares eight to 12 months in advance of your departure date. You may get cheap tickets at the last minute but this is rare, even if seats are still available. Unfortunately, many of the best deals will require you to pay in full soon after booking. And special or bargain fares often don't allow changes or carry heavy change penalties (which are rarely covered by your travel insurance).

Maximum Time Limits

If you are volunteering for more than a year, it is likely you won't be able to use the return portion of your ticket. This is because it is virtually impossible to find a ticket that allows you to be away for more than 12 months. It may still be cheaper for you to buy a return (rather than a single fare) and simply not use the return flight. However, before you go down this route, do some research on the Web to see how much it'll cost to buy a ticket home from your placement.

Cancellation Penalties

These vary considerably but cancelling your ticket once it's booked may mean you lose the entire value of your ticket. (Most travel insurance policies protect against unavoidable cancellation fees but only if the reason for cancelling is one covered by the particular policy you took out.)

Refund Policy

Sometimes volunteers want to extend their placements when in the field. If you do this and don't use a certain portion or sector of your airline ticket, it is unlikely you'll get a refund. Most airline tickets are sold on a 'non-refundable if part used' basis. And don't rely on what you're told about refund value by overseas travel agents or airline office staff – staff in Nairobi, for example, don't know all the rules of a discounted ticket sold by an agent in another country. If you are entitled to a refund, this can usually be arranged only through the travel agency where your ticket was purchased (and it may take several months). This isn't terribly useful if you're volunteering in the middle of Africa somewhere.

Change Penalties

There are three main types of changes: name changes, date changes and route changes. It's very rare that a name change will be permitted. As regards dates, there are usually restrictions on changing your departure date from your home country. However, if volunteering is only a part of a much longer trip, the dates of onward flights can often be changed (subject to seat availability). Although in many cases date changes are free, quite hefty fees can be levied depending on the rules of the ticket (and the policies of the travel agency and the airline(s) concerned). In some cases, tickets will allow no date changes at all. Route changes may be possible but usually attract a fee, and where they are permitted there is likely to be a stipulation as to how many route changes you're allowed (often only one).

Stopover Limits

Most fares restrict the number of stopovers permitted. Again, this is mostly relevant for volunteers who intend to travel independently before or after a placement.

Types of Tickets

You could write an entire book on the many types of airline tickets (although it might not be a very interesting one). But there are four main categories of ticket that international volunteers might want to buy: discount return, open-jaw or one-way tickets, and air passes.

Discount Return Tickets

If you plan to fly in and out of one country, all you need is a normal return ticket. However, if you want to see a little more of the world, either on the way out or the way back, then you can usually add in some stopovers – often at no extra cost.

Open-Jaw Tickets

With these tickets you fly into one destination and out of another. Again, this is an option if you want to volunteer and also do a bit of travelling. You can fly straight to your volunteer project and afterwards do some good old-fashioned overland travel before flying home.

One-Way Tickets

These might be an option if you are volunteering for more than one year. Proportionally, a one-way long-haul ticket is expensive – almost always costing a lot more than half the price of a return. In fact, they are sometimes even more expensive than a return. If you only want a one-way ticket, check in case a return is cheaper. If it is, buy the return and simply don't use the homeward leg.

One drawback of one-way tickets is that you often have to show how you're going to get out of a country before you can get in (immigration officials may want to see an onward ticket). Often, if you can prove that you've got sufficient funds for your stay and enough to purchase an exit ticket (whether by air, land or sea), you should be fine.

Air Passes

To explore a large country in depth (eg Brazil, India or Malaysia), ask your travel agent about air passes. These offer you a certain quota of flights within a single country. The flights are worked out either using a points system, a total mileage limit or a number of flights within one region. Air passes are often very good value, so long as journeys involving plane changes are not counted as separate flights.

For the international volunteer, these passes can be a cheap way of seeing more of the country on weekends. However, there are two drawbacks: they are usually valid for 30 days only (which means you have to do most of your travel in the first few weekends after your arrival) and you usually have to buy them in advance of getting to the country.

Buying Your Tickets

Buying from Airlines

For short-haul flights buying from airlines is almost always the best plan. For long-haul flights it's almost always the worst plan. Firstly, airlines use travel agencies to sell tickets at less than you can buy direct. Secondly, airlines won't tell you about deals that their competitors are offering. An agent's job is to compare the best deals on different airlines for you.

Buying from Specialist Travel Agents

There are regular travel agents and then there are specialist travel agents. For a week in the sun you're better off visiting the former, but to book your flight to a volunteering destination it's best to go through a specialist travel agent. A good specialist travel agent will be familiar with all routes that airlines fly and will have up-to-the-minute information on discounted fares around the world.

On the whole, all specialist travel agents have access to the same fares, so there isn't much to be gained by talking to a long list of them. Where there might be a difference is in how quickly they react to new fares on the market.

Specialist travel agencies in the UK include:

~ **Flight Centre** (☎ +44 (0) 844 800 8660; www.flightcentre.co.uk)

~ **Trailfinders** (☎ +44 (0)845 058 5858; www.trailfinders.com)

~ **TravelBag** (☎ +44 (0)871 703 4700; www.travelbag.co.uk)
~ **Travel Mood** (☎ +44 (0)800 011 1945; http://www.travelmood.ie/)

North American volunteers should try:

~ **Liberty Travel** (☎ +1 888 271 1584; www .libertytravel.com)

~ **Travelosophy** (☎ +1 800 332 2687; www.itravelosophy.com)

In Australasia, try:

~ **Flight Centre Australia** (☎ 133 133; www .flightcentre.com.au) or New Zealand (☎ +64 0800 24 3544; www.flightcentre.co.nz)

~ **Student Flights, Australia** (☎ 1800 046 462; www.studentflights.com.au)

~ **STA Australia** (☎ +134 782; www.statravel .com.au) or New Zealand (☎ +64 0800 474 400; www.statravel.co.nz)

Buying Online

If you are doing nothing more complicated than flying in and out of the same country you can find some good bargains online.

Here are some of the main UK online travel providers:

~ **ebookers** (www.ebookers.com)

~ **Expedia** (www.expedia.co.uk)

~ **Opodo** (www.opodo.co.uk)

~ **Travelocity** (www.travelocity.co.uk)

There are several solid online options in Canada and the USA:

~ **Airtreks** (www.airtreks.com)

~ **Cheaptickets** (www.cheaptickets.com)

~ **Hotwire** (www.hotwire.com)

~ **Kayak.com** (www.kayak.com)

~ **Orbitz** (www.orbitz.com)

In Australasia, try:

~ **Travel.com.au** (www.travel.com.au)

~ **Zuji** (www.zuji.com.au)

Not Booking Your Own Ticket

If you are volunteering on an organised programme, you will be sent details of your flights, accompanied by any other information you need.

Sometimes, an organisation will book flights on your behalf but require that you pay for them. This often happens on a group-based project where team members fly out together. This can be a good arrangement, because it often means the organisation has block-booked seats at a discounted group rate (sometimes up to 20 per cent off) and the savings are passed on to you.

Passports, Visas & Travel Insurance

Passports

Identity theft is one of the world's fastest-growing crimes. To help combat it, many countries around the world have started issuing biometric passports containing embedded microchips (also known as electronic passports or e-passports). If you applied for a new passport or renewed an old one in the last few years in the UK, US, Australia or New Zealand, you will have received a new biometric passport (or e-passport). Canada will begin issuing e-passports in July 2013. If you have a passport in the old style, don't worry – in most cases your current passport will remain valid until its expiry date. For up-to-date information about UK passports log onto the **Identify and Passport Service** (http://www.homeoffice.gov.uk/agencies-public-bodies/ips). US citizens should access the Department of State's **Bureau of Consular Affairs** (http://travel.state.gov). For Canadian passport information, **Passport Canada** (www.ppt.gc.ca) is the place. The Australian equivalent is the **Australian Passport Information Service** (☎ 131 232; www.passports.gov.au).

However, there are other things to bear in mind as you're are dusting off your passport:

~ **Expiry dates** Check your passport's expiry date – it has a habit of sneaking up on you. Also, make sure that your current passport is valid for at least six months after you get home from volunteering, as some countries are suspicious of passports that are approaching their use-by date.

~ **Blank pages** If you do a lot of travelling, you may run out of blank pages in your current passport. Many immigration officials around the world refuse to issue visas, entry or exit stamps on anything other than crisp, clean, unsullied pages. If you have few of these left, apply for a new passport. You can do this at any time during the life of your current passport.

~ **Volunteering in the US** There are specific passport requirements for entering the US without a visa under the Visa Waiver Programme (VWP). Passports issued after 26 October 2006 must be electronic; those issued after 26 October 2005 must bear a digital photo, and any issued earlier must be machine-readable. For information see http://travel.state.gov.

Visas

As you know, a visa is a stamp or document in your passport that says you may enter a country and stay there for a specific amount of time. Countries usually have five or six main categories of visa and one of them may be a volunteer visa. However, even if a volunteer visa does exist for the country you're going to, it is rare that you will need to obtain one to volunteer there.

You must get advice on this matter from your sending agency or local grassroots NGO but, nine times out of ten, you will be asked to obtain a standard tourist visa. There are a few reasons for this. Firstly, there's nothing wrong with doing some volunteering on a tourist visa. Secondly, you're not officially working: you've not got a contract of employment and you're not earning a salary. Thirdly, volunteer visas are sometimes more difficult to obtain because they can raise suspicion and lead to all sorts of petty officialdom. As a result, volunteers tend to travel on tourist visas and can be found at the weekends popping over to their nearest border post to renew them.

Having said that, there are some organisations that prefer you to volunteer on a volunteer visa. They will either arrange one for you or ask that you obtain one. In addition, many of the charities or sending agencies that dispatch skilled volunteers overseas for long periods of time will either obtain the proper volunteer visa or a working visa on your behalf.

If you are obtaining your own tourist visa, here are a few things to bear in mind:

~ The majority of tourist visas last for between three to six months and they are usually valid from the date of issue. This means you need to think carefully about when you obtain your visa, particularly if you are volunteering for a couple of months.

~ Visa requirements can sometimes be affected by the transport you've used to enter a country. For instance, if you fly into Cambodia or Laos you can get visas on arrival but if you go overland you must arrange them in advance (usually in Bangkok).

~ In some instances, you can get a visa for a longer period of time if you apply before you travel. For instance, Romania will give you six months if you apply in your home country but only 30 days if you rock up at the border.

~ If you've got an Israeli stamp in your passport from earlier travels, it can cause problems when entering countries like Syria and Lebanon (Jordan and Egypt are OK). If you are volunteering in the Middle East and have evidence of a visit to Israel in your passport, then consider getting another passport.

~ If you need to extend your visa while you're volunteering, remember that many over-land border crossings are open for a relatively short time during the day, so try to find out the 'opening hours' in advance. Also, they are often closed during religious holidays.

~ If you want to travel after your volunteer placement and plan to obtain visas on the road, take lots of passport-sized photographs with you. Many countries require two to four photos to process a visa and it's a hassle finding photo booths abroad.

Travel Insurance

Obtaining travel insurance for international volunteering is not the same thing as getting it for your annual vacation. For starters, you will probably buy a different insurance policy, because it must cover the specific activities and tasks that you will be performing.

If you volunteer with a sending agency, they will advise which insurance companies to approach. However, it will also be made clear that your travel insurance is ultimately your responsibility. As such, you need to ask the right questions and be aware of the main issues.

When discussing with an insurance company which policy you need, be upfront about what you are doing and where you are going. They need to be left in no doubt that you are volunteering and that you need to be covered for anything that happens to you while you are doing this. Also be aware that if your volunteer position is regional in scope, you may be asked to travel to other nearby countries. If you intend to volunteer in a developing country, medical cover up to £2 million/US$3.1 million/A$3.05 million should suffice but if you volunteer in Canada, the USA or parts of Europe then it is wiser to opt for a policy with up to £5 million/US$7.9 million/A$7.6 million or more.

On the subject of medical cover, check that the policy includes repatriation: in some cases evacuation to your home country might be safer than to being taken to the nearest regional medical facility. Also, if you are volunteering in the developing world, note how large the medical excess is. This is relevant because treatment in a first-class hospital in-country will be significantly cheaper than in other parts of the world: look at policies with an excess of around £50/US$80/A$75, rather than £150/US$240/A$230 or more.

Mark Jacobs, CEO of Azafady (p132), advises:

When taking out travel insurance, it is a good idea for volunteers to provide a couple of hypothetical scenarios to ensure they're covered for full medical costs and transport to an appropriately equipped hospital. I advise volunteers on our projects to give the following scenarios:

Would I be covered if…

1) I was crossing a 'bridge' (often a slippery log), two hours away from the nearest hospital, and inadvertently broke my leg?
2) I got malaria in a rural village and the standard methods of dealing with it did not get my temperature down to a safe level?
3) I was working with local communities making a beehive on an income-generating project and accidentally sustained some injury?

Explaining to your insurance company exactly what you'll be doing when volunteering is key. It is particularly important to tell them if you expect to do manual labour, because you will probably need to pay an extra premium per day for this activity. And, even then, you will probably be covered only for manual labour at ground level and for the use of hand tools only. In most cases, you will not be covered for the use of heavy machinery or for anything that requires a licence to operate.

If you are volunteering on a project involving animals, make sure you grill the insurance company on what you are covered for. Monitoring, surveying and observation are usually fine but close contact with wild animals is in a class of its own.

When asking your travel insurance company volunteer-specific questions, it is also wise to bear in mind some of the following more general travel insurance points:

~ **Ageism** Many policies are unashamedly ageist – often the price of travel insurance will double if you're 65 or over and on some policies restrictions apply even below that age.

~ **Repatriation** Ensure this means you'll be flown home and not to the country where you bought the travel insurance (if these differ).

~ **Pre-existing medical conditions** If you've got high blood pressure, diabetes, asthma etc, make sure you are covered. Usually you're OK if your condition is diagnosed and stable but all policies vary.

~ **Activities** If you are working with children (or even if you're not) look at the list of sports you're allowed to play. Also, if you plan to travel at the weekends, switching from volunteer to tourist, you may want to be covered for a few adventure activities. Often you'll be allowed one or two bungee jumps within a policy but have to pay twice as much if, for instance, you want to go gliding. If you want to try snowboarding or scuba diving, ask about these activities, because often they're not included.

~ **Geography** Make sure that you and your insurance company are talking the same language when it comes to geography. What do they understand by 'Europe', for instance? Are Turkey and Russia included? Cover for Europe, Australasia and most other destinations is reasonable. Premiums go way up when you are volunteering in Canada and the US.

~ **Extending cover** Most travel insurance policies cover you only for one year. However, you can purchase some policies for longer periods of time. If you are volunteering abroad and want to extend your placement, ensure that you can: a) extend your policy while you're away; and b) only pay for the difference between the two periods rather than needing to buy a fresh policy for your additional time away.

~ **Baggage and personal effects** Keep receipts at home for anything you might lose or have stolen while volunteering.

~ **Government travel warnings/advisories** If you go to a country that your government has advised against visiting, this will usually invalidate your travel insurance. Make sure you understand your insurance company's exact policy on this. Some insurance policies will still pay out if your claim is within seven days of your destination being named and others won't. This means you need to regularly check your government's relevant website when you're away: the **Foreign & Commonwealth Office** (www.fco.gov.uk) for UK volunteers, the **US State Department's Bureau of Consular Affairs international travel page** (http://travel.state.gov), **Canada's Consular Affairs Bureau** (www.voyage.gc.ca), or the **Australian Department of Foreign Affairs and Trade** (www.smartraveller.gov.au). This is particularly important if you are volunteering without the support of a sending agency based in your home country.

~ **Acts of war and terrorism** No-one will give you cover for nuclear, chemical or biological warfare but some policies do insure you against acts of terrorism.

If your sending agency has not advised which travel insurance companies to approach, or if you are arranging your own placement directly with a local NGO, try contacting the following in the UK:

~ **Campbell Irvine** (www.campbellirvine.com; ☎ +44 (0)2079 376 981)

~ **Christians Abroad** (www.cabroad.org.uk; ☎ +44 (0)870 770 7990)

~ **Insure & Go** (www.insureandgo.co.uk; ☎ +44 (0)844 888 2787)

~ **STA Travel** (www.statravel.co.uk; ☎ +44 (0)8712 300 040)

North American options include:

~ **Gateway Plans** (www.gatewayplans.com; ☎ +1 800 282 4495)

~ **HTH Worldwide** (www.hthworldwide.com; ☎ +1 610 254 8700)

~ **IMG** (www.imglobal.com; ☎ +1 800 628 4664)

~ **Travelex** (www.travelex-insurance.com; ☎ +1 800 228 9792)

~ **Wallach & Company** (www.wallach.com; ☎ +1 800 237 6615)

Australasian options include:

~ **Cover-More** (www.covermore.com.au; ☎ +61 1300 72 88 22 in Australia)

~ **World Nomads** (www.worldnomads.com; ☎ +61 1300 787 375 in Australia; and in New Zealand ☎ +64 0800 110 202)

What to Pack

There is an old travellers' adage, particularly relevant to international volunteers, that advises, 'Pack it and halve it; time it and double it.' Kerry Davies, who volunteered in Cambodia, agrees wholeheartedly with the first piece of advice:

Most people pack far too many things. It is tempting to visit a travel shop and buy lots of expensive gadgets. Most things can be obtained in the country you are working in. You will save money and support the local economy. Some things, though, are essential to take with you but this depends on your country. In Cambodia you can't get Western-sized bras and the knickers are nylon. And I still like to pack earplugs for the wedding season!

Just like Kerry, returned volunteers mostly advise that you take items you know you can't easily buy locally. Jacqueline Hill who went to Bangladesh says:

I took a sharp kitchen knife, vegetable peeler and Swiss Army knife. Bangladeshi cooks use floor knives which it takes quite some practice to master. Due to the abundance of fresh food, there is also little call for tins, and consequently tin-openers. I sometimes shopped in foreign food shops for treats (tins of tomatoes when the fresh ones were not in season) so the Swiss Army knife tin-opener came in handy.

Deborah Jordan and David Spinney, who volunteered in Ethiopia, pick up on the 'kitchen knife' theme and have a few additional suggestions:

Baggage allowance at 25 kilograms concentrates the mind. Check the climate and what is available locally to avoid taking two years' supply of tea bags or deodorant unnecessarily. And remember, family members are good at sending parcels. Invaluable was our sharp knife – all knives in the developing world bend. We also took a good supply of reading matter, a laptop (if you can use it in your placement) and some DVDs (TV serials can keep you going for weeks). We took our duvet in the second year and it was a great comfort on cold evenings.

Clothing is another hot topic. Emma Campbell, who volunteered in Ecuador, says:

There is no point packing clothes for volunteering. I went to the market and bought two cheap T-shirts and cheap shorts when I got there. They were ready for the bin, or the next set of volunteers, after one month.

And Jacqueline Hill had a good solution for culturally sensitive clothing issues:

Returned volunteers had lots of useful advice. Recognising that most of my Western clothes would be inappropriate, I bought a couple of *shalwar kameez* (long tunics with pants worn underneath).

Michelle Hawkins, who volunteered on one expedition in Costa Rica and another in Ghana, found that one of the most precious things she packed was a diary:

Even though certain memories do remain clear, the little details will fade. Journals are the best things for recalling what you felt at the time. They can also be therapeutic: writing down problems or issues you may have can help clarify your thinking and suggest solutions. Or else, sometimes writing in a diary is just like sharing a problem with a friend.

Most importantly, don't pack things that are inappropriate for where you are going. Diane Turner, who volunteered with Coral Cay Conservation (CCC, p134) in the Philippines and in Fiji, remembers:

Despite the list supplied by Coral Cay Conservation, one person still brought a hairdryer to a site that had no electricity!

Diane brings up a valuable point: if you are volunteering with a sending agency you will usually be sent a detailed kit list, specific to your destination and project. However, following is a suggested packing list that assumes that you will not only be volunteering but doing some travel at the weekends or after your placement. It is divided into eight sections: security; sleeping; eating and drinking; hygiene; health; travel essentials; clothing and footwear.

Security

~ **Money belt** A money belt is the safest way to carry your valuables. It's wise to have one for when you're out and about in the evenings or on weekends, particularly in towns or cities. Think about its fabric: plastic sweats while leather is heavy and will smell. Cotton or polycotton are the best bet, as they're washable and the most comfortable.

~ **Padlocks and a chain** Good for securing your luggage and fastening the door of hotel rooms. Chains are useful for attaching a backpack to the roof of a bus or the luggage rack of a train.

~ **Personal security** There are loads of personal security items on the market like personal alarms, internal door guards, a Pacsafe for your backpack (a steel mesh which covers your backpack to make it unslashable and which locks onto things) and packable safes for your room (attach them to a radiator or other fixed object). Check out what's on offer at your local travel specialist.

~ **Waterproof pouch** Consider taking one of these for your documents and money so that you can keep them on you if you choose to go swimming, diving or snorkelling.

Sleeping

~ **Alarm clock** To make sure you get up in time to start your volunteering day. If you usually use your mobile phone as an alarm clock, take into consideration that you may not always be able to keep it charged.

~ **Mosquito net** In risky places you will be provided with one, but it's good to have your own because it is crucial that your net is treated with a mosquito killer (such as permethrine) and has no holes.

~ **Pillow case** Nab one from home, just in case you stay anywhere that's a tiny bit unsavoury.

~ **Sleeping bag liner/sleeping bag** A sleeping bag liner is essential. You'll use this all the time either in dubious hotels and hostels or to keep your sleeping bag clean.

~ **Torch** Essential for those volunteer moments when the electricity packs it in or you're trying to read a book at night in the jungle. There are basically two types. The Maglite is the toughest but the bulbs and batteries run out quickly. Check out LED (light-emitting diode) torches, because the bulbs don't blow and the batteries last much longer. You can get an LED miner-style lamp that straps to your forehead and frees up both your hands.

~ **Tealight candles** During a power cut these are safer than regular candles.

Eating & Drinking

~ **Water bottle** Most water bottles are one litre, but two litres is what you'll probably need when you're volunteering. Buy the collapsible bladder type of water bottle, as they take up very little room in your luggage when not in use.

~ **Water purification** See the Food, Water & Hygiene section (p68) for details of what to take.

~ **Cup and spoon** If you're travelling at the weekends, your own cup and spoon will help you avoid catching or spreading disease.

Hygiene

~ **Bath plug** A rare commodity in some parts of the world. Wide-brimmed universal rubber or plastic plugs will fit most plugholes.

~ **Contraception** Condoms are sold in most countries but the quality can be variable (always check the use-by date). It's safer and easier to bring a supply with you. If you use the pill, bring enough to cover your whole time overseas, as it is difficult to get in many countries. However, you need to exercise extreme caution and restraint in sexual matters when volunteering overseas. This is especially so in any relationship with a local person in a culture that you don't completely understand.

~ **Tampons, sanitary napkins or menstrual cups** Depending on your destination, these might be hard to find.

~ **Toilet paper** It's best to learn how to use your hand and water, because toilet paper often blocks sewage systems in developing countries. Otherwise, take toilet paper but think about how you're going to dispose of it. Squash the roll down and put it in a plastic bag for packing.

~ **Toiletries** Most items are widely available (and often cheaper than at home) but take any speciality products with you. Shower gels travel much better than soap and will often do hair and body. Decant large bottles into smaller ones if you're volunteering short-term. Plus, you can now get concentrated travel soaps which will keep both you and your clothes clean. Make sure your travel soaps are biodegradable.

~ **Towel** There are two types of travel towels – ones made from chamois (which work wet and pack down to the size of a small tin of beans) and ones made from microfibre (which work dry and pack down to the size of a can of beans). Which sort you take will depend on your bathing routine. If you love wrapping up in your towel after your shower then the microfibre one is for you, but if you want pure towelling performance and don't mind something real weeny then take a chamois one.

~ **Washing detergent** See Toiletries, above.

~ **Washing line** A piece of string or even dental floss will do the job at a pinch, but there are relatively cheap lines on the market that don't need pegs and have suckers, hooks (or both) on the ends, making them more versatile.

~ **Wet wipes & no-water washes** Both are handy where clean water is in short supply.

Health
~ **Medical first-aid kit** See the section under Health & Hygiene (p66) for details.

Travel Essentials
~ **Address book, travel journal and pens** No explanation needed.

~ **Batteries** Bring spares for all your equipment and put new batteries in everything before you depart. Be mindful how you dispose of your batteries.

~ **Books and DVDs** Important entertainment if you're volunteering long-term overseas.

~ **Camera** Although print cameras are going the way of the dodo, be aware that digital cameras are not necessarily good for long-term volunteering unless you can easily download your photos and recharge, or you have a very large memory card.

~ **Earplugs** You'll never regret these if you're volunteering in a city or need a break from the blare of loud music on a 10-hour bus ride.

~ **Eye wear** Take your glasses (in a hard case) and contact lenses. If you wear prescription glasses or contact lenses, take the prescription with you, along with extras such as a case and contact-lens solution. Contact-lens wearers should also take a supply of 'dailies' (disposable contact lenses) – really useful in an emergency.

~ **Family photos and postcards of home** When you're volunteering, the people you work with will really appreciate seeing and learning more about your life back home.

~ **Kitchen knife** For all volunteers who want to do their own cooking.

~ **Lighter or matches** You'll need something to light your campfire, mosquito coils or candles (when the electricity blacks out yet again).

~ **Short-wave radio/MP3 player/smartphone** You might be able to tune into the BBC World Service, the Voice of America or Radio Australia and it will be good to listen to something familiar on your MP3 player if you're feeling down or homesick. If you ordinarily use your phone for music, be aware that it may be difficult to keep it charged in areas with no or unreliable electricity.

~ **Pocketknife** A Swiss Army knife (or good-quality equivalent) has loads of useful tools: scissors; bottle-opener; tin-opener; straight blade and all those strange gadgets that you don't know the use of (remember not to keep the knife in your hand luggage, though, as it'll be confiscated).

~ **Sewing kit** Needle, thread, a few buttons and safety pins are enough to mend clothing, mosquito nets, tents or sunglasses.

~ **Gaffer tape** As Maggie Wild, who has volunteered on lots of environmental projects, says, 'It fixes everything: torn tents; torn trousers; hanging-off vehicle parts and much, much more.'

Clothing
~ **Keeping cool** If you're travelling in hot climates you'll need a lightweight, loose-fitting wardrobe. Cotton clothing will absorb sweat and help keep you cool. Synthetic clothing doesn't get so creased and dries out quickly but can sometimes make you feel clammy. It's your choice. Trousers that convert into shorts are good because you get two for the price of one and you can also get trousers which convert into pedal pushers. Take a hat but make sure it protects the back of your neck from sunburn.

~ **Keeping warm** Several layers topped by a good-quality jacket will give you the versatility you need. For starters, pack some thermal underwear. Particularly good are lightweight, cycling-style T-shirts or merino wool vests. Both will allow your body to breathe while offering good insulation. Then you need a fleece or fibrepile jacket which is lighter and less bulky than a thick jumper. Most fleeces and fibrepile jackets are not fully waterproof or windproof so you'll also need a lightweight, breathable, waterproof jacket. If you're travelling in an extremely cold environment then consider the more expensive Gore-Tex mountain jackets. Take some polypropylene or merino wool long johns and then wear your usual travel trousers over the top. Don't forget mittens or gloves and a hat.

~ **Waterproof ponchos** Whether you're going hot or cold, think about one of these. You can use it to cover you and your pack, as a groundsheet, a sleeping-bag cover, on your bed as a barrier between you and a mouldy mattress or as a shade awning.

Footwear

~ **Boots or shoes** You've got the choice of three styles: a full-on high-leg boot; a mid-height boot (a cross between a shoe and a boot); and normal shoes or trainers. Unless you're going on an expedition or doing a lot of trekking, you probably don't need a high-leg boot. If you want versatility then the mid-height boot is good because it gives you ankle support without being too heavy. Whatever you choose, non-waterproof is better than waterproof (unless you're going somewhere really cold), as your feet will breathe better. However, at the end of the day, buy what your feet feel most comfortable in. And remember to break in your footwear before you leave, so that you can deal with any blisters or rubbing in the comfort of your own home.

~ **Watersport sandals** These are ideal for day-to-day wear in warm climates, even if you're doing a lot of walking. You can also wear them in dodgy showers or in the sea and leave them on your feet to dry out.

Health & Hygiene

Needless to say, you don't want to get sick while you're volunteering overseas. If you take the right precautions both before you go and while you're abroad, you'll probably experience nothing more serious than 'Delhi belly' or 'Montezuma's revenge' (travellers' diarrhoea). Jacqueline Hill, who volunteered in Bangladesh for a year, advises:

Be careful, not paranoid. I was only ill once – a 24-hour stomach bug in my first couple of weeks. Follow sensible precautions, especially those recommended by the volunteering agency and their in-country representatives.

Pre-departure Check-ups

Visit a travel clinic six to eight weeks before you depart. Your sending agency will usually advise on which vaccinations to get, but they will not be as up-to-date as a travel health specialist. They should also be able to advise whether you need an HIV test for where you're going.

Ensure that all your vaccinations are recorded on a vaccination certificate and take this away with you – proof of immunisation against certain diseases (yellow fever, for instance) might be needed at particular borders. Also, check that you're up-to-date with routine immunisations like tetanus and diphtheria, polio and any childhood ones like MMR (measles, mumps, rubella).

It is a good idea to check in with your doctor prior to departure and definitely with your dentist and optometrist. Tooth trouble, in particular, can be painfully inconvenient when you're in the field. At the optometrist, you may want to buy a spare pair of glasses, as you might end up wearing them more frequently than contact lenses when you're overseas.

Some charities and sending agencies will arrange all of this for you. Others might ask you to fill out a very detailed medical form and then follow up if there are any areas of concern. Mostly, however, you are responsible for your own health-related check-ups.

Ten Top Tips from Two Volunteers

Elaine Massey and Richard Lawson have volunteered on 15 projects with Earthwatch: seven times on Sea Turtles of Baja; twice on Costa Rican Sea Turtles and twice on Behind the Scenes of the Grey Whale Migrations in Bath. They volunteered once each on Mammals of Wytham Woods in Oxford; Grey Whale Migrations in Canada; Lions of Tsavo in Kenya and Elephants in Tsavo. Here are their tips for volunteers:

1. Read the Online Briefing Several Times

This way you can make sure that the project is right for you. For example, if you don't like the heat, don't join a project in the desert and if you like home comforts, don't join a project where the accommodation is described as 'rustic'. If you're unhappy about the prospect of sharing a dormitory with members of the opposite sex, make sure you know what the sleeping arrangements are. If the project isn't right for you, not only will you have a miserable time, but those around you will too.

2. The Weather

Make sure you know what types of weather you may experience and take appropriate clothing. For instance, if the project is in a hot area, shorts may come in handy. And, don't assume that suntan oil will be any good in a desert (believe it or not, we've seen it happen!). Don't forget sunglasses and a good hat.

3. Travel Arrangements

If the journey to your destination includes a long flight, try to allow some recovery time before the project starts – jet lag can seriously impair your enjoyment of the first couple of days! If you're travelling alone, why not try contacting some of the other people on the team list? You may be able to share accommodation before or after the project.

4. Clothing

Take clothing that you don't mind getting ruined – not your Sunday best! Most research will involve getting dirty or wet, and you won't enjoy it as much if you're worried about spoiling your clothes.

5. Camera and Film

Don't forget your camera and take lots of film if you're going with print rather than digital. Also, if you're doing a water-based project, consider getting a polarising filter to reduce glare.

6. Currency

In remote villages, the shops are unlikely to be able to change US$100 notes, so try to take a supply of small denomination notes. Don't assume that travellers cheques and credit cards will be accepted!

7. Your Feet (Part One)

If the project is sea based, there's a good chance that your feet will get wet and sandy. This can leave you with open cuts where your sandal straps rub your feet. Try to take a couple of different styles of sandals, so they don't all rub in the same place!

8. Your Feet (Part Two)

If the project involves lots of walking, make sure your boots are properly worn in and that you have plenty of plasters! Also, get a supply of good socks. We recommend Thousand Mile socks, which have double layers – the outer layer moves with the shoe, and the inner layer with the foot, so the friction is between the two layers. They guarantee no blisters!

9. Reading List

If the project briefing includes a reading list, try to get hold of some of the books. A little background knowledge will enrich your enjoyment of the project.

10. Packing

Try to pack light – there may not be much room to store or transport your belongings. (But make sure you've read the 'what to take' section of the briefing!) You may have to live out of your bag, so taking a small bag for dirty washing isn't a bad idea.

Elaine Massie & Richard Lawson

First-aid Courses

Many returned volunteers advise that first-aid skills are invaluable, whether you're working on a development or conservation and wildlife project.

Some of the best courses in the UK are run by:

~ **St John Ambulance**
(www.sja.org.uk)

~ **Lifesigns Group**
(www.adventurelifesigns.co.uk)

~ **Wilderness Expertise**
(www.wilderness-expertise.co.uk)

~ **Wilderness Medical Training**
(www.wildernessmedicaltraining.co.uk)

In North America, sign up for classes at:

~ **American Heart Association**
(www.americanheart.org)

~ **American Red Cross** (www.redcross.org)

~ **Canadian Red Cross** (www.redcross.ca)

~ **Wilderness Medical Associates**
(www.wildmed.com)

Australians should get in touch with **St John Ambulance Australia** (www.stjohn.org.au; ☎ +61 1300 360 455).

Medical Kits

Some large sending agencies suggest you purchase specific medical kits especially designed for the needs of their volunteers. If this is the case, you will be told where you can buy them. If not, travel clinics sell a range of medical kits to suit all types of travellers (and therefore volunteers) – overland, expedition, independent etc. Good ones cost in the range of £30 to £50/US$50 to US$100/A$50 to A$100. Otherwise, what you'll pack will depend on where you're going and what you plan to do.

Basics

Following is a list of basic requirements:

~ Any prescription medicines, including antibiotics and antimalarials.

~ Painkillers like paracetamol (acetaminophen) and aspirin for pain and fever and an anti-inflammatory like ibuprofen.

~ Insect repellent (DEET or plant-based) and permethrin (for treating mosquito nets and clothes).

~ Antidiarrhoeals – loperamide is probably the most effective.

~ Indigestion remedies such as antacid tablets or liquids.

~ Oral rehydration sachets and a measuring spoon for making up your own solution.

~ Antihistamine tablets for hay fever and other allergies or itches.

~ Sting-relief spray or hydrocortisone cream for insect bites.

~ Sun block and lip salve with sun block.

~ Water-purifying tablets or water filter or purifier.

~ Over-the-counter cystitis treatment (if you're prone to this).

~ Calamine lotion or aloe vera for sunburn and skin rashes.

~ Antifungal cream.

~ Cough and cold remedies and sorethroat lozenges.

~ Eye drops.

~ Laxatives (particularly if you're headed to an area like Mongolia where there's little fibre in the diet).

First-aid Equipment

Remember to stow your first-aid kit in your luggage for flights, because anything sharp will get confiscated as hand luggage:

~ Digital (not mercury) thermometer.

~ Scissors.

~ Tweezers to remove splinters, cactus needles or ticks.

~ Sticking plasters (adhesive bandages).

~ Gauze swabs and adhesive tape.

~ Bandages and safety pins.

~ Non-adhesive dressings.

~ Antiseptic powder or solution (eg povidone-iodine) and/or antiseptic wipes.

~ Wound closure strips.

~ Syringes and needles – ask your doctor for a note explaining why you have them to avoid any difficulties.

If you're really going remote then you'll also need:

~ Antibiotic eye and ear drops.

~ Antibiotic pills or powder.

~ Emergency splints (eg SAM splints).

~ Elasticated support bandage.

~ Triangular bandage for making an arm sling.

~ Dental first-aid kit (either a commercial kit or one you've put together yourself – ask your dentist to advise you).

Hopefully, you'll end up not using three-quarters of what you've packed. However, you never know. Phil Sydor volunteered to build a teenage-orphan teaching centre in Zambia and recalls:

I sustained a head injury – a steel bar dropped on my head and I needed stitches. The local hospital sewed me up using the sutures we'd brought with us as part of our medical kit. This way the local supplies weren't depleted and we were confident that the equipment was sterile.

Malaria

Sian Davies, who volunteered as a general coordinator with Doctors of the World (p142) in Tanzania, says:

Don't be too paranoid about getting sick. If you live in a place you have a lot more control over issues such as food, water and mosquitoes than if you're just passing through. However, having said that, I had malaria four times (despite taking prophylaxis).

Malarial risks and antimalarial drug-resistance patterns change constantly. If you're headed to a malarial area, you need to get expert advice from your travel clinic on how to avoid catching this potentially fatal mosquito-borne disease.

There are a number of antimalarial medicines on the market and they all have their pros and cons (see www.fitfortravel.scot.nhs.uk for a full list). A travel clinic will discuss these with you and come up with the best solution for where you're going and the type of volunteering you're doing. Remember, if you need to take antimalarial pills, they generally have to be started at least one week before you arrive at the destination and continued for four weeks after you depart the malarial area.

It is easy to forget that antimalarials do not stop you getting malaria, they just suppress it if you do. This means that you always need to combine antimalarials with proper precautions against being bitten in the first place. These should include:

~ Changing into permethrin-treated long-sleeved tops, long trousers and socks at dusk.

~ Using a DEET-based inspect repellent on any exposed skin at dawn and dusk. Reapply every hour in hot and humid conditions.

~ Using electric insecticide vaporisers or burning mosquito coils in your room or under restaurant tables.

~ Spraying your room with a knock-down insect spray before you bed down for the night.

~ Sleeping under a permethrin-treated mosquito net.

~ Volunteering in the height of the dry season – the risk of being bitten and therefore catching malaria is far less at this time.

How do you know if you've caught malaria? You'd think this was an easy question to answer. It isn't. What you need to remember is that any flu-like symptom could be malaria. If you're feeling off colour in a malarial area then go and get a blood test. In many parts of the developing world, local hospitals will test you on the spot – it takes 20 minutes and costs almost nothing. However, there are now a couple of self-testing malarial kits on the market (ask your travel clinic about these), which can be useful if you're far away from medical help.

Long-term Use of Antimalarials

Travellers normally take antimalarial tablets for three months. However, if you're volunteering for longer in a malarial area, you will need to take your antimalarial medicine for longer. With the exception of chloroquine which has been known to cause retinal problems, there is no evidence that the extended use of antimalarial medication will increase side effects or decrease effectiveness. It is best to take all the antimalarial medicine you'll need with you from your home country (check expiry dates), although sometimes these drugs will be available where you're going.

Other Insect-borne Diseases

It isn't only malaria which is transmitted by mosquitoes but also diseases like yellow fever, Japanese encephalitis and dengue fever. This last disease is an increasing problem because the carrier is a daytime mosquito, which means you have to practice bite avoidance (eg covering up and reapplication of insect repellent) during the day, which can be hard. Dengue fever is especially prevalent in Central America, Malaysia and Queensland (Australia) and there are no prophylactic tablets or treatment for the disease. As most of these areas are also malarial, it means you'll have to make sure you're not bitten 24 hours a day.

Food, Water & Hygiene

On your volunteer placement you will mostly prepare your own food, accept the hospitality of people you know or eat in local restaurants that you trust. However, what happens at the weekend when you travel or after your placement?

Hepatitis A, typhoid, diarrhoea and dysentery (bloody diarrhoea) are all transmitted by poorly prepared food and impure water. As you never know what might be buried in your food, here are a few tips to inwardly digest:

~ Always wash your hands prior to eating.

~ Avoid food that has been peeled, sliced or nicely arranged by other people because it means it's been handled a lot.

~ Remember that food can get contaminated by dirty dishes, cutlery, utensils and cups. Blenders or pulpers used for fruit juices are often suspect.

~ Raw fruit and vegetables are hard to clean. Eat them only if you know they've been washed in clean water or if you can safely peel them yourself. Bananas and papayas are safe to eat in the tropics.

~ Eat only food that's freshly prepared and piping hot – avoid hotel buffets like the plague.

~ Be wary of ice cream and se afood – although for different reasons.

~ Think twice before you drink water from the tap or brush your teeth in it.

~ Drink sealed bottled water or canned drinks where possible.

~ Avoid ice cubes in drinks: they may have been made from contaminated water.

~ The simplest way of purifying water is to bring it to a 'roaring boil' for three to five minutes; otherwise use chlorine, iodine or a water purifier.

Despite all these precautions, it's likely you will get a stomach upset. When you do, drink as much as you can to ensure you don't become dehydrated. In addition, use oral rehydration salts to rehydrate more quickly and drink sweet milkless tea and eat salty crackers (if possible).

Health-related Documents

When volunteering, keep the following information in a safe place in your room (or under your hammock):

~ Vaccination certificate.

~ Travel insurance emergency number and the serial number of your policy.

~ Summary of any important medical condition you have.

~ Contact details of your doctor back home.

~ Copy of prescription for any medication you take regularly.

~ Details of any serious allergies.

~ Your blood group.

~ HIV test documentation (if applicable).

~ Prescription for glasses or contact lenses.

~ Letter from your doctor explaining why you're carrying syringes in a medical kit to avoid any hassles.

More Information

Although self-diagnosis is never a good idea, it might be wise to invest in a practical book on travellers' health. Lonely Planet publishes a range of small *Healthy Travel* books, or try *Travellers' Health: How to Stay Healthy Abroad* by Dr Richard Dawood. If you're volunteering off the beaten track, one of the best books is called *Where There Is No Doctor: A Village Health Care Handbook* by David Werner.

Also, before you go, do as much research as you can online. The useful **Australian Travel Doctor** website (www.tmvc.com.au) has free online travel health advisory reports with recommended vaccination lists for every country based on the time of year and the duration of stay.

Money

There are three main ways of taking or accessing your money while abroad: debit and credit cards; travellers cheques; and cash. If you are volunteering in a town or city you might be able to use all three. Whichever combination works for you, remember to keep receipts in case they're needed as proof either within the country you're volunteering in or when you leave.

If your volunteer placement is rural, it is possible that you'll rely mainly on cash (make sure to get some small-denomination notes). Robin Glegg, who has volunteered in Siberia, Namibia and Oman, advises:

Take cash in US dollars. Most people will accept US dollars in developing countries. You can usually exchange hard currency for local currency when you arrive at the airport.

And from Mike Laird, who volunteered in Bolivia:

I would advise people on two things: take US dollars and American Express travellers cheques. I have been in situations where UK travellers cheques and pounds sterling have not been accepted. The greenback is welcome everywhere. Clean, crisp notes are sometimes worth more.

But, on a day-to-day basis, what do you do with your cash? Where do you put it? Sharon Baxter, who volunteered in Tibet, remembers:

In Yushu itself, there was no way to cash travellers cheques or change money. Whilst there, I just kept my cash under the mattress. My bedroom door had a lock, so I kept it locked most of the time.

Top Ten Safety Tips for Female Volunteers

1: Pack your common sense and have your wits about you at all times. If you wouldn't normally walk down a dark alley or deserted street at night in your home town, don't do it when you're volunteering overseas. Jacqueline Hill remembers the following incident in Bangladesh:

I was careless one evening and had my bag strap around my shoulders with the bag on full view as I travelled through Dhaka on a rickshaw. A taxi drove up alongside me and a hand came out of the window and attempted to snatch my bag, resulting in my being pulled out of the rickshaw as the taxi tried to make off. I was badly shaken and bruised but hung onto my bag.

2: Be informed about where you are going, so that you have a rough idea of a town's layout and any areas that may be unsafe. (This is particularly relevant if you travel to a larger town to change money or if you travel at the weekends.) Poonam Sattee, who volunteered in Guatemala City recalls:

There are a lot of areas within the city that are incredibly unsafe and without prior knowledge, it is easy to accidentally wander into these. Gang rivalry also operates within the city and you don't want to get caught up in their activities.

3: Pay close attention to your instincts. If you're in a situation that feels wrong, even if you don't know why, move to a place where you feel more secure. Michelle Hawkins, who volunteered in Ghana and Costa Rica, remembers:

I was suddenly surrounded by four little old ladies. They were all muttering Americana. Being British, I was a bit confused. I was confused further when they started pushing in on me from all sides, with hands grabbing my waist for my money belt. After a comic half-hearted fist fight, I fought my way out of the ambush. Had I really been overrun by little old ladies? I took my daypack off, and saw that it had been slashed with a knife – just centimetres from my ribs.

4: If you feel like having a few too many drinks then do so in a safe environment (your room, your friend's house or the bar at your hotel).

Kerry Davies, who volunteered in Cambodia, was in a similar position:

I kept my money locked in my house, as my landlady and the dogs were always around.

In fact, volunteers who are placed in remote locations become adept at operating in a cash society and hiding their money just becomes part of everyday life. Jacqueline Hill, who volunteered in Bangladesh, recalls:

There were no ATMs in the town where I lived and I did not set up a bank account. My stipend was paid monthly in cash (the equivalent of £80) and I kept little stashes of notes all over the flat. When in Dhaka, I could use ATMs to withdraw local currency.

Volunteers in rural areas often have to make a special trip to a city to use an ATM or change some travellers cheques. In Tibet, this was Sharon Baxter's experience:

The nearest place to get money was Xining, which was a 16- to 22-hour bus ride away. I took some cash from England and the rest of my money in travellers cheques which I cashed in Xining. When travelling, the cash was in a secret pocket in my jeans, sewn inside the cuff of one leg. The only way anyone could have got that was to take my jeans off and, if it came to that, I didn't think money would be my main concern.

Security is an issue that Ian Flood was concerned about when he volunteered in Bolivia. He says:

5: If you're going out at night on your own, tell someone (another volunteer, your host family etc) where you're going and what time you expect to be back.

6: Instead of going out after dark on your own to explore, make the most of your waking hours and get up really early in the morning.

7: If you're a self-funding volunteer and fixing up your own accommodation, make sure you do so in a safe part of town. If you're on a trip at the weekend, pay a little extra to stay in a hotel in a better area. Poonam Sattee advises again:

> Guatemala City is not safe and I do not recommend that anyone lives in the city. It is better to live in Antigua, which is a 45-minute commute on a bus. Although Antigua is touristy, it has none of Guatemala City's problems, due to the high levels of tourist police operating there.

8: Pay attention to what you wear and cover up. In many regions of the world, skimpy shorts and T-shirts relay a very different message to what you may be used to at home. Poonam Sattee again:

> Don't wear jewellery of any type – even if it is only studs in your ears or religious symbols. It attracts attention – I was mugged a number of times and on one occasion, had the studs taken out of my ears (they weren't even gold or silver).

9: Take a taxi more frequently than you might at home but make sure it is bona fide. Ensure you always have enough cash on you to get home this way if you need to.

10: Think about doing a course in travel safety before you leave your home country. In the UK you can arrange one through **Objective** (☎ +44 (0)1788 899029; office@objectiveteam.com; www.objective gapyear.com; Bragborough Lodge Farm, Braunston, Daventry, Northants NN11 7HA). In the US, the **School for Field Studies** (☎ +1 800 989 4418; admissions@fieldstudies.org; www.fieldstudies.org; 100 Cummings Center, Suite 534-G, Beverley, MA 01915) offers a variety of international health and safety courses year round. Australians can prepare themselves for difficult situations by doing a course with **RedR** (☎ +61 2 6273 6544; www.redr.org.au) which offers intensive personal security in emergency training. The Australian Department of Foreign Affairs and Trade (DFAT) produces a brochure with tips for solo women travellers; Australians can visit www.smarttraveller.gov.au to request a free copy.

I used ATMs all the time without problems. However, take a friend to stand next to you when taking money out, as sometimes the money can be snatched right out of your hands.

And security was also very important to Poonam Sattee when she accessed her money while volunteering in Guatemala City:

I opened up a bank account on arrival and got money transferred from my UK bank account to the Guatemalan account (the transfer instructions were set up before leaving). I had a passbook and used this to withdraw money from the bank. There were branches everywhere. The only drawback was that I had to take my passport as ID, which I didn't like doing in Guatemala City as it is not safe. So I got a copy of my passport stamped and signed by a lawyer in Guatemala (this guaranteed it was an authentic copy) and I used this to withdraw money instead. But I didn't put my money in a money belt because thieves there know all about money belts. After withdrawing cash, I would stuff it in my shoes, socks, bra, wherever, and if I'd withdrawn a large sum, get a cab home (from a trusted source – not just hailing one).

Kate Sturgeon avoided taking out large sums of money when volunteering in Zimbabwe:

We received our stipend to live on in the field once a month in US dollars. We then gave it to the project coordinator or logistician, who would change it for us. Because inflation was so high, we would change money on a weekly basis rather than all at once. This is definitely advisable in countries where the currency is unstable.

However, what happens if you volunteer with a charity or sending agency on an organised volunteer programme? David Grassham, who volunteered in rural India, remembers:

As everything was included, the only thing I bought was the occasional chocolate bar or soft drink.

If you are volunteering on a conservation or wildlife project the situation will be similar. The reason for this is summed up nicely by Vikki Cole, who volunteered on a conservation project in the Borneo jungle:

We were quite literally miles away from civilisation so taking credit cards or substantial amounts of cash was futile. We were advised to bring only a tiny amount of local currency. We were told we'd need this for the last day when we were able to access a bar in a motel. We drank them dry within an hour!

The organised skilled volunteering programmes offered by the Australian Government provide volunteers with a monthly allowance which is deposited into an Australian account. Overseas withdrawal fees start at A$4, so it's worth considering how you're going to access your cash if you're on a long-term assignment, and compare rates across banks. Also, if you find yourself in Asia trying to secure long-term accommodation, you may have to pay up to three to six months rent in advance, so a cash contingency plan is essential.

Credit & Debit Cards

If you want to find out how near your volunteer programme is to a local ATM, log onto an online ATM locator. The one for MasterCard is http://www.mastercard.us/cardholder -services/atm-locator.html and for Visa it's www.visa.com/atmlocator.

The rate of exchange for cash withdrawals from ATMs is often pretty good but it's offset by hefty transaction charges. What you need is a card which doesn't charge you each time you get cash out. At present, the best option in the UK is a Nationwide Select Credit Card (www.nationwide.co.uk). These cards will not charge you for cash withdrawals while you're abroad, and with Nationwide you get to keep your savings in a relatively high-interest-bearing account. The only problem with the Nationwide card is that it can't be replaced from abroad should it be lost or stolen. In Australia, one of the best-regarded travel credit cards is currently the 28 Degrees MasterCard (www.28degreescard.com.au), which charges no annual fees, no currency conversion fees and no international transaction fees.

Travellers Cheques

Experienced international volunteers (and travellers generally) know that one of the disadvantages of travellers cheques is that you're usually charged a commission when you buy them, a commission when you convert them, and on top of that they rarely attract a decent rate of exchange. Nevertheless, if you are volunteering somewhere remote you might rely heavily on travellers cheques.

In the UK you can buy American Express travellers cheques in US dollars commission-free from post offices (www.postoffice.co.uk). In the States and Canada, they're sold at many banks and credit unions and all AAA offices and American Express Travel Service branches (see http://www.aetclocator.com/wheretobuy/travelerscheques/ for a list of locations). Australians and New Zealanders should check out www.americanexpress. com/australia and www.americanexpress/newzealand respectively to find out where to exchange their cash for cheques. American Express travellers cheques can be exchanged commission-free at most American Express offices while you're away. However, remember to ask for a good quantity of cheques in smaller denominations, so you have the choice of changing either a large or a small amount of money. Needless to say, the equivalent of US$100 in some local currencies is a lot of money.

Keeping in Touch

The Yahoo! Mail Internet Cafe Awards were held in 2004 to celebrate 10 years since the opening of the first internet cafe. At the time, the award for the most remote internet cafe went to Télé Centre Polyvalent (TCP) in Timbuktu, Mali. Since then, internet cafes have sprung up in increasingly remote places, which is good news for the international volunteer. Clodagh O'Brien, who volunteered in the jungles of Borneo, says:

Email is the best thing that was ever invented for keeping in touch, not only with people from home, but also those you meet along the way.

The social networking revolution has made it easier than ever for travellers to keep friends and family up-to-date with their adventures. Forget the days of spamming your loved ones with epic group emails: Facebook and mobile apps such as Instagram allow for easy sharing of information and images, and Twitter is perfect for bite-sized missives.

Make sure that you are aware of your volunteer program's social networking policy (if it has one) and when you're online always be mindful about how you are representing the organisation for which you are working. Also beware of uploading photos of people, especially children, without their or their guardian's permission.

Some organisations even utilise volunteers in maintaining their social media presence, so do include this in your application if it is something you are interested in doing as part of your volunteer work.

As you would imagine, email is how the majority of volunteers keep in touch with friends and family. In Bangladesh, Jacqueline Hill remembers:

I mostly kept in touch through emails and my online diary. I would go to the internet cafe, download my emails onto a disc and reply to them on my PC at the flat. I would then copy my replies, go back to the internet cafe and attempt to send them. Erratic opening times, phone lines and electricity supplies made this a lengthy and often frustrating process.

There are two interesting things about Jacqueline's experience. Not only did Jacqueline write a blog (for more on this, see p75) to keep people in the loop about her experiences, she also beat the problem of erratic electricity supplies in a developing country. If you don't take a laptop overseas, you can still avoid writing lovely long emails only to lose them when the internet connection drops out: write in Word, then copy and paste the text into an email when you've finished.

Ann Noon, who volunteered in Peru, used internet cafes as chat rooms – but she wasn't chatting to strangers:

Thank goodness for MSN Messenger. It makes you feel like your family are just across the road somewhere rather than thousands of miles and three flights away. Skype's another handy invention…

Indeed it is. Online chat platforms such as Skype provide a cheap and easy way of keeping in touch and staving off any pangs of homesickness. They do rely on access to a reliable internet connection, but in this digital world internet cafes are springing up in even the farthest-flung places. (For more information on chat services, see p75.)

The question of whether to pack your mobile phone is not straightforward to answer. If you have a tri-band GSM handset then it will work in most parts of the world, including some of North America. If you've got a dual-band phone, you may want to think of upgrading before you depart. For more detailed information on where your phone will and won't work, check **Mobile World Live** at (http://maps.mobileworldlive.com/). This will also let you know if the country you're volunteering in has a GSM 'roaming agreement' with your service provider. Having said this, Phil Sydor, who volunteered in Lusaka, Zambia, had no problems:

We walked down to the end of the garden and the reception was quite good. Land lines were terrible, but many people had mobile phones. We bought a local SIM card and used that as it was cheaper than 'roaming'.

Unless you want to shell out a fortune paying an 'international roaming' tariff, local SIM cards are a must for international volunteers. Before departing, find out whether your mobile is SIM locked. If it is, get the code to unlock it so that you can purchase a local pre-paid SIM card when you're abroad – it will make your mobile calls significantly cheaper. You can buy local SIM cards almost everywhere in Asia and Africa and in most other places from telephone or service-provider shops.

Be aware that using online or location features on smart phones will chew through data frighteningly quickly. Investigate what the data charges are on a local prepaid SIM or international roaming plan before using your phone overseas to avoid any expensive headaches later on. It's also a good idea to turn off data in your phone's network settings while you are away and only turn it on when you need to access features that use it. (You will still be able to get text messages.)

However, if you're volunteering on a conservation or wildlife project, your mobile might not be so useful. Robin Glegg, who volunteered in Siberia, Namibia and Oman, points out:

In the Altai mobile phones did not work in the mountains, as we were fairly remote from civilisation. Biosphere Expeditions operates a satellite internet and phone link, so you can send and receive urgent messages or make urgent phone calls. Remember you may be going to remote places and you don't want mobile phones ringing every five minutes (if they work at all) as it spoils the atmosphere.

If you want to communicate quietly (and cheaply) on your mobile phone then this is what Kerry Davies did in Cambodia:

Texting. After hating all those people with mobile phones at home I admit I am now addicted to texting. Often a text arrives so quickly you can have a conversation.

And then there's the humble land line. Jacqueline Hill had a good arrangement with her relatives:

My parents called me once a week at the office (I had no phone or internet connection in my flat) and, as it only had one phone, this had to be carefully timed.

If you can't arrange for incoming calls to a land line near you, don't underestimate the international calling card. These usually work by giving you a freephone number which connects you to another service provider who can offer you a better rate on your call than the local provider can. These cards are often sold in local newsagents and shops, particularly in touristy areas. There isn't one card which works everywhere, although the Global Phonecard from **ekit** (www.ekit.com) comes close; this company also has a few other communication services that may interest you.

To help cut the costs of calls, Mike Laird, who volunteered in Bolivia, has some good advice:

One of the best things is to have a cascade (or telephone tree) set up so you only have to make one phone call (ie you call your folks, they call your brother and sister, they call two of your friends etc). I know it means you don't get to speak to all your family and friends but there may be times when you don't have enough money .

In addition to these methods, many international volunteers rediscover the ancient art of letter writing. Robert Driver, who volunteered in the jungles of Belize, remembers keeping in touch this way:

By letter during the jungle phase and by phone and letter during the rest of the time. It was quite refreshing keeping in contact this way.

And, of course, if you're out in the wilds, you may agree with Michelle Hawkins, who volunteered in Costa Rica. She says:

In Costa Rica I didn't keep in touch, as there was no electricity or postal system. It was actually quite liberating not to be contactable by phone, email or post.

Blogging

If you want to share more than just the odd status update or photo with friends and family, you might want to start your own travel blog. These days there are lots of sites that allow you to publish a blog for free and most don't require more than basic computer skills to get it looking presentable. Blogger (www.blogger.com) and WordPress (www.wordpress .com) are the two most popular options for text-based blogging, or if images are more your thing, Tumblr (www.tumblr.com) is a good option (and it does pretty well with text, too). Blogging is a great way to get the word out there, not just about your experiences but also for the project on which you're volunteering.

If you are planning to use your smartphone while you are volunteering, you can download apps that will allow you to blog on the go rather than having to be in front of your computer. WordPress (for both Apple and Android devices) and BlogPress (for Apple devices only) are two of the best. Instagram is the most popular of the photo-blogging apps.

If you're not at all tech-savvy, you can purchase a travel blog package for a small fee per month. Blogging companies offer differing features and functions, but most include interactive maps, space for online entries, digital photo albums and personal message boards. Be sure to find out whether you can download the content of your blog or burn it to DVD once you are back home, as you won't want all those memories of your time volunteering to just disappear into the ether. Some companies offering travel blog services include: MyTripJournal (www.mytripjournal.com), Off Exploring (www.offexploring.com) and Travel Pod (www.travelpod.com).

Chatting Online

There is a range of 'Voice over Internet Protocol' (VoIP) services that use the internet to deliver phone calls. All are easy to sign up for and are user friendly. Services include the following:

~ **Skype** (www.skype.com) Still the most popular, can be used for video and voice calls to others on Skype, as well as calls to mobiles and landlines.

~ **Google Talk** (www.google.com.au/talk) User-friendly chat app that works on almost any platform; can integrate with Gmail.

~ **Oovoo** (www.oovoo.com) Works across platforms, including Apple and Android devices.

~ **Yahoo! Messenger** (http://messenger.yahoo.com) Offers free text, voice and video chat, as well as budget international phone calling.

~ **Facetime** (www.apple.com/ios/facetime) Only works on Apple devices and relies on access to wi-fi or broadband connection.

~ **Mumble** (http://mumble.sourceforge.net) Originally created as a voice chat service for gamers but works for these purposes, too.

If you have a laptop or smartphone and a broadband connection, you can use your device to chat. If you're relying on internet cafes, keep at eye out for the terminals with headsets: they're for accessing chat services. You can chat face-to-face via a video call if the internet connection is fast and stable and there's a webcam; if not, keep it to just a voice call to help prevent frustrating 'freezing', lags between image and sound, and connection dropouts.

Services that utilise VoIP (Voice over Internet Protocol) are able to deliver either very cheap or free phone calls. In the case of Skype, if the person you're chatting with also has the app on their device, the calls are usually free; if they don't, you can buy credit at a per-minute charge or purchase a subscription that allows unlimited calls to landlines throughout the world.

If It All Goes Wrong

In everyday life it isn't often that you have to get used to a new job, a new culture, a new country, new living arrangements, new colleagues and a new support network all in one go. But this is what you do when you become an international volunteer.

At first it can be hard. During the first few days (and often weeks) you will need to give your mind and your body time to adapt. In all likelihood you will also have to reassess your personal expectations and those related to the job. Jacqueline Hill, who volunteered for a year in Bangladesh, wisely advises:

Find out as much as you can but be prepared for all your learning and assumptions to be challenged once you are there. Recognise that you are not single-handedly going to change the world in one trip and that what you expect to do may not be what you actually do once you get there. Don't expect lots of feedback on how you are doing or what impact you're having but recognise that just by being there and sharing you are helping the people to understand one another better. Accept that you will feel that you probably got more from the experience than the people you went to work with did.

As mentioned before, nine times out of 10, the reason why an international volunteer placement goes wrong is because the expectations of a volunteer do not match the reality of the placement. This doesn't mean there's anything wrong with the placement, or anything wrong with the volunteer. However, it might mean that the volunteer and the placement were ill-matched and that the volunteer was ill-advised and/or inadequately prepared. This is why it is so important to make sure that you volunteer with a reputable organisation that knows both you and their partner programmes well.

In addition, it is one of the reasons why patience, flexibility and adaptability are all key skills to have as an international volunteer. If your volunteer programme is significantly different to the one you signed up for, you will definitely need all three to see if you can still make things work for both you and your host organisation.

However, if you have given your situation time and you genuinely can't make the placement work, you do have a few options. If you have volunteered with a sending agency in your home country, you need to talk to their in-country representatives. Assuming there is no improvement, you will then need to contact the organisation itself in writing. If you asked for a job description prior to departure (see p26) you will be in a better position to point out the mismatch between the volunteer programme you were sold and the one you ended up with. You will then need to decide whether to go home early. This is not a decision to be taken lightly.

However, if coming home is your choice, any reputable volunteering organisation should discuss with you either a refund or free placement on another volunteer programme in the future. If this does not happen, you might like to forward your complaint to one of the professional or self-regulatory bodies that the organisation is part of. In the UK, for instance, this might be **The Year Out Group** (☎ +44 (0)1380-816696; www.yearoutgroup.org; Queensfield, 28 Kings Rd, Easterton, Wiltshire SN10 4PX). While **Volunteering Australia** (☎ +61 3 9820 4100; www.volunteeringaustralia.org) and **Volunteering New Zealand** (☎ +64 4 3843636; www.volunteeringnz.org.nz) are peak bodies concerned mostly with national volunteering, they might be able to offer advice. There's no all-encompassing volunteer organisation association in the US, but the **International Volunteer Programs Association** (☎ +1 201 221 4105; www.volunteerinternational.org) does count several dozen major organisations as members and might be able to offer advice on how to deal with uncooperative operators.

Useful Websites

~ **CIA World Factbook** (https://www.cia.gov/library/publications/the-world-factbook/index.html) Find out everything you ever wanted to know about the country you're volunteering in.

~ **ClimateCare** (www.climatecare.org) Offset the CO_2 emissions of flying to and from your volunteer placement by funding sustainable energy and reforestation projects.

~ **Department of Foreign Affairs and Trade (Australia)** (www.smartraveller.gov.au) Travel advisories for Australians listed by destination, travel bulletins, information on getting help overseas plus the low-down on visas and passports. The site also offers general travel and travel health tips. Register for email notification about changes to the safety status in the country you're volunteering in.

~ **eBay** (www.ebay.com) For the UK replace '.com' with '.co.uk' and for Australia add '.au'. Wherever you live, you could raise money to participate in your volunteer programme by becoming a seller.

~ **Embassy World** (www.embassyworld.com) There's a lot more to this site than just the location of embassies around the world.

~ **Kasbah.com** (www.kasbah.com) Flight bookings, car rentals, and thousands of local travel guides.

~ **Lonely Planet's Thorn Tree** (www.lonelyplanet.com/thorntree) Join one of the largest online travel communities and hear first-hand what you can expect in the country you're volunteering in.

~ **Lonely Planet's WorldGuide** (www.lonelyplanet.com/destinations) This site has information on nearly every country in the world.

~ **Malaria Foundation International** (www.malaria.org) Keep up-to-date with the latest news and views on this potentially fatal disease.

~ **New Zealand Ministry of Foreign Affairs and Trade – Manatū Aorere** (www.safetravel .govt.nz) Log on for travel advice and New Zealand passport and visa requirements. Travellers from the 'Land of the Long White Cloud' can register so the Ministry can contact them in an emergency.

~ **Global Electric & Phone Directory** (http://kropla.com) Everything you wanted to know about keeping in touch while you're away.

~ **Timeanddate.com** (www.timeanddate.com) Offers a world clock and also the times of sunrise and sunset, international country codes and city coordinates.

~ **Tourism Offices Worldwide Directory** (www.towd.com) This is pretty self explanatory.

~ **The Travel Doctor** (www.tmvc.com.au) Health reports, email notification service of health issues and details of clinic locations across Australia and seven locations in New Zealand.

~ **xe.com** (www.xe.com/ucc) Monitor the rate of exchange in the country you're volunteering in with this universal currency converter.

~ **Universal Packing List** (http://upl.codeq.info) Check your packing list against this one.

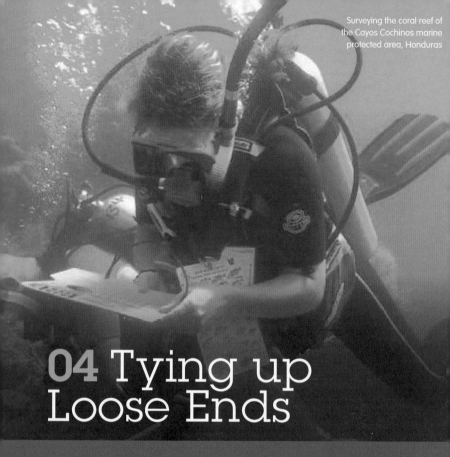

Surveying the coral reef of the Cayos Cochinos marine protected area, Honduras

04 Tying up Loose Ends

Whether it's sorting your moggie or your mortgage, planning is the key to a successful volunteering venture. This may be a once-in-a-lifetime experience, so you don't want to spoil it by leaving loose ends trailing at home. This chapter outlines some of the 'life stuff' that may need finalising before you go, but for more detail see Lonely Planet's *Career Break Book*.

Job

Negotiating time out from work is the most important, and potentially hardest, loose end to tie up. Bungle your approach to the boss and you could blow your volunteering dream out of the water – unless you've decided that you'll resign anyway. Planning your conversation carefully is crucial, especially if you work for a company that doesn't have a policy on volunteering or where no precedent has been set.

Before doing anything else, do your homework. If you work for a large organisation, consult your company's staff handbook, staff intranet and human resources department to get yourself up to speed on its leave provisions. Investigate if anyone else has taken time out and, if so, discreetly sound them out. Find out the company's general attitude to people taking extended periods of leave: is it openly supportive or the reverse? Armed with this information, you can plan your negotiation strategy accordingly.

Work out exactly what you're going to ask for and what you can offer in return. Do you want the same job once you return? Smaller companies may be able to accommodate this, but larger ones are unlikely to unless you're only going for a short period. Instead they will normally only promise employment at the same level and salary. If your company won't give you what you want, are you willing to quit? If so, are you going to be upfront about this, or will threatening to resign be the secret weapon that will give you leverage in your negotiations? If you opt to keep your job, are you asking for unpaid or paid leave or a mixture? How much time off do you need to volunteer? If the company doesn't agree to the period of time you are requesting, will you settle for less and, if so, how much less? Evaluate your worth to the company, as this will determine how accommodating they are likely to be. Have you worked there for long enough to prove your worth? (Many companies set two years as a minimum requirement for negotiating extended leave.) Draw up ways in which you can be replaced temporarily so that continuity is ensured and minimum expense incurred by the company. In this way you will be making life as easy as possible for your boss by doing the thinking and planning for them. Finally, put your case for how volunteering abroad is going to benefit both your company and you: in many cases a volunteering stint teaches you skills that are crucial in the workplace (such as communication skills, leadership and diplomacy skills). The aim is to present your volunteering as a win-win situation.

How long in advance should you pop the question? Antonia Stokes, a conference organiser who took a four-month break to work for Raleigh International in Namibia (p108), found her employers wanted over a year's notice. She says:

I would advise giving as much notice as possible about your plans, even up to a year in advance, so they can arrange proper cover for you. Be as honest and accommodating as possible, especially if you want your old job back.

The danger of giving plenty of notice is, of course, that you might be left out of any forward-planning meetings and effectively replaced long before you go. To avoid this scenario, other volunteers suggest giving only three to six months' notice.

Amanda Allen-Toland, who volunteered with the Thailand Business Coalition on AIDS (TBCA) as an Australian Youth Ambassador for Development (AYAD, p112), was fortunate that her workplace was well disposed to her proposed time off:

I gave four weeks' notice. I work for a public service agency that encourages staff to enhance their skills in either volunteer or paid roles which can add value to the government's work.

When negotiating it's wise to stick with well-worn tactics such as listening, expressing your wishes without being aggressive and showing that you can see things from your employer's point of view. Even if you've decided to quit if you don't get what you want, leaving on good terms will pay dividends in the future.

Once you've got agreement in principle from your employers, get it in writing. Make sure this includes the dates of your leave of absence, how much of your time off is paid or unpaid, what position (or level of position) and salary you'll return to and whether your pension or other company benefits are affected (see also the following 'Finances' section).

Of course, you may just decide to resign. Jacqui Pringle volunteered in Sri Lanka as an AYAD and worked as a communications adviser for the Sewalanka Foundation (a rural development agency). She adopted the following tactics when leaving her job:

I wanted to run straight to my boss and tell her that I would be leaving, as volunteering overseas was something I had always wanted to do and I wasn't enjoying my job at the time. There could be no guarantees the placement would go ahead, though, so I put off telling my employer just in case any last-minute hitches occurred. In the end I gave them two weeks' notice giving myself a week off before leaving for Colombo.

Of course, if you get wind of the fact that your company is looking to cut costs and staff, get in first and offer to take a voluntary redundancy package and you might just leave with a nice, fat cheque to help fund your volunteering adventure.

Finances

Once you've decided you're heading off to volunteer, it's crucial to sort your finances out well in advance. This may not be the most scintillating part of your preparations, but if your affairs aren't in order it could ruin your time away or leave you confronting a messy situation once you return. It's wise to get the ball rolling by discussing your affairs with an independent financial adviser. Whatever financial arrangments you make, it's important to keep some savings for when you get back, as that will make settling back in much easier. A small number of volunteering organisations offer resettlement grants when you return home but it's a good idea to make your own provision too.

Below are some particular financial issues you may want to address.

Pension and Superannuation

Even if they don't excite you, you must check how your pension or superannuation scheme will be affected by your time out of the workforce. If you're taking extended leave to volunteer and you're part of a pension or superannuation scheme at work, get all the details in writing. If you've quit your job, ask your scheme trustee or financial adviser what the options are – there are numerous different schemes and they all have different rules and regulations.

In New Zealand, for instance, people with National Super and participating in recognised volunteer programmes like Volunteer Service Abroad (VSA, see p123) can generally keep their entitlements for three years if volunteering overseas. In the UK, personal pension and stakeholder schemes are the most flexible for those volunteering, as you can often reduce your contributions or take a complete pension 'holiday' without penalty. And in the US, for breaks of two years or less, most employees with some seniority can easily alter their contribution levels without incurring any penalties. If you're considering leaving the company permanently, rolling your 401(k) assets into a Roth IRA is probably your best option. In any case, it's essential to consult a financial adviser about your specific situation and needs.

Company Share Save Schemes

If you work for a large company you may belong to a share save scheme. In the US these are called ESRP (Employee Stock Retirement Plans) or ESOP (Employee Stock Ownership Plans). If you are going away but intend to return, you should check how your scheme will be affected by a break in employment and ask for the advice to be put in writing. You will almost certainly have to opt out of the scheme while you are away, but your goal should be to re-enter it as soon as you return. Many companies require employees to have worked for two years before they qualify for such schemes, so you may decide to wait until you've notched these up before volunteering overseas. Some also have set dates during the year on which you can enter the scheme, so, again, take this into account.

Mortgage

See the 'House' section (p83) for details on the best way to deal with your mortgage while you're away.

Investments

Sometimes friend, sometimes foe, it is impossible to predict whether the stock market will be up or down when you return from volunteering. If you own stocks and shares and are counting selling them when you return, it may be prudent to transfer some of your money to more secure investments. Again, it pays to consult your financial adviser when considering the options. If you are likely to be away for more than three years, most financial advisers will recommend that you invest in a mixture of bonds and cash as well as equities.

If you live in the UK and your volunteering placement is shorter than a full tax year, think about buying a minicash ISA (individual savings account) up to the value of £3000 and you'll get your interest tax-free. However, if you are going away for a full tax year, fill in an R85 form, declare yourself a non-UK taxpayer with your regular savings account provider and your interest will be credited gross into your account.

Loans

If you have loans, make sure you have standing orders or direct debits in place to pay these while you are away and that you have left enough funds in your account to cover the payments. You can try to freeze them but lenders are unlikely to allow this.

If you are a young volunteer with a student loan, check whether your student loan lending agency has any special arrangements for international volunteers. For instance, in New Zealand, legislation grants interest-free status to the student loans of New Zealanders volunteering on specific programmes. Australians should check their HECS-HELP status at http://studyassist.gov.au/sites/StudyAssist or contact the **Australian Taxation Office** (www.ato.gov.au). UK volunteers could contact the **Student Loans Company Ltd** (www.slc. co.uk) for further information on assessment of any income they earn while overseas. In the US, federal and many private student loans allow principal and interest deferment during periods of unemployment (and self-funding volunteer trips fall into this category) or public service (such as work with the Peace Corps and other qualifying organisations). Click over to the **Department of Education** (www.ed.gov) or check with your lender for details.

Bank Accounts

You might want to allow a family member or friend to access your account while you're away. To do this, you need to nominate them as a signatory to your account by filling out forms held by your local bank branch. However, to be on the safe side, you probably wouldn't want this to be your main bank account with your entire worldly wealth in it.

Telephone & Online Banking

Thanks to online banking, tracking your finances from another country has never been easier. Online banking lets you check balances, pay bills, transfer money between accounts, set up direct debits and standing orders, and increase an overdraft. Most banks also have a telephone backup service which you can ring 24 hours a day if you experience any problems with online banking. Check if your bank can text you your bank balance – this could be useful, particularly if you have limited access to the internet and you're in danger of becoming overdrawn.

Security, however, may be a concern. There are email scams directed at banks' online operations designed to trick users into disclosing their online banking password, so beware of any suspect emails. If you receive an email purportedly from your bank that links you to a site asking for your full security information, treat it with suspicion and contact your bank directly. Do NOT divulge any personal information. Internet cafes are notoriously insecure environments to do your banking in, so consider using your own laptop with internet access or telephone banking instead. Also, ask your bank for its international helpline numbers in case something goes wrong.

If there's no alternative to an internet cafe in the middle of Mali or Madagascar, be cautious. Even if your memory is the size of a pea, think of different passwords to access your bank account: using the same one increases the chances of fraud.

Bills

If you are keeping your house and car, think ahead and make advance payments for items such as insurance, tax or registration and other ongoing bills. Alternatively, set up direct debits online. For more details relevant to house and car owners, see 'Mortgage' (p80) and 'Vehicle' (p86).

Paying your credit card bills while you are away is simple. There are three ways to do it: you can arrange for them to be paid by a friend who has access to one of your accounts; you can set up a direct debit for either the minimum payment, the full amount or a fixed amount; or you can pay the bills online. It's a good idea to alert your credit card company before you go abroad, because your user pattern will change and you don't want your card provider to assume the card has been stolen and cancel it.

Amanda Allen-Toland, who volunteered in Thailand for a year, found credit card fees to be a headache:

Unfortunately I didn't plan well and got stung by overseas credit card withdrawal fees. As a volunteer, that really hurts. Before you go, look into setting up an account with a bank that doesn't charge steep fees.

Direct Debits & Standing Orders

Go through any reccurring payments you have and reassess them; cancel ones you don't need and set up new ones. Have you remembered to sort your car repayments, for example?

Insurance Policies & Income Protection

Check your life or private health insurance policy for any exclusions before you go, as certain insurance companies deny cover if you are going to 'undesirable' areas like South America or Africa. Be aware that getting insured after you've returned home from these areas can be difficult – although don't let this deter you from going! It is unlikely that you'll be able to suspend payments while you are away, as most policies become void if you fail to make regular payments, but some companies are more flexible. In Australia, check with your tax adviser regarding suspending private health insurance, as pausing payments may have implications at tax time.

Maintenance Payments

Before you go abroad you should notify your child support agency, if relevant, other-wise you risk building up arrears. Your payments will be reassessed on the basis of your

Photo: www.biosphere-expeditions.org

Say 'ah' – a volunteer assists with cheetah monitoring in the Namibian savannah

volunteer status. You should also contact the agency again on your return. In the USA, the 1998 Deadbeat Parents Punishment Act stipulates jail time for those with child support obligations unpaid for longer than one year; check with your state's enforcement agency about how to continue payments from abroad.

Subscriptions

If you're going away for a long time remember to cancel subscriptions to newspapers and magazines. If you're going to be volunteering in a developing country, of course, your media diet may be limited, so consider taking out subscriptions to international publications like *The Economist* or *TIME Magazine*.

Taxation & National Insurance

Tax

Completing a tax return is the last thing you want to be doing while you are volunteering overseas. If you can, deal with it before you go. If you do need to file a tax return while you are away, work out exactly how you're going to do this. If possible, pick up a form from your local tax office, fill it in and post it off before you go or complete one online. In the UK, you can file your return online via the **HM Revenue & Customs** website (www.hmrc.gov .uk). US and Canadian citizens can 'e-file' their federal income tax payments online using privately produced software (some of which you can obtain for free). For Americans, the **Internal Revenue Service** website has comprehensive information (www.irs.gov); Canadians should check out the **Canada Revenue Agency**'s site (www.cra-arc.gc.ca). Australians can file their tax returns online with the **Australian Taxation Office** (www.ato.gov.au). The Australian Taxation Office also has a guide for volunteers called *Volunteers and Tax* (www.ato .gov.au/content/downloads/SME8729_nat4612.pdf) which will be helpful. New Zealanders should check out their **Inland Revenue** website (www.ird.govt.nz).

Your tax status is unlikely to be changed by volunteering internationally if the break is for less than a complete financial year, but check this with a tax adviser or your local tax office. You should also seek advice if you intend to earn money abroad to support your volunteering, or if you intend to dispose of any assets (eg your home or shares) before leaving or while abroad.

If you are resigning from your job, your employer will give you a certificate which shows your total taxable earnings and the amount of tax paid for the current tax year. Hang onto this as you'll need it to claim any tax refund and future employers may also need it.

National Insurance

For UK residents, sorting out your National Insurance (NI) situation before volunteering internationally for an extended period is vital. If you don't catch up on payments you miss, you may not be entitled to full maternity or unemployment benefits, or to a full state pension upon retirement. If you are volunteering abroad for less than a year, however, it is unlikely to affect your national insurance history. If you are going abroad for longer you may have to make voluntary contributions while you are away. An organised volunteering programme like VSO (p94) will pay your contributions for you.

House

If you're an older volunteer, you may own a house or flat that you'll be leaving behind. In this case you may choose to let it, leave it empty (rather dodgy, particularly as regards your insurance) or even sell it. If you're renting, you'll probably simply give notice and put your stuff into storage.

Mortgage

If your mortgage won't be covered by rent from tenants while you are away, think about switching to a flexible mortgage with online facilities. This is the perfect mortgage for international volunteers as you can pay bigger monthly payments before you leave or after you come back, and in return make smaller payments or even take a complete mortgage 'holiday' while you are abroad. Ideally, you should start making additional repayments a year in advance so that the pressure is off, both while you volunteer and once you return.

Selling

The beauty of selling your home (and maybe some possessions too) is that you're free of worries; you have no truculent tenants to potentially make your time volunteering any more challenging than it may already be. If you invest the money in a high-interest earning account, you may be able to keep your savings safe so that you are in a position to buy another home on your return. The risk is that if property prices rise faster than your savings, you may be forced to downsize when you buy back into the market. Don't underestimate the cost of buying again either – taxes, agent and legal fees all add up. For these reasons, selling your home is probably only a sensible option for long-term volunteers.

Letting (Leasing) Your Home

Most international volunteers who own property decide on this option. With luck your tenants' rent will cover your mortgage, your bills and even give you a modest income while you are away. Bear in mind, though, that rental income is taxable.

Here are some things to consider when letting your house or appartment.

Tell Your Mortgage Lender

Look carefully at the small print in the terms and conditions section of your mortgage document and it will invariably stipulate that you need to notify the lender if you let your home.

Finding Tenants & an Agent

You may decide to let privately and to find your tenants by advertising in local papers, shops or websites (universities often have websites that are referred to by visiting teaching staff, for example). Remember to obtain character references and bank statements (or payslips from an employer) and a watertight tenancy agreement. Although renting to friends can seem the easiest option, it can be disastrous: if something goes wrong with the rental arrangement, your friendship may be knocked on the head forever.

The other option is to let your property through a reputable agent. Although this will cost you more, it can be a safer option. Check the agent is well-established and affiliated to a respected industry body which imposes minimum standards. Whether you use an agent or go it alone, you should start looking for tenants around four to eight weeks before leaving.

Safety Issues

When you let your home in the UK you need to comply with certain legal obligations regarding safety. These usually entail having your gas, electrical appliances and fixed electrical installations tested for safety. If you are letting through an agent they will normally arrange for these checks to be carried out, for a fee.

Tax

If you let your home while you are abroad, remember that you'll be taxed on any profit, minus expenses like wear and tear, decorating and repairs. If you are going away for more than six months, you will probably have tax deducted from your rental income. Whether you own another house, whether you let it, and whether you live in your home again on your return will also have an impact, so check out your status with a tax adviser.

Decorating

Sprucing up your property before letting it will often ensure a better rent. The agent, if you are using one, will often suggest ways in which your property could be made more attractive, such as new carpets or a lick of paint.

Removing Items of Value

It goes without saying, but if you're letting your property fully furnished, take out items that are of sentimental value or items that you cannot replace like photos and antiques. Always assume the worst-case scenario; the contents of your home will not be treated as well as you would treat them.

Storage of Personal Effects

Should you decide to put your personal effects into storage, shop around, get quotes and ask lots of questions. For instance, find out how much notice is needed to collect your stuff; what insurance cover is offered; if insurance is included in the price; if the price includes tax; what the storage conditions are like; and if you can see the place where it will be stored (look out for damp areas that could damage your valuables). It could also be relevant to find out whether you can get access to your belongings while they are in storage and, if so, how much it costs. It's normally cheaper if you book storage for a long period of time (rather than constantly renewing) and don't need access. Never put precious items like jewellery, money or documents into storage – put them in a safe-deposit box instead.

Inventory

An inventory is essential for avoiding potential conflict when you reclaim your home. You can draw one yourself or pay an agent to do it as part of their service. If you are doing it yourself be meticulous: for example, write down the exact make and model of stoves and fridges and make a note of every blemish so there's no dispute later. It's a good idea to take electronically dated photographs of your contents as a backup, but don't rely on them: they are no defence in court as dates can be tampered with.

Building & Contents Insurance

If you tell your insurer that you're letting your house, they will almost certainly not want to know about contents insurance. However, do not despair: there are specialist insurers who will cover both buildings and contents. Premiums will probably be around 10 to 20 per cent more; ask an insurance broker to get quotes. It's hard, however, to get cover for a period of less than three months.

Tenancy Agreement

This agreement between you and the tenant (also known as a rental or lease agreement) is the key safeguard of your precious asset, so make sure it's done properly. If you are letting through an agent, they will issue their own version. If you are letting privately in the UK, you can buy off-the-shelf agreements from high street stationers or newsagents. In the US, major chain stores like **OfficeMax** (www.officemax.com) do sell standard rental agreements, but smaller outfits won't carry them. Far better, however, is to get a solicitor to draw up a watertight agreement. Make sure you have agreed who is paying contentious costs like water rates and council rates. There is usually no legal minimum period to let a property, but there may be a minimum notice period if you wish to end a tenancy agreement.

Rent

When the tenancy agreement is signed, you or the agent will probably ask for a month's rent in advance, plus one or possibly two months' rent as a deposit against damages or unpaid bills. In the UK you can insist that the tenant sets up a standing order for rent payment, which will give you far greater peace of mind. If you are paying an agent to manage your property, they will collect rent monthly and forward it to your bank.

Utilities

If you are using an agent, in the UK they will transfer accounts for utilities like gas, electricity and water into the tenant's name. Otherwise, the tenants will need to do it themselves once you have arranged for utilities to be disconnected. If you are volunteering only for a short time, you may prefer to leave accounts in your own name and get bills forwarded to the tenant to pay. The risk, though, is that the tenant won't cough up, in which case the responsibility is yours. The telephone is the biggest gamble; you may decide to stipulate that the tenant use their mobile and stop your line or switch it to incoming calls only.

Inspections & Repairs

If you are letting privately, you would be wise to appoint a friend to be on stand-by should anything go wrong, such as the hot water service breaking down. Ask them to inspect the property – every three to six months is the norm for real estate agents. If you are employing a managing agent, they will normally do this, but it is still advisable to ask a friend to be your agent's main point of contact while you're away.

Leaving Your House Empty

If you are volunteering for a short period, it may not be feasible to let your house and you may decide to leave it empty. If so, be sure to appoint a friend to keep a regular eye on it. One of the biggest problems with leaving a house empty is insurance. Most normal policies state that a house must not be left empty for more than 30 days (some say 60).

House-Sitters

Another option is to get a friend or relative to look after your house, pets and garden in return for rent-free accommodation. There are also a number of companies that provide professional house-sitting services, but this is an expensive option and probably not feasible for more than a couple of weeks.

Vehicle

What you do with your car, van or motorbike depends on how long you intend to be away. If it's just a few months, your best option is to leave the car in the garage or at a friend's or relative's place and ask them to drive it around the block once or twice. Note that they need to be nominated drivers on your insurance policy.

Amanda Allen-Toland was in Bangkok volunteering while her car stayed behind in Sydney with her mother. Amanda says:

She turned on the engine occasionally and looked after it. Fortunately, sorting out things like insurance and registration was a piece of cake because it's done online.

Many volunteers going away for a year or two decide to sell their cars, adding welcome cash to their volunteering funds. Another option is to lend the car to a friend while you are away. Again, there can be insurance snags but they are not insuperable.

Other Transport

If you have an annual or seasonal rail, bus or tram pass and are leaving before it expires, you can try applying for a refund by returning to the ticket office where it was bought. Your refund is typically calculated from the day you show up at the issuing office.

Photo: www.biosphere-expeditions.org

Turtle tagging around the Azores archipelago in the Atlantic Ocean with Biosphere Expeditions

Partner & Children

If you have a partner and children, you may need to time your volunteering to fit in around them. In the case of your partner, there may be an optimum time for you to volunteer abroad simultaneously, or you may decide to spend the time apart. Antonia Stokes, who spent four months in Namibia, had just started a relationship when she left the UK:

I'd been planning the trip for over a year so decided to go ahead with it and leave my boyfriend behind. A break of three or four months can improve a relationship, or at least expose the issues in it. It definitely pushes you to make decisions about your future.

Alternatively, of course, you may be wanting to volunteer abroad because you have just split up with a partner. Travel can be a great healer and spending time away an ideal way to cement the break.

Volunteering with children is slightly more complicated, depending on their ages and whether they are at school or not. Some parents decide to volunteer during the school holidays, which is easier than longer-term volunteering where you'll need to make decisions about schooling your child abroad. Teaching your children yourself is not an easy option if you are volunteering full-time. For information about international schools or local schools, contact your embassy in the country you plan to be in. And, as always, health and safety issues will be paramount with children. Lonely Planet's *Travel with Children* contains more information on being abroad with a family.

Making a Will

It may not be the cheeriest subject, but if you don't already have a will you should make one before you depart (the country that is, not this world). If you don't make one and you die intestate (ie will-less), your family and loved ones could end up with little. Your partner is particularly vulnerable if you are cohabiting but not married.

You can buy a DIY will kit from stationers or newsagents. However, solicitors claim they make more money out of unravelling DIY wills than they do drawing them up. So, for a fee, why not do it properly and get yourself a solicitor? Whatever method you choose, give your friends and relatives copies of your will, or tell them where copies are kept – your will is of little use if it's never found.

Power of Attorney

If you are volunteering long-term, you might want to think about giving a trusted friend or relative power of attorney over your affairs while you are away, in case you are incapacitated or out of contact. It's not a step to take lightly, as it gives the person power to do anything from selling your house or taking out a mortgage in your name to skinning your dog. If you are thinking of taking such a step the rule is, as ever, seek professional advice first.

Voting

If you're leaving for a while but still want a say in how your country is run, decide how you're going to vote. In the UK, consult the **Electoral Commission** (www.electoralcommission.org.uk). The **Federal Voting Assistance Program** website (www.fvap.gov) has information on absentee voting for Americans (also see www.fec.gov), and Canadians should consult **Elections Canada** (www.elections.ca). In Australia, **Australian Electoral Commission** (www.aec.gov.au) covers frequently asked voting questions for anyone heading overseas. If you're from New Zealand, get the low-down from **Elections New Zealand** (www.elections.org.nz).

Technology & Communications

You may want a break from routine, but not necessarily from friends, colleagues and family. Think well ahead about how to stay in touch while in another country: if you haven't engaged with social media as yet, now might be a good time. And don't forget to send out change-of-address cards or emails before you go.

While you are away, your local mail authority may be able to forward your mail either to your address abroad (if you have a fixed one) or to a reliable friend or relative in your home country who is willing to sift through it for you.

For advice on what to do about staying in phone contact while you're away, see p73.

Useful Websites

The following list of websites may help you get organised and on your way sooner:

UK Websites

~ **The Career Break Site** (www.thecareerbreaksite.co.uk) Everything you ever wanted to know about putting your life on hold while you are abroad.

~ **Carers UK** (www.carersuk.org) Information for those who look after elderly relatives.

~ **Driver & Vehicle Licensing Agency** (www.dft.gov.uk/dvla) Check with the DVLA when deciding what to do about your vehicle while you're away.

~ **Education Otherwise** (www.educationotherwise.net) A useful site about home schooling if you decide to do this with your kids.

~ **Home Education Advisory Service** (www.heas.org.uk) This organisation produces an informative leaflet on your options for home schooling abroad.

~ **Post Office** (www.postoffice.co.uk) Contact the PO for details on having your mail redirected while you're away.

North American Websites

~ **Canada Post** (www.canadapost.ca)

~ **Care Pathways** (www.carepathways.com) For those who look after elderly relatives, this site hosts a searchable database of recommended providers of assisted living, continuing care, independent living and nursing-home care.

- ~ **Kelley Blue Book** (www.kbb.com) Kelley's online Blue Book is full of practical advice about how to price, sell or trade in your car.

- ~ **Nolo Press** (www.nolo.com) Nolo Press publishes superb plain-English self-help legal books and provides a wealth of free online information on everyday legal topics.

- ~ **United States Postal Service** (www.usps.com) Information on how to organise redirecting your mail.

Australasian Websites

- ~ **Association of Superannuation Funds of Australia** (www.superannuation.asn.au) Information on different types of funds.

- ~ **Australian Furniture Removers Association** (www.afra.com.au) AFRA-registered businesses to take care of your beloved belongings in transit.

- ~ **Australia Post** (http://auspost.com.au) Australia Post will hold or forward your mail for up to a year at a time.

- ~ **Carers NSW** (www.carersnsw.asn.au) For those who look after elderly relatives, Carer Resource and Carer Respite Centres exist in each Australian state; they are all linked through this website.

- ~ **Drive** (www.drive.com.au) Check this site out before you put up a 'for sale' sign on your car.

- ~ **Australian Department of Human Services** (www.humanservices.gov.au/customer/themes/ families) You may lose your Family Tax Benefit if you leave Australia without notifying the FAO. Check the website for details.

- ~ **Law Council of Australia** (www.lawcouncil.asn.au) The Law Council of Australia represents 40,000 legal practitioners across the country (who can provide power of attorney and other legal advice).

- ~ **National Insurance Brokers Association** (www.niba.com.au) Find around 500 brokers in Australia who specialise in everything from car or house and contents insurance to travel, life and terrorism insurance.

- ~ **Self Storage Association of Australasia** (www.selfstorage.com. au) The SSAA represents 600 storage centres across Australia and New Zealand.

- ~ **Your Mortgage** (www.yourmortgage.com.au) The online version of Australia's *Your Mortgage* magazine, with broker listings and all sorts of mortgage advice.

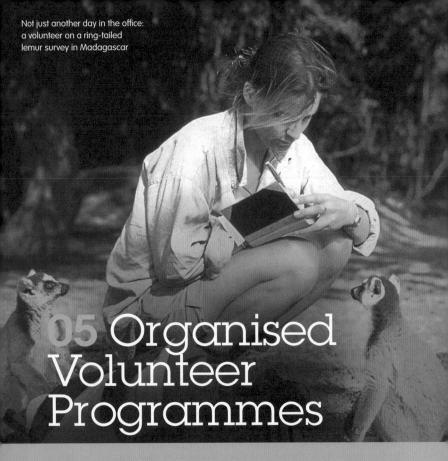

Not just another day in the office: a volunteer on a ring-tailed lemur survey in Madagascar

05 Organised Volunteer Programmes

If you've picked this book up, chances are that a little voice may have asked, 'Can I really do it?' The prospect of volunteering abroad can seem daunting, but it can be made much less so when it's arranged through a structured, organised programme. Choosing this route to a volunteer placement means that, in most cases, you'll pay a single fee and – voilà – everything from the pre-departure orientation to the little bag of peanuts on the flight home is arranged for you. Whether your calling is to tag turtles in Greece or teach grammar in Bangkok, there's a wide assortment of organised placements to choose from, offering opportunities to those who take comfort from a 'packaged' approach.

Most of these organisations have a few key characteristics in common, offering as part of the package pre-departure and in-country support and accommodation and food. Some also include travel insurance and visas, and others will organise your international airfare. But beyond these basic characteristics, the permutations are many and varied.

In many cases, the costs of organised programmes are high. However, it is difficult to generalise, because a number of voluntary organisations sending skilled volunteers abroad do not charge for placements and even offer a small monthly stipend. There are differences in the scale of organisations too. Some organisations, like AFS Intercultural Programmes (p98), have offices and programmes around the world, and send legions of people abroad on projects of every stripe. Others, like Skillshare International (p139) or Lawyers Without Borders (p141), send highly skilled professionals in very limited numbers. Some organisations specialise in particular fields, only offering placements in conservation or education, for example, while others allow participants to pick and choose from a smorgasbord of offerings. It's these variations in size, scope and types of project that can make or break your volunteering experience. One volunteer's dream placement doing hands-on entomology research is another volunteer's nightmare assignment swatting at bugs.

Some of the volunteering organisations listed in this chapter have programmes for everyone. Others are suitable only for people wanting to volunteer long term or for those trained in a particular profession (eg medicine). However, the offerings in this chapter can easily be sorted into two broad categories: expeditions and placements. We'll start by defining these terms.

How Do They Work?

Expeditions vs Placements

Anyone who has dipped a curious toe into the volunteering world knows that jargon and acronyms abound. In this book, the word 'expedition' is not to be confused with the kind of solo caper that involves slashing your way through the jungle with a machete. In volunteering parlance, expeditions are usually team-oriented exercises, where participants live, travel and work together in groups of 10 or more volunteers, accompanied at all times by qualified staff. Expeditions of this type often combine a service-based experience with an adventure element – activities such as trekking, climbing or rafting. Organisations offering these kinds of combined packages include Outlook Expeditions (p114), Madventurer (p106), Quest Overseas (p107) and Raleigh International (p108). Personal development is usually a key component of expedition-style volunteering. Laurence Gale travelled to Ghana with Raleigh International and says:

I did a 10-week expedition. As soon as we arrived in Accra we went to base camp and were immediately put into groups. The first week was spent doing icebreakers and learning basic first-aid and camping skills. Then we had three projects to work on: community, adventure and environmental projects. My community phase was spent on the border with Burkina Faso building pit latrines in a village. The adventure phase involved doing 260 kilometres over land and lake Volta in two and a half weeks. It was an awesome challenge and great fun for someone like me who loves running around outdoors. We also spent a lot of time in village schools teaching HIV/AIDS awareness. In my final (environmental) phase I spent the nights combing a sandy beach for olive ridley and giant leatherback turtles. By the way, we slept in big army tents along with various bugs, snakes and grass rats. Woohoo!

However, most organisations in this chapter offer placements, not expeditions. Simply put, for a placement the organisation acts like a temping agency, matching your requirements, skills, abilities and interests with projects in need. You may work independently, but more often than not you'll work alongside a handful of fellow volunteers. Placements are more self-determined than expeditions; you can have more freedom to shape your placement and make what you will of it, though you can still expect a high standard of in-country support. For example, most organisations have a local staff member who looks after a number of volunteers in a particular area and, in addition, there is a representative in the country of origin who is little more than a satellite phone call away should you need help. Two such placement organisations are The Leap (p105) and Projects Abroad (p100). Louise Ellerton, who travelled to Ghana with Projects Abroad, describes her experience of being part of an organised placement:

I did voluntary work in a veterinary practice, as this is the field that I will be going into. You have to be prepared for things to be different and accept that it's not always what you expected. I found the people very laid-back and a lot of the day was spent sleeping. At first this frustrated me, as I was there to gain experience, but you learn that this is how they are and you make the most of the times when you do get to see a case or an operation. I went alone but in the knowledge that I was going with a gap-year company who would be there for me when I arrived and had sorted out my placement and accommodation for the year. It was very easy to meet other volunteers doing the same thing through the company and you had ready-made friends who knew the country better than you did.

Claire Fulton, who volunteered in Kenya with The Leap, appreciated the in-country support during her placement:

The in-country staff were invaluable and they made it that much more enjoyable. They prevented many near-catastrophes from happening! They would have done anything for us, and I know that, as a group, we were all so glad that they were there.

Costs

While some of the more selective programmes like the Peace Corps (p96) don't charge for their placements, many of the programmes mentioned in this chapter are expensive. In many cases, the price covers a truckload of inclusions, sometimes incorporating flights, in-country support and pre-departure training. A proportion of the (often hefty) price tags attached to expeditions allows for first-class equipment, whether this comes in the form of a tent that won't leak or a guide who can read a map. Want to feel a warm inner glow from shelling out your life savings? Just keep in mind that all development and conservation and wildlife projects rely on volunteers' money to keep their projects afloat.

Selection & Eligibility

Some of the programmes in this chapter – particularly the ones in the 'Skilled Volunteering' and 'Emergency & Relief' sections – are selective, requiring such highly specialised training that they're simply not an option for many people. Others – particularly those in the 'Volunteering Holidays', section – require little more than an interest in the project and a financial commitment.

Length of Programmes

There are organised programmes of every length: from a volunteering stint during a week-long vacation to an assignment that will last several years. Be sure you have a general idea of the time commitment you'd like to make before you begin your research because, while some programmes offer flexible time frames, others require very structured time commitments.

What to Look for

Make sure you check whether costs such as airfares and travel insurance are included in the programme fee. Also, if you think you might like to do some independent exploring, find out how much time you'll be allowed off from the volunteer programme. As always, it's a good idea to request the contact details of former participants, who can provide objective answers to any specific questions you might have.

Pros & Cons

Regardless of whether you choose an expedition or a placement, there are some significant pros and cons attached to organised volunteer placements that you should weigh up before committing yourself.

Pros

You're guaranteed a structured and packaged volunteering experience

By definition, organised volunteer placements offer inclusive packages that take care of almost everything. In exchange for a sizable financial commitment, usually in the form of a flat fee, you're relieved of spending months trawling through guidebooks and foreign-language websites for information about your destination. You're also relieved of much of the burden of pre-departure planning, because your accommodation, food, local support and the project itself are all usually prearranged for you.

High standards of in-country support make you feel more secure

Safety is often a chief consideration for anyone about to jet off to an unfamiliar part of the world. Obviously, no-one can guarantee that things won't go wrong, but placement organisations have systems in place to prevent a crisis from turning into a tragedy. Expeditions are accompanied by experienced team leaders and sometimes a doctor or a nurse. If you're on a placement there will be in-country representatives who can provide support in an unfamiliar setting and who will follow established procedures in the event of an emergency.

You'll get thorough pre-departure training & briefings about your project

Many organisations take great pride in thoroughly preparing volunteers for their expeditions or placements. Many have training weekends, workshops on cultural awareness, language training, risk-assessment sessions and lengthy discussions on health and safety issues. Students who attend these training sessions are better prepared when they arrive at their destination and most hit the ground running from day one.

Also, when you live and work in the developing world where living conditions are, well, developing, it's important that you understand what to expect. Living without electricity or running water shouldn't come as a shock to you, as it did to Claire Loseby, who volunteered in China. She says:

Everything seemed a bit daunting at first because I never expected to live in such horrible conditions (no toilets, for example) but you soon adapt to it.

You'll work with like-minded volunteers & local communities

Programmes that attract school-leavers or recent graduates can be great places to make new friends. Volunteers who live and work together, alongside their local partners, can become like tight-knit family groups. Tabitha Cook, who taught English and worked at an orphanage in Sri Lanka with Travellers Worldwide (p114), really appreciated being around like-minded people her own age and says:

If you're thinking of volunteering, look at who you'll be living with, whether you're placed in a homestay or living with other volunteers. I chose to live with other volunteers because I wanted to be around people that I could moan to if it all got on top of me, and so if I made a cultural faux pas I wouldn't offend those I was living with. It was the best decision I have ever made. I made so many friends and learnt a lot, plus we had some great house parties.

You can find programmes geared toward personal development

Providing personal development opportunities for volunteers is a goal of many volunteering ventures aimed at young people. Encouraging volunteers to develop their skills, whether as part of a team or in a leadership capacity, is a key component of organisations such as Raleigh International (p108).

Your nearest and dearest are less likely to have a nervous breakdown worrying about you

Organisations aimed at the under-30 set are used to dealing with hand-wringing parents while you are halfway around the globe. Some go to great lengths to ensure that both you and your parents are kept happy while you're away, for example providing secure blogs on their websites so that friends and family can track your itinerary.

Cons

The costs

As we have mentioned, some of these programmes are expensive, though many organisations offer help in raising the programme fees. But if you get a thrill from not knowing where the next meal is coming from or where the next bus is going to, there are plenty of programmes that offer a less structured approach, along with a more affordable price tag.

You're locked into a pre-paid commitment for a rigid period of time, and you may be too coddled

Programmes vary in length, but some, like Project Trust (p107), require very specific and restrictive time commitments. If you're fresh out of school or college, these structured commitments might feel too institutional. Consider this carefully, because with many organisations, if you decide to pack up your bags and leave early, it's very unlikely your money will be refunded.

You're worried about not interacting enough with local people

Sometimes a group-based volunteer experience might not provide you with enough exposure to the local people and culture. Are you sure you want to be surrounded by compatriots when you go abroad? A good way to ensure interaction with local people is to live with a host family, so check if this is an option with the programme you're interested in. Otherwise, an immersive placement, where you work on your own or in pairs, might be more your cup of tea.

You came halfway around the world to do volunteer work, not for this personal development nonsense

If you're serious about rolling up your sleeves and committing your time to a charitable organisation in the developing world, you might be better off volunteering with an outfit that's focused on intensive volunteer work, rather than on a combination of volunteering and personal development.

Major International Placement Programmes

When you think of volunteering abroad, a handful of well-established, long-standing organisations probably spring to mind. Agencies like VSO and the Peace Corps are heavy hitters with well-organised programmes, elaborate support systems, and decades-old relationships with their host countries. It's worth bearing in mind, however, that smaller, grassroots organisations usually offer more flexibility than these large organisations.

VSO (Voluntary Service Overseas)

VSO, an international development charity working to alleviate poverty, is the largest independent volunteer-sending agency in the world. VSO sends skilled volunteers who pass on their expertise to local people. They accept applicants between 20 and 75 from a variety of professional backgrounds, such as medicine, engineering, small business, social work, health, management consulting, arts and crafts, accounting and agriculture. VSO pays your airfare and insurance, and provides accommodation, a small local wage, a resettlement grant when you return and other benefits. The average age of most volunteers is 38. Postings are usually for two years, although shorter placements do exist.

For people without professional expertise, VSO has two volunteering programmes aimed at people aged between 17 and 25: Youth for Development (YfD) and the International Citizen Service.

Youth for Development Programme (YfD)

By concentrating on six areas – education, HIV & AIDS, disability, health & social well-being, participation & governance and secure livelihoods – VSO's Youth for Development Programme helps young people get their first taste of intensive international volunteer service. The projects themselves are immensely varied. Volunteers on education placements may go to Kathmandu to run workshops and activities for disadvantaged children. Volunteers on secure livelihoods placements might be sent to Mongolia to help with small-scale farming projects. Participants are expected to develop a global education project before, during and after their placement. There are examples of these on the VSO website.

To qualify for this programme you need to:

~ Be between 18 and 25.

~ Be a resident of the UK or Ireland.

~ Have a year's volunteering or community-service experience under your belt.

Placements start in August, September and October of each year and you're expected to raise £900 towards placement costs. Apart from that, all other costs including airfares, accommodation and food, are paid by VSO. There's a competitive assessment procedure for this programme and approved applicants undertake four compulsory training courses. You need to apply giving at least 10 months' notice. Alice Tedd, a successful YfD volunteer, describes her experience with the programme:

I went to the Philippines and after three weeks of training (in language and culture etc) the six of us youth volunteers were let loose. I was working with a small NGO in Manila which implemented renewable energy projects in remote communities. Simple electricity can make a huge difference to people's lives. I was lucky because I was able to travel to the project sites, dotted all around the country, and then go back to Manila and relax in the relative luxury of the house there. I felt that I got to know the country and the people very well. I learnt about the contrasts that exist in Filipino culture: from the very wealthy people in the capital frequenting plush malls to the poorest of the poor in the remote villages with nothing to their name but a small patch of land to feed a large family. It was fun and supportive having the VSO network in the country – especially at holiday times when our group of YfDs met up to travel around together.

For more information on VSO and YfD call ☎ +44 020-8780 7500, log onto www.vso.org.uk or email enquiry@vso.org.uk.

International Citizen Service

Another VSO initiative, the International Citizen Service (formerly known as Global Xchange) offers participants a more team-oriented experience than YfD, giving young people opportunities to work in teams on development projects around the world on six-month placements. Twice a year, nine individuals are paired with nine overseas participants to spend three months together in the UK, followed by three months working on a practical project in the country that the overseas participant comes from. Community projects include such things as working with older people, children, marginalised communities or on global education and advocacy projects. On each leg of the exchange the pair live with a host family.

To qualify for this programme you need to be:

~ Between 18 and 25.

~ A resident of the UK; although residents of the EU, Norway, Liechtenstein or Iceland qualify if they've lived in the UK for a year or more, and residents of other countries can apply through partner organisations, which are listed on the website, www.vso-ics.org.uk.

~ Able to communicate in English.

Placements start in March and September and you need to raise at least £600 towards your costs. VSO pays for medical costs, training, international travel, accommodation, food, visas and a basic allowance. Again, competition is tough and the selection process is demanding. Check out their website (www.vso-ics.org.uk/pages/whats-involved.aspx) to get an idea of the complete programme. There are two application periods, both six months before departure. Successful applicants attend two compulsory training courses before working with volunteer partners from India, Indonesia, Kazakhstan, Kenya, Malawi, Mongolia, Nigeria, Pakistan, the Philippines and South Africa.

Peace Corps

For Americans, the Peace Corps (www.peacecorps.gov) is to volunteering what McDonald's is to fast food. Founded in 1961, the organisation is an independent federal agency of the United States Government, and has sent almost 200,000 people on 27-month development, humanitarian and relief assignments around the world. Even though there was a whiff of Cold War politics behind its founding, these days the Peace Corps' focus is on providing long-term volunteers to needy regions around the globe (currently 70 countries worldwide). Any US citizen over 18 can apply, and while there is no upper age limit, most volunteers are in their mid 20s.

Placements vary widely. You may work with subsistence farmers in a remote African village or end up living in air-conditioned comfort in an Asian metropolis mentoring college students – it all depends on the current needs of the programme and your skills. Volunteers range from bright-eyed college grads to professionals who want to escape the corporate doldrums.

New Yorker Ryan Andersen joined the Peace Corps as a break from a career in finance:

I served as a Peace Corps volunteer for two years in the Dominican Republic and transferred and extended for a third year to help launch a new project in Zambia. The overarching goal of my project in the

An old mission house used by Azafady volunteers for capacity-building in St Luce, Madagascar

DR was to teach business skills to farmers, women's groups and youth groups. In Zambia I lectured at a college on farm management and worked with the Zambian Ministry of Education to develop a new distance-learning programme for orphans and vulnerable children.

The experience surpassed my expectations – almost every week I get emails and handwritten letters that have traversed half the world carrying a stamp that cost a quarter of a day's wages. These letters reaffirm the bonds that I went to Zambia and DR to build. I've recently returned to the States and I'm still searching for that perfect job, but Peace Corps gave me a great new perspective. In some ways it made me more motivated to take advantage of all the opportunities that I have here and it also made me reassess what is truly important in life and where I should focus my priorities.

The Peace Corps is not a soft option – there's a three-month training programme before a full two-year assignment. To smooth the way, the US Government provides a monthly living allowance, dental and health insurance, flights and a lump sum of around US$7400 to help volunteers readjust to life back home at the end of their placement. Volunteers can also defer, or apply for reduced payments on, many student loans.

With all these perks, it's no surprise that competition for placements is fierce. The tough selection process includes reams of paperwork, a convincing personal statement about your motivations for applying, an in-depth interview (possibly including questions about what your partner thinks of your application), and a medical exam. Assuming you are up to scratch, you'll be assigned a placement matching your skills – which could be anywhere in the world doing almost anything. The whole process – from sending off the application to leaving the tarmac – can take six months.

European Voluntary Service (EVS)

EVS is funded by the European Union and will basically pay you to volunteer in another European country. Placements are coordinated by the volunteer, a sending organisation (usually from the volunteer's home country) and a host organisation (usually the one with which volunteers do their service). Placements are normally between two and 12 months, but shorter ones are available for people with special needs. The wide variety of placements include work in the social, environmental or cultural sectors.

EVS provides lots of assistance to their volunteers. They pay an allowance of approximately £100 per month and cover accommodation, food, insurance, language training and international travel costs. To qualify, you need to be between 18 and 30 and live in an eligible country – which includes EU member countries, the UK, Iceland, Liechtenstein, Norway, Romania, Bulgaria and Turkey. In addition, some projects take place in partner regions of the EU throughout Eastern Europe and the Caucasus, southeastern Europe and even Latin America.

In the UK, the scheme is administered by **Youth in Action** (☎ +44 (0)20-7389 4030; c/o the British Council, 10 Spring Gardens, London SW1A 2BN; www.britishcouncil.org/youthinaction; yia@nya.org.uk), but you need to apply locally through EVS-affiliated sending organisations. There's a list of these on the Connect Youth website.

As you might imagine, getting paid to travel and volunteer makes this scheme immensely popular. The organisation makes about 600 placements per year and successful applicants are subjected to a rigorous assessment process. To increase your chances of being selected, apply at least nine months in advance of your intended departure, have some foreign-language skills (or at least demonstrate an interest in learning the language of your destination), and make it evident that you're dedicated to your project.

This programme also allows volunteers who have completed an EVS placement to apply for a Future Capital grant to devise and manage their own project in programme countries. You need to apply within two years of completing an EVS placement.

Options for the Under 30s

Even though it's less common in the US than in most of Europe and the UK, many youngsters take a year out to see a bit of the world, either before starting higher education or after completing it. The following organisations (often referred to as 'gap-year organisations') cater mostly to the under-30 set, and send as many as 200,000 young people abroad every year. While some of the following opportunities are tailored to 17- to 25-year-olds looking for a taste of the world beyond academia's walls, many also accommodate older volunteers.

International Organisations

AFS Intercultural Programmes

71 West 23rd Street, 6th Floor, New York, NY, 10010-4102 USA
☎ +1.212.807.8686
fax +1.212.807.1001
www.afs.org

With over 70 years of experience and volunteering opportunities around the world, AFS has its hands in many placement projects. AFS sends volunteers from many countries; to investigate AFS volunteering opportunities in your country or region visit www.afs.org/contact. You might work with children in Brazil, rebuild communities in Honduras or work in an orphanage in Peru. Because cultural exchange and immersion are considered to be as important as the development work itself, all volunteers live with a local family. Ness Sellers, who was with the programme for six months, says, 'I worked alongside the two directors in planning and implementing projects within the Tumbes community which were aimed at the development of the community through education. Initially I worked on a project for the prevention of HIV/AIDS, which involved training 150 volunteers and then visiting house to house within deprived areas to give information on HIV/AIDS prevention, treatment and where to go for support and help. I then began my own project aimed at prevention of domestic violence. As coordinator of the project I was responsible for all the logistics, administration, visiting schools, giving talks, running workshops, trips with the children and much more.'

Status: International, voluntary, non-government, non-profit organisation.
Timing & Length of Placements: Placements range from three to six months with departures in January/February and July/August. Apply six to seven months in advance.
Destinations: Worldwide, there are over 50 different member countries in the AFS network.
Eligibility: Most applicants must be between 18 and 29 but some countries accept older volunteers.
Groups or Individuals: Individuals.
Annual no. of Volunteers: AFS sends 11,000 students, young adults and teachers annually.
Annual Projects: Teaching, conservation and development projects.
Partner Programmes: AFS has partnerships with hundreds of NGOs, community programmes and schools worldwide.
Selection & Interview Process: Initial applications through AFS offices are followed by a selection interview. Following the interview, final forms are completed and sent to the host country to help them decide project and family placement.
In-country Support: AFS has a thorough in-country support system.

AIESEC

Teilingerstraat 126, 3032 AW Rotterdam, The Netherlands
☎ +31 10 443 4383
info@ai.aiesec.org
www.aiesec.org

AIESEC is an international student platform in over 2400 universities and has over 86,000 members, and as such is the world's largest student organisation. Focusing on leadership development, AIESEC offers more than 60,000 leadership opportunities each year to facilitate its International Internship Programme, which sees the exchange of over 4000 students each year to live and work in another country.
Status: Not-for-profit organisation.
Timing & Length of Placements: To go on an exchange through the International Internship Programme, recruitment takes place usually at two or three points in the year. Those wishing to take part need to be involved with AIESEC activities for a period of time prior to their departure.
Destinations: Spin a globe and drop your finger at random – chances are AIESEC has a programme there. They currently have placements in 95 countries worldwide,

everywhere from Bosnia-Herzegovina to Qatar (and most countries in between).

Costs: There are small administration fees for the internship programme; contact your national chapter for specific costs. The majority of internships are paid positions and the salary provides interns with enough money for basic living costs in the country in which they will be working. Development traineeships are usually unpaid, however, accommodation is provided free of charge. The administration fees cover assistance with getting your visa, finding accommodation and cultural preparation and integration. Airfares are not included.

Eligibility: Volunteers must be 18 or over. There are no age restrictions, but most members are between 18 and 30. Each internship position requires a range of skills and experience based on academic or professional backgrounds. The organisations and companies who have agreed to hire an international intern are aware that members are students, so a lot of experience is generally not required.

Groups or Individuals: One of the goals of doing an exchange through AIESEC is to challenge your world view and experience a new culture. For this reason, travelling to work in a familiar place to visit friends, or accompanied by partners or family, is discouraged.

Annual no. of Volunteers: 5000

Annual Projects: 4000

Partner Programmes: Over 3500 organisations at the local, national and international level.

Selection & Interview Process: If you're interested, attend an information session run by the local AIESEC chapter at your university. You'll need to submit an application, then attend an assessment centre and an interview with a review board.

In-country Support: Support structures vary, depending on placement.

BUNAC (British Universities North America Club)

16 Bowling Green Ln, London EC1R 0QH, UK
☎ +44 (0)20 7251 3472
fax +44 (0)20 7251 0215
enquiries@bunac.org.uk
www.bunac.org/volunteer-abroad

Better known for working holiday and camp counselling programmes, BUNAC also offers seven volunteer programmes. Among these are school-based projects in Ghana, rainforest conservation in Costa Rica and community work in South Africa or China.

Status: Non-profit organisation.

Timing & Length of Placements: Placements last from five weeks to 6 months and run year-round (there are monthly group departures). Apply at least 10 weeks prior to departure.

Destinations: Cambodia, India, China, Ghana, South Africa, Peru, Costa Rica and USA

Costs: Five weeks from about £799, usually including: programme literature, an arrival orientation course, UK and in-country support, accommodation and food (check with BUNAC for full details). Flights, travel insurance and pocket money are not covered.

Eligibility: Minimum age is 18 and some programmes require you to be a student or recent graduate. South Africa and Cambodia are only open to British or Irish nationals; all programmes require that you be a UK resident. For the Peru and Costa Rica placements, you need to speak conversational Spanish.

Groups or Individuals: Individuals.

Annual no. of Volunteers: 300 to 500.

Partner Programmes: In all six regions, BUNAC partners with local NGOs.

Selection & Interview Process: All participants complete a written application form and are interviewed, either in-person at one of their London offices, or over the phone. Application deadlines are at least 10 weeks prior to departure.

In-country Support: BUNAC places importance on independent experiences and different projects have varying levels of in-country supervision. In all cases volunteers will receive an arrival orientation and our local partners will provide guidance and supervision throughout the trip. Emergency phone lines are operated 24/7 both in-country and also in the UK.

Cross-Cultural Solutions

UK: Tower Point 44, North Rd, Brighton BN1 1YR, UK
☎ +44 (0)845 458 2781/2
fax +44 (0)845 458 2783
US: 2 Clinton Pl, New Rochelle, NY 10801, USA
☎ +1 800 380 4777
fax +1 914 632 8494
info@crossculturalsolutions.org
www.crossculturalsolutions.org

Cross-Cultural Solutions offers volunteer programmes in 16 regions around the world. Placements are based on an individual's skills and interests and the needs of the local community. All work is with locally designed projects, usually in the fields of education, healthcare and social service. Strong emphasis is placed on cultural exchange, and participants are given the chance to be immersed in the culture of their host region through travel, activities and seminars.

Status: In the UK, Cross-Cultural Solutions is a registered charity and limited company. In the US it's a non-profit organisation.

Timing & Length of Placements: Placements are from one to 12 weeks and can be extended. There are start dates throughout the year. Apply 60 days in advance.

Destinations: Brazil, China, Costa Rica, Ghana, Guatemala, India, Peru, Russia, Tanzania and Thailand.

Costs: The cost of a two-week programme is approximately £1930 and each additional week comes in at around £350. This includes lodging, meals, in-country transportation, airport transfers, full staff support, medical insurance, language training and cultural excursions (but not international flights).

Eligibility: The minimum age of volunteers is 18 when unaccompanied by an adult, but some programmes accept 16- and 17-year-olds, at the discretion of the programme manager. The minimum age for a child travelling with a parent or guardian is eight. If a volunteer is between the ages of eight and 16, the accompanying adult must be a parent, legal guardian, or a person appointed by that parent or guardian.

Groups or Individuals: Depends on placement.

Annual no. of Volunteers: Over 3000.

Partner Programmes: Over 200 partner programmes worldwide.

Selection & Interview Process: Anyone with a desire to volunteer internationally is encouraged to apply and placements are designed to accommodate all kinds of skills and levels of experience. Volunteers wishing to apply their specific skills to local community projects may do so through a customised placement developed by the country director.

In-country Support: Professional, local staff to provide orientation, safety, supervision and guidance throughout each volunteer's stay. A staff member is always present and available and the country director is available in case of emergency at all times. For the convenience of friends and families of volunteers, there is a toll-free 24-hour emergency hotline in the US.

Projects Abroad

Aldsworth Pde, Goring, Sussex BN12 4TX, UK
☎ +44 (0)1903 708 300
fax +44 (0)1903 501 026
info@projects-abroad.co.uk
www.projects-abroad.co.uk

Another large organisation with multiple international offices, Projects Abroad deploys armies of volunteers as English teachers in China, rainforest defenders in Peru, turtle researchers in Mexico, journalists in Romania and medical assistants in India – these are only some of the hundreds of positions available. For every three months of voluntary work with Projects Abroad, it's possible to take two weeks off for travel, and independent travel is possible before or after a placement.

Status: Limited company.

Timing & Length of Placements: Placements can be from one to 12 months and you can move from one placement to another, if you wish. There are programmes year-round and departure dates are flexible. Try to give at least three months' notice.

Destinations: The many destinations include Argentina, Bolivia, Cambodia, China, Ethiopia, Ghana, India, Jamaica, Mexico, Mongolia, Nepal, Peru, Russia, South Africa and Thailand.

Costs: Two-week projects start from £900 and three months from £2100, which includes food, accommodation, comprehensive insurance and in-country backup. International flights are extra.

Eligibility: Those from 16 to 70 are eligible.

Annual no. of Volunteers: 5000

Annual Projects: 150

Partner Programmes: 50

Selection & Interview Process: After being selected on the basis of their application forms, participants reserve placements with a £320 deposit that goes toward their fundraising target.

In-country Support: There are full-time, paid and trained staff in every destination.

Photo: www.biosphere-expeditions.org

Volunteers with Biosphere Expeditions talk to local people about surveying Arabian leopards in Oman

Restless Development

2nd Floor, Faith House, 7 Tufton Street,
London, SW1P 3QB, UK
☎ +44 (0)20 7976 8070
fax +44 (0)20 7233 0008
info@restlessdevelopment.org
www.restlessdevelopment.org

Restless Development is an international development charity (which runs the International Citizen Service in partnership with VSO, see p103) that trains young people to work as peer educators on programmes that address urgent health and environmental issues in Africa and Asia. Restless Development offers the chance to work in rural communities, developing young people's life skills and changing attitudes about health and environmental issues. There are two programmes: health education and community resource work. You may run HIV/AIDS workshops in South Africa, set up sustainable organic farming initiatives in Uganda or work with a Green Club in Nepal. Volunteers from the UK are paired with volunteers from a host country. There are information days every two months in London, and accommodation is provided for international applicants (see the website for details).

Status: Charity.

Timing & Length of Placements: Volunteers leave every September and January. The assignments are four to nine months long, depending on the programme. Apply as early as possible.

Destinations: India, Nepal, Sierra Leone, South Africa, Tanzania, Uganda, Zambia and Zimbabwe.

Costs: Each volunteer is asked to fundraise a minimum of £3600, regardless of the length of placement. This fee covers all costs, including your international airfare.

Eligibility: Applicants should be between 18 and 28 and open to living in a different culture.

Groups or Individuals: Individuals.

Annual no. of Volunteers: In 2007, 800 volunteers were in the field reaching 400,000 young people.

Annual Projects: Hundreds of educational and development programmes worldwide.

Partner Programmes: UNICEF, UNAIDS, World Bank, Swedish International Development

Agency, New Zealand Aid, UK Department for International Development, Danish International Development Agency, Irish Aid, UNDPA, UNDP and more.

Selection & Interview Process: Applicants are selected on the basis of their application form, personal statement, references, assessment at a selection day and interview. Non-UK residents can opt for a phone interview.

In-country Support: Field staff resident in each country work from one or more permanent offices and regularly visit placements to organise training and offer general support. Workshops bring together volunteers from the region to refresh their training.

UK Organisations

Brathay Exploration Group

Brathay Hall, Ambleside, Cumbria LA22 0HP, UK
☎ /fax +44 (0)15394 33942
admin@brathayexploration.org.uk
www.brathayexploration.org.uk

Brathay Exploration Group was set up in 1947 and is now a charitable trust that runs overseas educational expeditions for young people. Some expeditions focus on fieldwork, others on trekking. In 2006, one expedition spent a week in a Himalayan village building a classroom before trekking through the desert region of Spiti. The average size of an expedition is 15 people. Parts of the Duke of Edinburgh's Award can be completed on these expeditions.

Status: Registered charity.

Timing & Length of Expedition: Two to four weeks, departing in July or August. Apply as soon as the programmes are advertised on the website.

Destinations: These vary each year but may include the Channel Islands, China, the French Alps, Italy, the Lake District, Morocco, Mull (Scotland), South Africa and Tanzania.

Costs: Expedition costs range from around £300 to £2000, excluding international flights. This includes comprehensive insurance, all accommodation, food, group equipment and in-country travel. Brathay will arrange flights and pass costs along to volunteers.

Eligibility: Members 15 to 25 years old, voluntary leaders of 21 and older.

Groups or Individuals: Volunteers can join up as individuals or with one or more friends. They join an expedition of between 10 and 20 members and up to four leaders.

Annual no. of Volunteers: 50-100

Annual Projects: Up to 10.

Selection & Interview Process: After submitting an application form, medical questionnaire and membership fee with your deposit, applicants are selected by the expedition leader.

In-country Support: Groups are led by paid and volunteer staff.

British Schools Exploring Society

The Royal Geographical Society, 1 Kensington Gore, London SW7 2AR, UK
☎ +44 (0)20 7591 3141
fax +44 (0)20-7591 3140
info@britishexploring.org
www.bses.org.uk

Founded in 1932 by a surviving member of Scott's Antarctic expedition, BSES aims to provide opportunities for young explorers to access remote areas of the world. It runs five-week summer expeditions for those aged 16 to 20 and longer two-month gap-year expeditions for anyone aged 18 to 23. Explorers work within groups of 12 on a variety of environmental and research projects. Expedition destinations vary each year but typically include the Amazon, Arctic, Himalayas and desert environments. Alice Hughes, who went to the Amazon, says, 'I think the trip has made me grow up and confirmed my desire to "preserve animals in their natural state" as a career. I have had a wonderful time and will definitely go back one day.'

Status: Charity.

Timing & Length of Expedition: The gap-year expeditions are for roughly two months and departure dates vary (check the website). The four- to six-week summer expeditions depart in mid-July. For deadlines and how to apply, please see the website.

Destinations: Vary from year to year. Traditionally expeditions were to Arctic and sub-Arctic destinations, but over the last 16 years they have expanded to include India, Kenya, Morocco, Papua New Guinea and the Peruvian Amazon.

Costs: The costs for expeditions average around £3250 plus flights. Fundraising support is given and BSES runs a mentoring scheme.

Eligibility: Applicants for the summer expeditions must be aged 16 to 20 at the time of the expedition but are encouraged to apply up to 18 months in advance. Gap-year expeditions are open to 18- to 23-year-olds. Some experience of camping, hill walking and outdoor activities is desirable but not a prerequisite.

Groups or Individuals: Individuals.

Annual no. of Volunteers: 200

Annual Projects: Vary, but always combine adventurous activities with environmental conservation projects.

Selection & Interview Process: All participants complete a written application and an interview, either in-person with a regional interviewer, or over the phone.

In-country Support: A qualified doctor accompanies every expedition, in addition to a chief mountaineer, chief scientist, base-camp manager and two leaders for every group of 12. Also, there is a 24-hour UK response team, International SOS repatriation and emergency cover.

Changing Worlds

11 Doctors Lane, Chaldon, Caterham, Surrey CR3 5AE, UK
☎ +44 (0)1883 340960
ask@changingworlds.co.uk
www.changingworlds.co.uk

Changing Worlds offers the experience of integration – you live with a local family and work with local people. It offers a variety of paid and volunteering experiences, including teaching, farming, law, journalism and medical placements. James Patterson, who was placed at a school in Ghana, says, 'It really was an amazing all round experience and I loved every minute of it. I will definitely be back to visit all the friends I made as soon as I can find the time. Its a cliché to say the words "life changing experience" but it's true in every way and I think the thing I learnt most about in my whole trip was me.'

Status: Limited company.

Timing & Length of Placements: Placements are for three to six months but can be extended. Departures are year-round.

Destinations: Argentina, Australia, Brazil, China, Dubai, Germany, Ghana, Honduras, India, Kenya, Madagascar, New Zealand, Romania, Serbia, South Africa, Thailand and Uganda.

Costs: Prices for three- to six-month placements start at £1595, including flights, accommodation, food and in-country support. A full pre-departure course covering, among other things, safety, health and cultural

awareness, is also included in the price. Some placements are paid.

Eligibility: The minimum age is 17; most volunteers are school and university leavers but some are on a break from careers.

Groups or Individuals: Individuals, but you can go out as part of a group in September January or April.

Annual no. of Volunteers: 100

Annual Projects: 40

Partner Programmes: 2

Selection & Interview Process: Participants complete an online application before being invited to one of the company's regular interview days. There they undergo a formal interview and perform some practical activities. Selectors are looking for initiative, adaptability, determination and good social skills.

In-country Support: All participants have a short orientation before being transported to their placement, where support is provided by destination managers who live and work in the country.

International Citizen Service

Carlton House, 27A Carlton Drive, Putney, London, SW15 2BS, UK
☎ +44 (0)20 8780 7500
fax +44 (0)20 8780 7577
enquiry@ics-uk.org.uk
www.vso-ics.org.uk

Photo: Azdady

Madagascan children peer through the window of a volunteer-built pharmacy

One of the youth programmes of VSO, the International Citizen Service gives 18- to 25-year-olds the chance to live and work in partnership with another young person from a developing country for six months, spending three months in the UK and three months in their partner's country. As well as doing work of practical benefit to local communities, the programme aims to build solidarity between youth in the UK and developing countries and promote strong and active participation in civil society in each of the countries involved. For more information on the International Citizen Service, see p95.

Inter-Cultural Youth Exchange UK

Latin America House, Kingsgate Pl, London NW6 4TA, UK
☎ +44 (0)20 7681 0983
fax : +44 (0)20 7916 1246
info@icye.co.uk
www.icye.co.uk
ICYE-UK is a user-led charity working in the field of personal, social and community development. ICYE is part of the ICYE International Federation, which has been recognised as an 'International Peace Messenger' by the UN General Assembly and has earned consultative status with Unesco. Volunteer placements include working in HIV clinics and orphanages, with disabled people and in primary schools. If you're interested in volunteering in Europe, ICYE-UK is an EVS-affiliated sending organisation (see p97).
Status: Charity.
Timing & Length of Placements: Placements last from three weeks to 12 months. The shorter placements run year-round but the longer ones (six or 12 months) depart in January and August. Apply with three months' notice.
Destinations: Many around the world, including Bolivia, Brazil, Colombia, Costa Rica, Europe, Ghana, Kenya, Mozambique, Nepal and New Zealand. Also Mexico, Honduras, Uganda, Morocco, Nigeria, India, Taiwan, Japan, Indonesia, Vietnam and South Korea.
Costs: A six-month placement costs from £3795 and a 12-month one from £4495, including international flights, living costs, health insurance, pocket money, a language course and pre-departure, on-arrival and evaluation training seminars. If you're 18 to 30 and going to Europe then your trip could be funded through the EVS.

Eligibility: Long-term international placements are open to those aged 18 to 30; EVS is open to 18- to 25-year-olds; and shorter term placements to those 18 and above.
Groups or Individuals: Individuals.
Partner Programmes: Unesco, European Commission's 'Youth In Action' Programme, the Council of Europe (European Youth Directive) and Mobility International.
Selection & Interview Process: Many applicants start with informational recruitment days. Contact the organisation for details.
In-country Support: After an orientation with in-country staff, volunteers have the full support of paid local staff.

Lattitude Global Volunteering

42 Queens Road, Reading, RG1 4BB, UK
☎ +44 (0)118 959 4914
fax +44 (0)118 957 6634
www.lattitude.org.uk
Established in 1972, Lattitude offers experiences teaching English, caring for the disadvantaged and working in medical clinics. Lattitude also runs a bursary scheme for individuals needing help with the fees. Preparation courses on teaching skills and language skills are provided along with an orientation programme. There is also a business partnership scheme: a number of large UK businesses have access to the Lattitude volunteer database and target former volunteers with offers of summer jobs for university students and graduate employment opportunities.
Status: Registered charity.
Timing & Length of Placements: Placements can be year-round but most start in September, January and March. They last from between three and 12 months. Applications and interviews take place year-round, but you must apply two months in advance.
Destinations: In 17 different countries, including Argentina, Australia, Brazil, Canada, China, Ecuador, Fiji, Ghana, India, Japan, Malawi, Mexico, New Zealand, South Africa, Tanzania, Vietnam and Vanuatu. Applicants from abroad can also apply to volunteer in the UK and Poland.
Costs: Fees vary depending on project, but they range from £3160 to £4460 depending on length, location and type of placement.

Eligibility: Applicants from the UK must be aged at least 17 at the time of departure and hold a British or Irish passport. Citizens of other countries are also eligible to apply.

Groups or Individuals: Individuals, sometimes pairs.

Annual no. of Volunteers: On average Lattitude globally places 1500 volunteers from around the world in placements around the world.

Annual Projects: In excess of 800 placements globally each year.

Partner Programmes: Around 20 worldwide, providing both pre-departure training as well as volunteer placements.

Selection & Interview Process: Submit an application via online form or post and pay an application fee. Lattitude conducts interviews at its offices in Belfast, Dublin, Glasgow, Leeds or Reading. Depending on the time of year, you will receive an offer of a placement within two weeks and then be contacted by a project manager, who will discuss details of the placement with you.

In-country Support: The support network includes in-country representatives and an emergency 24-hour phone line. Lattitude is a member of the Foreign and Commonwealth Offices 'Know Before You Go' campaign, which helps prepare British travellers for their trips overseas.

The Leap

121 High St, Marlborough,
Wiltshire SN8 1LZ, UK
☎ +44 (0)1670 519922
fax +44 (0)1672 519944
info@theleap.co.uk
www.theleap.co.uk

The Leap specialises in team volunteer placements that combine conservation, community and ecotourism projects. Each placement offers a variety of environments (eg beach, rainforest, mountain) and volunteer work, including teaching English and sport, caring for orphans, building clinics and wells, assisting rangers on safari and taking part in reforestation projects. In addition some placements also include language lessons and an adventure expedition element.

Status: Limited Company.

Timing & Length of Placements: Placements are for six and 10 weeks. Some departures are flexible, while others take place in January, April, July and September. You need to apply at least a month before you leave.

Destinations: Kenya, Tanzania, South Africa, Borneo, Cambodia, Argentina, Costa Rica, Ecuador and Venezuela.

Costs: Starting from £1843 depending on whether you stay for six or 10 weeks. Everything except flights and insurance is included. Approximately 60% of this fee goes straight to the place where you are volunteering.

Eligibility: You must be at least 17 at the time of departure; solo volunteers are usually between 22 and 60 years old.

Groups or Individuals: Individuals and team placements are available.

Annual no. of Volunteers: 300

Annual Projects: 10

Partner Programmes: 10

Selection & Interview Process: Each Leaper is called on application and invited to attend a comprehensive training and selection course. The course has two main aims: the first is for you to meet The Leap and your teammates, and secondly it allows us to ensure you are joining the most suitable placement.

In-country Support: Each placement is co-ordinated by an in-country manager who will ensure that your projects are completed, your time is spent efficiently and, most importantly, that you keep safe.

Link Overseas Exchange

The Hayloft, Wards of Keithock, Nr Brechin, Angus DD9 7PZ, Scotland
☎ +44 (0)1356 629134
fax +44 (0)1382 226087
info@linkoverseas.org.uk
www.linkoverseas.org.uk

Link has an emphasis on informal teaching; volunteers work in pairs, mainly teaching conversational English to children in schools, girls' or boys' homes, and orphanages. An effort is made to place volunteers with skills in music, drama, arts or sports accordingly. Other options include teaching English in Tibetan monasteries or helping with community projects. Past community projects include the building of a women's development centre and an HIV/AIDS awareness programme.

Status: Registered charity.

Timing & Length of Placements: Placements are for six months (including up to six weeks of leave). Applications are taken year-round but departures are limited to February and August. Apply three months in advance of departure. Six-week medical electives are also available in India and Sri Lanka.

Destinations: Include China, India, Romania and Sri Lanka.

Costs: The six-month package costs £2750, which accounts for everything, including international flights. The medical elective cost is £2000, all-inclusive.

Eligibility: Applicants must be aged 17 to 25.

Groups or Individuals: Individuals.

Annual no. of Volunteers: Up to 60.

Annual Projects: 12 to 15 projects, twice a year.

Partner Programmes: 12

Selection & Interview Process: After applications are received, applicants are invited to attend an information day in Dundee, Scotland.

In-country Support: There are local English-speaking representatives in the cities nearest to volunteer locations.

Madventurer

Newcastle University Students' Union, King's Walk, Newcastle upon Tyne, NE1 8QB, UK
☎ +44 191 232 0625
team@madventuer.com
www.madventurer.com

Madventurer combines volunteering activities in urban and rural areas of the developing world with a travel adventure. You choose how long you want to volunteer and how long you want to travel to create a customised experience. Projects range from building schools and teaching in rural communities to coaching sports and working on conservation initiatives. There are also opportunities for individuals to work in specialist fields, including medicine, journalism and in orphanages. Some adventure travel opportunities include travelling the entire length of Africa or visiting the mountain gorillas of Central Africa.

Status: Private limited company.

Timing & Length of Placements: You need to apply between three and nine months in advance of travel but late applications can sometimes be accommodated. Projects last anything from two weeks to 12 months and run year-round. Adventure travel components last from 15 to 77 days.

Destinations: Australia, Brazil, Costa Rica, Ghana, Guatemala, India, Kenya, Peru, Tanzania, Thailand, Togo, Trinidad & Tobago and Uganda.

Costs: A two-week volunteering project costs from £500, four weeks cost from £750 and 8 weeks from £1250, including all food and accommodation overseas, a donation to the communities that you'll be supporting, full-time overseas project support crew and in-country travel (international flights, visas, insurance and personal kit are not included).

Eligibility: Open to those aged 17 and over.

Groups or Individuals: Individuals and groups may apply; project work takes place in groups of five to 12 people.

Annual no. of Volunteers: 1000

Annual Projects: 100

Partner Programmes: 'Sportventurer' coaching projects, 'Gap Jobs' work experience placements and 'CareerBreaker' projects.

Selection & Interview Process: You can book over the phone or online through the Madventurer website.

In-country Support: Volunteers on rural projects will have full-time crew members looking after their needs 24 hours a day. Those on urban placements receive support from a full-time crew member at a regional HQ.

Outreach International

Bartlett's Farm, Hayes Rd, Compton Dundon, Somerset TA11 6PF, UK
☎ /fax +44 (0)1458 274957
info@outreachinternational.co.uk
www.outreachinternational.co.uk

Outreach International specialises in sending committed volunteers to a wide variety of small grassroots projects overseas. Most of the programmes involve conservation, education and social issues. Dale Hurd, who went to Cambodia, says 'Sitting here, back in the freezing English spring, I look at my hundreds of photographs and dream I'm back in Cambodia in Phnom Penh, dripping in sweat, dodging motodops, blinded by the radiant smiles of the enchanting Khmer people. Living in Phnom Penh was vibrant, at times frightening, sometimes depressing, but always fascinating. The drive to school, perched on the back of a motodop, at first cowering as we weaved – apparently at whim – across the traffic lanes, but later relaxed and chatty, was a revelation of street life: banana sellers with frames of green bananas; families eating breakfast on low plastic tables on the pavement; small pink-and-black pigs trembling in bamboo cages on the back of motor bikes.'

Status: Not-for-profit limited company.

Timing & Length of Placements: Projects are one to six months long, with departures in January, April, June and September. You should apply at least three months before, although last-minute applications may receive any empty places.

Destinations: Pacific coast of Mexico, Ecuador, the Galápagos Islands, Sri Lanka, Costa Rica Nepal, Kenya and Cambodia.

Costs: Refer to the costs page on the Outreach International website.

Eligibility: The minimum age is 18 and many volunteers are on their gap year, however, we also have many older career break volunteers. Volunteers must be fit, healthy and pass a criminal records check.

Groups or Individuals: Volunteers always work in pairs to maximise cultural integration and minimise cultural impact on the host community. However, approximately 15 volunteers are in the country at any one time. Outreach International projects are all located in the same geographical area, so meeting up with other volunteers is easy. You're also welcome to apply with a friend or partner.

Annual no. of Volunteers: 100

Annual Projects: 50

Selection & Interview Process: An effort is made to meet all potential volunteers in Bristol, London or Derby.

In-country Support: There is a full-time coordinator in every country, providing comprehensive support. All volunteers have unlimited health insurance, a 24-hour emergency line and full air evacuation in emergencies.

Project Trust

The Hebridean Centre, Isle of Coll, Argyll, PA78 6TE, UK
☎ +44 (0)1879 230444
fax +44 (0)1879 230357
info@projecttrust.org.uk
www.projecttrust.org.uk

Project Trust aims to provide young people with an opportunity to understand an overseas community through a full year of immersion and project work. Opportunities exist in teaching, journalism, social care, outdoor education and development.

Status: Educational charity.

Timing & Length of Placements: Project Trust currently runs a 12-month programme that departs during August and an eight-month programme that departs in either December or January.

Destinations: Twenty destinations, including Honduras, Dominican Republic, Jamaica, Guyana, Chile, Peru, Bolivia, Senegal, Namibia, South Africa, Swaziland, Rwanda, Lesotho, Uganda, India, Sri Lanka, China, Cambodia, Malaysia, Thailand, Hong Kong, Japan, Mauritius and Rodrigues Island.

Costs/Pay: The fee of £4950 for the 12-month programme and £4350 for the eight-month programme covers flights, insurance, training, accomodation and food.

Eligibility: Project Trust works with young people who are between the ages of 17 and 19 during their placement overseas.

Groups or Individuals: Individuals.

Annual no. of Volunteers: 260

Annual Projects: 120

Selection & Interview Process: After submitting an application volunteers attend a five-day selection course on the Hebridean Island of Coll. Those who are successful attend a five-day briefing and training course specifically for their country group.

In-country Support: There are in-country representatives on hand for emergencies.

Quest Overseas

15A Cambridge Grove, Hove, East Sussex BN3 3EDUK
☎ +44 (0)1273 777206
fax +44 (0)1273 204928
info@questoverseas.com
www.questoverseas.com

Specialising in gap-year projects and expeditions, Quest Overseas has been sending teams to South America and Africa since 1996. Three-month combined expeditions depart between January and April, and include time spent working on one of its long-term project partnerships, followed by an expedition such as trekking, scuba diving, jungle exploration or ice climbing. In South America, it also includes a language-training phase. Its shorter trips in July and August (four to six weeks) are either just a project or an expedition. Projects include working with children in a shanty town in Lima, Peru; caring for wild animals in the Bolivian Amazon; building sand dams in Kenya; working with orphans in Malawi, among others. Each project partnership has been established to ensure the work teams do is genuinely beneficial, and funds are provided to make sure they are sustained. **Status:** Limited company

Timing & Length of Placements: Three-month combined expeditions depart from January to April every year. Four- to eight-week projects or expeditions run in July and August.

Destinations: South America (Peru, Bolivia, Ecuador, Chile and Brazil) and Africa (Swaziland, Mozambique, South Africa, Botswana, Zambia, Kenya and Tanzania).

Costs: From £1700 for a four-week project, to £5150 for a three-week combined project and expedition. All expenses are included on the ground. Flights and insurance are not included.

Eligibility: No restrictions, however, typical age is between 18 and 24.

Groups or Individuals: Led group expeditions.

Annual no. of Volunteers: 180-200

Partner Programmes: Eight projects, all long-term partnerships.

Selection & Interview Process: After you decide on an expedition programme, apply via online applications to start the booking process.

In-country Support: Teams have project and expedition leaders with them, as well as an extensive local project and expedition support network.

Raleigh International

3rd flr, Prince Consort House, 27-29 Albert Embankment, London SE1 7TJ, UK
☎ +44 (0)20 7183 1270
fax +44 (0)20 7504 8094
info@raleighinternational.org
www.raleighinternational.org

Raleigh International is an international charity committed to the personal development of young people. Through its programmes in the UK and overseas, it works with young people from all backgrounds and nationalities to enable them to make a positive contribution and achieve personal and social development. Volunteers work in small groups alongside local communities to deliver three types of project: community, environmental and adventure projects. The five-week programme offers a choice of either a community or environmental project and a team-based adventure challenge.

Status: Registered charity.

Timing & Length of Placements: There are usually nine to 10 programmes throughout the year, including summer. Participants and volunteer staff choose from five-week or 10-week programmes. It's recommend you apply six to 12 months in advance to allow time for fundraising and a placement on your chosen programme. However, if you wish to join a programme that leaves in less than six months, the organisation will try to accommodate you.

Destinations: Borneo, Costa Rica, Nicaragua, India and Tanzania.

Costs: As a registered charity, the programme is completely dependent on fundraising activities to cover costs. The fundraising target for 10-week participants is £3150 and for five-week participants it's £1850. The fundraising targets for volunteer managers are the same. This includes all training, food, accommodation and in-country support.

Eligibility: Open to those aged 17 to 24.

Groups or Individuals: Individuals.

Annual no. of Volunteers: 700

Annual Projects: 45

Partner Programmes: 15

Selection & Interview Process: After completing an application and being selected, participants reserve their place with a £200 deposit that goes toward the fundraising target.

In-country Support: Raleigh has an extensive in-country support system, including medical professionals, 24-hour radio communications, in-country volunteer staff and a comprehensive emergency and evacuation plan.

Sporting Opportunities

The Clock House, Station Approach, Marlow, Buckinghamshire, SL7 1NT, UK
☎ +44 (0)20 8123 8702
fax +44 (0)16 2848 1065
info@sportingopportunities.com
www.sportingopportunities.com

Sporting Opportunities offers sporty people the chance to join sports coaching volunteer projects in Africa, Asia and South America, coaching disadvantaged children. Perfect for gap years, career breaks or volunteer holidays. Projects available in football, soccer, rugby, cricket, hockey, netball, swimming, athletics, basketball, tennis, baseball, ultimate frisbee, volleyball and more.

Status: Limited company.

Timing & Length of Placements: Departures take place every month of the year. Most volunteers join projects lasting from four to 12 weeks, although other durations are possible.

Destinations: South Africa, Ghana, India, Ecuador and Argentina.

Costs: Costs start from £620 for two weeks, with each additional week costing £130. This includes all accommodation, food, airport pick-up, training and induction, support and a donation to the project you work on. Fees do not include flights, travel insurance, vaccinations, visas and personal spending money

Eligibility: Applicants should be between 18 and 35.

Groups or Individuals: Groups and individuals are accepted on projects. There are also two-week sports and cultural tours for schools, colleges and university teams.

Annual no. of Volunteers: 500

Annual Projects: 50

Selection & Interview Process: Applications can be made online or over the phone. Criminal Records Bureau checks are made for some applicants who will be working with children. References are also required.

In-country Support: 24-hour UK and in-country support is available through project managers and in-country coordinators. Our resident in-country staff live nearby and are on call to make sure you are safe, secure and really enjoying your experience abroad. Full travel advice and inductions are provided pre-departure and during the project.

Youth for Development

Carlton House, 27A Carlton Drive, Putney, London, SW15 2BS, UK
☎ +44 (0)20 8780 7500
fax +44 (0)20 8780 7207
enquiry@vso.org.uk
www.vso.org.uk

As the other youth-oriented programme of the Voluntary Service Overseas (VSO), Youth for Development (YfD) provides an opportunity for young people to work with VSO partners and contribute towards the achievement of VSO's development goals. See p95 for more information on YfD.

North American Organisations

Amigos de las Américas

5618 Star Ln, Houston, Texas 77057, USA
☎ +1 800 231 7796, +1 713 782 5290
fax +1 713 782 9267
info@amigoslink.org
www.amigoslink.org

For over 40 years, Amigos de las Américas has run community service projects involving more than 20,000 youth volunteers and thousands of communities in Latin America. Through its programmes, high-school and college-aged volunteers jump in to lend a hand on collaborative projects working with a vigorous network of Pan-American partner agencies and local host communities. These same volunteers often return to lead programmes in Latin America as project staff. Amigos aims to be a youth-led organisation in which creativity, initiative and multicultural understanding are highly valued.

Status: Non-Governmental Organisation.

Timing & Length of Placements: Volunteers spend five to eight weeks living and working in one of nine Latin American countries. Project dates vary from year to year between the months of June and August (five-, six- and eight-week projects all have set dates, although these vary from summer to summer).

Destinations: Nine different countries in Latin America: Brazil; Costa Rica; Dominican Republic; Honduras; Mexico; Nicaragua; Panama; Paraguay and Uruguay.

Costs: Volunteers pay US$5150 as a participation fee, which goes directly towards training, equipment, transportation and support costs. The fee includes international airfares from Miami or Houston, all project-related expenses, materials, in-country lodging, transportation and meals. It also includes international medical insurance, staff training and a 24-hour on-call emergency system.

Eligibility: Participants must be 16 or older by 1 September of the year of service, and at least a sophomore in high school. They must also have at least two years of Spanish or Portuguese or an equivalent fluency level.

Groups or Individuals: Volunteers travel to and from their countries as a group.

Annual no. of Volunteers: About 750.

Raleigh International volunteers helping African communities

Photo: Samantha Cook/Raleigh International

Annual Projects: 14
Partner Programmes: Amigos partners with 21 other agencies.
Selection & Interview Process: Depending on whether the volunteer works with a local chapter, they will either have phone interviews or interviews in person.
In-country Support: Each project is equipped with a project staff member on call 24 hours a day. In many countries there are partnerships in place with the Ministry of Health, which assists volunteers when they are sick or in case of emergencies.

Amizade

4 Smithfield St, Floor 7, Pittsburgh,
PA 15222, USA
☎ +1 412 586 4986
fax +1 757 257 8358
volunteer@amizade.org
www.amizade.org

Amizade is a non-profit organisation dedicated to promoting volunteering, community service, collaboration and cultural awareness throughout the world. Amizade offers a broad range of international volunteer opportunities for individuals and families, and regularly customises programmes for groups.
Status: Non-profit organisation.
Timing & Length of Placements: Two or more weeks with regular departures throughout the year. Some placements can be extended for up to six months.
Destinations: Bolivia, Brazil, Mexico, Jamaica, Germany, Poland, Northern Ireland, Tanzania, Ghana and the United States.
Costs: Costs vary based on location, length and type of program.
Eligibility: The minimum age is 18, or 12 if you are accompanied by a parent or guardian; there is no nationality requirement. Some sites are more suitable than others for disabled volunteers; contact Amizade for details.
Groups or Individuals: Groups of six to 30 volunteers work alongside host-community members. Participants in customised group programmes serve with their group.
Annual no. of Volunteers: 350
Annual Projects: 50
Partner Programmes: 14 community partnerships in 14 different sites.
Selection & Interview Process: Volunteers are assigned to projects and communities that best match both their interests and skills and local needs.
In-country Support: Upon arrival in the country, on-site personnel provide a formal orientation to familiarise volunteers with the programme, location and logistics. A staff member remains with the group for the duration of the project to coordinate and provide assistance as needed.

Global Volunteers

375 E Little Canada Rd, St Paul,
MN 55117-1628, USA
☎ +1 800 487 1074
fax +1 651 482 0915
email@globalvolunteers.org
www.globalvolunteers.org

Global Volunteers is a large organisation that has placed more than 20,000 volunteers since it was founded in 1984. It offers short-term service programmes in 20 countries on six continents – at the invitation of local host organisations, under the direction of local leaders and hand-in-hand with local people. Volunteers teach conversational English; care for vulnerable and at-risk children; construct, repair, and paint community buildings; deliver healthcare and provide any other service requested by communities.

Status: Global Volunteers is a private, non-profit, non-sectarian international organisation.

Timing & Length of Placements: Programmes are one to three weeks long and are offered year-round. At present, extended stay options are offered in China, Ecuador, India, Ireland, Poland, Romania and Tanzania – for an additional per-week fee of between US$150 and US$300. There are specific departure dates throughout the year.

Destinations: Australia, China, India, Sri Lanka, Cook Islands, Brazil, Peru, Ecuador, Costa Rica, Mexico, Jamaica, United States, Ghana, Tanzania, Ireland, Poland, Hungary, Italy, Greece and Romania.

Costs: Fees are tax-deductible and cover all meals, lodging, ground transportation in the community, project expenses, an emergency medical evacuation service and the services of a trained team leader. Airfares are extra, however, all project-related costs, including airfares, are tax-deductible for US taxpayers. There are discounts for those who book online, students, returning volunteers and families and groups.

Eligibility: Children as young as five can serve and there are no upper age limits. You can serve as long as you are in good health, sufficiently mobile and have a curiosity about other cultures, a flexible attitude and a willingness to serve.

Groups or Individuals: Volunteers can work in teams of up to 20 or one-on-one with local people in the host country. Family and group applications are accepted.

Annual no. of Volunteers: Around 2000.

Annual Projects: Each year nearly 200 teams of short-term volunteers are sent to work on long-term development projects in over 100 communities in 20 countries on six continents.

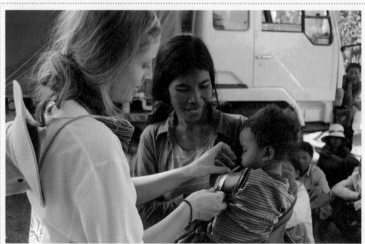

Photo: Briony Stevens

Australian Volunteers International set up a World Food Programme malnutrition workshop in Cambodia

Partner Programmes: Global Volunteers works with 30 community organisations in the United States and overseas.

Selection & Interview Process: Volunteers must fill out an application, attest that they are in good health and sufficiently mobile and provide three character references. They are then interviewed over the phone or via email.

In-country Support: The international staff is made up of indigenous, in-country team leaders and consultants. All team leaders and country managers are available 24 hours a day for medical emergencies and are acquainted with medical facilities in their communities.

Australasian Organisations

Australian Youth Ambassadors for Development

Lvl 1/41 Dequetteville Tce, Kent Town, SA 5067, Australia
☎ +61 (0)8 8364 8500, 1800 225 592
fax +61 (0)8 8364 858
info.ayad@austraining.com.au
www.ayad.com.au
www.ausaid.gov.au/youtham

The AYAD programme places young Australians aged 18 to 30 on medium-term assignments (of between three to 12 months) in developing countries throughout Asia, the Pacific and Africa. AYAD volunteers work with local counterparts in host organisations to achieve sustainable development outcomes through capacity building, skills transfer and institutional strengthening. AYAD assignments cover a diverse range of sectors including education, environment, gender, governance, health, infrastructure, rural development and trades.

Status: AYAD is an AusAID project managed by Austraining International Pty Ltd.

Timing & Length of Assignments: AYAD assignments are advertised three times per year across three intakes which are mobilised in March, July and October. Assignments are three to 12 months in duration.

Destinations: Bangladesh, Cambodia, China, East Timor, Fiji, Ghana, Indonesia, Thailand, Laos, the Maldives, Mongolia, Myanmar (Burma), Nepal, Papua New Guinea, the Philippines, Samoa, the Solomon Islands, Sri Lanka, Tonga, Vanuatu and Vietnam.

Costs/Pay: The AYAD programme covers the cost of airfares, medical expenses, visas and insurance. When in-country, volunteers receive a locally applicable living allowance to cover accommodation and other costs (from A$1000 a month). Upon return a resettlement allowance is paid. Special grants for suitable clothing are given to those going to extremely cold places in winter.

Eligibility: AYADs must be between the ages of 18 and 30 at the time of applying and must be Australian citizens.

Groups or Individuals: Mainly individuals, with some couples applying for separate assignments. AYADs work alone but are briefed and mobilised in groups, and there is generally a number of them in an area at any one time.

Annual no. of Volunteers: 400

Annual Projects: 400

Partner Programmes: AYAD partners with organisations in country and in Australia to support volunteers and develop assignments across a broad range of sectors.

Selection & Interview Process: AYAD assignments are listed three times per year online at www.ayad.com.au. Applicants must apply for a specific position related to their skills and experience. The AYAD program has a staged selection process. The selection process is based on merit and AYAD works within the parameters of the Australian Equal Opportunities Act. For further information about the stages of selection, please see the AYAD website. All shortlisted candidates will be interviewed.

In-country Support: AYADs and host organisations are supported in country by an In Country Manager (ICM). The ICM is an AYAD programme staff member who lives in that country, often in the capital city. Each country has its own ICM. When AYADs arrive in country the ICM will run an In-country Orientation Program. The In-country Orientation Program includes information about the culture and history of the host country, banking, shopping, taking public transport, health and security issues. The ICM also helps volunteers find safe, affordable and appropriate accommodation, source appropriate language training and secure appropriate visas. If any issues arise while an AYAD is on assignment (both personal and professional), the ICM is the first point of contact.

Overseas Organisations

Kwa Madwala

PO Box 192, Hectorspruit, 1330,
Mpumalang Province, South Africa
☎ +27 (0) 82 779 2153 , +27 (0) 79 553 3420
fax +27 13 792 6735
gapyear@kwamadwala.co.za

Though tracking lions, identifying snakes and learning how to survive in the bush might not be everyone's ideal assignment, this organisation (based on a 'big four' private game reserve in South Africa) gives students personal development opportunities and a broader outlook on the world of wildlife conservation. Choose from a variety of placement durations (four, six, eight or 10 weeks). At the end of the experience participants receive a certificate in conservation competency.

Status: Limited company.

Timing & Length of Placements: The 10-week placements start at the begining of January, April, July and September. It also offers four-, six- and eight-week options that are more programme specific.

Destinations: Kwa Madwala Private Game Reserve in South Africa, located south of Kruger National Park close to the Mozambique and Swaziland borders.

Costs: A four-week placement with Kwa Madwala costs £1699; a six-week placement costs £2299; an eight-week placement costs £2699; and a 10-week placement costs £3499. This includes accommodation, meals, activities, entry fees, specialised courses and transfers from KMIA International Airport. It does not include international flights, insurance or airport transfers from Johannesburg.

Eligibility: Open to anyone aged over 17. You need to be fit, healthy and able to work in a team; placements are 'not for the faint-hearted'.

Groups or Individuals: Both.

Annual no. of Volunteers: 75

Selection & Interview Process: Applications are submitted online.

In-country Support: A field guide and an assistant work with the teams at all times. These are called Bush Buddies. Other professionals, including vets, lecturers, pilots etc also join the expeditions.

Volunteer in Africa

PO Box 602, Osu Accra, Ghana, West Africa
☎ +233 20 8731745
voluinafrica@yahoo.com
www.volunteeringinafrica.org

Formerly known as the Save The Earth Network, this organisation renamed itself in the hope of bringing more internet keyword exposure to its programmes promoting environmental preservation, sustainable development, international cultural exchange, solidarity and friendship through voluntary work placements and host family homestays in Ghana. Working four days a week, volunteers help teach children English or maths, care for orphans or abandoned children, educate people about AIDS, help with reforestation or work in healthcare clinics and hospitals.

Status: Not-for-profit organisation.

Timing & Length of Placements: Placements are from two to 12 weeks and you can join year-round.

Destination: Ghana.

Costs: A one-week stay costs US$377 and a four-week stay costs US$677, with the cost rising by US$77 for every week after the first four.

Eligibility: People from 16 to 60 without special skills, qualifications or experience may volunteer with all except the healthcare programmes (and a few other programmes). People with disabilities cannot apply.

Groups or Individuals: Applicants may apply in pairs, and will usually work in a group of between four and 30 people.

Annual no. of Volunteers: 250

Annual Projects: 24

Partner Programmes: 14

Selection & Interview Process: Applications and interviews are handled via phone and email.

In-country Support: Volunteers have 24-hour in-country support.

Volunteering Plus

'Volunteering Plus' listings are mostly aimed at people under 30. They combine service opportunities with structured classes in a wide variety of subject areas, including language and culture. For instance, Travellers Worldwide (see p114) may teach you to tango while at the same time allowing you to work on a conservation project. Asociación Pop Wuj (p119) will help you hone your Spanish skills while giving you the opportunity to do something for the common good, working on a community-development project.

UK Organisations

Outlook Expeditions

8-9 Chestnut Court, Ffordd y Parc, Parc Menai, Bangor, Gwynedd LL57 4FH, UK
☎ +44 (0)845 900 2989/+44 1248 672 760
fax +44 (0)114 275 5740a
info@outlookexpeditions.com
www.outlookexpeditions.com

Outlook Expeditions is the youth arm of Jagged Globe Ltd, the first British company to run guided expeditions to climb Mt Everest. It offers a wide programme of overseas educational expeditions; a typical itinerary includes a trek or mountain summit, a project with local school children, cultural visits and other challenging activities, such as river rafting and mountain biking. Expeditioners have the opportunity to develop new skills as they work in a team towards identifiable goals. The programme fulfils the expedition requirements of the Duke of Edinburgh's Gold Award and the Queen's Scout and Guide Awards.

Status: Limited company.

Timing & Length of Projects: 10- to 30-day adventures offer the option of joining a community project. Applications should be sent six to 12 months in advance of departure, though destination options are available year-round.

Destinations: Morocco, Tanzania, Kenya, Nepal, India, Kyrgyzstan, Borneo, Ecuador, Argentina, Peru, Bolivia, Canada, Corsica, Spain, Greenland, Slovakia and the Alps.

Costs: The adventure phase costs between £1500 and £2000, flights and in-country costs included. The volunteering phase costs roughly an additional £200 per month.

Eligibility: Applicants must be 16 or older; but most are school leavers.

Groups or Individuals: Groups of between 12 and 15 are most common. Larger groups can be accommodated, but may be split.

Annual no. of Volunteers: Varies.

Annual Projects: 18 expeditions throughout the year.

Partner Programmes: Thornbridge Outdoors, Undercover Rock, Young Explorers Trust.

Selection & Interview Process: Individual or group applications, beginning with an online query.

In-country Support: Groups are led by a team leader and an in-country English-speaking guide.

Travellers Worldwide

Suite 2A, Caravelle House, 17/19 Goring Rd, Worthing, West Sussex BN12 4AP, UK
☎ +44 (0)1903-502595
fax +44 (0)1903-708179
info@travellersworldwide.com
www.travellersworldwide.com

Although Travellers Worldwide offers the standard fare – teaching English or sports, working in conservation, medicine, veterinary medicine, journalism or law in the developing world – it also has a range of 'off-the-wall' projects like learning to tango, or doing photography, meditation or music courses abroad. You can even get a pilot's licence. People with two left feet or a fear of heights should check out Travellers Worldwide's conservation programmes, which are geared towards working with wildlife.

Status: Limited company.

Timing & Length of Placements: Placements can be as short as two weeks or as long as a year. Some can be arranged with only four weeks' notice but the most popular need to be booked between six and 12 months in advance. Programmes run throughout the year with flexible start dates.

Destinations: Argentina, Australia, Brazil, Brunei, China, Cuba, Ghana, Guatemala, India, Kenya, Malaysia, New Zealand, Peru, South Africa, Sri Lanka, Thailand, Zambia and Zimbabwe.

Costs: Projects start from £595 for two weeks. Costs vary depending on length and include accommodation, food, transport, airport pick up, induction and 24/7 support in destination and at home. International flights and travel insurance are not included.

Eligibility: Open to anyone over 17.

Groups or Individuals: Both.

Annual no. of volunteers: 1000

Annual Projects: 200

Selection & Interview Process: Online application, CV and motivational letter required.

In-country Support: There are support staff 24/7 in all destinations worldwide and a 24-hour emergency international telephone line direct to the head office.

Trekforce

☎ +44 (0)207 384 3028
info@trekforce.org.uk
www.trekforce.org.uk

Trekforce is a for-profit expedition company that evolved out of the UK-based charity Trekforce Expeditions. Keen to continue the charity's legacy of running conservation expeditions to remote and challenging destinations, the new company puts 20 years' worth of experience towards their expedition consultancy service, combining the challenge of expedition life with sustainable conservation projects in the most remote corners of the globe. In addition, participants can enhance their overseas experience by developing skills in languages, remote trekking, teaching and diving. You can find out more by attending one of their informal 'open days' or visiting their website.

Status: UK-based company.

Timing & Length of Placements: Each expedition lasts two months, with an option to extend to five months. Expeditions depart all year. There's no official deadline for applications but apply at least three months before you want to travel.

Destinations: Belize, East Malaysia, Guatemala, Guyana and Peru.

Costs: Volunteers are required to fundraise £2800 for the basic two-month expedition. This includes all costs except your international flights and insurance. The five-month combination placement (a two-month expedition plus intensive language course and teaching) costs from £4050 for all elements, bar international flights and insurance.

Eligibility: There is no upper age limit, but most volunteers are between 18 and 25.

Groups or Individuals: Individuals.

Annual no. of Volunteers: 60

Partner Programmes: In every country Trekforce partners with myriad scientific research and conservation agencies.

Selection & Interview Process: As long as you are medically fit, joining an expedition is by self-selection. You pay to play: in the eyes of the organisation, anybody who can fundraise the amount needed has shown the determination, motivation and discipline required to participate.

In-country Support: Each expedition team is accompanied by an experienced expedition leader, assistant leader, two medics, satellite phone and emergency position indicating radio beacon (EPIRB), as well as an in-country base.

VentureCo Worldwide

Lockyer House, Paddon's Row,
Tavistock, PL19 0HF, UK
☎ +44 (0)182 261 6191
www.ventureco-worldwide.com

VentureCo's multi-phase travel programmes incorporate development projects, expeditions, language classes and adventure travel. For example, a South America project may combine a Spanish-language phase with a volunteer project phase and an expedition phase. Volunteering projects are all community based, with each project having specific aims – from rehabilitating manatees in Central America to working on housing and orphan projects with the monks of the Life and Hope Association in Cambodia.

Status: Limited company and registered charity.

Timing & Length of Placements: Departures are year-round, with ventures lasting between four and 15 weeks. The trips include two to four weeks of volunteering work.

Destinations: South America, Central America, Asia and Africa.

Costs: Costs vary greatly – from £500 to £5000 – depending on length of trip and whether the airfare is included.

Eligibility: No experience is required and people with disabilities can apply. School projects run for people aged 17 to 18, and there are 'gap-year' programmes for people aged 18 to 21 and career-break programmes for those aged 21 and over.

Groups or Individuals: You are welcome to volunteer with friends or partners and work within the groups, which usually comprise 10 to 16 people. Volunteers work with a group and the local community.

Annual no. of Volunteers: 200-300

Annual Projects: 12

Selection & Interview Process: There is an application form online.

In-country Support: Volunteers have two VentureCo guides with them at all times and project partners present during the

continued on p118

An AYAD Tells Her Story

I first looked into volunteering as a university graduate. At the group interview we gathered around a laminex table and talked about installing a water facility in a fictional African village. On the same day, I met someone working at Lonely Planet and I guess the urge to work there, and understand the world before trying to change it, won out. It wasn't until many years later that I found myself volunteering overseas.

Taking in Mekong sunsets, slurping up watermelon shakes and meandering through markets were some of the experiences I had become accustomed to while backpacking through Asia. But I also became increasingly aware of the environmental issues facing developing countries. Once while travelling through northern Laos in the back of a pick-up truck, I saw nonbiodegradable rubbish being tossed into the lush forest. Everywhere there was beauty, but I wondered how it could be preserved for the future. I wanted to be part of the solution.

Some seven years on, I found myself in Bangkok, Thailand, as an Australian Youth Ambassador for Development (AYAD) with the World Conservation Union (IUCN), the world's largest environmental knowledge network. It has helped over 75 countries prepare and implement national conservation and biodiversity strategies. My communications position was regional in scope, which suited me, because I would have struggled to choose one country over another.

Asia is one of the most ecologically and culturally diverse regions in the world. It is also one of the most fragile. With a population topping 3.4 billion, freshwater depletion and water pollution are rife. Native species continue to decline. Around 72 per cent of Asia's forests have been lost, and urbanisation is like an express train carving up the landscape. From Bangladesh to Cambodia, some of the poorest people are also the most dependent on the environment for their livelihoods. The modern age has left a massive environmental footprint. Hello 21st century!

Seated next to my Pakistani colleague who proudly showed me screensaver images of the Karakoram, I plunged myself into the world of 'environmental flows', sustainable livelihood approaches and more acronyms than my head

could hold. On the international organisation scene, one goes on 'missions'. My first was to Laos PDR (as it's known in development-speak). I edited my way through the wetlands of Cambodia and the health statistics of Mekong River dwellers.

I also worked on a six-country project concerning forest law enforcement and governance (FLEG), which took me to Vietnam and Sri Lanka. The affable Mr Pham Quang Hoa greeted me in Hanoi and we travelled to the imperial capital of Hue to visit the proposed project site. With a penchant for newspapers and sporting a wide-brimmed hat, Mr Hoa was the most delightful of travelling companions. By day we talked about tactics for involving local NGOs in the forestry project and by night Mr Hoa told me about his childhood during the 'American War'.

Professor Shantha Henayake is a breezy Sri Lankan with a love of discussion. I worked with him in Sri Lanka's Knuckles Ranges conservation zone, and later in Colombo. Again, working with a committed local was one of the highlights of my time volunteering. We did a series of rapid rural assessments which would become the building blocks of a communications strategy. We talked with farmers, shared biscuits with village women and bonded during a series of very long drives (getting anywhere in Sri Lanka takes time and it's only 435 kilometres long by 225 kilometres wide).

These experiences were my most memorable. I found linking people with action is what motivates me. The bureaucracy I encountered proved tedious, but between whizzing home on the back of a motorbike and lunching with Thais, my working days were never monotonous. My senses were on high alert for the sights, sounds and smells around every corner.

I had dabbled with the idea of volunteering in Mongolia only to discover Ulaanbaatar is the coldest city on the planet! East Timor was high on my list, but there were no suitable positions at the time. When I first visited Bangkok, I'll admit that I wanted to get out of there, yet slowly but surely, this mega melting pot of hedonism, humidity and humility crept its way into my heart.

It was a defining, exciting and stimulating

Sarah Wintle in the field in Sri Lanka

year, mostly because of the people I met. Going out with people from around the world was commonplace: across the dinner table I'd be chatting with an Indian, a Malaysian and a Swede. I discovered I could be myself anywhere. And I took more of an interest in Australian affairs, seeing my own country differently from afar. I was looking at the world up-close through a set of wide-angle binoculars.

Being conveniently situated in the travel bargain basement of Southeast Asia, I travelled from Myanmar to Malaysia. And each time I returned, Bangkok felt like a home away from home. I fell in love, saw more photogenic things than my camera could capture, and enjoyed Sunday walks at Bangkok's Lumpini Park amid chanting Hindus, sword-wielding exercisers and couples ballroom dancing. The year was like a jigsaw puzzle of experiences which came together in an unexpected and pleasing way.

The 'think global, act local' mantra rings true but for the past decade the world has been my backyard. Someday I would like to work with indigenous communities in Australia, and I plan to check out Indigenous Community Volunteers (www.icv.com.au).

I learnt a lot about people and power as a volunteer. My job description was tossed aside, there were occasional tears and, at times, I wondered if it was all worth it. But eventually I came to the realisation that people are the same the world over – they strive for peace, happiness, wellbeing and a place to call home. I also came to understand good fortune and how it can be used for the common good. My volunteering stint enabled me to work in Asia and internationalised my CV. But the greatest legacy of volunteering is the friendships you make along the way. And I know a good green curry when I taste one.

Volunteering has its moments but it's those moments that make life worth living.

Sarah Wintle

Sarah Wintle, a co-author on this book, was an AYAD in Intake 14 and worked as a Communications Officer for the Ecosystems & Livelihoods Group at the World Conservation Union's (IUCN) Asian Regional Office in Bangkok, Thailand.

volunteering stages. All groups have an emergency satellite telephone and a major incident plan involving in-country staff and the offices in Warwick.

North American Organisations

PEPY

105 Schrade Rd, Briarcliff Manor NY 10510, USA
☎ +1 914 762 2705
fax +1 646 514 0853
contact@pepycambodia.org
http://pepycambodia.org

PEPY (Protect the Earth, Protect Yourself) offers fundraising cycling and volunteer tours in Cambodia that combine teaching opportunities and building projects with visits to local organisations and sites of interest. Travellers interact directly with the areas and people who benefit from their financial support.

Status: Non-profit organisation.
Timing & Length of Projects: Volunteer and cycling trips last one to three weeks; projects are conducted year-round. Custom group tours and internships are also available.
Destinations: Cambodia.
Costs: Varying trip fees cover housing, meals, local transportation, administrative costs, and entry charges; volunteers must also make a minimum donation to their project organisation. Participants cover their own airfares and insurance.
Eligibility: Minimum age is 17, or seven if accompanied by a parent or guardian; no nationality restrictions apply. For cycling tours, riders must be in good physical shape and able to ride a bike for up to five hours per day in high temperatures. Most noncycling volunteer tours can be adapted to suit a wide range of travellers, including those with disabilities.
Groups or Individuals: Cycling trips accommodate six to 15 participants; volunteer tours are for six to 35 people. Volunteers work in pairs or groups on various projects at the volunteer site.
Annual no. of Volunteers: 150
Annual Projects: 11
Partner Programmes: PEPY partners with educational, environmental and health organisations in Cambodia, and works in rural Siem Reap Province supporting schools and child clubs through educational programs.
Selection & Interview Process: Interested parties can apply on the PEPY website. Interviews will be conducted for longer term internship placements.
In-country Support: All trips begin with an orientation meeting. Staff guides and local partners accompany volunteers during rides and tours.

Australasian Organisations

AFS Intercultural Programmes – Community Service Programme

PO Box 5, Strawberry Hills, NSW 2012, Australia
☎ +61 (0)2 9215 0077, 1300 131 736
fax +61 (0)2 9215 0088
ausafs@afs.org
www.afs.org.au

AFS offers international community service volunteering opportunities, with a focus on gaining work experience, learning another language and fostering intercultural understanding. There's a range of experiences on offer, from the challenging (eg working in a women's shelter in Honduras), to the purely cultural, such as assisting in a Danish folk high school. Volunteers are either housed with a local host family or with other international volunteers on a project site.

Status: Not-for-profit organisation.
Timing & Length of Assignments: Various departure dates, with assignments spanning four weeks to 12 months.
Destinations: Belgium, Bolivia, Brazil, China, Costa Rica, Denmark, Dominican Republic, Ecuador, Egypt, Ghana, Guatemala, Honduras, Hong Kong, Malaysia, Mexico, Panama, Paraguay, Peru, South Africa, Thailand and Venezuela.
Costs: Starting from A$7000, including all flights, visas, medical insurance, food and accommodation with a local family, orientation in Australia and overseas, and airport pick-up.
Eligibility: Applicants must be 18 years or over; some projects have specific age and language requirements.
Groups or Individuals: Volunteers travel individually and then join groups in-country. People with a disability can apply.
Annual no. of Volunteers: 23 in 2005.
Annual Projects: Over 30.
Partner Programmes: AFS has offices in 53 countries and each country runs various community-service programmes.

Selection & Interview Process: Applications close four months before departure dates and the selection process includes a face-to-face interview.

In-country Support: 24-hour emergency phone assistance and offices in 53 countries.

Overseas Organisations

Asociación Pop Wuj

Primera Calle, 17-72, Zona 1,
Quetzaltenango, Guatemala
☎ /fax +502 7761 8286
info@pop-wuj.org
www.pop-wuj.org

Owned and operated by a cooperative of teachers, the Pop Wuj school offers immersive Spanish classes with the option of volunteering on development or medical programmes in the city and surrounding countryside of Quetzaltenango, Guatemala. The classes last 4½ hours a day, five days a week. During the rest of the time, participants are encouraged to practice their Spanish while working alongside local people. The five programmes offered include a basic Spanish-language immersion course, a Spanish for Teachers programme, an excursion programme that includes language study and cultural field trips, and two specialised programmes geared towards students and professionals in the healthcare or community-development fields. All programmes feature volunteer work projects. Nick Van Buskirk spent a month in the programme and says, 'I was a complete beginner at the start of my travels, but the small class sizes and great instruction really helped me get a strong foundation. More useful even than the Spanish classes, though, were the field projects. I spent much of my time outside class working on a construction site building an agricultural storage structure outside the city limits.'

Status: Non-profit organisation.

Timing & Length of Placements: Participants are encouraged to stay for at least three weeks.

Destinations: Guatemala.

Costs: The tuition for the immersion programme is approximately US$185 per week (with a one-off US$65 registration fee), covering classes, room and board with a host family, and school activities. Students who elect to find accommodation themselves have a slightly reduced fee. The excursion programme is US$1000, which doesn't include food or hotel tariffs.

Eligibility: Minors need to be accompanied by a guardian. Most students are college age.

Groups or Individuals: Both individuals and groups are encouraged to apply.

Annual Projects: Approximately 50.

Selection & Interview Process: Applications begin online. The school only has space for 32 students at a time, so early applications are encouraged, especially for the popular summer months. Medical and social work programmes require extra supporting materials.

In-country Support: In-country support is provided by school staff and the host family.

Institute for Central American Development Studies

Apartado 300-2050, San Pedro de Montes de Oca, Costa Rica
☎ + 506 225 0508
info@icads.org
www.icads.org

ICADS is a Central American research and learning centre, dedicated to social and environmental issues. Its main areas of focus are women's issues, economic development, environmental studies, public health, education, human rights and wildlife conservation. With the four programme areas in ICADS you may study Costa Rica's rich flora and fauna, Spanish conversation with an ecological bent, or work to protect threatened rainforests, all while earning academic credit. Spanish classes have a four-person size limit; field courses have a 12-person limit. People enrolled in the Spanish immersion programme are only allowed to volunteer if they have sufficient language skills and spend a month or more with the programme.

Timing & Length of Placements: Placements start at two weeks, though most are a month long. There are programmes year-round. Apply at least two months in advance for the popular summer months.

Destinations: Costa Rica and Nicaragua.

Costs: Tuition for the four-week programme includes room and board and is approximately US$1850. There are additional fees for transferring college credits to your academic institution.

Eligibility: Minors need to be accompanied by a guardian. Most students are college age.

Groups or Individuals: Projects are typically group-oriented work.

Annual Projects: There are four ongoing projects.

Selection & Interview Process: There is no selection process; interested applicants can submit an enrolment form with a deposit to secure placement.

In-country Support: Teachers, staff and project leaders are on hand at all times.

Jubilee Ventures

Main Office: PO Box 10477-00100 GPO, Nairobi, Kenya

☎ +254 203 42929

www.jubileeventures.org

Jubilee Ventures offers volunteer opportunities in schools, orphanages, health clinics and relating to animal welfare, mostly to students on leave. Placements run the gamut of possibilities: from HIV education to helping local women weave baskets. It also offers medical and dental experts opportunities in Kenya, Zanzibar and Tanzania. There's an optional two-week language and culture programme and jungle adventure safari.

Timing & Length of Placements: Projects can run for anything between a week and a year. There are two start dates per month. Apply at least one month in advance.

Destinations: Kenya and Tanzania, but expanding to other African countries and Asia.

Costs: Placement costs begin at US$340 for one week, US$400 for two weeks and US$110 per week thereafter. This includes pick-up from the airport, accommodation, field visits, communication and food. A non-refundable registration fee of US$350 also applies.

Eligibility: Applicants must be aged over 16, but younger volunteers are accepted with a parent or guardian.

Groups or Individuals: Both.

Annual no. of Volunteers: 175

Annual Projects: Varies.

Selection & Interview Process: Enquiries and applications are conducted online.

In-country Support: There are weekly or bi-weekly field visits at the project or host home.

Volunteering Holidays

For people who prefer to tip the ratio of volunteering to touring in favour of the latter, the following organisations represent solid options in the burgeoning field of 'voluntourism'. These 'companies of conscience' have been spawned by travellers' demands and it's now easier than ever to book a trip doing something more rewarding than snoozing under a palm tree. The organisations in this section focus primarily on travelling rather than volunteering. As such, you'll find that most have less rigorous application procedures than traditional volunteering organisations, allowing anyone with the funds and the motivation to participate.

International Organisations

i-to-i

England: Woodside House, 261 Low Ln, Leeds LS18 5NY, UK

☎ +44 (0)871 781 1123

www.i-to-i.com

Ireland: Exploration House, 32 Grattan Square, Dungarvan, Co. Waterford

☎ +353 (0)58 40050

www.i-to-i.com

North America: 190 E 9th Ave, Ste 350, Denver, CO 80203, USA

☎ +1 800 985 486

info@i-to-i.com

www.i-to-i.com

Australia: Level 4, 380 Lonsdale St, Melbourne, VIC 3000, Australia

☎ +61 1300 884 270.

australia@i-to-i.com

www.i-to-i.com

As one of the largest volunteer-sending organisations in the world, i-to-i sends scads of international volunteers abroad, mostly on teaching placements. Really, they're huge: there are over 500 placements in 22 countries. Placements are available teaching English and on conservation, health and other development projects. An online TEFL (Teaching English as a Foreign Language) course is even included for those hoping to teach English but who don't wish to attend one of the TEFL weekend courses run in the US, UK, Australia, Ireland or New Zealand. It's also possible just to take their TEFL course alone and arrange travel independently.

Status: Limited company.

Timing & Length of Placements: Placements can be arranged in four weeks but it's recommended that you apply three months in advance. Placements last from one week to six months and begin year-round.

Destinations: A veritable geography test, including Argentina, Australia, Bolivia, Brazil, China, Costa Rica, the Dominican Republic, Ecuador, Ghana, Guatemala, Honduras, India, Kenya, Malaysia, Mexico, Nepal, Peru, South Africa, Sri Lanka, Thailand, the UK and Vietnam.

Costs: Costs vary greatly depending on placement, but travellers can expect to pay £1000 to £1200 for a four-week placement. In most cases this includes accommodation, meals, information packs, travel insurance, TEFL training for teaching placements, airport pick-up, orientation and fundraising advice. Fees do not include airfares to the country of your placement.

Eligibility: Open to anyone aged 18 to 80.

Groups or Individuals: Most placements are for individuals, though school group and family travel options are available in some cases.

Annual no. of Volunteers: 5000

Annual Projects: 500

Selection & Interview Process: Applications can be made online or over the phone. Criminal Records Bureau checks are made for UK applicants who will be working with children.

In-country Support: After in-country orientation, support includes a local in-country coordinator and a 24-hour emergency phone line, manned at all times by i-to-i staff. i-to-i also retains the services of crisis management specialists in case of large-scale emergencies.

UK Organisations

Go Differently

Flat 1, The White House, 24 Third Avenue, Hove BN3 2PD, UK
☎ +44 (0)127 373 2236
info@godifferently.com
www.godifferently.com

Go Differently specialises in short-term volunteering and 'voluntourism' adventures in Southeast Asia, with particular emphasis on Thailand. Opportunities include working with elephants, teaching English in remote villages and assisting with one-off projects including tsunami relief, village construction or reforestation work.

Status: Limited company.

Timing & Length of Placements: Adventures are normally between one and four weeks long, although longer stays can be arranged. Some of the small-group 'voluntourism' itineraries do have set departure dates throughout the year, but most volunteer projects can be joined at any time, subject to availability.

Destinations: Thailand, Laos, Cambodia, Vietnam, India and Bali.

Costs: These vary depending on the project, itinerary and duration but start at £320 for a one-week stay. This covers project fees, administration, accommodation and all meals whilst at the project. Airfares are not included.

Eligibility: The minimum age is 18, although those under 18 are welcome if accompanied by an adult. Families with children are also welcome. There is no maximum age as long as volunteers are relatively fit and healthy. People with disabilities can be placed on suitable projects. Fluency in English is required for those wishing to teach English.

Groups or Individuals: With the exception of 'voluntourism' itineraries, most volunteers join projects individually, although several volunteers work on each project at any one time. Maximum numbers vary but are not usually greater than 10. Participants are welcome to volunteer with a friend, partner or family members.

Annual no. of Volunteers: 200

Annual Projects: 10

Selection & Interview Process: Prospective volunteers should complete a questionnaire providing information about their background, experience, abilities and expectations, and motivations for joining the project. In-person interviews are normally not conducted.

In-country Support: Local support staff are available at all times and in most cases are based at the projects. All volunteers are provided with local contact telephone numbers that they can call in case of emergencies or day-to-day queries.

Hands Up Holidays

61 Parkstead Rd, UK
☎ (UK) +44 (0)207 193 1062
☎ (US) +1 201 984 5372
info@handsupholidays.com
www.handsupholidays.com

Hands Up Holidays was created to allow tourists to enjoy meaningful interaction with different cultures and to give something back through a volunteering 'taster'. Most accommodation is four-star, and is always with local operators. The volunteering portion of a holiday accounts for approximately one-third of the trip duration, and may include house building, repairs and renovations, teaching English, environmental assistance etc. Hands Up Holidays is committed to environmental sustainability and to contributing a portion of profits to sustainable development projects in the communities with which it interacts.

Status: Limited company.
Timing & Length of Projects: Due to the tailor-made nature of the trips, the timing and length of projects are up to you, although typically, guests spend three to five days volunteering and the remainder of the time exploring their chosen destination.
Destinations: Argentina, Australia, Belize, Bolivia, Borneo, Brazil, Cambodia, China, Colombia, Costa Rica, Ecuador, Fiji, Ghana, Guatemala, India, Indonesia, Kenya, Laos, Libya, Malawi, Mexico, Morocco, Mozambique, Namibia, Nepal, New Zealand, Peru, Portugal, Romania, Rwanda, Slovakia, South Africa, Thailand, Vanuatu, Vietnam and Zambia.
Costs: Because trips are tailor made, the cost depends on a variety of factors, including destination, level of accommodation, length of trip and time of year. The average cost per person for a 14-day trip in four-star accommodation is US$4000 per person, excluding flights.
Eligibility: Clients' skills and interests are matched with volunteer projects. There is a minimum age of 18 unless accompanied by a guardian. Many trips are specifically recommended for families.
Groups or Individuals: Both.
Annual no. of Volunteers: 200
Annual Projects: 20
Partner Programmes: Hands Up is partnered with over 60 organisations throughout Africa, Asia, Latin America, Europe and the Pacific, including World Vision, Tearfund, Rotary International, and many smaller NGOs.
Selection & Interview Process: There is a questionnaire to be completed, and clients' skills and interests are matched with volunteer projects. For most volunteer projects there is no interview, but some do require it. A police check is required if the volunteer project entails interaction with children or other vulnerable people.
In-country Support: 24-hour in-country support is provided and local guides and trip coordinators are present throughout the trip (including the volunteer component); all are fluent in English. Training specific to the volunteer project is provided where necessary.

North American Organisations

Hoy Community

Rio Mexapa 130, Colonia Hacienda Tetela, 62160 Cuernavaca, Morelos, Mexico
☎ +52 (777) 176-7868
hoycommunity@gmail.com
www.hoycommunity.net

This US non-profit organisation, which is based in Mexico, engages travellers in 'participatory trips' to underprivileged Mexican urban and rural communities. Trips combine work on hands-on community projects with sightseeing and cultural activities.
Status: Non-profit organisation.
Timing & Length of Projects: One or two weeks; email inquiries regarding availability.
Destinations: Mexico urban setting: Cuernavaca; numerous rural settings in Morelos State.
Costs: One week at Casa HOY in Cuernavaca: US$600 per person, which includes hostel-type lodging, breakfast and lunch, local transportation and bus to and from airport, all arrangements for volunteer service, one guided excursion, wireless internet. Not included is the airfare to and from Mexico City, visas, travel insurance, meals other than those specified, and personal expenses.
Eligibility: Minimum age is 18; minors must be accompanied by a parent or guardian. Volunteers may be of any nationality, but must have a basic knowledge of Spanish and a willingness to discover a new culture. No accommodation is available for people with disabilities.

Groups or Individuals: Trips are arranged for groups: minimum of four, maximum of 15.
Annual no. of Volunteers: 40 to 50.
Annual Projects: 6
Partner Programmes: 10
Selection & Interview Process:
Organisation founders Katy Barnhart and Gerardo Jaime personally select programmes and projects and work with partners to identify short-term volunteer activities. Feedback from volunteers and organisations determines whether the partnership continues. Participatory travellers are placed mainly according to their interests and past volunteer experiences (if any); their level of Spanish may also inform the decision.
In-country Support: A preparatory orientation covers logistical, cultural, linguistic and safety issues. Volunteers have 24-hour access to a local contact person.

Australasian Organisations

Volunteer Service Abroad (VSA)

PO Box 6144, Thorndon, Wellington 6144, Aotrearoa, New Zealand
☎ +64 (0)4 472 5759
fax +64 (0)4 472 5052
vsa@vsa.org.nz
www.vsa.org.nz
New Zealand's leading international volunteer agency, Volunteer Service Abroad (VSA) offers people the chance to pitch in on a short-term community project overseas.
Status: Registered Charity.
Timing & Length of Assignments: VSA projects are offered twice to three times a year. Each project usually runs for a couple of weeks, with time allowed to explore the particular destination.
Destinations: Cambodia.
Costs: VSA asks volunteers to fundraise NZ$2000 for two-year assignments and NZ$1000 for projects that will run for 12 months or less. Costs of flights, visas, insurance and accommodation are covered by VSA and volunteers receive a living allowance.
Eligibility: VSA volunteer applicants have to be New Zealand citizens, permanent residents, or have right of re-entry to New Zealand.
Groups or Individuals: Groups and individuals welcome. Up to 12 people per group.

Annual no. of Volunteers: 24-36
Annual Projects: 2-3
Partner Programmes: 3
Selection & Interview Process: Applicants download a form from the website and email it back with a cover letter and a CV. Shortlisted applicants are asked to attend a two-day interview process in Wellington, with VSA contributing towards any travel costs.
In-country Support: Groups are accompanied by a New Zealand and local tour guide and link with staff at the local VSA office and VSA volunteers working in Cambodia.

World Expeditions

Australian Office: Lvl 5, 71 York St, Sydney, NSW 2000, Australia
☎ +61 (0)2 8270 8400
fax +61 (0)2 8270 8401
info@worldexpeditions.com.au
New Zealand Office: Lvl 2, 35 High St, Auckland, New Zealand
☎ +64 (0)9 368 4161
fax +64 (0)9 368 4162
enquiries@worldexpeditions.co.nz
www.worldexpeditions.com
World Expeditions is an Australian adventure-travel outfit which offers community project trips to developing countries while enabling travellers to enjoy a cultural experience in stunning terrain. Part of the trip payment helps pay for the materials on projects, which include installing piping for sewerage and renovating a school in Nepal. World Expeditions promises an 'interactive, philanthropic, educational and uplifting' experience. Certainly working alongside villagers on the 'roof of the world' could lend a new meaning to the term 'workplace high'.
Status: Limited company.
Timing & Length of Assignments:
Departure dates are advertised on www.worldexpeditions.com. Trips range from seven to 18 days; there are departures year-round for selected projects.
Destinations: Arnhem Land (Australia), Nepal, Peru, Tanzania and Laos.
Costs: A$1800 to A$4000.
Eligibility: Participants must be over 16 and fit and healthy, as some trips entail two-day treks to remote communities.
Groups or Individuals: Individuals are placed on group trips; private group arrangements are possible.
Annual no. of Volunteers: 100
Annual Projects: Varies.

Partner Programmes: World Expeditions works alongside on-the-ground operators and remote communities.

Selection & Interview Process: A normal trip-booking process applies, with no selection prerequisites or interview necessary. A medical clearance is required.

In-country Support: Experienced on-the-ground operational staff and crew.

Overseas Organisations

Buffalo Tours

94 Ma May Street, Hoan Kiem District, Hanoi, Vietnam
☎ +84 4 3828 0702
fax +84 4 3826 9370
info@buffalotours.com
www.buffalotours.com
www.educationaltravelasia.com

Buffalo Tours is one of the leading tour operators in Vietnam and has established a very good reputation for inclusive tours since 1992. To its credit, it has pioneered many adventure travel opportunities, such as trekking in Mai Chau and kayaking in Halong Bay, and it also advocates responsible tourism, supporting worthy projects such as Binh Luc Orphanage, medical treks in Mai Chau and 'friendship village' visits for victims of Agent Orange.

Status: Limited company.

Timing & Length of Placements: Project length can vary, however, a minimum of one week is normally recommended, but ideally 10 to 14 days. Projects are also offered for longer periods of time.

Destinations: Locations throughout Vietnam, Cambodia, Thailand and Laos.

Costs: Costs are subject to length of stay and programme.

Eligibility: This is dependent on the nature of the project or experience, but generally the age minimum is 13 years.

Groups or Individuals: Buffalo Tours specialises in groups and caters to many schools, clubs and universities.

Annual no. of Volunteers: 453

Annual Projects: 53

Selection & Interview Process: Selection is dependent on group interest, size, age and dates of travel.

In-country Support: A full time, experienced Volunteer and Educational Travel team is available in-country to operate group projects and experiences from start to finish.

Voluntourists Without Borders

22/8 Moo 4, Mahidol Rd, Nonghol, Amphur Muang, Chiang Mai 50000, Thailand
☎ +66 (0)53 801 257
fax +66 (0)53 801 674 ext 1
info@track-of-the-tiger.com
www.track-of-the-tiger.com

VWB is a non-profit initiative established in 1986 in Chiang Mai, Thailand. The initiative sends volunteers to rural Thai villages, where they participate in sustainable agricultural and agroforestry programmes, attempting to save existing forest cover, augment degraded forest areas and retain biodiversity. Local communities must agree on project plans, the project must be accessible for all participants and must have potential for replication by other communities. Projects include the Ban Pang Daeng Nai and Pang Soong nature trails – both comprised of several ecotourism components including nature trail development, forest augmentation and interaction with local people. VWB's long-term goal is to build a sustainable ecotourism company in the region that will be owned and operated by the local villagers.

Status: Ltd company/not-for-profit arm.

Timing & Length of Placements: Programmes for individuals and families range in length from one day to one year. Other 'gap' programmes run significantly longer, ranging from four predetermined timelines to two weeks or two months.

Destinations: Thailand.

Costs: Costs vary greatly depending on length of stay, but are around US$75 per day. This covers all meals, wages for local workers and accommodation, but not airfares.

Eligibility: The minimum age is over 18 years. Volunteers under 18 must be accompanied by parents or be with a school or youth group.

Groups or Individuals: Both.

Annual no. of Volunteers: 200

Annual Projects: 4-5

Selection & Interview Process: The selection process is conducted via email.

In-country Support: All programmes are suported by our commercial arm and are based at the Pang Soong Lodge, Outdoor & Environmental Education Centre.

Volunteering as a Staff Member

If you enjoy working in a leadership capacity, or are looking to get into the expedition business, you might consider volunteering as a staff member for an expedition-based gap-year organisation to gain experience. Raleigh International (see below), for example, takes on about 300 volunteer staff every year to help run its expeditions, including team leaders, drivers and project managers. However, you need relevant skills for these positions – for example, six months' experience in youth work or team-leading to apply for a project manager role – and you must pay for your own flights.

Greenforce (see below) regularly recruits staff to assist with its programmes, and others, like Trekforce (p115), take volunteer medical personnel on expeditions. If you're interested in participating in an expedition as a doctor or nurse, it wouldn't hurt to contact whatever organisation catches your eye, as there may be openings.

Greenforce

21 Heathmans Rd, London SW6 4TJ, UK
☎ UK +44 (0)207 384 3028
info@greenforce.org
www.greenforce.org
Greenforce rewards its field staff by providing international flights, food, accommodation, medical insurance and a stipend. Also, staff who complete the programme may receive annual awards that can be used to help fund additional training. Those interested in applying for staff positions need to be

prepared to commit to at least 12 months. Applications are sometimes accepted as late as three months prior to departure and positions for dive instructors, expedition leaders or scientists might be offered, for example. For more information about Greenforce programmes, see p131.
Status: Registered charity.

Raleigh International

3rd flr, Prince Consort House, 27-29 Albert Embankment, London SE1 7TJ, UK
☎ +44 (0)20 7183 1270
fax +44 (0)20 7504 8094
info@raleighinternational.org
www.raleighinternational.org
Every year about 300 volunteer staff work with Raleigh's volunteers and local community members on projects in three areas: community, environment and adventure. For more information on non-staff volunteer placements, see p108. Staff volunteers can be field-based, in roles such as administrator, communications officer, finance manager or logistics manager. Alternatively, project-based roles include medics, interpreters, project managers and builders. Staff volunteers are required to attend a selection weekend in the UK to assess their suitability.
Status: Registered charity.
Destinations: Borneo, Costa Rica, Nicaragua, India and Tanzania.
Eligibility: Raleigh looks for volunteer staff who are over 25 and can offer appropriate skills.

Development Placements

As you'll see, development can mean almost anything – this multidisciplinary field can encompass digging latrines one day and playing soccer with orphans the next. But the common goal of all these organisations is to alleviate difficult living conditions through sustainable social programmes and increasing the effectiveness of healthcare and educational institutions and infrastructure (that's where the latrines come in). The experiences offered by very large organisations like Inspired Breaks (p126), who send thousands abroad annually, are very different from those offered by small outfits like the Village Education Project (p127), which sends only six volunteers abroad per year.

UK Organisations

Cuba Solidarity Campaign

c/o Unite Woodberry, 218 Green Lanes, London N4 2HB, UK
☎ +44 (0)20 8800 0155
fax +44 (0)20 8800 9844
office@cuba-solidarity.org.uk
www.cuba-solidarity.org.uk

Conservation volunteering can help repair the effects of slash and burn agriculture, seen here in Madagascar

CSC organises volunteers for International Work Brigade camps near Havana. British volunteers (or *brigadistas*, as they are called) work alongside Cubans and groups from other countries. Volunteers carry out light agricultural work (such as picking oranges on a local cooperative farm) or construction work. There is a full programme of activities, including visits to factories, hospitals, trade unions, schools and educational or political events. A preparatory weekend takes place four to six weeks before departure.

Status: Non-profit organisation.

Timing & Length of Placements: The camps last for three weeks and are run twice a year, in summer and winter.

Destinations: Cuba.

Costs: The trip costs around £1000, which includes flights, accommodation and food.

Eligibility: Applicants must be 18 or over.

Groups or Individuals: Both.

Annual no. of Volunteers: 70

Annual Projects: 2

Selection & Interview Process: Those interested must complete an application form, send in £100 deposit, two passport-sized photos and become a member of the Cuba Solidarity Campaign (£20 waged/£8 unwaged).

In-country Support: The trip is organised in conjunction with ICAP (Instituto Cubano de Amistad con los Pueblos) who run the programme in Cuba and provide full support.

Inspired Breaks

1st flr, 1 Meadow Rd, Tunbridge Wells, Kent, TN1 2YG, UK
☎ +44 (0)1892 701881
fax +44 (0)1892 523172
info@inspiredbreaks.co.uk
www.inspiredbreaks.co.uk

Inspired Breaks specialises in career breaks and voluntary work for people over 30. They offer a range of placements covering a range of paid and voluntary work, tailor-made trips and language courses.

Status: Limited company.

Timing & Length of Placements: Departures take place year-round for the majority of projects, though some have limited departure dates (to fit in with turtle breeding seasons etc). Programmes range in length from one week to a year and all programmes can be tailored to fit in with specific time lengths requested.

Destinations: 40 countries worldwide, covering Africa, Australasia, Eastern Europe, the USA, Canada, Central America, South America and Asia.

Costs: Projects vary in cost from £399 upwards, and cover all accommodation, meals, on-site support and more. Airfares are not included.

Eligibility: No specific skills are required; a basic level of fitness is necessary.

Groups or Individuals: Volunteers are allowed to travel in pairs or small groups and will usually work in small groups.

Annual no. of Volunteers: 5000
Annual Projects: Hundreds.
In-country Support: There is a 24-hour emergency phone number in the UK. Full support on-site is provided by English-speaking staff.

IVS GB (International Voluntary Service)

Thorn House, 5 Rose St, Edinburgh EH2 2PR, Scotland, UK
☎ +44 (0)131 243 2745
fax +44 (0)131 243 2747
info@ivsgb.org
http://ivsgb.org

IVS promotes peace and social justice through volunteering. The projects focus on conservation, inner-city children, orphanages, community arts projects and people with disabilities. Some of our projects have a strong study element on peace, human rights and climate change. Volunteers join a team of six to 20 volunteers who live and work together on the project. IVS works on the principle that the more understanding there is between people, the less conflict there will be.

Status: Registered charity and limited company.

Timing & Length of Placements:
Short-term projects are two to four weeks long. Long-term projects are two to 12 months. Most of the short-term projects run between April and October.

Destinations: Projects are located in over 70 countries in Europe, Asia, Africa, the Americas and Australia.

Costs: Projects abroad cost £150 to £245 and projects in Britain cost £55 to £155. Food and accommodation are provided by the host. Volunteers pay their travel costs.

Eligibility: Volunteers need to be at least 18 to go abroad. There are some places on British projects for those aged under 18 and residents of Great Britain.

Groups or Individuals: Volunteers travel alone to their placements, but work in groups. In some cases it's possible for volunteers to work with requested partners.

Annual no. of Volunteers: 200
Annual Projects: 1000
Partner Programmes: Approximately 90.
Selection & Interview Process: Selection is by application form. Volunteers must attend a preparation day and an evaluation day. Extra information is needed when the project is in the North/South Programme.

In-country Support: All projects are sourced locally by the local branch. The local branch and local host work closely together to provide in-country support.

Village Education Project (Kilimanjaro)

Mint Cottage, Prospect Rd,
Sevenoaks, Kent TN13 3UA, UK
☎ +44 (0)1732 743000
project@kiliproject.org
www.kiliproject.org

Village Education Project is a registered charity dedicated to improving education in the Kilimanjaro region of Tanzania. Each year a handful of volunteers teach in village primary schools 1500m up the slopes of Mt Kilimanjaro. Volunteers also accompany pupils on school outings to national parks and the Indian Ocean. Rented accommodation is provided in one village. Sue Davies chose this programme because she saw the larger sending agencies as 'money-grabbing organisations, who use the fact that volunteers are willing to work (albeit often illegally) for the duration of their holiday permit, and charge obscene sums of money.' Placed with the programme for nine months, Davies says, 'I lived in Mshiri village which is approximately 5000 feet above sea level. The village is in the most beautiful setting and wherever you walked there was always the summit of the mountain as a backdrop. The village itself consisted of a church, a school and a couple of bars, which sold the very bare essentials and some local produce, which varied according to the seasons. The nearest marketplace and town was Marangu Mtoni, which was reached by foot through some of the most beautiful scenery imaginable. From Marangu Mtoni you could catch *dala dalas* (local buses) to the nearest major town, Moshi, for the luxuries of pasta and wine!'

Status: Charity.
Timing & Length of Placements: Placements run from January to August/September. The set departure date is therefore early January each year.
Destination: Mshiri village on the slopes of Mt Kilimanjaro, Tanzania.

Photo: Azafady

It's a dirty job, but someone's got to do it - building wells in Madagascar with Azafady

Costs: A placement costs £3250, which includes airfares, a two-week training course in the UK in the November before departure, accommodation in Mshiri village, administration costs and two school outings. Not included is accommodation on the training course held in Sevenoaks, Kent, and spending money in Tanzania.

Eligibility: The minimum age 18 and volunteers must be native speakers of English, preferably with a UK passport. The programme cannot accommodate people with disabilities.

Groups or Individuals: Volunteers work individually but live in the same village as other volunteers. Friends can apply together.

Annual no. of Volunteers: An average of six.

Partner Programmes: The Tanzanian Ministry of Education and the District Education Office for Moshi Rural – the work in the primary schools is fully authorised.

Selection & Interview Process: All applicants are interviewed in person in Sevenoaks, Kent.

In-country Support: The project director is on site in Mshiri village about half of the time (January to April, then July to September) and project staff are available 24 hours to provide assistance. Phone and email contact, and 4WDs, are available for emergencies. Volunteers provide a lot of mutual support, as they all live within five minutes' walk of each other.

Winant Clayton Volunteer Association

St Margaret's House, 21 Old Ford Rd,
Bethnal Green, London E2 9PL, UK
☎ +44 (0)20 8983 3834
info@winantclayton.org.uk
www.winantclayton.org.uk

For more than 50 years this charity has placed British volunteers in social projects, working with the homeless, inner-city children, HIV sufferers or the elderly. There are about 12 to 15 places available each year. There are two weeks of independent travel at the end of each placement.

Status: Charity.

Timing & Length of Placements: Placements are for two months from late June to August, with two further weeks at the end of the placement allocated for travel around the US. The programme runs once a year, with volunteers departing their home country in late June and returning in early September.

Destination: UK volunteers work mostly in New York City; US volunteers work mostly in London.

Costs/Pay: Though participants pay for airfares, WCVA arranges discounted group flights. Accommodation is provided and there is a stipend for food, essential transport and pocket money.

Eligibility: British and Irish passport-holders aged 18 and over.

Groups or Individuals: Volunteers travel as a group, but work individually or in pairs on different placements. Up to 20 volunteers are sent each year, depending on placement availability and funding. Volunteers are welcome to apply with friends, partners and family members but each will be interviewed separately and the success of one does not guarantee the acceptance of others.

Annual no. of Volunteers: Up to 20.

Annual Projects: 1

Partner Programmes: In 2006, UK volunteers were placed with 10 different organisations in New York City.

Selection & Interview Process: Candidates must complete and return a written application form by the end of January. If short-listed, candidates are called for interview in February.

In-country Support: A US coordinator and members of the US Management Committee support volunteers in New York. There is always someone available in the event of an emergency. Volunteers have their own supervisor on each placement responsible for inducting them and supporting them during their stay.

Australasian Organisations

Australian Volunteers International

71 Argyle St (PO Box 350), Fitzroy, Victoria 3065, Australia
☎ +61 (0)3 9279 1788, 1800 331 292
fax +61 (0)3 9419 4280
info@australianvolunteers.com
www.australianvolunteers.com

The best known of Australia's volunteer programmes, Australian Volunteers International (AVI) has been operating since 1951 and has recruited more than 7000 Australians for volunteer placements in over 70 countries in Asia, the Pacific, Africa and the Middle East. AVI is mindful of sustainable development and works with a range of partner organisations overseas to guarantee that the work of volunteers is responding to the needs of those organisations and the communities they represent. AVI volunteers are recruited based on their technical skills and experience to assist in reducing poverty, promoting human rights and gender equality, protecting the environment, promoting better health and education, and fighting HIV/AIDS.

AVI has just the right mix of organisation and benefits for volunteers, while leaving room for volunteers to plot their own course through the volunteer journey. Many Australians now working in development started off as international volunteers with AVI.

Status: A company limited by guarantee, registered as a charity and a not-for-profit organisation.

Timing & Length of Assignments: Volunteers work on long-term placements that are 18 to 24 months, departing year round. There are some opportunities to participate in shorter term assignments.

Destinations: Up to 40 countries in Asia, the Pacific, Africa, the Middle East and Latin America.

Costs/Pay: All volunteers receive travel, living and accommodation allowances, visas and medical insurance.

Eligibility: Volunteers can be aged from 18 to 80 but are required to have at least two years' work experience in their field or profession. Volunteers need to be Australian or New Zealand citizens or hold permanent residency status. People with disabilities are encouraged to apply.

Groups or Individuals: Most AVI assignments are for individuals.

Annual no. of Volunteers: Up to 400.

Annual Projects: Up to 400.

Partner Programmes: AVI has a range of partner programmes including the AusAID-funded Volunteer Program, the Cambodia Midwives Project and Hamlin Fistula Hospital project, the AVI/VSO Partnership, and the Global Futures Program, which is run in partnership with Macquarie University. We also have partner programmes with the Planning Institute of Australia, the Planet Wheeler Foundation, Intrepid Travel, FaCHSIA and Lawyers Beyond Borders.

Selection & Interview Process: Positions are advertised on www.australianvolunteers.com in February, May, August and November for three weeks. Prospective volunteers can apply for specific positions or send in a general application. AVI's recruitment process involves making sure applicants meet the selection criteria, doing a skills assessment and expertise evaluation, and checking personal and professional references. If selected, a candidate must attend a three-day pre-departure briefing in Melbourne.

In-country Support:AVI has support staff for each country they work in, as well as in-country offices in East Timor, Cambodia, Vietnam, Fiji, Johannesburg, the Solomon Islands, Papua New Guinea and Indonesia.

Volunteer Service Abroad (VSA), Te Tuao Tawahi

PO Box 12246, Thorndon,
Wellington, 6144, New Zealand
☎ +64 (0)4 472 5759
fax +64 (0)4 472 5052
www.vsa.org.nz
Volunteer Service Abroad (VSA) is New Zealand's main volunteer agency working in the field of international development and is always on the look-out for people with the diverse skills needed by its partner organisations overseas (from beekeeping to nursing).

Status: Registered charity.

Timing & Length of Assignments: Most VSA assignments are for two years, with volunteers departing throughout the year.

Destinations: VSA operates in 12 countries in Africa, Asia and the Pacific. It works in Zambia, South Africa, Tanzania, Cambodia, Lao PDR, Timor-Leste and Vietnam. Over half of the assignments take place in the Pacific, in the Autonomous Region of Bougainville, Papua New Guinea, the Solomon Islands, Tokelau and Vanuatu.

Costs/Pay: VSA volunteers are paid a monthly living allowance during their assignment. An establishment grant is offered and at completion a resettlement grant is provided for each month the volunteer was away on assignment. Accommodation, flights, insurance cover, medicals, visas and permits are also paid for.

Eligibility: VSA volunteer applicants have to be New Zealand citizens, permanent residents, or have right of re-entry to New Zealand. They need experience in a specialist field, or a recognised professional, trade or commercial qualification.

Groups or Individuals: VSA volunteers are individually assigned to partner organisations.

Annual no. of Volunteers: VSA places 150 new volunteers in assignments annually.

Annual Projects: 150 plus assignments.

Partner Programmes: 200

Selection & Interview Process: Generally, potential volunteers apply for advertised assignments on www.vsa.org.nz. Successful applicants are invited to an interview that runs over two days, and includes group exercises, one-on-one interviews, and panel interviews. Once selected, they must undertake a three-day-long briefing before departing. Couples may apply, and where there's a skills-fit, a volunteer's partner can be placed on the same assignment. VSA volunteers range from 20 to 75 years of age.

In-country Support: VSA has field officers in 10 of its 12 countries. The remaining two countries are visited regularly by VSA programme staff.

Volunteering for International Development from Australia

Lvl 1, 41 Dequetteville Tce,
Kent Town, SA 5067, Australia
☎ +61 (0)8 8364 8500, 1800 995 536
fax +61 (0)8 8331 8944
info@vidavolunteers.com.au
www.vidavolunteers.com.au
Established in 2005, VIDA places skilled Australians in developing countries in the Asia-Pacific region. VIDA volunteers work with local counterparts to reduce poverty and achieve sustainable development in the communities in which they work. This programme attracts people with a bit of life experience and professional clout.

Status: VIDA is an AusAID project managed by Austraining International Pty Ltd (an NGO).

Timing & Length of Assignments: Volunteer assignments are one month to three years in length. The average volunteer assignment duration is 18 months. VIDA volunteers are mobilised throughout the year.

Destinations: Bangladesh, Cambodia, East Timor, Fiji, Indonesia, Laos, Nepal, the Philippines, Papua New Guinea, Samoa, the Solomon Islands, Thailand (regional assignments), Tonga, Tuvalu, Vanuatu and Vietnam.

Costs/Pay: VIDA supports volunteers with airfares, a living allowance, an accommodation allowance, medical costs and vaccinations, comprehensive insurance cover, pre-departure training, in-country support and a debrief on return.

Eligibility: VIDA volunteers must be over 18 years at the time of application and Australian citizens or permanent residents.

Groups or Individuals: Volunteers are placed individually; VIDA will place couples and there is also some support available for dependants of volunteers.

Annual no. of Volunteers: Approximately 110.

Annual Projects: Each volunteer works on a separate project, so up to 200 projects each year.

Partner Programmes: VIDA partners with organisations in-country and in Australia to develop volunteer assignments across a range of sectors.

Selection & Interview Process: VIDA advertises new assignments every month. Applications are processed for compliance and assessed against the selection criteria for the position. Selected applicants are interviewed and required to comply with all stages of the recruitment and selection procedure.

In-country Support: VIDA has in-country managers in all countries who are the first point of contact and support for volunteers in the field.

Conservation & Wildlife Placements

To be honest, it's rare to find large organisations that *don't* have conservation or wildlife management programmes in their portfolio of opportunities. But the following organisations all have a conservation-centric bent. Burgeoning Dr Doolittles will delight in the plethora of hands-on wildlife management opportunities, like protecting endangered sea turtles with Archelon, the Sea Turtle Protection Society of Greece (p137). For animal-lovers who want to stay on dry land, organisations like the African Conservation Experience and Greenforce (both this page) offer placements in the African grasslands. If your taste is for trees rather than cheetahs, look to the many ecological programmes – from Rainforest Concern's work in the Amazon (p136) to The Centre for Alternative Technology's inspiring efforts in the UK (p133).

International Organisations

Greenforce

21 Heathmans Rd, London SW6 4TJ, UK
☎ UK +44 (0) 207 384 3028
www.greenforce.org

Greenforce runs a series of environmental projects around the globe, focusing on wildlife conservation. The work ranges from tracking elephants in Africa to collecting scientific information in the Ecuadorian rainforest or monitoring species on coral reefs in Borneo. All training is provided, including scuba diving training for marine volunteers. Open evenings are held once a month in London and there are pre-departure training days. Teams comprise 16 people.

Status: Registered charity.

Timing & Length of Placements: Most programmes last from four weeks to six months, though there are some that last only a week or two. There are four or five departures spread throughout the year. Apply six months in advance so that you don't miss out on pre-departure training.

Destinations: Marine expeditions go to the Bahamas, Borneo and Fiji. Terrestrial expeditions go to Africa, Ecuador and Nepal.

Costs/Pay: The costs of programmes vary greatly, but everything is included except international flights. For a year-long teaching programme in Ecuador you may earn a small wage, but most 10-week expeditions cost about £2500. Other two-week excursions cost approximately £1500.

Eligibility: People aged 18 to 70.

Groups or Individuals: Many placements will work in small teams, though teaching projects are more independent.

Annual no. of Volunteers: Varies.

Annual Projects: Dozens; of varying length, cost and intensity.

Partner Programmes: Greenforce partners with many international organisations, including the Marine Conservation Society, the World Wildlife Fund, World Conservation Union and the United Nations General Assembly.

In-country Support: Greenforce staff live and work on location to give support to volunteers.

UK Organisations

African Conservation Experience

Unit 1, Manor Farm, Churchend
Lane, Charfield, Wotton-Under-Edge,
Gloucestershire, GL12 8LJ, UK
☎ +44 1454 269 182
www.conservationafrica.net

This programme offers conservation placements in game and nature reserves in southern Africa. These are ideally suited to anyone interested in botany, biology, environmental sciences and veterinary science – especially those on leave from school and students considering a career in conservation and environmentalism. Postgraduates are able to carry out specific field research.

Status: Limited company.

Timing & Length of Placements: Placements are available year-round and usually last from one to three months. You need to apply three to four months in advance.

Destinations: Southern Africa, Botswana and Zimbabwe.

Costs: Between £3000 and £5000, including flights from London to Johannesburg, transfers, all meals and accommodation.

Eligibility: Applicants must be over 17 and enthusiastic about conservation. There's no upper age limit.

Groups or Individuals: Couples can be placed together and families can be accommodated on a case-by-case basis.

Annual no. of Volunteers: Approximately 250.

Annual Projects: 10

Partner Programmes: None.

Selection & Interview Process: There's no interview, but a comprehensive application form must be filled out.

In-country Support: An African Conservation Experience staff member is available 24 hours a day, and coordinators are based on each project continually. Full support is given in emergencies in terms of first aid and transport to a doctor or hospital. A staff member accompanies volunteers at all times. They have a Major Incident Protocol and chain-of-communication in place to deal with emergencies.

Azafady

Studio 7, 1a Beethoven St,
London W10 4LG, UK
☎ +44 (0)20 8960 6629
fax +44 (0)20 8962 0126
info@azafady.org
www.madagascar.co.uk

'Azafady' is a Malagasy word meaning 'please'. This registered charity sends volunteers to help with grassroots conservation and sustainable development programmes in Madagascar. Founded in 1994, placements are available on conservation, development and sustainable livelihoods projects in southeastern Madagascar. Projects focus on local needs, human or otherwise, and the work is extremely diverse, ranging from digging wells and latrine pits, to teaching English, to conducting field studies on endangered species.With Azafady you can volunteer from two to 10 weeks on the award-winning Pioneer programme, the Azafady Conservation Programme, or short-term programmes in English teaching or school-building. Volunteers work closely with locals and Azafady staff and have the opportunity to learn basic Malagasy. Programmes can also be taken as internships.

Status: Registered charity and Malagasy NGO.

Timing & Length of Placements: Assignments last from two to 10 weeks and start in January, April, July and October. Apply giving at least one month's notice.

Destination: Southeast corner of Madagascar.

Costs: Volunteers are required to fundraise a minimum donation between £595 and £2000 depending on the programme. As this is a direct charitable donation, volunteers are encouraged to actively fundraise this with the hands-on help of the UK team, while raising awareness about Madagascar. The fee excludes flights, vaccinations and visa.

Eligibility: Must be 'able bodied' and over 18.

Groups or Individuals: Volunteers work within a team of approximately 15 to 20.

Annual no. of Volunteers: Approximately 100.

Selection & Interview Process: All volunteers must fill in an application form and send it in to the Azafady London office, which may request answers to further questions or an interview before the assessment process is completed.

In-country Support: Each team is accompanied by a field coordinator and supported by an administration coordinator. They have a team of Malagasy guides and work closely with specialists for support on specific projects. Azafady's staff are trained in all types of potential emergency response; risk assessments are updated quarterly and teams always have supervision.

TCV (The Conservation Volunteers)

**Sedum House, Mallard Way,
Doncaster DN4 8DB, UK**
☎ +44 (0)130 238 8883
fax +44 (0)130 231 1531
information@tcv.org.uk
www.tcv.org.uk

TCV is the UK's largest practical conservation charity, annually involving volunteers in projects to care for the environment. Though the majority of the projects are domestic placements in the UK, a range of placements – through TCV Conservation Holidays or their partner NGOs – involve international travel. Among the many options are managing wetlands in Japan, building footpaths in Iceland or even olive picking in Italy. With an ethos of 'environments for all', TCV requires no specific skills or experience, though an adequate level of fitness is required. Volunteers are accepted from around the world, but should speak enough English to understand and follow safety instructions. Those with special needs are accommodated where possible following discussion.

Status: Registered charity.
Timing & Length of Placements: Most holidays last between one and two weeks and run year-round. You can book up to the week before the start date.
Destinations: Worldwide, but many placements are in Europe.
Costs: The price depends on where you go and what you're doing, so could cost anything between £210 and £1190. This does not include flights. Special offers apply when booking on more than one project.
Eligibility: Minimum age 18.
Groups or Individuals: Expeditions place volunteers together in small groups.
Annual no. of Volunteers: 300
Annual Projects: 30
Partner Programmes: 20
Selection & Interview Process: There is no selection process.
In-country Support: Pre-project contact is by phone or email with the leader. All TCV

leaders are trained in leadership, technical aspects and health, safety and welfare, and they accompany every project, as do local leaders. There's a 24-hour emergency contact for volunteers and family members, 24-hour organisational back-up for emergencies and a trained leader on-site. Fully developed safety management and risk assessment systems are backed up by TCV's full-time professional team.

Centre for Alternative Technology

Machynlleth, Powys SY20 9AZ, Wales, UK
☎ +44 (0)1654 705950
fax +44 (0)1654 702782
www.cat.org.uk

CAT is Europe's leading ecocentre, which inspires, informs and enables people to live more sustainably. Key areas of work are renewable energy, environmental building, energy efficiency, organic growing and alternative sewerage systems. There are two volunteer schemes. One is for long-term volunteers who come for six months and work in a specific area or department – including biology, building, engineering, gardening, information, media, publications or visitor centre management. The second is for short-term volunteers who come for a week or two and help with general outdoor, practical work (mostly gardening).

Timing & Length of Placements: The short-term programmes are for one or two weeks and run during particular weeks in the spring or summer. The long-term six-month placements begin either in spring or autumn. Due to the popularity of the programme, it's a good idea to apply six months in advance.
Destination: Powys (Wales).
Costs: Short-term volunteers pay £10 per day for full board. Long-term volunteers pay £105 per month if they are staying on site and an additional £110 per month for food, laundry, fuel etc. Some long-term volunteers cannot be accommodated on-site so there's no fee payable to CAT (although you obviously need to pay rent to someone else). Long-term volunteers must also take a minimum of one of CAT's courses which are running during their stay.
Eligibility: For those aged 18 and over.
Groups or Individuals: Individuals; groups by negotiation for specific projects.

Annual no. of Volunteers: 64 short-term volunteers and approximately 20 long-term volunteers.

Annual Projects: Ongoing construction, installation and research projects are possible, such as the production of woodland walk display boards.

Partner Programmes: European Voluntary Service (p97).

Selection & Interview Process: Long-term volunteers spend a trial week with the department they wish to assist, following submission of their CV.

In-country Support: Support is provided by the personnel department and a friendly, supportive atmosphere. Many long-term staff are former volunteers.

Coral Cay Conservation

The Granary, Shoelands Farm,
Puttenham, Surrey GU10 1HL, UK
☎ +44 (0) 207 620 1411
fax +44 (0)148 381 0223
info@coralcay.org
www.coralcay.org

Coral Cay Conservation (CCC) runs expeditions to collect scientific information in some of the most beautiful coastal areas of Cambodia, Tobago and the Philippines. Participants help to protect some of the most endangered marine and tropical habitats in the world on cutting-edge programmes that work hand-in-hand with NGOs from the host countries. CCC runs projects at the invitation of local governments and in collaboration with in-country NGOs, so it is purely coincidental that the locations happen to look like a slice of paradise.

Status: Non-profit organisation.

Timing & Length of Placements: Most CCC projects run continuously throughout the year and volunteers can choose to join an expedition ranging from two weeks upwards. Ongoing projects have 13 start dates a year.

Destinations: Current projects run in Cambodia, the Philippines and Tobago, with the option of combining Cambodia & the Philippines in one expedition.

Costs: Costs start from £315, though CCC pricing is defined by project costs and location. The minimum commitment for volunteers is one week for terrestrial expeditions and two weeks for marine expeditions, which includes UK briefing sessions, field accommodation, food, buoyancy control devices, dive training, tanks, air, weight belts, expedition and research training and field staff supervision. Fees do not include international flights, manuals and dive certification, insurance, airport departure taxes or your personal diving or trekking equipment.

Eligibility: There is no upper age limit, but volunteers must be 16 or over. The ability to speak and read English is important, as all expedition training is given in English. No previous experience is required since professional CCC expedition staff will provide all necessary training on-site, including scuba training.

Groups or Individuals: Volunteers are never on their own. Typically, you'll work in expeditions of between five and 40 people. If there is space available on the desired expedition, volunteers can be placed together. Groups of six people or more will also secure a 10% fee reduction and a free place for the organiser.

Annual no. of Volunteers: 300

Annual Projects: 3

Partner Programmes: 20

Selection & Interview Process: For volunteers there is no selection process. For staff that are office-based, interviews are conducted at the CCC head office in London.

In-country Support: All expedition sites have a full-time staff team comprising an expedition leader, project scientist, medical officer, educational officer and scuba instructor, plus local staff. All sites have a comprehensive medical inventory, an up-to date evacuation plan and a CCC crisis management plan for major emergencies.

Operation Wallacea

Wallace House, Old Bolingbroke, Spilsby, Lincolnshire PE23 4EX, UK
☎ +44 (0)17 9076 3194
info@opwall.com
www.opwall.com

Operation Wallacea is a series of biological and social science expedition projects that operate in remote locations across the world. These expeditions are designed with specific wildlife conservation aims in mind – from identifying areas needing protection, through to implementing and assessing conservation-management programmes.

Status: Limited company and charitable trust.

continued on p136

Memories of Maqui

'Ever since arriving in Maqui there was a little spot by the river that I loved,' wrote Kerri McGuinness of her placement with Outreach International, spent mostly at the Maquipucuna Ecological Reserve, two hours north of Quito, Ecuador. 'The song of the river and the view from it are awesome.' But there was a problem: there was nowhere to sit to admire them. Taking the situation in hand, Kerri and another volunteer decided to build a bench from bamboo. But that wasn't enough – they weeded the surrounding ground, constructed a small rock staircase and landscaped the area, so that everyone else who visited the reserve might have a place to relax and listen to the river's song. This story perfectly illustrates the rewards of ambitious self-determination that many development projects, like those of Outreach International, offer. Kerri initially signed up with the London-based charity for a three-month volunteer project, but stayed on for four. When Kerri is asked what her typical duties were, she replies, 'What were not my duties is far easier to answer! Normally I'd rattle off what a 'typical' day was, but the beauty was that every day was unpredictable!'

Even though she admits there was little structure to her particular programme, she found that freedom liberating, and says that the more she put in to the work, the more she got out of it.

'I immersed myself in the local community working with the craftswomen, teaching in schools and painting murals in the school playground. Then I went to the organic coffee farm affiliated with Maquipucuna for a few weeks, and lived with a typical family,' she says. 'Aside from helping with coffee-growing, I took on the other aspects of farm life. By 6am every morning I was across the valley herding the cows (a handful on your own!) and after milking them I herded them back over, cowgirl style. We then drank their milk in our home-grown coffee at breakfast time. For the final month of my stay I had the run of the place, and helped construct trails and build signs, and I taught English, helped in the kitchen, waited on guests, translated and built a bench from bamboo, to name just a few projects!'

But she was hardly slacking during her days off. She rafted the Amazon, climbed volcanoes and explored local hot springs. She even found time to take the famous train ride down the 'Devil's Nose', said to be one of the most dangerous rail journeys in the world. 'We rode on the roof like peasants!' she says.

When Kerri finished in Maquipucuna she toured the region, topping off her trip with a visit to the Galápagos islands, 'No better way of ending my out-of-this-world adventure. I was 30 metres under, diving with sharks, turtles, rays and sea lions.'

All told, it was her trust in the Outreach International staff that helped her choose the programme and she describes the placement as unforgettable, gratifying and eye-opening. 'One only sees so much when travelling but volunteering with Outreach International allowed me to go to places no backpacker would even know about and do things that they'd never think of doing. I feel fulfilled, refreshed and hungry for more already.'

Kerri McGuinness at the Maquipucuna Ecological Reserve

Photo: Kerri McGuinness

Timing & Length of Placements: Expeditions run from late June until early September. Volunteers can stay from two to 10 weeks.
Destinations: Cuba, Egypt, Honduras, Indonesia, Peru and South Africa.
Costs: Ranging from £1075 (US$1750) for two weeks to £3500 (US$5500) for eight weeks. All food, accommodation, transfers and training courses are included in the price. Airfares and insurance are not included.
Eligibility: General surveyors must be 16 years and over and have an interest in conservation and biodiversity and a good fitness level. People with disabilities can apply.
Groups or Individuals: Volunteers work in teams according to the area of interest. Minimum and maximum numbers also depend on the scientific component (for example, volunteers interested in the howler monkeys in Honduras work in teams with a maximum of five members). Individuals who wish to volunteer with friends or partners are welcome.
Annual no. of Volunteers: Over 1000.
Annual Projects: There are hundreds of different projects in six countries.
Partner Programmes: More than 10.
Selection & Interview Process: Most applicants come via universities and are undertaking a biology or geography degree, however, any volunteer who shows an interest in conservation and biodiversity is welcome.
In-country Support: All volunteers are accompanied by staff members both at all the sites and whilst out in the field. All sites are staffed by qualified scientists and have a medical officer. There are well-rehearsed evacuation procedures.

Rainforest Concern

73 Great Pulteney St, Bath BA2 4DL, UK
☎ +44 (0)122 548 1151
info@rainforestconcern.org
www.rainforestconcern.org
Rainforest Concern's objective is to conserve threatened rainforests and the biodiversity they contain. In Ecuador, volunteers might assist with scientific research, species auditing, surveying to compile flora and fauna lists, trail maintenance, reforestation, socio-economic work with local communities, teaching English and conservation issues to schools. Volunteers who work for shorter periods are typically placed in Costa Rica and

Panama at coastal reserves for the protection of the leatherback turtle.
Status: Registered charity.
Timing & Length of Placements: Volunteers are sent to the Ecuador project year-round and length of stay depends on availability of places. In Costa Rica and Panama the minimum stay is two weeks and volunteers are accepted from mid-March to early June.
Destinations: Ecuador, Costa Rica and Panama.
Costs: See cost and availability details for individual projects on the website.
Eligibility: An interest in conservation is a must. As some programmes require hiking to work sites, a degree of physical fitness may also be required, depending on the placement.
Groups or individuals: Volunteers work in teams according to the project and the area of interest. Individuals who want to volunteer with friends or partners are welcome.
Annual no. of Volunteers: 75-100
Annual Projects: 19
Partner Programmes: GVI, AV, Aqua-Firma, Steppes Discovery.
Selection & Interview Process: Some placements with Rainforest Concern are made in partnership with GVI, AV, Aqua-Firma; other projects can be applied for on the website.
In-country Support: Volunteers work with trained staff who often live and work with volunteers.

Scientific Exploration Society

Expedition Base, Motcombe, Shaftesbury, Dorset SP7 9PB, UK
☎ +44 (0)1747 853353
fax +44 (0)1747 851351
www.ses-explore.org
SES shares the same ethos as Raleigh: to take up a challenge and build teamwork skills. Expeditions have a scientific purpose: for example, mapping reefs or conducting an archaeological survey. Often SES is invited by host governments and local communities to achieve a specific goal.
Status: Registered charity.
Timing & Length of Placements: Expeditions leave throughout the year and generally last three weeks. Applications need to be in at least two to three months before departure so volunteers can attend a briefing day six weeks before departure.

Destinations: Bolivia, India, Mongolia, Philippines, Ecuador and many more.
Costs: A three-week expedition costs approximately £2500 to £3000, depending on the location, and includes everything, bar international flights.
Eligibility: No skills required. Applications welcome from anyone aged 18 and over. Best suited to fit, healthy individuals who are happy working in a team and learning new skills.
Groups or Individuals: Volunteers work in teams of about eight to 14 people.
Annual no. of Volunteers: 60-80
Annual Projects: 6
Partner Programmes: In-country scientific organisations and the British charity Just a Drop.
Selection & Interview Process: Application form, interview by phone or in person, briefing day.
In-country Support: All teams have an expert related to the project, and an expedition team doctor and dentist (to assist the local community).

Australasian Organisations

Cape Tribulation Tropical Research Station

PMB 5 Cape Tribulation, Qld. 4873, Australia
☎ +61 (0)7 4098 0063
fax +61 (0)7 301 1853
www.austrop.org.au

If doing ecological and animal research in paradise appeals to you, look into this station on the Coral Coast of Queensland, which is considered to be the jewel of the Australian Wet Tropics World Heritage Area. The station is focussed on issues of adaptation to climate change, both as it affects the environment and the human community. You might be radio-tracking bats, counting figs, stomping grass for forest regeneration, constructing station buildings, digging holes or manning the visitor centre. This is a very special area of rainforest sandwiched between the fringing reef and the coastal mountain range, and is home to a wide variety of animal habitats, from coastal reefs to tropical rainforest.
Status: Non-affiliated, funded by the not-for-profit, tax-exempt Austrop Foundation.
Timing & Length of Placements: Typically two

to three weeks, but extensions are rarely denied.
Destinations: Australia.
Costs: Volunteers pay about A$35 per day, which covers accommodation and food. Airfares are not covered.
Eligibility: The station prefers volunteers over 20: people with trade skills are especially welcome. Minor physical disabilities are OK. Volunteers must be proficient in English.
Annual no. of Volunteers: About 45.
Selection & Interview Process: Email CV and application form. Applicants are rarely refused.
In-country Support: Station staff support volunteers 24 hours a day.

Overseas Organisations

Archelon, The Sea Turtle Protection Society of Greece

Solomou 57, 104 32 Athens, Greece
☎ +30 210 523 1342
fax +30 210 523 1342
volunteers@archelon.gr, stps@archelon.gr
www.archelon.gr

If rescuing turtles and spending time on the shores of Greece sounds palatable, this could be the opportunity for you. The primary aim of Archelon is to protect sea turtles in Greece through monitoring and research, management plans, raising public awareness and rehabilitating sick and injured turtles. Volunteers must bring their own tents to stay on designated free campsites, restricted to Archelon volunteers. Archelon was instrumental in the establishment of the National Marine Park of Zakynthos, and is a world leader in its specialised area of marine wildlife research. When asked about his most memorable experience on the programme, Mian Vich, who was with the programme for a month, says it was 'the sensation you have the first time you see a turtle getting out the water and see her laying that huge amount of eggs, just 40cm from you'.
Timing & Length of Placements: The advised participation length is six weeks departure times vary according to the type of volunteer work, and are listed on the website.
Destinations: Greece, particularly in Crete and in Kyparissia Bay in Peloponnesus.
Costs: Once accepted, applicants pay a non-refundable participation fee of €250. A minimum amount of €15 per day should

Photo: Paul Dymond/Getty Images ©

A snapshot of conservation – a man meets a mangrove tree on Cape Tribulation, Queensland, Australia

cover basic food needs. Airfares to Greece are not included.

Eligibility: No special qualifications are required, although a driving licence, English-language skills or a boating licence will be appreciated. Volunteers need to be over 18 years old.

Groups or Individuals: Participants work in teams but applicants are not accepted in groups larger than two.

Annual no. of Volunteers: 500

Annual Projects: 5

Partner Programmes: Archelon is a member of the European Union for Coastal Conservation (EUCC), the European Environmental Bureau (EEB) and a partner to UNEP/Mediterranean Action Plan. Also, members of Archelon participate in the IUCN Marine Turtle Specialist Group.

In-country Support: Volunteers are trained and supervised by field leaders and experienced project members.

Skilled Volunteering

Fancy escaping the rat race and the daily grind of a nine-to-five lifestyle? Salvation could lie in a volunteer placement that will dovetail with your individual skill-set and culminate in a rewarding escape. This is a particularly attractive option for professional career-breakers or students who have just completed a degree programme. From programmes offered by Challenges Worldwide (CWW, listed right) to the fairly self-explanatory Lawyers Without Borders, the following listings are only a smattering of career-specific opportunities. If you don't see a good fit with your professional skills, don't worry – with a few well-aimed internet searches you're likely to find that there are niche opportunities out there for almost anyone.

International Organisations

Voluntary Service Overseas

Carlton House, 27A Carlton Drive, Putney, London, SW15 2BS, UK

☎ +44 (0)20 8780 7500

enquiry@vso.org.uk

www.vso.org.uk

VSO is an international development charity that works to alleviate poverty in the developing world by recruiting professional volunteers from countries around the world. Participants in the international volunteer programmes are typically skilled professionals who spend two years living abroad and applying their skills training and advising colleagues in an area of expertise. For more information about VSO, see p94.

UK Organisations

Challenges Worldwide (CWW)

54 Manor Pl, Edinburgh EH3 7EH, UK
☎ toll free +44 (0)845 2000 342
fax +44 131 225 9549
info@challengesworldwide.com
www.challengesworldwide.com

CWW is a charity based in Scotland that matches individual volunteers with three- to six-month assignments in developing countries. All placements are carefully planned to meet the specific needs of CWW's host partner organisations overseas, and therefore volunteers are matched according to their professional experience and work backgrounds. Volunteer assignments use the skills from a wide range of professions including legal, strategy, IT, communications and finance, to provide services in renewable energy, civic governance, fair trade, health and education.

Status: Registered charity.
Timing & Length of Placements: Departures happen year-round. Length of placement varies depending on the work but will be a minimum of three to six months for individuals. The length of personal and professional development assignments can range from six weeks to six months.
Destinations: Belize, India, Sri Lanka, Tanzania and Kenya, with plans to extend further into Asia and Africa.
Costs: £1500 contribution which covers end-to-end support, including pre-departure training and weekly appraisals; a logistics advisory service and fundraising support. Additional costs will be necessary for extras such as Chartered Management Qualification.
Eligibility: The average age of volunteers is 35, although volunteers can be aged 18 to 65. Volunteers are required to have some level of relevant education and experience and will be matched according to their skills and work backgrounds.
Groups or Individuals: Project work is designed for individuals, however, attempts will be made to find two projects within close proximity if partners wish to travel and stay together. Project work depends on the needs of the host partners in the developing country and their capacity to work with a given number of volunteers.
Annual no. of Volunteers: 100 plus.
Annual Projects: 100 plus.
Partner Programmes: Over 60.
Selection & Interview Process: Applicants submit a full CV and supporting documentation. Successful applicants will have a phone or face-to-face interview and be invited to attend the two-day predeparture preparation and training session in Edinburgh.
In-country Support: Support is provided through a local in-country placement leader. Full mentor support is provided by CWW recruitment and an overseas officer with 24-hour contact is available in emergencies.

Skillshare International

Imperial House, St Nicholas Circle, Leicester LE1 4LF, UK
☎ +44 116 2541862
info@skillshare.org
www.skillshare.org

Skillshare International works to reduce poverty and inequality in Europe, Africa and Asia by recruiting professionals to share their skills and experience with local communities to further economic and social development. Projects cover a wide range of activities and general management, agricultural, technical, educational and medical skills are all required.
Status: Registered charity.
Timing & Length of Placements: Recruitment takes place throughout the year. The average length of placement is 18 months.
Destinations: Botswana, Cambodia, Lesotho, South Africa, Nepal, Namibia, Swaziland, Mozambique, India, Uganda, Tanzania, Kenya, Mali and Burkina Faso.
Costs/Pay: Development workers are encouraged to raise £500 towards their placement cost. Skillshare International offers return flights, a small living allowance, free accommodation and comprehensive medical

Photo: www.biosphere-expeditions.org

Monitoring porcupines and other wildlife in the Namibian savannah with Biosphere Expeditions.

insurance, as well as ongoing support and supervision.

Eligibility: People with two years of relevant work experience can apply, including those with disabilities.

Groups or Individuals: The placements are for individuals. Occasionally it is possible for a partner and/or dependents to accompany.

Annual no. of Volunteers: Approximately 30.

Annual Projects: Approximately 65.

Partner Programmes: 65

Selection & Interview Process: Skillshare does not accept CVs. You can apply online at www.skillshare.org, either as a general applicant or in response to a specific role advertisement. The selection process includes an interview, referencing, medical and police checks. Candidates do not have to be based in the UK in order to be considered.

In-country Support: In-country staff provide ongoing support, including orientation, periodic reviews and help with medical emergencies. Full support is also available in rare cases of national emergencies.

North American Organisations

IESC Geekcorps
1900 M St NW, Ste 500
Washington DC 20036, USA
☎ +1 202 326 0280
fax +1 202 326 0289
iesc@iesc.org
www.iesc.org/geekcorps

This international non-profit organisation disseminates information and communication technology (ICT) in the developing world. IESC Geekcorps' volunteers and consultants aim to teach communities how to be digitally independent: able to create and expand private enterprise with innovative, appropriate and affordable ICT.

Status: Non-profit organisation.

Timing & Length of Projects: Four months; extensions and shorter projects are also available. Volunteers are needed year-round on a rolling basis.

Destinations: Bulgaria, Romania, Armenia, Kyrgyzstan, Mongolia, Thailand, Ghana, Rwanda, Zimbabwe, Senegal, Mali, Lebanon and Jordan.

Costs/Pay: All volunteer expenses are covered, including airfares, lodging, immunisations and basic medical insurance. A monthly stipend is also issued to each volunteer to reimburse them for meals and incidental expenses in the host country.

Eligibility: Volunteers must be in good health and have at least five years of professional experience. No nationality restrictions apply.

Groups or Individuals: Depending on the project, volunteers may work independently or in groups. All volunteers work with local counterparts to ensure project sustainability.

Annual no. of Volunteers: 15-20

Annual Projects: 4-5, with multiple volunteers on each project.

Partner Programmes: Four regional programmes, in collaboration with the US Agency for International Development (USAID).

Selection & Interview Process: The organisation designs its own programmes and identifies trusted partners at the outset. Skills, experience and adaptability are considered when matching volunteers to programmes.

In-country Support: Volunteers are given information about their host country prior to departure, and work with local partners on the ground. In-country personnel are responsible for volunteers' safety and wellbeing; if there are no local programme staff, the volunteer's primary contact is the home office in Washington, DC.

Lawyers Without Borders

750 Main St, Hartford CT 06103, USA
☎ +1 860 541 2288
fax +1 860 525 0287
info@lwob.org
www.lwob.org

This organisation is dedicated to connecting rule-of-law projects and initiatives, legally oriented issues in the human rights arena, projects and programmes involving capacity-building for emerging nations and regions emerging from strife or conflict, and situations calling for neutral observers and lawyers willing to serve pro bono.

Status: Registered charity.
Timing & Length of Placements: One week to one year.
Destinations: Latin America, the Caribbean, Africa and Eastern Europe.
Costs: Dependent upon the project and funding parameters. Some projects are entirely self-funding by the individual, some offer airfares but with all other costs borne by the volunteer.
Eligibility: All volunteers must have a law degree or be currently enrolled in law school. Eligibility of volunteers aged 22 to 30 depends upon their international experience. International experience is not required for volunteers aged 30 and over.
Groups or Individuals: Typically travel is solo or in small teams of two or more, rarely in groups.
Annual no. of Volunteers: 30
Annual Projects: 50
Selection & Interview Process: Written applications are followed by interview over the phone. In-person interviews are required under some circumstances. References must be supplied.

Operation Smile, Inc.

6435 Tidewater Dr, Norfolk, VA 23509
☎ +1 757 321 7645
www.operationsmile.org

Throughout the world, Operation Smile volunteers repair childhood facial deformities while building public and private partnerships that advocate for sustainable healthcare systems for children and their families. Their goal is to create smiles and change lives. Each Operation Smile international mission includes a student team consisting of one student sponsor and two student educators, who perform free evaluations and surgery to children with cleft lips, cleft palates, tumours and burns. Student educators teach oral rehydration, burn care and prevention, proper nutrition and dental care to patients and families.

Status: Not-for-profit organisation.
Timing & Length of placements: International medical missions are conducted year-round and are typically two weeks in length.
Destinations: Bangladesh, Bolivia, Brazil, Cambodia, China, Colombia, Democratic Republic of Congo, Ecuador, Egypt, Ethiopia, Haiti, Honduras, India, Jordan, Kenya, Mexico, Morocco, Nicaragua, Panama, Paraguay, Peru, the Philippines, Russia, South Africa, Thailand, Venezuela and Vietnam.
Costs: Each team member (both medical and non-medical) pays a team fee of US$500 per mission trip. Operation Smile arranges for air transportation, accommodation and most meals.
Eligibility: All medical volunteers must complete a credentialing process; requirements depend on the medical discipline. Student volunteers who travel on international missions must be 16, attend an Operation Smile International Leadership Conference and a Mission Training Workshop.
Groups or Individuals: Volunteers with partners and dependents are welcome.
Annual no. of Volunteers: Around 1200.
Annual Projects: In 2005, medical volunteers provided free surgery for 9334 children through international and local medical missions in more than 20 countries.
Selection & Interview Process: Medical volunteers should complete an application and submit it to be reviewed by the medical officer. All students can attend the International Leadership Conference. Applying for mission training is competitive and extensive.
In-country Support: Mission teams are hosted by Operation Smile International Foundations, which are responsible for all in-country mission logistics.

Azafady volunteers take a break on the Madagascan beach

Peace Corps

Paul D Coverdell Peace Corps Headquarters,
1111 20th St, NW, Washington, DC 20526, USA
☎ +1 855 855 1961
www.peacecorps.gov

In the US, the Peace Corps is one of the most readily recognised names in international volunteering. The organisation's roots go back to then-US Senator John F Kennedy's challenge to students at the University of Michigan to serve their country in the cause of peace by living and working in developing countries. Eventually, his vision gave rise to an agency of the Federal Government devoted to world peace and international friendship. Today, a placement with the Peace Corps could find you doing almost anything – from working in emerging and essential services in cutting-edge fields like information technology and communications, to the most basic community programmes in the developing world. For more information on the Peace Corps, see p96.

Emergency & Relief

If your interest in volunteering stems from dilettantish daydreaming about spending the school break parachuting in with a box of plasters to save the day, then don't bother reading on. The organisations listed below are definitely not for the casual volunteer looking for a good way to while away the summer. These opportunities are strictly for skilled volunteers dedicated to a life on the frontlines of humanitarian relief. For such individuals, working on the international stage with organisations such as those listed here is a worthy long-term goal.

This list includes many of the most selective volunteering opportunities in the world. Given the fact that they mostly operate in extremely unpredictable and difficult locations – often shattered by natural disaster or military conflict – the rigorous selection criteria that apply are a necessity for the safety of everyone involved. Since factors such as destination, length of placement and in-country support vary on a case-by-case basis, this information can't always be listed.

International Organisations

Doctors of the World

French Office: Médecins du Monde
62 Rue Marcadet, 75018 Paris, France
☎ +33 1 44 92 15 15
fax +33 1 44 92 99 99
www.medecinsdumonde.org

UK Office: 6th flr, 1 Canada Square, London E14 5AA
☎ +44 (0)20 7515 7534
fax +44 (0)20 7515 7560
www.doctorsoftheworld.org.uk
Like other organisations in this category, Doctors of the World is an international humanitarian organisation that sends medical and non-medical volunteers abroad to provide healthcare to vulnerable populations around the world. The organisation was formed in 1980. Today Doctors of the World's work is divided into three categories: emergency response to war and disaster, post-emergency rehabilitation, and long-term development projects. In addition to providing medical support, Doctors of the World's volunteers give a voice to the most marginalised people worldwide.

Status: Registered charity in the UK.
Timing & Length of Placements: Doctors of the World requires a commitment of a few weeks up to three months for emergency projects and six to 12 months for long-term development projects.
Costs/Pay: Transportation, housing and insurance are covered by the organisation. In addition, staff receive approximately £100 to £250 per month as a local allowance and a monthly compensation of between £600 and £800, deposited into their bank account at home.
Destinations: 60 countries worldwide.
Eligibility: Volunteers need to have at least two years of professional experience. This could be as a doctor, a nurse, a medical coordinator, an accountant, a logistician or a project manager. Aside from their projects in London, Doctors of the World does not accept medical students.
Groups or Individuals: Teams are composed of two to 12 international staff, along with 20 to 100 national staff.
Annual no. of Volunteers: 300
Annual Projects: 160
Selection & Interview Process: Send a CV and cover letter stating your availability and interests to the UK office by email or post. If shortlisted but no role, applicants are placed on a waiting list. If there is a matching role, candidates have final interviews in Paris.
In-country Support: All volunteers attend a three-day pre-departure training at our headquarters in Paris. They are also briefed individually on the context and the project's situation.

International Federation of the Red Cross and Red Crescent Societies (IFRC)

PO Box 372 CH-1211, Geneva 19, Switzerland
☎ +41 22 730 42 22
fax +41 22 733 03 95
www.ifrc.org
Depending on where you live, the Red Cross might bring to mind any number of community services. In the UK and the US, the Red Cross is concerned with disaster relief and mitigation, blood services or emergency preparedness and response. In other areas of the world, the Red Cross may operate ambulance services, provide wartime medical service or run orphanages. The IFRC is a non-religious organisation and, with millions of volunteers, the largest relief organisation in the world. Those interested in participating in domestic disaster relief should contact their local chapter. Those interested in joining international relief operations should be aware that it can literally take years (sometimes decades) of training and experience to be deployed on an international operation with the IFRC. That said, the organisation is often among the first on site delivering aid, setting up sheltering operations and distributing essentials in times of international crisis.
Status: World's largest humanitarian organisation, comprised of hundreds of International Red Cross and Red Crescent societies in almost every country in the world, including the American Red Cross and the British Red Cross.
Timing & Length of placement: Dependent on operation.
Destinations: Global.
Costs: The Red Cross usually funds all transportation and accommodation while a volunteer is on assignment.
Eligibility: Organisations under the IFRC umbrella have varying eligibility criteria.
Annual no. of Volunteers: Millions globally.
Selection & Interview Process: If you wish to volunteer with the Red Cross, begin by contacting your local chapter. The interview, training and eligibility requirements of international relief operations are extremely rigorous.

International Medical Corps

US Office: 1919 Santa Monica Blvd. Suite 400, Santa Monica, CA 90404 USA
☎ +1 310 826 7800
fax +1 310 442 6622
inquiry@internationalmedicalcorps.org
www.internationalmedicalcorps.org
UK Office: 3rd Floor, 254-258 Goswell Road, London EC1V 7EB, UK
☎ +44 (0) 207 253 0001
fax +44 (0) 207 250 3269
info@internationalmedicalcorps.org.uk
www.internationalmedicalcorps.org.uk

IMC is a private non-political, non-sectarian organisation that assists with healthcare training and relief services in the developing world. Though it might not have the recognition that Doctors Without Borders does, IMC is a major player in the field of international voluntary medical work, currently saving lives in Afghanistan, Chad, DRC, Iraq, Somalia, Sudan and Uganda (among others).
Status: Non-profit organisation.
Timing & Length of Placements: Assignments to various locations are for a minimum of six to eight weeks, though with highly technical positions a two- to four-week placement is sometimes possible.
Costs/Pay: In general, volunteers cover the cost of travel to their assignment. Per diem allowances, shared housing and emergency medical evacuation insurance are usually provided. In some instances, depending on funding, duration of contract and the person's speciality, the volunteer may be eligible for a monthly stipend.
Eligibility: Emergency roster volunteers are required to be ready for deployment within 24 to 72 hours and be professional doctors, nurses, lab technicians, nutritionists, EMTs, engineers or various medical administrators. There are other domestic opportunities in the US and UK that don't require medical training.
Selection & Interview Process: Submit a CV and cover letter via email or post. Promising applicants are then interviewed.

Médecins Sans Frontières (Doctors Without Borders)

78 Rue de Lausanne, Case Postale 116, 1211 Geneva 21, Switzerland
☎ +41 22 849 8484
fax +41 22 849 8404
www.msf.org

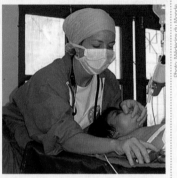

Photo: Médecins du Monde

A Médecins du Monde staff member bringing emergency relief following the 2005 Pakistan quake

With offices in 19 countries and operations around the world, MSF is one of the best-recognised international voluntary medical relief organisations. It delivers emergency aid to people affected by armed conflict, epidemics and natural or man-made disasters and has been doing so for over a quarter of a century. MSF is one of the first organisations to arrive on the scene of a disaster, dispatching teams with specialised medical equipment specifically suited to the assignment. Each year, MSF-affiliated doctors, nurses, water-and-sanitation experts, logisticians and other medical and non-medical professionals tackle more than 3800 field assignments in over 70 countries, working with over 22,000 locally trained staff.
Status: International collective of non-governmental, non-profit volunteer organisations.
Timing & Length of Placements: Physicians are required to be available for a minimum of six months, though surgeons and anaesthesiologists may be accepted for shorter assignments.
Destinations: MSF works in more than 70 countries.
Costs/Pay: The organisation covers all transportation and accommodation costs and pays a monthly stipend of approximately €900 and a per diem allowance in local currency.
Eligibility: The general criteria for working abroad are: at least two years of professional

experience in a relevant, usually medically related field; availability for at least six months; current professional credentials; and relevant work or travel experience outside the US. Medical students are not accepted.

Groups or Individuals: An average field project team has four to 12 international volunteers working in collaboration with up to 200 local staff members.

Selection & Interview Process: After eligible applicants complete an application form, a motivation letter and a current CV, they will be contacted for an interview. Applicants who advance past that stage are moved into a pool of active volunteers and considered for deployment based on their qualifications.

In-country Support: Volunteers are briefed on the region's security situation before going to the field and are given specific security protocols on-site.

An Emergency Relief Experience

Over the years, my work has taken me around the world, and as I travelled to more and more developing countries I began to appreciate just how lucky we in the West really are. As a backpacker travelling through places, there was never enough time to do more than just sightsee, and I never felt I was helping the poorer people I encountered. When I got home I wanted to do something more, so I completed an advanced course in first aid and started investigating humanitarian organisations that I could volunteer with. I had a background in arduous adventure sports, so I was looking for an organisation that would test my limits. I found out about a small Australian medical NGO called Australian Aid International (AAI; www.aai.org.au).

AAI appealed to me because of its small size. This makes it a very flexible, nimble and effective organisation in the wake of a disaster, where, in the first few critical weeks, everything is mayhem. AAI is a non-profit Non-Government Organisation, committed to mitigating the double burden of poverty and poor access to quality healthcare in regions where healthcare systems and medical infrastructure have collapsed. AAI regards healthcare as a fundamental human right, and strives to make it available in some of the most remote and dangerous regions of the world, targeting those communities where the need is greatest.

In October of 2005, an earthquake measuring 7.6 on the Richter scale hit northern Pakistan, resulting in over 86,000 fatalities and almost three and a half million people being made homeless. I decided to go with AAI to Pakistan, leaving my wife and two small children behind in Australia. I was worried that I might not be effective, as I had no medical training and it was my first time volunteering, but AAI were looking for determined, fit and eager young individuals to provide logistical support and first-aid services to their team of medical personnel in the most remote and dangerous places in Kashmir, and I fitted the bill.

Once in Pakistan, we were sent to the remotest villages that had received no aid. We were either choppered in or trekked for hours to reach villages cut off by landslides. Most vulnerable were the young, the old and the traumatised, who were unwilling or unable to seek help due to the remote location and various social and cultural barriers.

What I saw was complete devastation. As far as the eye could see, homes had been flattened and people wandered around aimlessly. Whole mountains had opened up and moved. Hillsides had collapsed and swallowed up roads, making crossing them dangerous, even on foot, as aftershocks were still being felt weeks after the initial quake. But what struck me the most was talking to people. Everyone I met had lost someone in their family; some were the only survivors. We would talk to each other despite the lack of a common language, but I couldn't get over the empty look of sadness and mourning in their eyes. We slept in tents only metres from freshly dug graves, as they were the only safe places to camp.

For mile upon mile, the hills, ridges and valleys were dotted with fallen houses. Poorly built to begin with, these structures stood no chance against the earthquake's fury; their occupants possessed even less hope of survival. The dwellings in these remote villages were built without effective foundations; they were just large rocks piled on top of each other to act as walls, and roofs made of the same large stones and foot-wide wooden beams held together by two feet of mud. When the earthquake struck, there was no time for people to evacuate their homes, as most buildings toppled in the first few seconds, burying people alive or killing them instantly as heavy roof beams and 100kg rocks fell on top of them.

The hardest thing for me was dealing with the children. Having two children of my own, it was hard not to become emotional when little boys and girls wandered up to me with deformed limbs due to untreated broken bones. Large wounds were common among children, and so were scabies and acute respiratory infections –

Paul Piaia about to be airlifted into a remote Pakistani village to bring emergency relief following the 2005 earthquake.

not to mention the emotional trauma of losing parents, brothers, sisters and friends. One boy was stuck under the rubble for eight hours when his school collapsed. He had seen his friends die and heard their screams only feet away. He had broken his hip in three places, and when he went to the hospital they told him to go home and sleep on it and it would get better. We found him after a week in bed, in agony, unable to move. We stabilised his leg and got him to a hospital to be properly treated. Another case was of a boy who had a large open wound that had become infected. We came across his father by accident, who told us about him (in very broken English), and told us he was going to amputate his son's leg. We quickly walked the two hours to his house to find him, but luckily the wound was healing well and the leg did not require amputation.

I returned home after a few weeks and instantly got the guilt feelings that so many experience once they return to their own country. Thoughts such as, 'Did I do enough?' 'I should have stayed longer.' 'I wonder how the people we treated are.' 'Did they survive?' whirled around my brain. Once home I continued monitoring events in Pakistan but it wasn't long until I was needed again, this time in East Timor in June 2006.

Today, I continue to volunteer with AAI, helping with their website and public relations. The time I spent volunteering abroad was one of the most fulfilling things I've done. It's hard to stay focused at the scene of a disaster as, at first glance, the work you do seems too insignificant to make a difference. I firmly believe, however, that if everyone does their little bit, situations as a whole can be improved. The camaraderie in these places was fantastic, as people from all over the world rushed to the aid of innocent victims who, without our help, would definitely have perished.

Paul Piaia, Formerly Special Cartographic Project Manager, Lonely Planet

Volunteers assist with
climate change research at
the Arctic's edge

06 Structured & Self-Funding Volunteer Programmes

Instead of following a leader down a plotted trail, would you rather just be handed a map and allowed to find your own way? Rather than having a portion ladled into your bowl, would you prefer to dig into the dish yourself, making sure you've snagged a little extra of your favourite bit? If you've answered 'yes' to these questions, then structured volunteering programmes may be the best option for you.

Structured programmes are the middle ground between organised and DIY programmes. They mark X on the map for you, but reaching X and deciding what to do once you arrive there are often left up to you. The majority of structured programmes are run by small, grassroots organisations who don't have the capacity (or desire) to develop and run all-inclusive, package-style programmes. Many of these organisations are based overseas in the country in which they operate, and are therefore run by locals. Volunteers usually work in very small groups or individually in conjunction with these organisations.

Structured programmes are great for people who want flexibility in their placement and don't feel the need to have their hand held. Consequently, they're popular with older volunteers, people who are taking a career break, and those who have previously travelled or volunteered overseas. These programmes can provide some of the most rewarding volunteering experiences. However, to enjoy this kind of programme you need to have particular character traits: you need to be independent and self-motivated, have initiative and relish a challenge.

Nayna Wood volunteered as a teacher with Development in Action in India (DiA, p165). Her motivation for choosing a structured programme echoes that of many other volunteers who've chosen the same option:

I had travelled overseas independently before and wasn't looking to have my hand held or to be restricted by a strict programme of activities. However, I wasn't sure how easy it would be to be introduced to an organisation I could volunteer with myself, or even where to start in a country as vast as India. Plus, it was good to know that there was some extra support in terms of logistics or if I needed help in an emergency situation.

A desire for independence, cultural immersion and insights into grassroots development work are also common reasons for choosing a structured programme. Tom Wilmot, who worked as an engineer in India, explains why he chose to volunteer with Development in Action:

There were many reasons for not volunteering with a packaged expedition. I wanted the experience of working in development but without the group mentality of a working party. I felt this option would give me much more scope for engaging with the local culture. I looked at the packaged expeditions and felt that while they would have been very enjoyable, they would have offered me much less independence. Also, I wouldn't have got a well-rounded experience of development work. I like the fact that DiA is a non-profit organisation which is no frills and down to earth.

Ben Donaldson volunteered in Thailand as a teacher and helped install a water system with the Karen Hilltribes Trust (p169). He had similar reasons for volunteering with a grassroots, structured programme:

I wanted to be part of a smaller, more tightly knit group so I could grasp the full impact of the charity's work, and not get lost in bureaucracy and other behind-the-scenes action. I wasn't looking for a highly organised operation with no surprises or flexibility, and I didn't get one. The experience far exceeded my expectations – it was far more hands-on and offered plenty of scope for improvisation and creativity, and you could get as involved as you wanted to.

The fluid, self-determined nature of structured programmes can be daunting to people who haven't travelled or volunteered before. If you're considering taking this route, you need to be sure you're comfortable with the level of self-reliance expected of you by the organisation you're considering volunteering with. To help ease the burden, most organisations will be happy to give you tips and advice on making your travel arrangements and can put you in touch with past volunteers who can also give you pointers.

How Do They Work?
Costs

A major feature of structured programmes is that they're self-funding. This means that volunteers not only make their own travel arrangements but also cover all their travel-related costs, including insurance. Structured programmes do charge fees but these are often much less than those of organised programmes. The amount you'll pay covers things such as organising your placement, a short orientation upon your arrival and your room and board during the placement. That's usually about all they do cover, though.

The cost of a placement depends largely on the country in which it's based, how long you go for and what work you'll be doing there. Fees charged by organisations based overseas tend to be lower than those charged by conservation projects, which need to cover equipment, training and running costs, while fees for community development projects can be next to nothing.

Some volunteers raise funds to cover the costs of their placement and travel, but as fees are often low, many volunteers can afford to pay out of their own pockets. If you do decide to fundraise, be prepared to put in a lot of time and energy. For fundraising advice see Raising the Money (p48), and the Fun, Fun, Funds box on the next page for more ideas.

Fun, Fun, Funds

Thinking of fundraising to cover the costs of your placement? Consider these tried-and-tested methods:

~ Bring the noise and organise a night of live music.

~ Add some humour to the raffle idea (see p52).

~ Hold a car-boot or garage sale.

~ Toast your endeavour with a pub night.

~ Sing or play your way overseas by busking.

~ Display your creative side and sell home-made goods.

~ Get energised with a sponsored swim, bike ride, run or dance-a-thon.

Selection & Eligibility

The selection process for structured placements largely depends on the type of work you will be doing and where the organisation is based. Organisations based in the volunteer's home country will often hold telephone or face-to-face interviews, while those based overseas are usually restricted to online applications. In the latter case, it is very important that you make a special effort to find out whether the organisation you're applying for a placement with is one you'd be happy working with and that seeks to match your interests and abilities with its needs. Wherever possible, talk to people who have volunteered with the organisation in the past; most organisations are happy to give out these contacts.

For skilled positions, the selection process is fairly strict – proof of qualifications is often required and references checked – but for many structured programmes, the only requirement is that you are at least 18 years old. Some organisations state a preference for experience in a particular field, but most welcome volunteers from a wide range of backgrounds and ages. Instead of specific skills, many structured programmes list attributes like commitment, enthusiasm, a spirit of adventure and flexibility as necessary qualities. However, the two most important qualities you'll require are motivation and initiative, as the nature of these placements generally means that it is up to you to determine both what kind of involvement you want to have and your level of involvement.

Tom Wilmot's experience of volunteering in India with Development in Action (p165) illustrates just how important these qualities are:

I found that I needed to be proactive in choosing and finding jobs to do. DiA doesn't specify what work volunteers will do, since it's entirely up to the partner organisations. At Barli it was really a case of communicating what sort of thing I wanted to do, appearing keen and motivated, and then getting on with it. This was the secret of my success as a volunteer. There were plenty of opportunities to do a wide variety of work and, depending on their skills, volunteers could exploit these opportunities and contribute in many different ways.

Michele Moody took up a manual labour placement with Volunteer Africa (p171). She speaks of the necessity of self-motivation in a placement:

Once on site and participating in the project, we had complete freedom over what we did and this motivated us to push ourselves harder than we may have done if we had specific tasks each day. We knew what the goal of the project was and were keen to make our mark.

Matthew Sykes, who taught in Brazil with the Association Iko Poran (p157), also found that being pushed to take initiative was very motivating:

Iko Poran places a lot of emphasis on individual volunteers making a unique contribution by using their particular skills and experiences. This was very challenging, but far more rewarding than simply being told what to do.

Length of Programmes

While some structured programmes offer two-week placements, most ask for a minimum commitment of at least a month and others require volunteers to stay for a minimum of three to six months. Almost all programmes prefer longer-term commitments. Because of their flexible nature, many organisations will allow you to extend your stay.

Heather Graham did exactly this when she volunteered at Casa Guatemala (p160) on the Rio Dulce in Guatemala:

Originally, I was only planning to stay for six months, but I ended up staying almost three years, and I still go back every year. Because of this I have participated in almost all aspects of the project, from being farm supervisor to store manager to working in the administration of the orphanage.

What to Look for

This depends entirely on what you're after. One of the first things you need to determine is whether to volunteer through an organisation based in your home country or one based overseas. Both options have their advantages. Sending agencies and organisations in your home country can offer face-to-face assistance prior to the placement and pre-departure support. It's often easier to discuss expectations and potential hurdles with someone from your own culture and to check out the reputation of an organisation located in your own country. On the other hand, overseas organisations often charge cheaper rates and you can be pretty sure that all of your fee is going directly to the local community. The programme is likely to be very grassroots, with all aspects of the project run and managed by locals.

It's important to have clear expectations of your experience: do you want to undertake a certain type of work; use a particular skill; be immersed in a new culture or have the opportunity to accomplish something on your own initiative? If so, will the organisation enable you to achieve your aim(s)?

Gemma Niebieszczanski volunteered in Thailand with the Karen Hilltribes Trust (p169) and gives this advice:

Think about what you want to get out of your volunteer experience, where you'd like to go and what you'd like to do. For me, the aim of the trip was to get some work experience in a developing country in order to pursue a career in overseas development. Therefore, I wanted a long-term project and ideally something that would give me the opportunity to do more than just teach.

In pinpointing a programme that suits you, try and determine what the primary aims of a given programme are. For example, is the programme focused mainly on cultural exchange and learning about development work, or on practical work? To what degree is it able to offer opportunities in these areas? As structured programmes are generally more loosely organised and grassroots in nature, volunteers are often in a great position to gain an insight into development work, which is the focus of many placements. For volunteers who were hoping for a placement focused more on practical work, this can be frustrating: many complain of feeling 'useless' and of being unable to use their skills or get their teeth into any 'real work'. Others are happy to simply go with the flow, experience the culture and exchange knowledge, and see working as a bonus.

Peggy Melmoth took this perspective when volunteering in India with Indian Volunteers for Community Service (IVCS, now called Volunteers for Rural India (VRI), p168):

What I liked about IVCS was the emphasis on observing and learning. You are a 'project visitor', not a 'volunteer'. This allowed me to try out lots of different types of work: I painted murals, helped with English conversation classes, taught hypnotherapy and joined yoga and Hindi classes. The overall experience was very fulfilling.

Most volunteers look for a balance between giving through work and receiving something in return. Katie Hill, who taught in India through Development in Action (p165), feels that she found the right balance:

DiA is a small organisation that depends on volunteers, but it focuses on development education. It's not just about going out, doing the placement and then coming back. The work done with partner organisations in India is realistic, and is as much about learning and bringing experiences back to the UK as helping out in India. I learnt far more than I could have ever given in such a short space of time. I gained an insight into development work that I wouldn't have had with a big, packaged expedition. I think this will be valuable to me, those around me, and my future career.

Oliver Middlemiss, who taught tribal children in rural India with Dakshinayan (p157), also feels the scales were well balanced:

The education went both ways. While the children were learning English, I was learning that kids are kids wherever you are in the world. Through Dakshinayan, I learnt first-hand what rural India and rural development are really about.

Look at how many partners or projects the organisation works with. If it's only one or a few, then it's easier to determine whether the organisation can offer you what you're after. With structured programmes, particularly with overseas, grassroots organisations, having lots of partners is not necessarily a negative factor – it can be an asset. So long as the organisation has an ongoing, proven relationship with these partners, you may find exactly what you're after. As Matthew Sykes discovered in Brazil:

The number of contacts that Iko Poran has means they can find a good fit with the skills and interests of volunteers.

While the best way to determine if an organisation is right for you is by getting in touch with some of their past volunteers, in the end you should trust your instincts. When asked why he chose to volunteer with Cultural Destination Nepal (CDN), Michael Best says:

I didn't have any real reasons for choosing CDN over another organisation. The picture that CDN painted for me appealed to me as a person. It was all very natural from the moment I received their letter of acceptance.

Expectations

According to an ancient Chinese proverb, 'The one who goes with an empty cup may have it filled. The one who goes with a full cup leaves no room for new experience.' In other words, be open to the unexpected and don't head off with such a full agenda that you miss out on opportunities to learn things or to make a difference. Volunteering with structured programmes generally means that there won't be a clearly defined task awaiting you. How the placement evolves is, to a large extent, left up to you and it's unlikely you will be guided every step of the way. Therefore, you need to expect as many stumbles as successes.

After volunteering in India, Katie Hill advises:

Be realistic. This is difficult to begin with because of all the excitement, but soon enough reality will hit and it's best to be prepared. Things aren't going to be easy, and there are going to be days of self-doubt and frustration. Achieving anything in such a short space of time is difficult. People spend their whole lives doing work such as you may be doing – a few months is nothing really. Be realistic about why you're volunteering. You will not change the world, but you will learn a whole lot. It probably won't 'change your life', but it will be an experience that will stay with you, influence future decisions and hopefully those around you for the rest of your life.

Structured programmes are more about the overall experience, especially as they often involve a high level of cultural immersion. It's likely that what you accomplish and take away with you – what you will look back on as your most rewarding experience – will not be what you expected.

Thinking back to his placement in Brazil, Matthew Sykes says:

It probably sounds corny, but I really did take a lot of pleasure from how chuffed the kids were when they were able to make themselves understood in English. Even when lessons didn't go quite so well, you could tell that it meant a lot to them that two foreigners had come to spend time with them. They also gained a lot of confidence – even teaching us a bit of Portuguese.

It's worth questioning how reasonable your expectations are at the outset. Michael Best, who volunteered in Nepal, was in need of a reality check:

I went away thinking that the trip would change me so much, that I would come back in a Zen state and everything would be right with the world. Well, that didn't happen. I got involved in the trivialities of life in Nepal as if I were still at home. So in a way the trip taught me one big thing: no matter where in the world you go, whether to Africa, Asia or America, you're always you. There is no big change, maybe just a little growth.

Pros & Cons

As with other types of volunteering experience, there are pros and cons to structured placements. While these vary between organisations, there are some common ones that can affect your volunteering experience. Consider the following information when deciding if a structured placement is for you and, in particular, if a specific organisation meets your needs.

Cost

The low cost of structured placements is a drawcard for many volunteers. Far less expensive than most organised placements, structured programmes open up international volunteering to those without a fat wallet. Even when airfares, insurance and any necessary in-country travel, accommodation and food costs are tacked on to the placement fee, structured programmes are still considerably cheaper. This is largely due to the DIY factor; you're not paying anyone to book transport for you or to act as a guide etc.

Matthew Sykes's experience of volunteering through a structured placement in Brazil reassured him that he chose the best deal:

We thought that the fully packaged expeditions seemed overpriced for what they offered and this was confirmed after a while in Rio. Iko Poran also acts as the local coordinator for packaged firms so, essentially, we were cutting out the middle man and saving quite a lot of money. We are very independent people and didn't want any of the hand-holding that might come with a packaged scheme.

If you are comfortable taking on the role of middle man and prefer to hunt down the best deals for flights and insurance yourself, then you may find that structured programmes suit your personality as much as your finances.

Of at least equal appeal is the fact that most organisations offering structured placements are small and do not have large overheads. Because of this, volunteers often feel that more of their money is going directly to where it is needed most. They also feel that their role as a volunteer isn't simply to feed money into the organisation, but to make a genuine contribution through both a modest placement fee and actual on-the-ground activity.

Gerrard Graf, who taught at an orphanage in Tanzania through Volunteer Africa (p171), chose a structured placement for this reason:

I wanted to be part of a volunteer project where I could see that I was making a real and tangible difference to the people I was working with and for. With some of the fully packaged expeditions, it is questionable whether you are actually providing any real benefits aside from money. And this money in itself can sometimes be misspent or used inappropriately. The Volunteer Africa programme was extremely transparent.

Edwin Griffiths had a similar experience when teaching in Brazil with Iko Poran (p157):

A lot of the other volunteering organisations appeared to be very money-orientated; this one was a lot cheaper and I knew that half of the money I paid was going directly to the project.

Freedom & Flexibility

Structured programmes offer volunteers the opportunity to create and tailor their placement to suit their own interests and skills. This appealed to Nayna Wood when she taught in India with DiA (p165):

A DiA placement is very flexible, and the fact that I could have an input into where I was placed and a relatively large degree of independence during my placement was also a great bonus. I really enjoyed the freedom I had and it allowed me to make much better use of my very short time than I might have done in a more tailored environment. Some of the most interesting and enjoyable experiences I had came out of using my initiative and from being the only volunteer at the time.

Gerrard Graf has similar memories of his time spent teaching in Africa:

The main benefits were that you could see a real difference being made and could work within a flexible and rewarding environment. The fact that we were able to introduce and develop new and existing ideas and projects meant we could readily utilise all our skills to assist where we felt help was most required. Overall, the experience exceeded my expectations – it was one of the most enjoyable and rewarding things I have ever done.

However, the freedom to determine the course of your placement can also pose problems. Volunteers left to their own devices in communities where they don't speak the language, and may be suffering culture shock, can find themselves feeling bored or frustrated. The onus is often on the volunteer to plan a course of action, and if this is something they've never done before, it can be daunting. It's well worth putting some time and energy into researching and preparing for your placement to head off these potential problems.

The way in which structured placements are set up also means that volunteers have much more flexibility with their travel itineraries. As volunteers book their own transport and travel, most tack some independent travel on to the beginning or end of their placement. This gives them the chance to round out their experience of a country, seeing it through the eyes of a short-term resident as well as those of a tourist. And as most volunteers manage to pick up a little of the language while on their placement, as well as an understanding of the culture and day-to-day practicalities, it's easy to gain the confidence to travel independently after their placement is over.

Cultural Immersion

Most volunteers on structured programmes are placed individually or in very small groups within a local community, so cultural immersion often plays a large role in their experience. Almost all volunteers find this a rewarding part, if not the highlight of, their placement.

Michael Best speaks highly of his cultural experience in Nepal:

I was completely embraced by the local population. As far as I'm concerned this was the 'experience'. There would have been no point in me travelling to Nepal (a country vastly different from my own) and surrounding myself with anybody except the local people. The most rewarding aspect of the experience was the sense of being integrated into the community. Over the course of the placement I got to know the parents of the children I was teaching: I bought my papers from them in the morning, sat on the bus with them in the afternoon and shared a Coke with them while watching the sunset in the evening.

Nayna Wood's experience in Africa also highlighted the importance of cultural interaction:

I don't see how you can learn anything meaningful about a place without interacting with the locals; you may as well be watching them on television. Even with a language barrier it is amazing how much you can learn about a place and its people with a bit of effort.

Past volunteers recommend that those after in-depth cultural immersion choose a programme that offers homestays, as it is gives you the chance to join in the everyday life of locals.

Gemma Niebieszczanski describes her experience of living with a Karen hilltribe family in Thailand:

All volunteers with KHT live with a Karen family in their house. I shared a room with another volunteer, but we ate meals and spent our free time with the rest of the family. We really became involved in village life and gained a sense that the teaching was only one part of our experience. A lot of it was about cultural exchange and really getting to know how these people live. People were always keen to talk to me and I made many friends, both from my village and other villages nearby; this definitely enhanced my experience: I felt I was part of the village and could really get to know the Karen lifestyle. I don't think there was any way I could have had more interaction with the local population, and I certainly wouldn't have changed that.

Ben Donaldson also lived with a Karen Hilltribe family and found it equally rewarding:

Living with a local family was probably the most special part of the whole experience. Being welcomed as a child of their own was quite amazing. Socialising with the locals was an essential part of every waking minute, let alone every day. Privacy was a real rarity, but this suited me fine.

Even if the programme you're interested in doesn't offer homestays, the flexibility of structured programmes generally means that you will have free time to immerse yourself in the culture. As with most aspects of a structured placement, the level of cultural interaction you have is largely dependent on the initiative you take, as well as on your cross-cultural communication skills.

Oliver Middlemiss, who lived and volunteered with a rural community in India, describes how he got to know the locals:

You had to pitch the interaction at the right level. Kids were easy to get on with, as all you needed was a football or Frisbee and off you went! The adult villagers were naturally a lot more stand-offish, and you had to earn their respect. It is important not to dive straight into a community and start acting as if you've known everyone for years.

It should, of course, be noted that if the idea of being dropped on your own into a foreign culture with people who speak a different language makes you break out in a cold sweat, then you need to think carefully about which programme you choose. There are structured programmes that always place volunteers in pairs, and others (particularly those in conservation) where volunteers work in groups. Bridging a cultural gap alone is certainly not going to appeal to everyone. If this is the case for you, it's best to recognise this before you sign up. Also, if privacy is important to you, look for a programme that offers alternatives to homestays.

In-Country Support

Organisations offering structured programmes are generally small and have little infrastructure. While this can be appealing in regard to transparency and cost, when it comes to support in emergencies, structured programmes can suddenly appear rather less attractive. Most organisations are upfront about the support they're able to offer and the fact that the onus is often on the volunteer to be as self-reliant as possible. It pays to be aware from the outset about what help you can expect to receive in an emergency. If you're going to be placed in the middle of nowhere, at a considerable distance from a telephone or hospital, be sure to take all precautions necessary to ensure your safety in the event of something going wrong.

While a degree of isolation may sound adventurous and exciting, Ben Donaldson, who volunteered in Thailand, paints a rather different picture:

An emergency arose involving my mother back in England having a terrible stroke. Due to the remoteness of my village and my not teaching for a few days, there was no easy way of contacting me, so it was five days before I heard. It hit me very badly – she had been in intensive care almost a week before I spoke to my father.

Even if there is access to telecommunication networks, volunteers are often left largely to their own devices in an emergency. When volunteering in Africa, Michele Moody did not find a telephone a very comforting replacement for personal, in-country support:

We had a satellite phone that we could use in case of emergency, but I feel that as we were in such an isolated area, it would have been difficult to get help to us quickly. I would have been much happier if we had an experienced member of the organisation working with us at the project.

But don't let such stories put you off. Most organisations do take all possible precautions, ensuring there is first aid available on site, and that volunteers are placed within a reasonable distance from a hospital and given a 24-hour contact number for emergencies. Most volunteers are placed in pairs as well, and working and/or living with another volunteer offers a huge amount of support. Horror stories are extremely rare, but you should still make sure the programme offers a level of support you feel comfortable with. Once you're in the field, take note of any limitations in the in-country support available and be sure to have a plan of action in case any emergencies arise.

Nayna Wood describes the in-country support available to her while volunteering in India:

Two volunteer coordinators provide support to volunteers if needed. I found that they were very useful, but felt that they were not equipped to deal with a couple of situations of a more serious nature that arose. Ultimately, we dealt with these situations on our own, as if we were independent travellers. Perhaps a more tailored package would place a greater emphasis on the duty of care. I think that as long as volunteers are aware that they are ultimately independent travellers with additional support, then they should be fine.

Earthwatch volunteers helping preserve the precious coastal ecology of the Bahamas

Development Placements

The kinds of projects working in development are as diverse as they are numerous. Work in tsunami-affected regions of Thailand; erect community buildings in Cameroon; or teach in aboriginal communities in Canada's arctic north. The possibilities for development volunteering are almost inexhaustible and the destinations span the globe. This section lists some of the most worthwhile, stimulating and exciting projects in this field. It's divided into sections according to the type of work involved.

Overseas Organisations

Community Development

Association Iko Poran
Rua do Oriente, 280/201, Santa Teresa, Rio de Janeiro, RJ, Brazil
☎ +55 3852 2916
fax +55 3852 2917
www.ikoporan.org

Iko Poran works with local NGOs to tackle specific challenges identified by Brazilian community councils. Placements are incredibly diverse and developed according to volunteers' abilities and interests, but one of the main objectives is the exchange of experiences. Past volunteers have taught dance, music and circus skills; worked in health, translation, fundraising, business development and website development; and trained locals in film-making and photography. The organisation acts as a facilitator in the placement but stresses that volunteers must take an active role in planning their involvement.

Status: Not-for-profit organisation.
Timing & Length of Projects: Three to 24 weeks. Volunteers can join projects on the second or fourth Friday of every month.
Destinations: Brazil.
Costs: The programme fee is about US$1100 for up to four weeks and about US$100 per additional week, including a 20-hour intensive Portuguese course, airport pick-up, orientation and four weeks' lodging. Approximately half of the fee is donated to the partner organisation with which the volunteer is working.
Eligibility: The minimum age is 18 but no specific skills or experience are required. It's recommended that volunteers have basic Portuguese or Spanish. Those with physical disabilities are welcome to apply, but all accommodation has stairs.
Groups or Individuals: You can apply in a group of six to 30 or individually. Volunteers share accommodation in designated houses.
Annual no. of Volunteers: 500
Annual Projects: 40
Partner Programmes: 40
Selection & Interview Process: Online application and email discussion to agree upon an individualised placement.
In-country Support: Volunteer accommodation is situated near the organisation's office, with assistance available at all times.

Dakshinayan

F-1169, Chittaranjan Park, 1st Flr, New Delhi 110019, India
☎ +91 9836 596426, +91 9934 572399
info@dakshinayan.org
www.dakshinayan.org

This long-standing, very grassroots organisation works in remote communities in India's tribal state of Jharkhand. Its emphasis is as much on what volunteers gain as on what they give; participants teach basic English or maths to village children and come away having experienced the realities of development work first-hand. Volunteers live within the villages in basic conditions (no running water or electricity) and therefore experience a very high level of cultural immersion.

Status: Registered trust.
Timing & Length of Projects: Projects run throughout the year. Volunteers can join anytime but preferably towards the start of the month. The minimum period of stay is 30 days, with a maximum of five months.
Destinations: India.
Costs: The fee is US$300 per month, which includes food and accommodation. Volunteers cover all expenses to and from the project.
Eligibility: Participants need to be above 18 years of age. There is no age limit, but those who apply should be physically fit.
Groups or Individuals: Volunteers can participate individually or with a friend, partner or family. Volunteers are usually placed with one or two other participants.
Annual no. of Volunteers: 20-30

Annual Projects: 2

Partner Programmes: Dakshinayan does not partner with any organisation in India, but unofficially supports many.

Selection & Interview Process: Applications are accepted online. There will be an interview with at least one of the trustees in Kolkata. Briefing and travel instructions are given during this time.

Himalayan Light Foundation

GPO Box 12191, Dhumbarai (Peepalbot), Kathmandu, Nepal
☎ +977 144 25393
fax +977 144 12924
info@hlf.org.np
www.hlf.org.np

Working in the Himalaya and South Asia, this small, grassroots organisation aims to improve the quality of life in remote villages by introducing environmentally friendly, renewable-energy technologies. Through its Solar Sisters Programme (SSP), volunteers subsidise and work with local technicians to install solar electricity systems in community buildings like medical clinics or schools. During the installation, volunteers stay with a local family. HLF also runs a number of other projects which self-funding professionals with appropriate skills and training can occasionally join.

Status: NGO.

Timing & Length of Projects: Solar Sisters Programmes are typically 10 days long, but volunteers can choose to stay up to five months to support the community or other HLF projects. Projects are open year-round.

Destinations: Nepal, Sri Lanka, India and Bhutan.

Costs: The cost varies in each country; in Nepal the SSP costs US$1350 and in Sri Lanka it's US$1490. This includes accommodation, food, an administration fee and the cost of the Solar Home System that the volunteer installs.

Eligibility: The minimum age is 18. There are no required skills or experience for SSP, but volunteers must have sound health and be willing and able to trek and travel to remote areas. Volunteers must also have full insurance coverage for health and emergency evacuation.

Groups or Individuals: Volunteers can work individually or in a family or group of up to 15.

Annual no. of Volunteers: Approximately 15.

Annual Projects: The number of projects depends on the demand from communities and the number of volunteers.

Partner Programmes: HLF works with local, grassroots partners as well as South Asia Regional NGO partners in Sri Lanka, Bhutan and India.

Selection & Interview Process: Apply via email or telephone.

In-country Support: Volunteers are accompanied by HLF staff who are able to provide first aid, and have access to a 24-hour contact person.

Kathmandu Environmental Education Project (KEEP)

PO Box 9178, Kersharmahal, Thamel, Kathmandu, Nepal
☎ +977 144 10952
fax +977 144 10292
keep@info.com.np
www.keepnepal.org

Originally established to inform travellers and local businesses how to minimise the negative effects of tourism, KEEP now places volunteers in Nepalese communities for an exchange of experience, culture and knowledge. Placements are mainly to teach English, but experienced applicants can also assist grassroots NGOs in conservation, health, community development, orphanages or with street children. Placements are also tailored to the interests and experience of volunteers.

Status: Registered NGO.

Timing & Length of Projects: Short-term placements are for a minimum of one week, and teaching placements for a minimum of two months. Placements can begin at any time of the year, however, teaching with KEEP's annual English-language course is from June to July and December to January.

Destinations: Nepal (Kathmandu or smaller communities).

Costs: The fee for two week placements is US$50 and for longer placements it's US$120, which covers orientation. Volunteers must be entirely self-funding.

Eligibility: There are no age restrictions. Preference is given to volunteers with relevant work experience or TEFL qualifications.

Groups or Individuals: A maximum of two volunteers are placed on each project.

Annual no. of Volunteers: 30

Annual Projects: KEEP works with a number of grassroots projects.
Partner Programmes: Some of KEEP's placements are with local NGOs.
Selection & Interview Process: Applicants complete a registration form and, if successful, are interviewed once they arrive in Kathmandu to find a suitable placement.
In-country Support: Prior to placing volunteers, KEEP evaluates the security in the region. Placements are in areas where KEEP has strong relationships with the local communities, and volunteers are in regular contact with the coordinator.

Mango Tree Goa

The Mango House, H.No 148/3, Karaswada, Mapusa, Bardez, Goa, India
☎ +91 9881 261 886
www.mangotreegoa.org
This charity aims to help children living on the streets and in slums in Goa. It provides outreach work, assists children to gain access to the registered school system and provides healthcare for up to 150 children. It has also recently established The Mango House, a base for children to receive healthy food, a safe and dry place to rest and a chance to join in creative, educational play. Volunteers help with all aspects of the project, including sorting and distributing clothes and maintaining the house and garden.
Status: Registered UK charity; registered trust in India.
Timing & Length of Projects: A minimum of three months; projects start year-round.
Destinations: India.
Costs: A £50 deposit is required and refunded on request after completing the minimum three-month duration. Volunteers are expected to be completely self-funding, including travel and accommodation.
Eligibility: The minimum age is 18 and volunteers need to be fit and healthy. A clear, recent police check from the applicant's country of origin is required.
Groups or Individuals: Volunteers can apply either individually or as a group. All volunteers work as a team on site.
Annual no. of Volunteers: 40-100.
Annual Projects: 1
Partner Programmes: None.

Selection & Interview Process: All applicants must supply a police check, two references, a CV, covering letter and photo. Selection is via post or email.
In-country Support: There is a modern hospital near the project and local staff are available 24 hours for emergencies.

Pina Palmera

Apartado Postal 109, CP 70900 Pochutla, Oaxaca, Mexico
☎ +52 9585 843147
fax +52 9585 843145
caipinapalmera@gmail.org
www.pinapalmera.org
For more than 20 years, Pina Palmera has been working towards the social integration and acceptance of people with disabilities, promoting independence and encouraging the development of their abilities. Located on the Pacific coast, Pina Palmera works in nearby rural and indigenous communities. Volunteers assist in all aspects of the project: the special care centre for teenagers with severe disabilities; arts, sports and handicraft projects; the garden and kitchen; and also work within teams of therapists focusing on community-based rehabilitation.
Status: Not-for-profit organisation.
Timing & Length of Projects: Placements are for a minimum of six months, preferably from the start of January, April, July or October.
Destinations: Mexico.
Costs: Volunteers must be self-funding. Accommodation and board are provided for a nominal cost of US$20 per month.
Eligibility: The minimum age is 19 and volunteers need to be flexible, open-minded, willing to integrate into the community and sensitive to the topic of disabilities in rural areas. Applications from disabled volunteers are welcome, but while the project has good wheelchair access, the surrounding towns and area do not.
Groups or Individuals: Volunteers are integrated individually within the project; it's possible to volunteer with a friend or family, but it's unlikely that you would work together.
Annual no. of Volunteers: 30
Annual Projects: A number of local, community-based projects.
Partner Programmes: 4
Selection & Interview Process: Interested volunteers should read the website and then

send an introductory email. The organisation then determines the candidate's suitability.
In-country Support: Volunteers live within the compound, where there is 24-hour support in case of emergencies. A doctor also lives on the grounds and there is a nearby hospital.

Rural Community Development Programme – Nepal

GPO Box 8957, Tasindole Marg-95/48, Kalanki-14, Kathmandu, Nepal
☎ +977 142 78305
fax +977 142 82994
info@rcdpnepal.org, info@rcdpvolunteers.org
www.rcdpnepal.org

This organisation works across four countries but remains small scale, offering placements in community development with a high level of cultural immersion. You might end up working and living in an orphanage, teaching English, helping in rural-health projects or working in environmental conservation. RCDP also offers week-long intensive language classes to get you started.
Status: Not-for-profit organisation.
Timing & Length of Projects: From two to 20 weeks with set departure dates on the first and third Monday of each month.
Destinations: This organisation offers placements throughout Asia, Africa and Latin America. (See website for a complete list.)
Costs: Prices vary according to the location and duration of the volunteer project.
Eligibility: No previous experience or skills are required, however, participants must be motivated and committed. Applications from those with disabilities are welcome.
Groups or Individuals: Volunteers work in small groups and can apply with friends or partners.
Annual no. of Volunteers: 130
Annual Projects: 15
Partner Programmes: 15
Selection & Interview Process: Via email and telephone.
In-country Support: RCDP is in continual contact with its volunteers and can take immediate action in case of emergency; the organisation has a vehicle that enables it to reach all volunteers within an hour. It also thoroughly briefs host families on how to support volunteers.

Volunteer Bolivia

Calle Ecuador E-0342, Casilla Postal 2411, Cochabamba, Bolivia
☎ +591 4452 6028
fax +591 4452 9459
info@volunteerboliva.org
www.volunteerbolivia.org

Volunteer Bolivia arranges placements with local organisations such as literacy centres, children's services, schools, health clinics and human rights groups. Previous placements have included working in orphanages, working in natural medicine clinics and providing physical therapy. Placements are determined following your arrival and a personal interview in Bolivia.
Status: Limited company.
Timing & Length of Projects: Placements are for a minimum of one month, year-round.
Destinations: Bolivia.
Costs: Fees are £1100/1300/1600 for one/two/three months. This includes a month of language classes and homestay accommodation.
Eligibility: There are no skill or age limitations.
Groups or Individuals: Volunteers usually work individually. Applications from friends, partners and families are welcome.
Annual no. of Volunteers: 60
Annual Projects: Volunteer Bolivia works with a wide variety of humanitarian and ecological projects in Bolivia.
Partner Programmes: 5.
Selection & Interview Process: Application is by email, sometimes followed by phone contact.
In-country Support: Support and assistance by local staff is available at all times.

Education & Training

Casa Guatemala

14 Calle 10-63 Zona 1, Guatemala City, Guatemala
☎ /fax +502 2331 9408
administracion@casa-guatemala.org
www.casa-guatemala.org

Casa Guatemala runs a children's village on the banks of the Rio Dulce, where it cares for 250 orphaned, abandoned or poverty-stricken children. Volunteer placements are generally teaching based but can also include caring for children outside school hours, working in the medical clinic, administration

Thinking of Taking the Kids?

When Clare Wearden and her husband set about looking for an organisation to volunteer with, they had more than the usual concerns to take into account. Along with their usual luggage allowance, they were also taking along their three children, aged 16 months, five and eight. In the end, they chose Volunteer Bolivia (p160), where Clare worked with a rehabilitation project for women recently out of prison, and then was an office administrator and evaluator for an NGO that installed water systems in small communities. In total, the family was overseas for over a year. Here, Clare gives some pointers on what to look for in an organisation if you're planning to volunteer with your kids, and how she prepared for the experience:

Make sure that the organisation is positive about children – we had definite negative vibes from two other organisations before we found Volunteer Bolivia. They put us in contact with people they knew with kids around the same age as ours, so that we could ask about schooling, the main concern for us. Also, they are willing to help with visa requirements for children if you are staying beyond the period that a tourist visa is valid for. You can't find out about these requirements easily from the UK and it was invaluable to us to have this information.

Make sure you decide how the voluntary work will fit in around your family time. I think it is very easy to get carried away and end up working full-time and handing your kids over to someone else. We decided to put our kids into the Bolivian education system, where schooling is only on offer for one four-hour session (either morning or afternoon) and then we worked it out between us to be with them in the afternoons. We also decided to live in a residential area with a garden, outside the town centre, so that the kids had neighbours to play with, as lots of poorer countries don't have playgrounds. We were very careful about food – especially with the baby – and did not eat any street food for a long time. We did all have occasional bouts of illness, but nothing serious.

Make sure the kids know where and why they are going and what the place is like, what the people look like, how it will be different etc. We got maps, videos and books about Bolivia for them. We even managed to get some children's films in Spanish – Buzz Lightyear and Toy Story – and we learnt a little bit of basic Spanish before we left. Taking them out of the UK system for five terms has had absolutely no ill effects. We did no home tutoring at all and they went to a Spanish-speaking school within two weeks of arrival. They settled in incredibly quickly. They are doing really well at school now and are eager to repeat the experience – with or without us.

We settled so quickly into life in Bolivia that the challenges were no greater than if we had moved within the UK – in fact it was probably less daunting, as we had so much more time together as a family. It is the best thing we ever did and a totally different experience of a country from going as a single person.

and helping on the farm or in the kitchen. All volunteers spend at least a week working at the project's hostel. Doctors and nurses are always required.
Status: Not-for-profit.
Timing & Length of Projects: Placements start year-round. Week-long placements are possible; longer term volunteers (three months plus) are welcome.
Destinations: Guatemala.
Costs: Long term: one-time tax-deductible donation of US$300; short term: US$235 per week. This covers food, lodging and transport

by boat to and from the orphanage.
Eligibility: The minimum age is 24. Skills or experience in teaching, medicine, computers, childcare, cooking, agronomy, animal husbandry or administration are preferred. Volunteers with minor disabilities may be accepted if possible.
Groups or Individuals: You can apply as an individual, with a partner or friend, or as a group. Volunteers work together in a group of up to 50.
Annual no. of Volunteers: Over 150
Annual Projects: 1

Partner Programmes: 1 (project-run hostel)

Selection & Interview Process: Apply online.

In-country Support: Support is available at all times, there is a volunteer co-ordinator and clinic on site.

Frontiers Foundation

419 Coxwell Ave, Toronto,
Ontario M4L 3B9, Canada
☎ +1 416 690 3930
fax +1 416 690 3934
www.frontiersfoundation.ca

This well-established charity sends volunteers to work on community-development projects in small, isolated aboriginal communities in Canada's far north, many of which are above the Arctic Circle. Most volunteers work as tutors and teaching assistants in schools, although it's also possible to work on recreation projects and assist in Band and Tribal Council offices. Volunteers are given the opportunity to immerse themselves in a unique culture and way of life.

Status: Registered charity.

Timing & Length of Projects: Placements are from early September until the end of June. Volunteers must commit to the full 10 months.

Destinations: Northern Canada: Northwest Territories, Nunuvat, Yukon.

Costs/Pay: There is a C$50 registration fee. Travel costs within Canada, food, living expenses and insurance are all covered and volunteers are given a living allowance of C$50 per week.

Eligibility: Minimum age is 19 and Frontiers prefers that volunteers have a university degree and experience teaching or working with young people. Volunteers must be outgoing and energetic and have a strong desire to learn about another culture.

Groups or Individuals: Volunteers are placed individually and in groups of up to five. It is possible to volunteer with a friend or partner.

Annual no. of Volunteers: 25

Annual Projects: 12

Partner Programmes: Frontiers works directly with schools, school boards and the communities. Each project has its own partner organisation within the community.

Selection & Interview Process: Application forms can be downloaded from the website and must be sent along with three recommendation forms. Interviews are in person whenever possible; otherwise by telephone.

In-country Support: Frontiers has offices in Vancouver and Toronto to offer volunteer support. In addition, each community appoints one local person as the volunteer's contact. Each community also has a health unit.

Volunthai: Volunteers for Thailand

86/24 Soi Kanprapa, Prachacheun Rd,
Bahng Sue, Bangkok 10800, Thailand
☎ +66 4481 3346
application@volunthai.com
www.volunthai.com

A grassroots organisation with projects in the most remote province of Thailand, Volunthai places volunteers in teaching positions in rural, underprivileged communities. Volunteers live with local families and teach for about three hours per day. Placements are in a close network of schools well-known to the organisation.

Status: Not-for-profit organisation.

Timing & Length of Projects: Placements are for one to three months and begin year-round.

Destinations: Thailand.

Costs: A fee of US$375 for a one-month homestay and US$200 for each additional month goes towards running the volunteer programme; the local communities offer accommodation and food free to volunteers in exchange for their services. All other costs are the responsibility of the volunteer.

Eligibility: There is no age restriction, however, most volunteers are between 20 and 30.

Groups or Individuals: Homestays and work placements are generally for individuals, with the opportunity to meet other volunteers on weekends. Couples and families are welcome to apply.

Annual no. of Volunteers: 100

Annual Projects: The organisation works with several projects for poor children, refugees and tsunami victims.

Partner Programmes: The number varies from year to year.

Selection & Interview Process: Application and interview is via email.

In-country Support: Local staff are available to answer questions and help both before you arrive and while you're at your homestay. Homestays have phone, internet, and nearby clinics and hospitals.

Photo: Michael Coyne/Getty Images ©

Burmese pupils arrive at the Bamboo School on the border of Myanmar and Thailand

UK Organisations

Volunteer Action for Peace

16 Overhill Road, East Dulwich,
London SE22 0PH, UK
☎ +44 (0)844 20 90 927
action@vap.org.uk
www.vap.org.uk

Working across all continents, VAP's standard workcamps bring together a group of international volunteers from different backgrounds to undertake unskilled tasks that would otherwise be impossible without paid labour. These can range from construction work on public buildings, to environmental conservation, to social projects involving children, the elderly or refugees. A main goal is to promote intercultural understanding between participants and the local community. VAP's North–South workcamps take place in developing countries, involve larger groups with many local participants and focus as much on cross-cultural cooperation as on practical work.

Status: Registered charity.

Timing & Length of Projects: Most placements are between two and four weeks, although there is the possibility for longer-term placements of three to 12 months. The majority of placements are between June and September but can take place year-round.

Destinations: 80 countries, including Kenya, Burundi, Peru, Italy, Palestine, Mexico, Zambia, Portugal, Argentina, Vietnam and France.

Costs: Standard Programme workcamps (projects in Europe, North America, Japan, South Korea and Taiwan) cost £160, including food and accommodation. North–South Programme workcamps (Africa, Latin America and other Asian countries) cost £195 plus a hosting fee for food and accommodation. Medium/long-term projects cost £210 plus a registration and hosting fee. All travel and personal expenses are borne by the volunteer.

Eligibility: The minimum age is 18 on most projects; there are a few projects open to 15 to 17 year olds, though. Some projects have a maximum age of 30. No skills or experience are required, but it's preferable that volunteers on North–South projects have previous experience volunteering in a workcamp setting.

Groups or Individuals: Volunteers are placed in workcamps of five to 25 participants. It is preferable that participants are individuals, although for larger projects, partners and friends can apply together. In such cases, these participants must make every effort to integrate into the group.

Annual no. of Volunteers: 100
Annual Projects: 1600

continued on p165

Volunteering Unwrapped

Eileen Bennicke didn't have the type of skills required by VSO or similar organisations, but wanted to volunteer overseas and have a gap-year experience nonetheless. So, armed with ambition and curiosity, she travelled alone to Ecuador. She had signed up for a three-month volunteering stint through the Experiment in International Living (EIL, p166), but had little idea what the actual work would be like once she got there. While this is a risky way of embarking on a volunteering placement, this element of the unknown challenged Eileen and spurred her on.

In many respects, Eileen was probably like most of the other volunteers working on EIL projects. It was her first time living away from home, she was filling a gap year, and was keen to do something meaningful with her time. But she was different in one respect: while the vast majority of her co-volunteers were around 20, Eileen had just turned 60. This trip was a retirement present to herself.

Eileen started her adventure by spending a month in Quito, having one-on-one Spanish classes and living with a family who included her in all of their activities, which gave her a window into day-to-day Ecuadorian life. Next, she volunteered with CENIT, an organisation that helps poverty-stricken children in Quito. For five mornings a week, Eileen would go out onto the streets or into the markets and engage children in games. She also helped out with elementary maths in a classroom and painted school furniture. The experience was not very fulfilling for Eileen, who felt that her interaction with locals was limited, and that she didn't really have a role that she could sink her teeth into.

Eileen then set out for the Ecuadorian cloud forest, where she lived and volunteered on a plantation named Santa Lucia. Eileen felt the organisation was a little dubious about her participating in a conservation project because of her age, but this didn't stop her. Initially, she tended an organic garden in the valley, then another one high in the hills. To finish, she assisted an American student with a research project. She found this part of her trip 'a truly wonderful and all-consuming four weeks in a magical environment with lovely people and some proper work to do'.

Upon her return to the UK, Eileen's friends commented that she must have missed her family. Eileen replied honestly that she hadn't 'because life was so full of new experiences'. Nevertheless, speaking very little Spanish and being a naturally chatty individual, Eileen found the language barrier difficult. She became very adept at getting her point across with a lot of energetic arm waving.

Another challenging, but rewarding, task was getting on with the younger people on the projects, particularly the other volunteers, who were from different countries and all about 35 years her junior. In the end, these interactions were a highlight of her placement: one of her most memorable moments was returning from a fiesta in a neighbouring village at 4am in the back of an open truck, with loads of locals and a few young volunteers.

Looking back on her volunteering placements, Eileen is adamant that her experience far exceeded her expectations: 'I really would encourage other people to have a gap experience like this between work and retirement. It really took me outside my comfort zone and I gained a lot of confidence knowing I could cope away from family and friends in a continent I had never visited, in a language I could not speak. Since returning, I have sent money back to the community and I stay in touch regularly with my family in Quito. I feel that my life has been greatly enriched by the experience. Go on – give yourself the pressie of a lifetime!'

Photo: Eileen Bennicke

Partner Programmes: 100

Selection & Interview Process: All participants must complete an application form. North–South Programme and longer-term participants should participate in a training weekend or an interview.

In-country Support: The in-country host organisation takes responsibility for volunteers. For North–South workcamps, the infrastructure is usually basic but safe.

Building & Construction

AidCamps International

483 Green Lanes, London, N13 4BS, UK
☎ +44 (0)84 5651 5412
info@aidcamps.org
www.aidcamps.org

AidCamps works in developing countries, assisting local communities in finding solutions to problems they've identified. Volunteers work alongside locals. In short-term Group AidCamps, volunteers help erect community buildings. With longer-term Independent AidCamps, volunteers are matched to suitable placements within partner organisations.

Status: Registered charity.

Timing & Length of Projects: Group AidCamps run for three weeks on set dates; Independent AidCamps can be organised for one week to three or more months at any time.

Destinations: Cameroon, India, Nepal and Sri Lanka.

Costs: Group AidCamps have a registration fee of between £300 and £350 plus a minimum donation of between £800 and £900, which covers accommodation, food, ground transport and excursions. Independent AidCamps have a £95 registration fee plus a £500 minimum donation for placements up to five weeks. After five weeks, each additional week costs £50.

Eligibility: The minimum age is 18, although those aged 16 to 18 can apply for Group AidCamps if accompanied by an adult. Children can accompany adults on Independent AidCamps. No specific skills are required.

Groups or Individuals: For Group AidCamps, volunteers travel and work as a group of 15 to 20, and you can apply to volunteer with your partner or friend. For Independent AidCamps, volunteers travel and work individually, although you can also do them with friends, partners or families.

Annual no. of Volunteers: 65

Annual Projects: 3-5

Partner Programmes: 5

Selection & Interview Process: Acceptance for Group AidCamps is on a first-come, first-served basis. For Independent AidCamps, interviews are in person in London where possible or by phone or email if not.

In-country Support: Group AidCamps are led by a UK member of the organisation who remains with the group at all times. Volunteers on Independent AidCamps are overseen by a member of the local partner organisation who provides logistical and personal support.

Community Development

Development in Action

78 York St, London W1H 1DP, UK
☎ +44 (0)7813 395957
www.developmentinaction.org

Since the 1990s, DiA has been supporting locally based NGOs in India by providing them with volunteers. Placements are very hands-on and can include informal teaching, research, fundraising, environmental conservation and working with deaf and blind children. The aim is for volunteers to learn from and with the local community, and while in India, participants are encouraged to produce resources (such as articles, photographs or worksheets) for development education in the UK.

Status: Registered charity.

Timing & Length of Projects: Placements are for two months in July and August, or for five months from September to February.

Destinations: India.

Costs: The fee for a two-month placement is £880; for five months it's £1600. This includes a pre-departure training weekend, in-country orientation and accommodation.

Eligibility: The minimum age is 18. There are no specific skills or experience required for most placements, but applicants must show an interest in learning about global issues.

Groups or Individuals: All volunteers live in groups of two to four. They also usually work in groups of two to four, although individual placements are possible.

Annual no. of Volunteers: Up to 28.
Annual Projects: Up to eight.
Partner Programmes: Up to 10.
Selection & Interview Process: Apply online.
Those initially selected are invited to attend a
further 'selection day' (usually in London) for
group activities, workshops and individual
interviews.
In-country Support: Volunteers are supported
by the partner NGO they are working with.
There are also two DiA coordinators based in
India who are contactable by telephone at all
times and able to travel to placements to deal
with emergencies.

Epiphany Trust

St Davids, Park Rd Sth, Newton-le-Willows,
Merseyside, Warrington WA12, UK
☎ +44 (0)1925 220999
fax +44 (0)1925 220179
gill@epiphany.org.uk
www.epiphany.org.uk
The Epiphany Trust has supported the
Romanian Lugoj orphanage for over 15 years,
helping to transform it from one of the country's
most appalling institutions to one of its best. As
an extension of this work, the Trust has recently
opened The Arc, a home for four young people
with minor learning disabilities who are of
an age to leave the orphanage. Volunteers
become part of the home's 'family' and assist
the residents in learning basic life skills such as
cooking, cleaning and computer literacy. The
Arc is located in the ski resort town of Sinaia. In
Sri Lanka, volunteers can work in either of two
projects: in a street-children centre in Kandy or
with preschool children in the tea plantations of
the hill country. Volunteers are also required to
work in Hong Kong with an international team,
redistributing surplus goods to areas of need
around the world.
Status: Registered charity.
Timing & Length of Projects: From three weeks
to up to a year for all projects.
Destinations: Romania, Sri Lanka and Hong
Kong.
Costs: Romanian placements for three weeks
cost £390 exclusive of flights and insurance,
but include transfers, accommodation and
food. Subsequent weeks cost £70. Flights
are from £120 to £220. Sri Lankan and
Hong Kong placements for three weeks cost
£1500 exclusive of flights and insurance, but

include transfers, accommodation and food.
Subsequent weeks cost £100. Flights are from
£600.
Eligibility: The minimum volunteer age is
18 years. There is no upper age restriction.
Volunteers need to have good interpersonal
skills and a willingness to learn some
conversational Romanian or Sinhalese/Tamil.
They must be enthusiastic and committed,
with an ability to empathise with young
people. Applicants with disabilities are
welcome. CRB or equivalent check essential.
Groups or Individuals: Volunteers usually
travel individually but often work in pairs.
Annual no. of Volunteers: Up to 10.
Annual Projects: 5
Partner Programmes: 5
Selection & Interview Process: Volunteers
can apply by post or online by application
form. References are taken up, and an
informal interviews are conducted either in
the northwest of England or at a mutually
convenient location in the UK.
In-country Support: Representatives of the
Epiphany Trust in Romania, Sri Lanka and
Hong Kong work closely with volunteers,
providing induction, traning and ongoing
support.

Experiment in International Living

Elphick House, 287 Worcester Rd,
Malvern, Worcester WR14 1AB, UK
☎ +44 (0)1684 562577
fax +44 (0)1684 562212
info@eiluk.org
www.eiluk.org
EIL is an educational charity specialising in
cultural-awareness programmes. Founded
over 70 years ago, it tailor-makes group
programmes and individual placements that
give volunteers the chance to work in rural
development, health clinics, children's groups
and conservation. Most placements include
homestays with local families.
Status: Registered charity.
Timing & Length of Projects: For European
destinations, placements are for two to 12
months. For most worldwide destinations,
placements are six weeks to one year.
Destinations: Argentina, Chile, Brazil, Ecuador,
Guatemala, Ghana, Morocco, South Africa,
India, Thailand and the European Union
member countries.

Costs: European volunteering is completely funded by the European Union. For placements outside Europe, room and board is provided but volunteers must be self-funding.

Eligibility: The minimum age for most projects is 18. For European placements, disabled volunteers receive extra financial assistance and sometimes another volunteer to provide support.

Groups or Individuals: Volunteers travel individually but often work within a group. Applicants interested in volunteering with a friend, partner or family should contact EIL about possibilities.

Annual no. of Volunteers: 50

Annual Projects: 40

Partner Programmes: Many, especially in Europe.

Selection & Interview Process: EIL prefers to interview in person in Malvern, however, interviews can also be arranged in other parts of the UK.

In-country Support: EIL has partners in all countries where volunteers are placed. Volunteers are given a 24-hour emergency number and support.

Independent Living Alternatives

Trafalgar House, Grenville Pl,
London NW7 3SA, UK
☎ +44 (0)20 8906 9265
fax +44 (0)20 8959 1910
paservices@ilanet.co.uk
www.ilanet.co.uk

ILA promotes the rights of disabled people to live independently by providing them with full-time personal assistance in their own homes in London. Volunteers work full-time, four days per week, supporting clients in day-to-day activities and necessities.

Status: Registered charity.

Timing & Length of Projects: Placements are for four months and occur throughout the year.

Destinations: UK.

Costs: Living expenses and accommodation are provided.

Eligibility: Minimum age is 21. Volunteers need to have a driving licence and empathise with the organisation's aims.

Groups or Individuals: Volunteers work individually but live communally.

Annual no. of Volunteers: 50, with about 90% coming from overseas.

Annual Projects: 10

Selection & Interview Process: Complete an application form; this will be followed up with a reference check and telephone or Skype interview.

In-country Support: Volunteers have access to the office and emergency support at all times. They also receive training on arrival which includes emergency policies and procedures.

MondoChallenge

Town Hall, Market Place,
Newbury RG14 5AA, UK
☎ +44 (0)1635 45556
fax +44 (0)1635 45596
info@mondochallenge.co.uk
www.mondochallenge.co.uk

MondoChallenge provides support to schools families and vulnerable communities in developing countries. Volunteers can teach children or adults, work in orphanages, or on support programmes for HIV-affected families. Volunteers' professional skills and experience are matched to a local partner's needs, leading to placements in business, medicine, sports, IT, science or art.

Status: Limited Company, with a separate registered charity, FutureSense Foundation.

Timing & Length of Projects: Typically from two weeks to six months, year-round.

Destinations: Tanzania, India, Sri Lanka, Nepal, Gambia, Senegal, Chile, Ecuador and Romania, with new projects in Thailand, Peru and South Africa being developed.

Costs: Fees range from £500 upwards. Local support, food, accommodation and airport pick ups are included.

Eligibility: The minimum age is 18. Many volunteers are career breakers and early retired.

Groups or Individuals: Both individuals and groups, and families and friends are particularly welcome.

Annual no. of Volunteers: 200

Annual Projects: 50

Partner Programmes: 100

Selection & Interview Process: Application Form, interview (by phone or in person) and references are required

In-country Support: In-country managers and deputies provide support (24 hours in most locations). Local partners manage health and safety issues.

Personal Overseas Development

Formal House, 60 St George's Place,
Cheltenham, GL50 3PN UK
☎ +44 (0)1242 250901
info@podvolunteer.org
www.podvolunteer.org

PoD is a leading not-for-profit organisation which has been sending volunteers abroad for the last nine years. It provides worthwhile placements that allow volunteers to make a difference overseas, while experiencing incredible parts of the world that are rich in culture, variety and natural beauty. Its placements range from marine conservation projects in Belize to teaching street children English in Vietnam and building in Tanzania. It has an array of opportunities throughout South America, Central America, Africa and Asia.

Status: Not-for-profit limited company.
Timing & Length of Projects: Projects run year-round, some with fixed departure dates. Placements are from one week to six months.
Destinations: Peru, Thailand, Tanzania, Nepal, Belize, Cambodia, Indonesia, South Africa and Vietnam.
Costs: Prices start at £375. An example project of three weeks in Nepal would cost £845 – this includes training, support and accommodation. Cost depends on the location and duration of the project. For some projects the cost also includes food and local activities.
Eligibility: The minimum age is 18. Volunteers must be energetic and in good health and have enthusiasm and a willingness to get involved. Applications from those with disabilities are welcome and considered on a case-by-case basis.
Groups or Individuals: Volunteers work in a group of two to 10. Volunteers can apply as friends, partners or families, with a discount per person for joint applications. In some locations it is possible to travel and live together but work on different projects.
Annual no. of Volunteers: 300-400
Annual Projects: 28
Partner Programmes: 21
Selection & Interview Process: Application form followed by a interview. A Criminal Records Bureau check (or equivalent) may be required.

In-country Support: In-country support staff are available 24 hours a day and live on-site or nearby the project. Each project also has a risk-management and crisis-management plan.

Volunteers for Rural India (VRI)

12 Eastleigh Ave, South Harrow,
Middlesex HA2 0UF, UK
☎ +44 (0)20 8864 4740
enquiries@vri-online.org.uk
www.vri-online.org.uk

This small organisation gives participants the opportunity to be immersed in village life and thereby learn about development first-hand. Placements are with grassroots NGOs throughout rural India, although all volunteers spend their first three weeks in the northern state of Uttar Pradesh. VRI has a strict policy of only employing local staff and the emphasis of all placements is on observing and learning. Volunteers are 'project visitors' who can assist in activities such as office administration, teaching and marketing. The level of involvement is very much determined by the motivation of the volunteers.

Status: Registered charity.
Timing & Length of Projects: Three weeks' orientation is offered, with the option to stay longer or move on to projects in other areas.
Destinations: India.
Costs: Project visitors pay all their own costs. They must become members of VRI (£15) and pay £250 placement fee, which includes literature, a short London orientation and three weeks' board and lodging at the project in India.
Eligibility: The minimum age is 18. There are no required skills or experience. The organisation cannot accommodate people with disabilities.
Groups or Individuals: Individuals, couples or a small group of friends (up to three people).
Annual no. of Volunteers: 30-40
Annual Projects: One main project but contacts with 15 others.
Partner Programmes: The Asian Foundation for Philanthropy.
Selection & Interview Process: Applicants send in an application form and membership fee. They are called for an interview, after which they decide whether to join. They then pay a placement fee and attend a

London orientation. Overseas applicants are interviewed by phone and orientation material is posted to them.

In-country Support: In India, project visitors are under the care and supervision of the Society for Agro-Industrial Education in India, plus at least one trustee from VRI.

Education & Training

Ecologia Youth Trust

66 The Park, Forres, Moray IV36 3TD, UK
☎ /fax +44 (0)1309 690995
info@ecologia.org.uk
www.ecologia.org.uk

Ecologia Youth Trust is a small charity through which volunteers can help support Kitezh, a self-contained rural Russian community that is home to orphaned and abandoned children. The project is very community oriented and in addition to teaching English volunteers can help out with all aspects of the programme, from childcare to construction. A second sister community, Orion, also accepts volunteers. The two communities are closely linked and there is a regular flow of adults and children between them.

Status: Registered charity.

Timing & Length of Projects: Placements are for two to three months and start every three months throughout the year.

Destinations: Russia.

Costs: Placements cost £1320 for two months, including the necessary visa support, in-country transport and all accommodation and food. The fee for three months is £1450. Airfares, visa and insurance extra.

Eligibility: The minimum age is 18, and while no particular skills are required, volunteers need to feel able to teach English. It is useful if you have some basic Russian. Other useful skills include being able to teach music or IT.

Groups or Individuals: There is a maximum of six volunteers at any one time.

Annual no. of Volunteers: 24

Annual Projects: 4

Partner Programmes: Ecologia also runs a volunteering programme in Georgia.

Selection & Interview Process: Applicants complete an introductory questionnaire, which is put before the Russian community for their approval. They then have an informal telephone interview and are sent a booking form.

In-country Support: Participants live within the community with 24-hour support from a resident volunteers coordinator, who also provides guidance for English teaching. Ecologia is available at all times by phone and email.

Karen Hilltribes Trust

88A Main St, Fulford, York YO10 4PS, UK
☎ +44 (0)1904 411891
fax +44 (0)1904 430580
www.karenhilltribes.org.uk

Karen Hilltribes Trust works with the hilltribes in northwest Thailand to help them develop their own social, educational and economic infrastructure. Volunteers are sent to remote villages to teach in primary and secondary schools, and also have the opportunity of spending three weeks helping to install a clean water system. Volunteers live with local families and are completely immersed in the local culture.

Status: Registered charity and limited company.

Timing & Length of Projects: Placements are from six to nine months, beginning mainly in October and sometimes January. Eight-week volunteering placements are available in July and August.

Destinations: Thailand.

Costs: A five-month placement is £2000, including accommodation and food.

Eligibility: The minimum age is 18, and teaching experience or previous work with children is desirable but not essential. People with physical disabilities can apply, however, the mountainous, remote location means placement is not always possible. Volunteers need to be motivated, self-disciplined and flexible.

Groups or Individuals: Volunteers are generally placed in pairs. Unmarried couples cannot be placed together.

Annual no. of Volunteers: 50

Annual Projects: 1

Partner Programmes: 1

Selection & Interview Process: Application form and then a personal interview in York.

In-country Support: A Karen manager and English member of staff are based in the area and can be contacted at all times. Volunteers are always placed within easy access of a hospital.

Sudan Volunteer Programme

34 Estelle Rd, London NW3 2JY, UK
☎ +44 (0)20 7485 8619
david@svp-uk.com
www.svp-uk.com

SVP organises volunteers to teach English in universities, schools and colleges in the developing country of Sudan. English is the second official language of Sudan, and while many locals have studied it, most have never had the opportunity to practice with a native speaker. Volunteers work approximately 30 hours per week. Outside teaching hours, there are also opportunities to work with children displaced by Sudan's civil war.

Status: Registered charity.
Timing & Length of Projects: Placements begin in January or October for a minimum of six months.
Destinations: Sudan.
Costs/Pay: A fee of £60 covers insurance and accommodation. A modest stipend is paid during the placement.
Eligibility: Graduates or undergraduates with English as their native language.
Groups or Individuals: Volunteers work individually or sometimes in pairs. Married couples may apply.
Annual no. of Volunteers: 20-40
Annual Projects: 1

Partner Programmes: 1
Selection & Interview Process: Potential volunteers are interviewed in person or by telephone.
In-country Support: A local support group is available at all times and organised to respond to emergencies.

Task Brasil

PO Box 4901, London SE16 3PP, UK
☎ +44 (0)20 7735 5545
fax +44 (0)20 7735 5675
info@taskbrasil.org.uk
www.taskbrasil.org.uk

Task Brasil's aim is to improve the lives and support the needs of children and pregnant girls living on the streets in Brazil. It does this by providing a clean, safe place to live and training in beneficial skills. Volunteers work alongside local educators and care-workers, helping the kids with things like sports, reading, writing, music, art and computer skills. Placements are either in Rio or with teenage boys on an ecological farm (called the Ecotour Farm Experience).

Status: Registered charity.
Timing & Length of Projects: Placements are for a minimum of one month and preferably at least three months and up to one year. Placements begin year-round.
Destinations: Brazil.
Costs: Volunteers must fundraise £1200 to £2500, which covers Portuguese classes, accommodation, food and a donation towards the projects. The Ecotour Farm Experience costs £245 to £495 (depending on accommodation) and participants must raise an additional £350.
Eligibility: Volunteers must be at least 21 and have a genuine interest in children. Skills in music, IT, teaching English, crafts, sports or lifesaving are an advantage, as is a working knowledge of Portuguese, Spanish or Italian. There are no age restrictions or requirements for Ecotour participants.
Groups or Individuals: Placements are made for individuals, although volunteers may work in groups of two to four on some projects. Ecotour participants are in a group of two to 15.
Annual no. of Volunteers: 20 (not including Ecotour participants).
Annual Projects: 6
Partner Programmes: Task Brasil has a number of trusts and companies supporting its work.

Dear Diary...

Even extended placements can zip past and morph into hazy recollections. Before you board that plane, consider the words of Tom Wilmot, who volunteered for six months as an engineer in India with Development in Action (p165):

So many stories spring to mind, and so many come flooding back on re-reading my diary. This, in itself, prompts me to highly recommend keeping a diary. It can become a chore, but approach it with good humour and try to record all those little events as regularly as possible. It really is worth it when you look back. It doesn't have to look beautiful (mine is barely legible), but looking back at it is one of those things MasterCard just can't buy!

Selection & Interview Process: Applicants apply in writing and interviews are conducted in person in London.

In-country Support: While on placements, volunteers work with Task Brasil staff. In-country, a volunteer coordinator, two volunteer leaders and an English-speaking farm manager are available for support.

Volunteer Africa

PO Box 24, Bakewell,
Derbyshire, DE45 1UP, UK
☎ +44 (0)162 964 0980
support@volunteerafrica.org
www.volunteerafrica.org

Volunteer Africa works with partner NGOs in Tanzania on sustainable community-initiated projects. Volunteers live and work in rural villages in the Singida region on community-development projects. Programmes are of varying lengths (four, seven or 10 weeks), with regular start dates throughout the Tanzanian dry season (May to October).

Status: Registered charity.

Timing & Length of Projects: Placements last from four to 12 weeks, year-round. The Singida programme only runs during the dry season.

Destinations: Tanzania.

Costs: Fees range from £600 to £1895, depending on the length and location of the placement. This includes food, accommodation, internal travel and one week of language and cultural training.

Eligibility: The minimum age is 18.

Groups or Individuals: Volunteers work in groups of four to 12.

Annual no. of Volunteers: 120

Annual Projects: 1

Partner Programmes: 1

Selection & Interview Process: Applications can be made via the website and are followed by a telephone interview.

In-country Support: Support is given by the host NGO, as well as by the volunteer coordinator, who is accessible at all times.

Conservation & Wildlife Placements

In addition to the listings in this section, many of the organisations included in the Development section have an environmental component. For example, see PoD (p168), KEEP (p158), or Rural Community Development Programme (p160). The Ecologia Youth Trust (p169) is also in the process of establishing a volunteer programme within a sustainable agriculture eco-village in Mexico's cloud forest – it might be worth getting in touch with them about this exciting project.

International Organisations

Earthwatch Institute

Mayfield House, 256 Banbury Rd,
Oxford, OX2 7DE, UK
☎ +44 (0)1865 318831
fax +44 (0)1865 311383
info@earthwatch.org.uk
www.earthwatch.org

Earthwatch is a global conservation charity that places volunteers on scientific research expeditions in over 50 countries, with the aim of promoting the understanding and action necessary for a sustainable environment. Past volunteer expeditions have included projects as diverse as looking at climate change in the Arctic, researching the habitat of the cheetah in Namibia, studying elephant behaviour and protecting turtle hatchlings.

Status: Registered charity.

Timing & Length of Projects: Expedition lengths vary from two days to three weeks, with departure dates throughout the year. You can also opt to go on two consecutive expeditions at different locations within the same country.

Destinations: Worldwide.

Costs: The cost varies from around £350 to £3195 (with an average of £1500), depending on the project and duration. This includes briefing, training, food, accommodation, in-country transport and carbon offsetting.

Eligibility: Depending on the project, volunteers need to be at least 16 or 18. There are also some family teams which can include children 10 years and older. No skills or experience are required. Earthwatch tries to accommodate all disabilities.

Groups or Individuals: Most Earthwatch volunteers travel alone but on an Earthwatch expedition you will be in a group of between four and 20 volunteers, depending on the project.

Annual no. of Volunteers: 3000

Annual Projects: 65

Partner Programmes: Earthwatch works with a large number of individuals, NGOs, government organisations and universities worldwide.

Selection & Interview Process: A telephone discussion is held with each participant to ensure an appropriate match between volunteers and projects.

In-country Support: Volunteers are supported by the Earthwatch research team throughout the project. A risk assessment is carried out for each project and volunteers are given a 24-hour emergency telephone number.

Greenpeace

Greenpeace International,
Ottho Heldringstraat 5, 1066 AZ, Amsterdam, The Netherlands
☎ +31 2071 82000
fax +31 (0)2071 182002
supporter.services.int@greenpeace.org
www.greenpeace.org

Started as a small, campaigning organisation in Vancouver, Greenpeace is now an international organisation with offices around the globe. Its mission has remained unchanged: to use non-violent, creative confrontation to expose global environmental problems and force solutions. All offices offer plenty of volunteering opportunities, from stuffing envelopes to public outreach, and from lobbying to Amazon survival training. Many offices also offer intern positions to applicants with appropriate skills. Contact the international office for current openings or get in touch with your local office.

Status: Varies between countries.

Timing & Length of Projects: There are various opportunities within each country, including short- and long-term placements.

Destinations: Worldwide, including aboard Greenpeace's ships.

Costs: Varies with placements and between countries.

Eligibility: Depending on the project, volunteers can be unskilled or may need specific training and expertise. A commitment to the aims of Greenpeace is essential.

Groups or Individuals: Varies.

Annual no. of Volunteers: All Greenpeace offices accept volunteers, with numbers depending on their current projects and needs.

Annual Projects: Each national office undertakes numerous projects.

Partner Programmes: Greenpeace works with various grassroots NGOs around the world but does not place volunteers through them.

Selection & Interview Process: The selection process varies between countries and depends on what the placement entails.

In-country Support: This also varies between countries and on the types of placements concerned.

Willing Workers on Organic Farms (WWOOF)

PO Box 2154, Winslow,
Buckingham, MK18 3WS, UK
www.wwoof.org

Well respected and long standing, WWOOF organisations compile lists of organic farms that host volunteers. Placements usually involve helping out with the farm work but can also include working in an outdoor centre. In winter, volunteers can prepare garden beds and orchards, help with composting, planting fallow crops or maintenance. The programme largely appeals to 'townies' looking for a rural experience and those interested in organic practices.

Status: Varies between countries, but most often not-for-profit.

Timing & Length of Projects: Each placement is unique and the duration and timing depends on the needs of the host. Placements are year-round, although there is less work in winter months. Volunteers generally work four to six hours per day, six days a week.

Destinations: WWOOF has organisations in 24 countries, including Ghana, Sweden, Mexico, Italy and Korea. They also have independent hosts in around 50 more countries.

Costs: Most WWOOF organisations charge a membership fee of about £15, which gives you access to a host list and a membership card. Other than that, volunteers are entirely self-funding, although room and board are generally provided for free by the host.

Eligibility: An interest in conservation, community development or environmental teaching.

Groups or Individuals: Volunteers must be over 18 years old.

Annual no. of Volunteers: As they only provide lists of hosts, WWOOF does not record this number.

continued on p174

Painted Lines

Peggy Melmoth spent three weeks in Amarpurkashi in northern India, volunteering with Indian Volunteers for Community Service (IVCS, now called Volunteers for Rural India (VRI), p168). She lived within the school compound, where she wielded a paintbrush to create two colourful murals in the primary school that could be used for ballgames by the kids. She also helped out with English-language conversation classes in the degree college and managed to squeeze in daily yoga and Hindi classes as well. Before she left India, Peggy captured her experience in the following poem:

A Day at APK

Cold sunrise, yoga, shawls,
Mandala classroom walls,
Breathing, concentration,
Pranayama, meditation,
Nibu garum pani hai?
Semolina, sunny day,
Mud-brick oven heating water,
Must remember wear *dupatta*.
Bucket washing clothes and wring
It out and tie with string
To stop the monkeys stealing them.
Say *Namaste* to Ian again.
Assembled children, sing and pray,
School bell starts the teaching day.
Greeting children, meeting teachers,
Learning Hindi words for creatures.
English teacher going to Delhi
For a marriage celebration.
Would we teach the next three days
Of his English conversation?
Balaji makes lunch for all,
Soneil serves it with a smile.
Sono brings the spicy veg,
Mohit brings chapatti bread.
After lunch in yard below,
School boys counting *ek* and *do*,

Photo: Rebecca Mills

Exercise and stand in lines,
Repeat the routine several times.
Hindi lesson starts at four,
Mukesh will teach the PVs more.
Your father's name, name of your brother?
After forty-two thalis I can't eat another!
At the dance competition we are
'visiting celebrities',
At the yoga competition we are
'foreign dignitaries',
And introduced to the crowd as 'distinguished personalities'.
Off to Bareilly to visit some galleries,
Graduate artists give a guided tour,
We join them for a picnic on the gallery floor.
We march with two thousand students to the paper mill and back again
To raise awareness for the Eradicate Polio Campaign.
Four men on an elephant just passing through
Need a place for the night, the schoolyard will do.
Discussion at six with Babuji,
Development and poverty.
But what did we learn at APK?
Hum India ko piyar kurte hai!
(We love India.)

Peggy Melmoth

Photo: Rebecca Mills

Annual Projects: Again, they do not keep track. All hosts are checked and usually visited by the country's WWOOF organisation.
Partner Programmes: 0
Selection & Interview Process: WWOOF does not select volunteers. Placements are offered at the discretion of the host. To apply, you must first join the WWOOF organisation of the country you'd like to volunteer in (via the website), after which you will be sent a copy of the list of available hosts. It's then up to you to contact the farms and make your own arrangements.
In-country Support: WWOOF does not supply any in-country support: it's up to the hosts and the volunteer to arrange this.

UK Organisations

Biosphere Expeditions

The Henderson Centre, Ivy Lane, Norwich, NR5 8BF, UK
☎ +44 (0)8704 460801
fax +44 (0)8704 460809
info@biosphere-expeditions.org
www.biosphere-expeditions.org
This group offers volunteers the chance to be involved in hands-on wildlife and conservation research alongside local scientists in locations around the globe. Promoting sustainable conservation, the group doles out 'adventures with a purpose'. Past projects have included snow-leopard research in the Altai mountains, whale studies on the Azores, human-elephant conflict resolution in Sri Lanka, and chamois, bear and wolf conservation projects in the Tatra mountains.
Status: Not-for-profit organisation.
Timing & Length of Projects: Project length is usually one or two weeks, but people can join for up to 10 weeks at a time. Start dates for different expeditions vary throughout the year.
Destinations: Project locations vary, depending on where there is a need, however, they generally include Oman, Honduras, the Azores Archipelago, Peru, Slovakia, Sri Lanka, Namibia, Brazil, the Altai Republic and Australia.
Costs: Between £960 to £1730, including all food, lodging and in-country transportation. At least two-thirds of this contribution goes directly into the conservation project to fund long-term sustainability.

Eligibility: Biosphere aims to be inclusive and there are no age or physical restrictions (the oldest participant so far was 87!). Expeditions vary in the amount of physical ability required and you must be confident that you can cope with the demands. Volunteers under the age of 18 must have parental consent.
Groups or Individuals: Volunteers travel in groups of up to 12 and work in smaller research teams of two to four once in the field. You can apply as an individual or with a partner, friend, family or group.
Annual no. of Volunteers: 400
Annual Projects: 9
Partner Programmes: 15
Selection & Interview Process: The process is self-selecting with the requirments that you can speak English and you are physically able to undertake the work of the project that you have selected. Two projects require a diving qualification. You can join a project immediately by completing an online form.
In-country Support: There is an expedition leader on every project who works and lives with the volunteers, liaises with the local partner organisation and deals with all emergencies.

Blue Ventures

Level 2 Annex, Omnibus Business Centre, 39-41 North Rd, London N7 9DP, UK
☎ +44 (0)207 697 8598
fax +44 (0)800 066 4032
enquiries@blueventures.org
www.blueventures.org
Blue Ventures runs projects and expeditions to research and conserve global marine life. Its volunteer programme is popular and has won a number of prestigious eco-awards. Volunteers carry out research with scientists and camp staff in southwest Madagascar. This includes diving to collect data, monitoring sites, surveying coral reef habitats and identifying new sites. Onshore, volunteers assist with social-research activities, surveys, community environmental education, awareness-raising initiatives and teaching English or French in local schools. Placements can be focused towards volunteers' interests.
Status: Not-for-profit organisation.
Timing & Length of Projects: Six weeks, although there are options to stay for three weeks or over six weeks. Projects begin year-round.

Destinations: Madagascar and Belize.

Costs: For nonqualified scuba divers, the cost is between £2200 and £2300 for six weeks, including all food and accommodation, training and diving.

Eligibility: The minimum age is 18. There are no skills or experience required. Those with disabilities are accepted whenever possible.

Groups or Individuals: Volunteers travel to the site as a group and work as part of a team, with a maximum number of 18. You can apply with a friend, partner or as a family.

Annual no. of Volunteers: 120

Annual Projects: 1

Partner Programmes: Blue Ventures works with a number of NGOs, private companies, community groups and national institutions like the Wildlife Conservation Society, WWF and the Fisheries Department of Madagascar.

Selection & Interview Process: Receipt of an application form is followed by a telephone interview.

In-country Support: Each expedition has a leader, medic and four local staff available at all times. Annual risk assessments are carried out and satellite communications mean emergency services are always contactable.

National Trust

Heelis, Kemble Dr, Swindon SN2 2NA, UK
☎ +44 (0)179 381 7400
fax +44 (0)1793 817401
volunteers@nationaltrust.org.uk
www.nationaltrust.org.uk/volunteering

The National Trust maintains over 248,000 hectares of land, which are home to over 200 historic buildings, coastline, countryside, gardens, houses and farms throughout the UK. It has been accepting volunteers since 1895 and a huge range of opportunities are available, from room stewarding at heritage properties to estate gardening. Some of its short-term programmes are geared towards younger participants but it also offers individualised long-term placements for older volunteers.

Status: Registered charity.

Timing & Length of Projects: Placements are available year-round and range from very short term (two to seven days) to full-time (meaning a minimum of 21 hours per week for three to 12 months).

Destinations: England, Wales and Northern Ireland.

Costs: Placement costs vary depending on location and duration of project. Full-time volunteers usually receive free accommodation but may need to cover some amenities (such as heating or electricity). Travel to and from projects is generally covered by the volunteer.

Eligibility: There are no restrictions, although some short-term programmes (called 'working holidays') are age specific. Acceptance is granted on a case-by-case basis.

Groups or Individuals: Most conservation tasks are carried out by groups. Short-term placements tend to be in groups of approximately 12.

Annual no. of Volunteers: 47,000

Annual Projects: There are 180 different types of volunteering roles available and many different projects.

Partner Programmes: The National Trust works in partnership with many organisations, including BTCV, Mencap, Scouts and RSPB.

Selection & Interview Process: Ideally, applicants for full-time placements will be interviewed in person at the volunteering location. Interviews for short-term placements are more flexible.

In-country Support: Volunteers are given an induction and consistent support, particularly in areas such as health and safety.

Orangutan Foundation

7 Kent Tce, London NW1 4RP, UK
☎ +44 (0)20 7724 2912
fax +44 (0)20 7706 2613
info@orangutan.org.uk
www.orangutan.org.uk

This well-respected charity actively conserves the orang-utan and its Indonesian rainforest habitat. Volunteer placements are generally construction based, such as building release camps or conservation health centres. While volunteers do not have hands-on contact with orang-utans, they are likely to encounter some of the free ranging, ex-captive orang-utans in the locality and will have the opportunity to accompany resident assistants into the forest to search for wild orang-utans. They're also given the chance to visit the orang-utan care centre.

Status: Registered charity.

Timing & Length of Projects: Three teams of six weeks in length between May and October, with set starting dates.

Destinations: Indonesian Borneo.

Costs: The fee is £850, including accommodation, food and materials but not in-country transport.

Eligibility: Previous field experience is desirable but not necessary. Volunteers must be at least 18, physically fit, in good health and a member of the Orangutan Foundation. Applications should note that the placements require a great deal of physical exertion. Due to the nature of the work, placements are not open to those with physical disabilities.

Groups or Individuals: Participants are given each other's contact details beforehand in case they wish to travel together. Volunteers live as part of a team of 12 but are sometimes divided into smaller groups for field work. Volunteers can apply as friends, partners or families.

Annual no. of Volunteers: 36

Annual Projects: 1

Partner Programmes: 0

Selection & Interview Process: Apply online. Interviews are held in London or over the phone.

In-country Support: English coordinators are on-site, speak the local language, are trained in first aid and provide support and assistance to volunteers. While all health and safety precautions are taken, the project is located in a very remote area. A satellite phone is available for emergencies.

North American Organisations

Caribbean Volunteer Expeditions

Box 388, Corning, NY 14830, USA
☎ +1 (607) 962-7846
fax +1 (607) 936-1153
ahershcve@aol.com
www.cvexp.org

CVE offers working and learning vacations in the Caribbean that focus on historic preservation. Programmes include archaeology, recording and photography, museum development and historic cemetery surveys.

Status: Not-for–profit.

Timing & Length of Projects: Projects are offered during the winter months and are usually of one- to two-week duration.

Destinations: Mainly the English-speaking Caribbean.

Costs: Participants arrange and pay for their own travel expenses, accommodation and meals. A small registration fee (which varies with the project) covers insurance, group leader expenses and programme transportation.

Eligibility: Participants must be aged 21 and over. Work is often physical, in tropical conditions.

Groups or Individuals: Small groups (five to 10 people). Individual or pair programmes can be arranged.

Annual no. of Volunteers: 15-20

Annual Projects: 5-6

Partner Programmes: CVE provides programmes for Exploritas (formerly Elderhostel) and can organise affinity-group programmes.

Selection & Interview Process: Register via the website.

In-country Support: CVE has knowledgeable and experienced group leaders as well as local community support and participation.

Oceanic Society

30 Sir Francis Drake Blvd, PO Box 437, Ross, CA 94957, USA
☎ +1 (800) 326-7491
fax +1 (415) 474-3395
www.oceanic-society.org

The Oceanic Society is a non-profit organisation dedicated to protecting wildlife and marine biodiversity. Research projects are sponsored in cooperation with selected universities; volunteers help fund and conduct fieldwork.

Status: Non-profit organisation.

Timing & Length of Projects: Projects last seven to 10 days; volunteers may also register for back-to-back sessions lasting up to a month. Some projects (such as humpback whale migration research) have seasonal departure dates, but others operate year-round.

Destinations: Belize, Costa Rica, Suriname and Brazil.

Costs: Project fees of US$1500 to US$2500 cover meals and lodging, research activity costs, and in some cases, airfares. Volunteers must provide their own insurance.

Eligibility: Minimum age is 16. Fieldwork is often physically demanding, and a doctor's approval may be required.

Groups or Individuals: Volunteers usually work side-by-side with research scientists in small groups.

Annual no. of Volunteers: 250

Annual Projects: 30
Partner Programmes: 7
Selection & Interview Process: The organisation commissions the fieldwork conducted by its partner programmes, which must share a responsible and sincere interest in conservation education and research. Volunteer openings for each project are limited.
In-country Support: Each project enforces unique volunteer safety protocols; partner programme staffers guide participants throughout the project.

Australasian Organisations

Conservation Volunteers Australia
National Office, PO Box 423,
Ballarat, Vic. 3353, Australia
☎ +61 (0)3 5330 2600/1800 032 501
fax +61 (0)3 5330 2922
info@conservationvolunteers.com.au
www.conservationvolunteers.com.au
From wildlife surveys to tree planting, Conservation Volunteers Australia's work in urban, regional and remote Australia is renowned. CVA also offers World Conservation Programmes, enabling volunteers to join team-based conservation programmes around the globe. The organisation is a founding member of the Conservation Volunteers Alliance (www.cvalliance.org), bringing together worldwide organisations which promote and manage conservation volunteer projects. In 2006, Conservation Volunteers New Zealand (☎ +64 (0)9 376 7030; www.conservationvolunteers.co.nz) was launched.
Status: Not-for-profit organisation
Timing & Length of Assignments: Projects take place year-round in Australia and New Zealand with weekly departure dates; set departure dates for programs in other countries are advertised on www.conservationvolunteers.com.au (under World Conservation).
Destinations: California, Costa Rica, Ecuador, France, Galápagos Islands, Greece, Italy, Japan, New Zealand, South Africa and Turkey (the Gallipoli project).
Costs: Programmes in Australia and New Zealand start from A$40 per day, including meals, accommodation and in-country, project-related transport (international airfares and travel insurance not included).

Eligibility: Volunteers must be aged 18 to 70 and should be in good health. Volunteers with disabilities are catered for where possible.
Groups or Individuals: Volunteers are placed in teams of up to 10, with a team liaison officer who provides on-site training and management.
Annual no. of Volunteers: 12,500
Annual Projects: 2500
Partner Programmes: 1000
Selection & Interview Process: A short application form covering pre-existing medical conditions, allergies or injuries which may affect participation must be completed.
In-country Support: Teams are managed by team leaders who provide on-site training and management. Volunteers are given comprehensive safety advice and orientation before commencing projects.

Overseas Organisations

Fundación Jatun Sacha
Pasaje Eugenio de Santillán N34-248 y Maurian, Urbanización Rumipamba, Quito, Ecuador
☎ +593 2243 2240
fax +593 2331 8156
volunteer@jatunsacha.org
www.jatunsacha.org
This environmental conservation organisation offers placements in eight biological stations, including one on the Galápagos Islands and others in tropical rainforests and highlands. Volunteers are involved in reforestation, seed collection, developing and teaching classes in environmental education, agroforestry, reserve maintenance and the development of organic agriculture.
Status: Not-for-profit organisation.
Timing & Length of Projects: Volunteers can join projects year-round, and participate for anything from two weeks to a year.
Destinations: Ecuador.
Costs: Details of costs can obtained via email.
Eligibility: The minimum age for volunteering is 18. An interest in conservation, community development or environmental teaching.
Groups or Individuals: Both.
Annual no. of Volunteers: 800
Annual Projects: 8
Partner Programmes: The projects work alongside a number of smaller, local organisations.

continued on p180

Way Down Deep…

Having gained a degree in zoology, Katie Yewdall packed her bags for a volunteering placement with Blue Ventures (p174) in Madagascar. She found herself doing everything from underwater marine surveys to teaching English and biology and even scrubbing down the decks. She loved it enough to extend the usual six-week placement to 12 weeks. Her experience highlights the freedom possible through structured placements, as well as the motivation and initiative required to turn these sorts of placements into fulfilling adventures.

My main reason for choosing Blue Ventures was that I wanted to take part in a research and conservation project, not just to travel for its own sake. I wanted to contribute to a project that was set up to really benefit the local community and research in the area and not solely to recruit gap-year volunteers, which many rival organisations appeared to be doing. The country appealed to me as a place I didn't know much about and because few tourists venture there – I liked the sense of adventure. Other attractions were the small size of the organisation and the fact that volunteers seemed to range from gap-year students to career-breakers.

Part of being a volunteer… means that you are expected to 'muck in' with the less pleasant tasks, such as scrubbing algae off the bottom of the dive boat, and live a less-than-luxurious lifestyle, including showering from bottles of water which were stored up during the rare occasions when the water was running! But these are small hardships compared to those suffered by the villagers just along the beach, and I found it a humbling experience. You are also expected to motivate yourself, work independently and take on sometimes difficult tasks. The main benefit is a sense of achievement when these challenges are overcome,

such as standing up in front of a group of non-English-speaking children and teaching English, or passing the tests enabling you to contribute to the projects' research.

I was very happy with my experience and I tried to approach it with few expectations, as projects such as these can often be a let-down. I did feel that the research we were doing was worthwhile but I was disappointed, being a zoology graduate, that the level of scientific knowledge and of the work was not as high as I had hoped. However, this is a common problem with volunteer-based research.

It's hard to select one standout experience – there were many. These included passing research tests, meeting research targets and socialising with the locals. The most challenging were also the most rewarding: such as travelling by myself afterwards on local transport and communicating in the little Malagasy that I had learnt. Letting off steam with the rest of the volunteers and staff at our weekly 'party night' was also fun and the 'snorkel challenge' – drinking a bottle of beer through a snorkel as quickly as possible – was indeed challenging!

One of the best parts of the trip was that we were given plenty of freedom to shape our own experience. We could take part in as little, or as much, of the research and conservation work as we liked and were encouraged to initiate smaller short-term projects. Although a few volunteers complained of being bored and not getting enough diving, I found that you really did get out what you put in. The volunteers who got involved and explored the culture by going on pirogue sailing lessons with the locals, going for walks into the baobab forests, hanging out in the village bars or going snorkelling and

Katie helps out with measuring the girth of a Madagascan baobad tree

swimming were the ones who got the most out of the experience. Accomplishing things independently in my spare time was the most rewarding part of it all.

We had a lot of interaction with the local population through the English and nature lessons, the fisherman's-catch and fishing-observation surveys. We were also encouraged to go into the village to buy drinks and chocolate and to socialise and, like much of the experience, we could interact as little or as much as we liked. There were also several local Blue Ventures staff. I felt that interaction with the locals immensely enhanced my experience; there are some real characters in the village, and the locals are the people I remember most fondly.

After my trip, I travelled around the north of the country for a week independently. I would highly recommend seeing more of the area as the Blue Ventures project only involved a tiny part of a very diverse country.

I returned from Madagascar over two years ago, but I often think about my time there. I had an amazing experience when I was out there, which I'll never forget. It has changed the way I look at the world. It's not something that I would recommend to someone who wants a relaxing diving holiday. There are difficulties and problems, and it's not for everyone, but if you are willing to get involved and don't expect to be handed the experience on a plate then you will find it very rewarding. The beaches are beautiful, the work is fulfilling and the locals are captivating!

Katie Yewdall

Selection & Interview Process: Volunteers should apply with a letter indicating experience in relevant activities, reasons for applying, future interests, preferred station and preferred dates, a CV, a doctor's note of fitness, two passport-sized photos and the application fee.

In-country Support: All stations are in permanent communication with the main office in Quito. All station staff are first-aid trained and have emergency plans.

Golondrinas Foundation – Ibarra Ecuador

Parroquia La Carolina, Sector Guallupe, Km 48 from Ibarra via San Lorenzo, Provincia de Imbadura, Ecuador
☎ +593 6264 8679
fgolondrinas@yahoo.com
www.fgolondrinas.org

Working to conserve Ecuador's highland cloud forest and regenerate deforested areas, this organisation places volunteers within local communities to implement organic farming techniques and assist with environmental education. Volunteers live in villages in the Ecuadorian Andes.

Status: Not-for-profit organisation.

Timing & Length of Projects: Year-round for one to three months.

Destinations: Ecuador.

Costs: The fee is US$280 per month, including meals and accommodation.

Eligibility: Volunteers must have a basic level of Spanish. Experience is preferred and participants should be willing to work hard.

Groups or Individuals: Volunteers are accepted individually or in a group.

Annual no. of Volunteers: 100

Annual Projects: 5

Partner Programmes: 5

Selection & Interview Process: Application is by email, followed by an interview.

In-country Support: Project staff have first-aid equipment and a contact person is available at all times in Quito.

Millennium Elephant Foundation

Radeniya, Hiriwadunna, Kegalle, Sri Lanka
☎ +94 (0)35 226 3377
fax +94 35 226 6527
volunteer@millenniumelephantfoundation.com
www.millenniumelephantfoundation.com

Dedicated to the welfare of retired and sick elephants, this foundation offers field management, animal care, a mobile vet and resolution for human-elephant conflict in a remote village. They also provide English lessons for locals and maintain an eco-farm for herbal medicinal plants and quality food for the elephants. Volunteers work on all aspects of the project.

Status: Registered charity.

Timing & Length of Projects: Placements are for one, two or three months and can be extended to six months. Start dates are flexible.

Destinations: Sri Lanka.

Costs: The fee is £510 for three weeks, £680 for one month, and £1020 for six weeks. This includes food, twin-share accommodation, an administration fee, excursion costs and transport to and from the airport.

Eligibility: Volunteers must be committed to the cause and willing to work hard. It is preferable for volunteers to have experience or qualifications in an allied subject, although anyone with a sincere affection for elephants is welcome to apply. It may not be possible for those with physical disabilities to undertake the work; cases will be considered on an individual basis.

Groups or Individuals: The organisation can take on up to 20 volunteers, however, tasks are undertaken in groups of up to six. It is possible to volunteer as a group, couple or family.

Annual no. of Volunteers: 90

Annual Projects: 5

Partner Programmes: The organisation works with around 15 local groups, including the University of Peradeniya, the National Zoological Gardens and the Department of Wildlife Conservation.

Selection & Interview Process: The initial application is by email, followed by a telephone interview.

In-country Support: Staff live on-site and are available at all times for support and in case of emergency. Local hospitals are well equipped.

Sunseed Trust

Apdo 9, 04270 Sorbas, Almeria, Spain
☎ +34 950 525 770
sunseedspain@arrakis.es
www.sunseed.org.uk

Established in a once-abandoned village in the drylands of southern Spain, this community works to develop low-technology methods of living sustainably in a semi-arid environment. They also practise what they preach, demonstrating a sustainable lifestyle complete with solar electricity, solar cookers and composting toilets. Volunteers help out with organic growing, dryland regeneration trials, appropriate technology development and day-to-day work in the community. It is also possible for students to undertake their own projects as part of a long-term volunteer placement.

Status: Registered charity.

Timing & Length of Projects: Sunseed offers short- and long-term opportunities year-round. Short-term volunteers work four hours per morning, Monday to Saturday; long-term volunteers stay for a minimum of five weeks and work seven hours per day, Monday to Friday, with occasional weekend duties.

Destinations: Spain.

Costs: Fees vary depending on the time of year, but the price includes food and shared accommodation, although not travel. Students and unemployed people may receive a discount. Contact Sunseed for cost information.

Eligibility: Sunseed welcomes anyone interested in learning about sustainable living, and has had volunteers up to the age of 82. Applicants aged 16 to 18 require parental consent. No specific skills are required.

Groups or Individuals: There is a maximum of 35 people at the project at any one time, including volunteers and staff. It is possible to volunteer with a friend, partner or family.

Annual no. of Volunteers: Approximately 130.

Annual Projects: Sunseed runs various projects at its site in Almeria year-round.

Partner Programmes: Sunseed works with a similar programme in Tanzania.

Selection & Interview Process: You can apply by email, however, the connection can be poor in bad weather. If you don't receive a response, try calling.

In-country Support: Volunteers and staff live together in a community and so have 24-hour support in emergencies.

Wild Animal Rescue Foundation of Thailand

Phuket: 104/3 M3 Paklock, Talang, Phuket 83110 Thailand
☎ +66 76 260 491
fax +66 76 260 492
Bangkok: 65/1 3rd flr, Sukhumvit 55, Klongton, Wattana, Bangkok 10110 Thailand
☎ +66 2 712 9715
fax +66 2 712 9778
volunteer@warthai.org
www.warthai.org

Operating for over a decade, WAR is a wildlife-conservation group with projects established throughout Thailand. Volunteers help with the day-to-day running of sanctuaries and can work with gibbons, macaques, elephants and sea turtles. Placements are very hands-on and volunteers prepare food, clean, and construct or repair buildings and enclosures. WAR does not offer opportunities for scientific experimentation or research.

Status: Not-for-profit NGO.

Timing & Length of Projects: Placements are for a minimum of three months and commence year-round.

Destinations: Thailand.

Costs: Fees vary according to the duration of the project and the kind of activities involved, but include orientation and accommodation. In-country transport is not included, but pick-up from the local airport and a weekly trip into town is.

Eligibility: The minimum age is 18 and fluent English is essential. No other experience is required, although participants need to have a genuine interest in the care of animals, good teamwork skills and must be physically fit. A number of vaccinations are required.

Groups or Individuals: Volunteers work in a group of up to 10. It is possible to apply with a friend or partner.

Annual no. of Volunteers: Approximately 50.

Annual Projects: WAR works within four different wildlife sanctuaries and places volunteers on three projects.

Partner Programmes: WAR works with a number of local NGOs and governmental organisations like the Royal Forestry Department. It also receives support from international agencies like the WWF and IWC.

Selection & Interview Process: Send an application form and short letter about your motivation, along with description of related experience or a CV and a recent passport-sized photo.

In-country Support: Local staff are available at all times for support and assistance and in case of an emergency.

Skilled Volunteering

In addition to the organisations listed here, many of the projects in the Development (p157) and Conservation & Wildlife (p171) sections are keen to accept volunteers with relevant skills, qualifications or experience and will sometimes tailor a placement for you.

UK Organisations

2Way Development

The Hub, 5 Torrens St, London EC1V 1NQ, UK
☎ +44 (0)207 148 6110
volunteer@2waydevelopment.com
www.2waydevelopment.com

This organisation arranges individual volunteer placements by matching the skills of participants with appropriate needs within grassroots development organisations in the developing world. Volunteers assist with project development, training or research. Past placements have included co-writing a key publication for a large environmental charity in India, setting up an accountancy training programme for NGOs in Fiji, training small-business owners in Morocco, and campaigning for changes to human rights policy in Cambodia.

Status: Social Enterprise.

Timing & Length of Projects: Three to 24 months (six months average), start dates are flexible.

Destinations: Latin America, Africa, the Middle East, Asia and the South Pacific.

Costs: The fee is £850, including placement arrangement, accommodation, pre-departure training and in-country greeting.

Eligibility: The minimum age is 21. A degree and/or two years' work experience is preferred. People with disabilities are welcome to apply.

Groups or Individuals: Individuals.

Annual no. of Volunteers: Up to 300.

Annual Projects: 150

Partner Programmes: As placements are most often for individuals, the organisation has as many partner programmes as projects. 2Way Development works closely with these organisations to ensure that volunteers are channelled into appropriate areas of need.

Selection & Interview Process: Interviews are in person whenever possible; otherwise by telephone.

In-country Support: Some projects are located in countries where a 2Way Development representative is based. For all projects, there is a local organisation which provides professional and personal support and which has guidelines to follow in emergency situations.

Junior Art Club

PO Box GP 1301 Accra, Ghana
☎ +233 2141 4223
kelvin@junior-art-club.org
www.junior-art-club.org

This organisation aims to give disadvantaged children and youth from Ghana's urban slums the opportunity to express themselves creatively. Volunteers help with workshops to guide kids in various art forms. Half of each placement is also spent collaborating with local, skilled artists and learning a new art form, such as carving, drumming, textile making, basketry or bead design.

Status: Not-for-profit.

Timing & Length of Projects: Placements can range from one week to a year and are open year-round.

Destinations: Ghana.

Costs: The programme fee is £650 for a month, £970 for two months, £1200 for three months and £240 for any additional months after that. This includes accommodation, food, airport pick-up and daily transport to projects.

Eligibility: Applicants should be aged 18 to 70. All volunteers are expected to have some skills in the arts. Core attributes required are self-motivation, creativity and commitment.

Groups or Individuals: Both.

Annual no. of Volunteers: 10

Annual Projects: 12

Partner Programmes: 5

Selection & Interview Process: Application is via email.

In-country Support: Volunteers have 24-hour support from the local JAC teams.

Karmi Farm Clinic

c/o Nomad Travel Store, Unit 34, Redburn
Industrial Estate, Woodall Rd, Enfield,
Middlesex EN3 4LE, UK
☎ +44 (0)845 260 0044
fax +44 (0)845 310 4475
cathy@nomadtravel.co.uk
www.nomadtravel.co.uk/
t-karmifarmcharityproject.aspx
www.karmifarm.com

This small, grassroots clinic is set up in a
guesthouse near Darjeeling, in the foothills
of the Himalaya. It offers medical assistance
to local farming families – volunteers will
find themselves dealing with machete cuts,
conjunctivitis, scabies and other day-to-day
injuries or illnesses common to subsistence
farmers living in basic conditions. The clinic
is the first port of call to locals and relies on
volunteers to keep it running.

Status: Not-for-profit organisation.
Timing & Length of Projects: Placements are
from two weeks to two months, year-round.
Destinations: India.
Costs: Volunteers pay £50 per week for food
and accommodation.
Eligibility: Applicants must be medically
qualified to either nurse or doctor level. There
are no other specific restrictions, however,
applicants should be aware that travel to
outreach patients is all by foot in a hilly
environment at 1200 to 1500 metres above
sea level.
Groups or Individuals: Volunteers are taken
on individually and work with the local
healthcare worker. The guesthouse where
the volunteer is accommodated offers cheap
rates for board and lodging for the family or
partners of volunteers.
Annual no. of Volunteers: 8
Annual Projects: 1
Partner Programmes: 0
Selection & Interview Process: Applicants
first send a CV, which is followed up by a
telephone interview. The volunteer is then
interviewed by a previous volunteer over the
phone. It is preferable that there is some
person-to-person contact in London prior to
departure.
In-country Support: The clinic is based at a
guesthouse which offers 24-hour in-country
contact.

Rokpa UK Overseas Projects

Kagyu Samye Ling Tibetan Centre,
Eskdaalemuir, Langholm,
Dumfriesshire DG13 0QL, UK
☎ +44 (0)1387 373232, ext 230
fax +44 (0)1387 373340
charity@rokpauk.org
www.rokpauk.org

Working mainly in Tibetan and Nepalese
communities, Rokpa is run almost entirely by
volunteers. Its soup kitchen in Kathmandu
serves 800 meals per day during the winter.
It also runs free medical clinics and supplies
Tibetan schools with English-language
teachers. Many of the placements are in
small and relatively remote communities.

Status: Registered charity.
Timing & Length of Projects: Placements in
Tibet are for a minimum of six months, usually
starting in March. Placements in Nepal are
open from December to March, however,
volunteers can specify their availability
between these dates.
Destinations: Nepal and Tibetan areas of
China.
Costs: All volunteers must be entirely self-
funding, with the exception of teaching
placements in Tibet, where accommodation
and food is provided.
Eligibility: The minimum age is 25. For
teaching placements in Tibet, a TEFL
certificate and some teaching experience
is required, with a preference for additional
experience living in a developing country.
Clinical placements require relevant medical
qualifications. For placements in Nepal,
volunteers must be physically fit and able to
cope well with stress. Placements are not
suitable for those with disabilities.
Groups or Individuals: Teaching placements
are for individuals or pairs. Medical
placements are usually in a group. In Nepal,
volunteers work in a group of up to six.
Annual no. of Volunteers: Varies according
to local needs, however, approximately 15
annually.
Annual Projects: Rokpa has over 120
ongoing projects.
Partner Programmes: Rokpa works with local
communities and local government for most
of its projects.

Selection & Interview Process: For teaching placements in Tibet, applicants are invited for an interview in Scotland, although where this isn't practical, telephone interviews are conducted. Volunteers for Nepal are selected via a questionnaire.

In-country Support: For Tibetan placements, volunteers rely on email communication with Rokpa, although there is a local project leader on-site. Medical volunteers work as a group and must be self-reliant. Volunteers in Nepal have a project leader responsible for training, who also provides support.

North American Organisations

ArtCorps Inc

240 County Road Ipswich, MA 01938, USA
☎ +1 (978) 998 7995
fax +1 (978) 356 3250
info@artcorp.org
www.artcorp.org

ArtCorps sends professional artists to Central America for one year to work with grassroots NGOs and local artisans. Volunteers train and engage local staff and communities, assisting them to communicate social messages through art.

Status: Non-profit organisation.

Timing & Length of Projects: One year; annual departures in January.

Destinations: Guatemala, Honduras and El Salvador.

Costs/Pay: Volunteers should bring US$1800 to US$2200 to cover any personal expenses such as internet, phone and vacation travel costs, including airfares to and from the host country.

Eligibility: College graduate with community work experience. Spanish fluency is required.

Groups or Individuals: Volunteers work individually.

Annual no. of Volunteers: 10, with future plans for 20 or more.

Annual Projects: 8

Partner Programmes: 8

Selection & Interview Process: Organisation staff visit prospective partners to present objectives and evaluate the local environment and proposed volunteer housing. Linguistic aptitude and professional background are considered when matching volunteers to host organisations. Read the Artist Information Packet, available online, for more details.

In-country Support: A three-day orientation in Guatemala is provided before artists travel to their sites. An in-country coordinator in Guatemala is available to support artists with questions or emergencies; volunteers are also required to be in weekly email contact with the US office.

Ecuador Volunteer Foundation

Yanéz Pinzón N25-106 y Av Colón,
Quito, Ecuador
☎ +593 (2) 255-7749
fax +593 (2) 222 6544
www.ecuadorvolunteer.org

This NGO offers volunteer opportunities in community development, environmental protection, health and education in Ecuador and Argentina.

Status: Non-profit.

Timing & Length of Projects: Short-term projects last two weeks; long-term projects range from one month to two years. Projects are available throughout the year.

Destinations: Ecuador and Argentina.

Costs: Volunteers are responsible for travel and insurance costs. 'Free projects' provide volunteers with lodging and meals; 'low-cost projects' involve hostel accommodation or a homestay with a local family and a monthly room-and-board fee of approximately US$360. An optional donation of US$250 to US$300 defrays programme administrative expenses.

Eligibility: Volunteers must be between 18 and 40 years old; no nationality restrictions apply. 'Free projects' require specific professional qualifications; 'low-cost projects' have no such requirements. No accommodation is available for applicants with disabilities.

Groups or Individuals: Both individual and group opportunities are available.

Annual no. of Volunteers: 130

Annual Projects: 25 in Ecuador and five in Argentina.

Partner Programmes: 3

Selection & Interview Process: Candidates are interviewed by partner-programme staff, then selected based on experience.

In-country Support: Upon arrival in-country, volunteers attend a brief orientation at the organisation's main office in Quito. Local partner-programme staff support volunteers throughout the project.

Health Volunteers Overseas
1900 L St NW, Ste 310,
Washington, DC 20036, USA
☎ +1 202 296 0928
info@hvousa.org
www.hvousa.org

Health Volunteers Overseas (HVO) works to increase healthcare access in developing countries through clinical training and education programmes in child health, primary care, trauma and rehabilitation, essential surgical care, oral health, infectious diseases, nursing education and burn management.

Status: Non-profit organisation.
Timing & Length of Projects: One month; longer placements are possible. Departures throughout the year.
Destinations: China, Cambodia, Vietnam, Bhutan, India, Moldova, Ethiopia, South Africa, Tanzania, Uganda, Malawi, Peru, Nicaragua, Honduras, Costa Rica, Guyana, St Lucia, Palau and Samoa.
Costs: Volunteers must bear travel and insurance costs. Most sites provide room, board and daily transportation for either a nominal fee or free of charge.
Eligibility: Qualified American health professionals of any age may apply. There are no health restrictions.
Groups or Individuals: Generally individuals; burn-management programmes require small groups. Family members may accompany volunteers.
Annual no. of Volunteers: 300
Annual Projects: 65
Partner programs: 52, both in the US and abroad.
Selection & Interview Process: The organisation requires prospective programmes to submit detailed project proposals, after which staffers will visit the programme in order to assess project suitability. Experienced programme directors screen volunteer applicants, taking into account prior healthcare and international experience.
In-country Support: Volunteers receive an orientation package several months prior to

Photo: Azdady

Protecting the Madagascan chameleon

departure. On-site contacts orient volunteers upon arrival and support them throughout their stay.

Australasian Organisations

Australian Business Volunteers
Unit 3 & 4, Association House, 71 Constitution Ave, Campbell ACT 2612, Australia
(PO Box 25, Deakin West, ACT 2600)
☎ +61 (0)2 6151 9999
fax +61 (0)2 6103 9129
info@abv.org.au
www.abv.org.au

ABV is an overseas development agency established in 1981, largely funded by AusAID. ABV focuses on assisting the development of the private sector as a 'sustainable engine for development'. At the request of clients in developing countries of Southeast Asia and the Pacific, ABV sends skilled and experienced Australian volunteers to undertake short-term training and advisory and mentoring assignments with client counterparts overseas, including micro-businesses and small- and medium-sized businesses, local government bodies, NGOs and civil society organisations.

Status: ABV Ltd is a not-for-profit incorporated company, limited by guarantee.
Timing & Length of Assignments: Volunteers are sent on assignments throughout the year, lasting between one and 12 months.
Destinations: Cambodia, East Timor, Fiji, Indonesia, Laos, Papua New Guinea, the Philippines, the Solomon Islands, Thailand, Vanuatu and Vietnam.
Costs/Pay: ABV pays all costs (visas, airfares and insurance) but encourages contributions from clients (who often provide

accommodation, food or allowances). Volunteers receive a weekly allowance.

Eligibility: No age restrictions (but ABV is unable to provide insurance coverage for those over 80). The average age of ABV volunteers is about 55. People with disabilities can apply.

Groups or Individuals: Individual volunteers. Some volunteers are accompanied by their partners (who travel at their own expense).

Annual no. of Volunteers: 260 volunteers in 2006/07.

Annual Projects: Between 200 and 250.

Partner Programmes: In-country organisations, business councils and chambers of commerce in the Asia-Pacific, and Australian professional organisations.

Selection & Interview Process: A CV with evidence of work skills and experience is required, along with recent work referees. This is followed by an interview which focuses on a set of core competencies.

In-country Support: There's an in-country manager in each country to provide support.

Engineers Without Borders Australia

PO Box 708, North Melbourne VIC 3051, Australia

☎ +61 (0)3 9329 1166

info@ewb.org.au

www.ewb.org.au

The ideal opportunity for engineers with a global conscience, EWB works with disadvantaged communities to improve their quality of life through education and the implementation of sustainable engineering projects. Collaborating with engineering students, professionals, industry and the broader community, EWB provides assistance to local communities on water, sanitation and energy projects, information and communication technology and disability access. EWB volunteers will continue to be in demand if the worldwide shortage of skilled engineers continues.

Status: Not-for-profit limited company.

Timing & Length of Projects: There are no set departure dates, as volunteers are sent overseas as projects arise. Projects are typically three, six or 12 months in length.

Destinations: Cambodia, India, Indonesia, Laos, Maldives, Nepal and East Timor. Projects are also run in remote areas of Australia.

Costs/Pay: Volunteers receive an allowance of around A$1000 a month, depending on the country. EWB covers all travel, insurance and medical costs.

Eligibility: Overseas positions are advertised and volunteers are selected based on merit. Applicants must be over 18 years of age.

Groups or Individuals: Volunteers are typically sent on their own, although some volunteers may spend time with other volunteers on ongoing projects.

Annual no. of Volunteers: EWB has sent 40 volunteers overseas since it started in 2003.

Annual Projects: In 2007 EWB managed over 25 projects overseas and in remote areas of Australia.

Partner Programmes: EWB works with partner organisations ranging from small grassroots organisations to the likes of Unicef.

Selection & Interview Process: All overseas positions are advertised on the website and are open to all paid EWB members (membership is A$50 for professionals; A$10 for students). You must submit a formal application for a position that outlines your experience and addresses project-selection criteria. Applicants are then interviewed and selected based on merit.

In-country Support: Volunteers are supported by EWB partner organisations and their safety is monitored by a EWB in-country support officer. In addition to financial support, volunteers receive pre-departure training.

Options for the Under 30s

Many people choose to volunteer soon after leaving school, either as a means of gaining work experience and directing career goals or simply as a way of contributing to the global community before heading into university or the workforce. The organisations listed in this section cater largely to younger volunteers. There are also organisations listed elsewhere in this chapter that aren't geared specifically to those under 30, but are nevertheless popular with younger participants. Check out Dakshinayan (p157), AidCamps (p165), the Karen Hilltribes Trust (p169) and the Orangutan Foundation (p175).

UK Organisations

Concordia

19 North St, Portslade, Brighton BN41 1DH, UK
☎ +44 (0)1273 422218
fax +44 (0)1273 421182
info@concordiavolunteers.org.uk
www.concordiavolunteers.org.uk
Concordia offers diverse volunteer opportunities to those over the age of 18. Past volunteers have undertaken tasks like painting orphanages in the Ukraine, organising art activities for kids in Mexico, working with disabled people in France and Germany, and constructing a health centre in Uganda. Other activities include restoration, archaeology, construction and nature conservation.
Status: Registered charity.
Timing & Length of Projects: Projects run for two to four weeks, with the majority operating from June to September. A smaller programme operates from October to May.
Destinations: Worldwide.
Costs: Volunteers pay a registration fee to Concordia of £180 and fund their own travel and insurance. Board and accommodation is free of charge for projects in Europe, North America, Japan and South Korea. For projects in Latin America, Asia, the Middle East and Africa, volunteers pay an extra fee on arrival of between £80 to £200 that covers food and accommodation, as well as funding the programme in the host country.
Eligibility: Volunteers must be at least 16. There are no required skills or experience, but volunteers must be motivated, and committed to the project. People with disabilities can apply, however, there is a limited number of suitable projects available.
Groups or Individuals: A maximum of two volunteers are sent from Concordia to any one project. Once there, volunteers work with a group of 10 to 15 participants from around the world. Volunteers can apply to be placed with a friend or partner.
Annual no. of Volunteers: 350
Annual Projects: Approximately 2000 projects are available.
Partner Programmes: 80
Selection & Interview Process: All projects are listed on the website with an application form. For projects in Africa, Asia and Latin America volunteers must attend a preparation weekend before departure.

In-country Support: During the project, volunteers are supported 24 hours a day by a local coordinator. On their return, volunteers give a report of their experience and any issues that arise are followed up.

North American Organisations

Youth Challenge International

555 Richmond St W, Ste 313, PO Box 1205, Toronto, ON, M5V 3B1, Canada
☎ +1 416 504 3370
fax +1 416 504 3376
generalinfo@yci.org
www.yci.org
Youth Challenge International builds the skills, experience and confidence of young Canadians by engaging them in overseas international development projects with local youth-serving organisations.
Status: Registered charity.
Timing & Length of Projects: Four to 10 weeks.
Destinations: Ghana, Tanzania, Kenya, Guyana, Costa Rica, Vanuatu, Guatemala and Nicaragua.
Costs: Applicants must fundraise between C$2800 (for four-week projects) and C$3900 (for 12-week programmes); this fee covers meals, lodging and in-country transportation, as well as a contribution to local administrative expenses. In addition, volunteers are responsible for the costs of their personal equipment, medical expenses, visas and airfares.
Eligibility: Canadian youth aged 18 to 30.
Groups or Individuals: Volunteers may engage individually or in a group project, with team sizes averaging from four to 12 people.
Annual no. of Volunteers: 17
Annual Projects: 32
Partner Programmes: 9
Selection & Interview Process: Prospective YCI volunteers can apply online through the website at www.yci.org. Once the application is received, it is reviewed by the volunteer programs team, and if successful, a phone interview will be scheduled with the applicant. Selection is not based on quotas – volunteers are selected on motivation, aptitude and attitude. Placement in a program will be determined by past travel, work, education and volunteer experience as well as skills and interest.

Tracking the behaviour and range of elephants in Tsavo National Park, Kenya

In-country Support: For the Africa programmes, YCI has a Country Program Manager responsible for overall programming and volunteer support. In some cases, there are also other locally identified staff supporting volunteers and programming. YCI staff do not live with or provide constant supervision to volunteers, but are always on-call. Groups function as a unit to deliver programming with ongoing support, risk and safety management and guidance from the Country Program Manager. In both Guyana and Central America, YCI has an International Program Manager (IPM) responsible for overall programming and volunteer support.

Australasian Organisations

World Youth International

PO Box 25, Hindmarsh SA 5007, Australia
☎ +61 (0)8 8340 1266
fax +61 (0)8 8312 3128
admin@worldyouth.org.au
www.worldyouth.org.au

WYI has an emphasis on supporting children around the world and enables young people to make a contribution in developing countries. There are two types of packages available. Flexible overseas service projects run in China, Kenya, Nepal and Peru. These involve general or professional teaching in a primary school and programmes are tailored to individuals' timing and style preferences. Overseas action programmes offer the chance to work in rural development, education, healthcare or environmental projects with communities in Kenya, Nepal or Peru. The focus is on cultural immersion and contribution to 'people less fortunate'. Volunteers work in leader-led groups. Approved by AusAID and a signatory to the Australian Council for International Development (ACFID), the organisation is also non-religious and non-political, and has a good reputation for safety and the variety of programmes on offer. It reputedly impacts on the lives of over 40,000 children each year.

Status: Not-for-profit organisation.

Timing & Length of Assignments: Overseas action programmes are five to 12 weeks long with an optional adventure package at the end.

Destinations: China, Kenya, Nepal, Cambodia, Uganda, India and Peru.

Costs: The overseas action programme costs from A$3780 to A$5370.

Eligibility: You will need to be aged between 18 and 30 years of age to participate on the team programme, the overseas action programme. The minimum age for our overseas service project is 18.

Groups or Individuals: Individuals, friends and families are encouraged.

Annual no. of Volunteers: 150

Annual Projects: 25

Partner Programmes: 30

Selection & Interview Process: To apply for an overseas placement, go to www.worldyouth.org.au and complete the application form (including an application fee of A$55). You will then be required to complete an online interview form followed by a 30-minute phone discussion which is designed to cover all elements of your programme. Once selected, you will then have two weeks to pay a deposit of A$550.

In-country Support: You will be guided by a professional in-country programme manager who will take you through an extensive orientation programme and provide regular ongoing support. Weekly meetings allow you to debrief your highs and lows for the week and plan for the week ahead.

Twelve Months in Uganda

Patrick Pringle, an economic consultant, wanted to do something worthwhile on his career break. He approached 2Way Development about working in international development. After three months of consultation, 2Way Development organised a 12-month voluntary placement for him in Uganda. He became a health project worker for a community development organisation that aimed to improve the people's quality of life in rural areas through poverty eradication. 2Way Development asked him to write a diary of his experience to demonstrate to new volunteers how his skills were used in a positive way, and to highlight some of the common challenges of working in a very different environment.

In the autumn of 2004 I decided that I wanted to take a break from my job as an economic development consultant to volunteer in a developing country. I got in touch with 2Way Development and met up for an informal chat about the possible options. I was keen to find a placement which would give me valuable professional experience while at the same time enable me to make a real contribution to reducing poverty in Africa.

I chose to work for an NGO called FUGA that works with rural communities in Uganda. FUGA aims to reduce poverty in rural communities in western Uganda through its healthcare, education and income-generation programmes.

March to April, 2004

My job with FUGA incorporates organisational development, project management, fundraising and liaison with donors, so already I'm getting a real variety of work. From designing new projects to driving the ambulance, in a small organisation you have to muck in and get on with whatever needs to be done.

The first few weeks have been quite a culture shock, but I have been made incredibly welcome. On my arrival, the staff at FUGA organised a party for me, then, at 5.30am on my first full day in Uganda, I was boarding a bus to visit the villages where FUGA works. I will be making regular visits to the project sites, which involves a six-hour journey to Ntungamo District, a hilly part of the country close to the

border with Rwanda. Visits to the villages are usually a little hectic and often involve buzzing around on a motorbike to visit the various projects, check on progress and speak to beneficiaries. Many of the villagers are surprised to see a *muzungu* (white person) and the children either come to hug me or run away in fear!

Even though I've only been in Uganda for a couple of months, I am really settling in to the lifestyle and my job. It's certainly very different from my life back in the UK. Adjusting to 'Africa time', keeping your temper in the face of Ugandan bureaucracy, and surviving the hot, dusty and chaotic taxi-parks all take some getting used to, but the rewards of living and working in Africa certainly make it all worthwhile.

May to June, 2004

After four months I'm getting used to life in Uganda, though there are still surprises every day! Working with a Ugandan NGO, much of my work has focused on organisational development and putting systems in place. While it would be great to start implementing projects, there is so much that needs doing first in terms of capacity-building within the organisation and getting things organised. I have been busy working with colleagues on a new strategy, undertaking staff reviews and also putting a development plan into place for the Health Centre.

It is strange how quickly you get used to seeing poverty, though every so often I see something that reminds me why I chose to volunteer. Recently I met a teenage girl who is blind and deaf because she was not immunised against measles. I also took the body of a mother of seven back to her family. She had walked five kilometres to get help for a potentially treatable heart condition, but by the time she reached the clinic she was past helping. While such images are distressing, it can be a powerful reminder of how much we take basic services for granted back home.

On a lighter note, I'm getting around a lot at weekends and meeting lots of people – both Ugandans and expats. I spent four days climbing Mount Elgon, which was a great escape from the heat of Kampala. While camping in a cave, my rucksack was attacked by fruit bats searching for the bananas that I'd carried for the journey, so for three days of the trip I stank of rotten bananas! I'm also getting used to the local diet, which largely consists of *matooke* (green bananas) or *posho* (maize meal) and some sauce, often peanut or meat. The *senene* (fried grasshoppers) are surprisingly good washed down with a few bottles of Nile beer!

July to August, 2004

The longer I work in Uganda the more I realise that progress has to be measured by the little steps forward rather than aiming for the lofty, if naïve, ambitions I had when I first arrived. It often seems to be the case that when progress is made in one area of work problems emerge in another! For example, FUGA are making significant advances with improvements in the performance of the Medical Health Centre, a key project for the organisation. We have received funding from the UK-based retailer MFI to renovate the Health Centre, the medical staff have moved into a rented house, providing more space for patient care, and a new midwife has joined the team. Patient numbers are up as a result of improved sensitisation within the local community, which has increased income for FUGA to deliver additional health services. To detract from all this positive news, this month we received only half the expected funding from a regular donor making my job of balancing the books nearly impossible!

I am continuing to meet so many interesting people, both Ugandans and expats. My social life in Kampala tends to be a mix of these two worlds. I feel very lucky that my day-to-day work is with Ugandans, as I am learning so much about African life and attitudes and have made some really good friends. A couple of weeks ago I spent the weekend with my good friend, Silver, in his village in central Uganda, and another good mate, Martin, is ensuring I make the most of the Kampala nightlife! It's also good to have a network of expat mates who can empathise with some of the frustrations of working in Africa and help put the bad days into perspective over a drink or two.

Perhaps the most inspiring person I have met this month is a young man who I shall call William. William was abducted by the Lord's Resistance Army (LRA) in Northern Uganda at the age of 13. After spending nearly five years with the rebels as a child soldier, he escaped. In retaliation for his escape, the LRA returned to his village and killed his family and neighbours, burning them alive in their houses. William survived, as he was undergoing rehabilitation at a government centre at the time. I met William in Kampala where he was living on the streets carrying luggage at the bus-park to pay for food. He is determined to get his life back on track, and has gained the support of his local member of parliament, who verified his story. We are now in the process of enrolling William in an electronics course so that he can start up a workshop mending radios, phones and other electrical goods, while his local member has provided enough money for him to rent a room. When I see his determination in the face of such adversity it really puts my frustrations into perspective.

September to October, 2004

FUGA, the NGO I am working for, currently has a proposal being considered by the Japanese embassy, so this has kept me pretty busy. If successful, it will be a great boost to the community and to FUGA and will involve the construction of a community hall and staff quarters for our Health Centre. However, there has been a lot of supporting evidence to gather to ensure we progress to the next stage. In Europe this task would be fairly straightforward, but not here! Chasing around for up-to-date statistics, quotes from construction companies etc was hot, time-consuming and pretty frustrating, but we got it finished in time.

Four good friends of mine have come out from the UK to visit me, so I'm making the most of

Paddy with the Tiger
Club Football Team

being a tourist! We've rafted the Nile, tracked mountain gorillas and visited some of the less classy Ugandan nightspots but had a great time. I thought seeing old friends might make me feel a bit homesick, but actually it made me realise what amazing experiences I'm having here compared to what I would be doing back home.

In the last few months I have been helping out with football coaching for the Tigers Club Project which works to improve the lives of street children and enable them to realise their potential. The football activities provide the kids with a much-needed break from life on the streets and is a key tool for outreach and relationship-building. The Tigers Club Project also provides a refuge, medical care, education and resettlement programmes, giving the children a permanent alternative to life on the streets. Going to Tigers every Thursday is a refreshing change and very different to my work with FUGA. The Tigers staff are great, and the boys are so full of energy and fun despite their difficult situations.

Less positive news for Uganda was the suspension of the Global Fund, a UN fund to fight HIV/AIDS, malaria and tuberculosis. Corruption is a real problem here and it seems that substantial funds have gone astray. For NGOs like FUGA this is really disappointing news, as we were hoping that we could use this money to help those who really need it. For example, malaria is the most common illness treated at our Health Centre and kills and disables hundreds of people in the area each year. The problems with the Global Fund illustrate just how complicated the delivery of effective aid can be. On one hand, it is essential to allow developing nations to determine their own priorities, but on the other, this corruption has to stop.

November to December, 2004

November was memorable for the rioting in Kampala. With campaigning for next year's elections beginning, the government arrested the leader of the opposition, Dr Kizza Besigye. This sparked riots in the capital and for a few days Kampala was a tense and worrying place to be. The chances of genuinely free and fair elections seem pretty slim right now. I just hope that Uganda doesn't destabilise further. At times like this I appreciate that I can always head back to England, but for millions of Africans, when drought or war strike, there is no plane out of here.

I have been helping FUGA to redesign its education programme. FUGA has been supporting orphans and vulnerable children (OVCs) to go to school for five years, providing school uniforms, books and stationery to over 90 children, and also helping with contributions towards school fees for secondary students. However, everyone at FUGA felt it was time to look at the issue of education in a more structured way. Having spoken to teachers, parents and children, we have now decided to focus on helping four UPE (Universal Primary Education) schools in Ntungamo district. These are government schools that provide 'free' education; however, many families can't afford the books, pens, pencils and uniforms to send their children there.

Christmas in Africa was brilliant! The whole country grinds to a halt and everyone in Kampala returns to their village. It's so refreshing that the Christmas hype doesn't begin until the 20th of December! I went to the carol service in Kampala Cathedral, then headed for Lake Bunyonyi, where I spent a great Christmas camping with friends. A group of over 20 of us took over an island, ate, drank, swam and had a great time. Yet again, we were made so welcome by the local people, especially Patrick, the manager of the Bushara camp.

January to February, 2004

I really can't believe that my time in Uganda is coming to an end. The New Year has mainly been spent tying up loose ends and making sure that the work is handed over properly to colleagues. I've also been making arrangements for another volunteer to take over from me. By February I'll be in trekking in Kenya, then on to Tanzania to laze on a beach… and eventually home to England.

I have learnt so much in the last year: about Africa, about development issues and most of all about myself. I think I've experienced just about every emotion in the last year – both good and bad. I've seen incredibly uplifting sights and those which leave me awake at night searching for answers. At times I've felt proud of my achievements, and at other times frustrated that I could not do more. But most of all, I feel inspired to keep helping people who are less fortunate than me, but who always seem to live life with a smile on their face.

Patrick Pringle

Polly Freer harvests local weeds to eat while working in a village community in Zambia with the Church Mission Society

07 Religious Organisations

Assisting those in need has long been the custom of faith-based and religious organisations. Many of these organisations, particularly from the three monotheist faiths – Christianity, Judaism and Islam – provide aid and relief through overseas missions, and often welcome volunteers to help them achieve their goals. The degree to which religion plays a role in volunteer work varies from organisation to organisation. Some focus mainly on specific hands-on projects and faith is more of an underlying element; others have a strong evangelistic mission, with the promotion of faith being their main aim.

So, although many of these organisations require you to belong to the faith in which they are rooted, the extent to which you need to be practising depends both on the organisation and the specific project. In general, though, you don't need to be devout to obtain a placement through a religious organisation. In some cases you don't even need to be a member of the faith in which the organisation is based. Many Christian organisations are nondenominational or inter-denominational, meaning that as long as you support the Christian basis of faith, it doesn't matter whether you are Catholic, Baptist or whatever. Christian organisations do offer the most opportunities for volunteers. Islamic relief organisations tend to rely on permanent staff, but several Judaist organisations place Jewish volunteers overseas, and there are also some Buddhist groups.

The types of work volunteers become involved in through religious organisations are similar to that offered by other charities and NGOs working in the development sector, taking in everything from medical aid to teaching, construction to running soup kitchens. Volunteering programmes also take various forms: some farm out groups of volunteers on short-term workcamp-style placements, while others send individuals to live and work in communities for extended periods (usually for a minimum of one year).

Why volunteer through a religious organisation? Perhaps you relish the thought of sharing and working through your faith overseas. Or perhaps you never made it past the first page of the Talmud, Bible or Quran but agree with the principles which motivate the work of these organisations. If you have an interest in volunteering and, in addition, are in tune with the beliefs and practices of a religious sending organisation, then combining the two may lead to your ideal placement.

This chapter takes a look at what kinds of volunteer placement are available through religious organisations. As these organisations run both structured and organised placements, it's worth reading the How Do They Work? and Pros & Cons sections of this chapter in conjunction with the equivalent sections in Chapters 5 (p91) and 6 (p149). Though we've pulled together a lot of information here, it's worth keeping in mind that your local faith communities can also be a good source of information, as many have links with overseas communities or NGOs that take on volunteers.

How Do They Work?

Costs & Length of Placements

Religious volunteering programmes generally work in the same way as secular programmes. The majority of religious programmes are well established and many have been running for a long time (we found one with a 200-year history!), so they are often exceptionally well organised. Depending on whether they're organised or structured, the cost and duration of placements vary. Many require you to fundraise a substantial chunk of the cost and then they make up the shortfall, providing anything from your airfare to a roof over your head. Others are totally self-funding – you're responsible for all costs. None of the religious organisations listed in this chapter is profit based; all money raised goes towards the cost of your placement, or is invested in the overseas community or the aims of the religious group itself.

While there are a few short-term placements, in general religious organisations are looking for an extended time commitment from their volunteers.

Selection & Eligibility

The eligibility criteria and selection processes for volunteers also vary greatly between organisations. However, almost all require you to have an understanding of the faith in which the organisation is rooted, and some may require a demonstrated devotion to it. Many of these organisations send only a handful of volunteers overseas each year and so competition for placements can be stiff. Interviews are generally conducted in person and references are required (sometimes these are from your local faith community). Depending on the type of work you'll be doing, qualifications or relevant experience may also be required.

The main qualities that religious organisations are looking for in a volunteer are: an understanding of the fundamental tenets of their religion; an ability to empathise; a capacity to live in basic conditions; and a willingness to take on various (sometimes not-so-pleasant) tasks as the need arises.

What to Look for

In choosing a religious organisation to volunteer through, there are a number of things to keep in mind. A fundamental point to consider is the level of evangelism required of you

This fragile vessel symbolises the precarious livelihoods of people in East Timor, where volunteers are welcomed.

in your placement, or the extent to which religion will play a role in the work. It's vital that you are clear about this in advance and feel comfortable with what's expected of you. Many placements are based in affiliated churches or organisations overseas and so you'll also need to consider the way in which religion is followed in the community you're going to. For instance, a not particularly conservative religious organisation in the UK might place you in a very orthodox community abroad, which could make for difficulties. It might also pay to find out whether or not the religion of your sending organisation is accepted or practised in the wider community you'll be placed in; you may find yourself working within a community of a different faith. Robin Dawson, for example, managed a community development programme in Afghanistan through the Church Mission Society (CMS, p206):

Afghanistan is an Islamic state and I was working for a Christian organisation. I knew that there would be tensions and limitations… and this proved to be the case. However, I was also aware of the rich exchanges that can be experienced as part of an international community… We are required by the protocols our organisations sign with the government not to proselytise. However, in a faith-dominated society such as Afghanistan, this does not prevent Afghans from asking questions about our religion (which they see as essentially corrupt and containing doctrines which are clearly both incorrect and illogical). It is most interesting trying to answer these questions. In many ways, I have felt more comfortable discussing matters of faith in Afghanistan than I have in secular Western society. God is not called upon to justify his actions in Afghanistan. Where I have felt uncomfortable is with the tensions that arise between those, like me, who see our protocols not to proselytise as a discipline to be adhered to, and others who feel that there should be more proclamation of the Christian message. The way these issues are dealt with can be a matter of life and death to Afghanis who may become involved.

It's also important to be clear about your expectations and goals and whether or not these are a good fit with the organisation's programmes. If you're hoping for very hands-on work and the chance to accomplish something tangible, you need to make sure that the programme has the kind of project-focused approach to enable this. On the other hand, if your main goal is to develop your faith through volunteering, be sure that there is adequate provision for you to practise it. Liz Bodner found this more difficult than she expected when volunteering with the Missionaries of Charity (p203) in India:

When I went to Kolkata, I thought that I would have a very spiritual experience and would grow in my faith. This was not the case, however. It was very easy to get into the routine of work without being spiritually aware or intentional. The Missionaries of Charity are service oriented and are focused on sharing God's love through acts rather than words… I had to make the decision to go to mass in the mornings and adoration in the afternoons in order to keep myself connected to my faith.

"Everyone has the power for greatness, not for fame, but for greatness, because greatness is determined by service."

Martin Luther King Junior

Pros & Cons

Volunteering with a religious organisation is not for everyone. However, if you're considering going down this path, the pros and cons in this section zero in on some of the defining features of these placements.

Support

A strong characteristic of most religious organisations, and one which is a drawcard for prospective volunteers, is the level of support they offer. This extends to many aspects of the placement. Firstly, there is the shared faith, which provides the foundation for the project as well as, in most cases, a corresponding community of faith into which volunteers are welcomed. Ben Martin worked with a renewable energies empowerment project in India through Karuna (p207), as well as fundraising for the organisation in London. While he is not Buddhist, he found the faith-based support impressive and constructive:

I have to admit that the fact that Karuna was a Buddhist organisation had little bearing on my decision to volunteer with them… Having said that, however, I cannot stress enough the benefits I gained from working with a group of people sharing a common bond of Buddhist faith. The atmosphere in the office is one of mutual respect and friendliness; office 'politics' simply don't come into play. Frank conversations about motivations, goals and personal contributions really helped me think more about myself, and also ensured that I did as much as I could to help the organisation.

Your faith can also act as a sort of security blanket, as it offers an element of the 'known' within a culture and country that may well be unfamiliar to you. If you are religious, you can also feel comfortable knowing that your beliefs and practices will be accepted in your placement. Ele Ramsey found this to be the case when she volunteered with Christian Aid (p212) in the UK and Nicaragua:

My placement working in 'new' evangelical and charismatic churches meant that I didn't feel, at any point, that I had to suppress my own interpretation of Christianity. All the congregations I worked with held the same set of beliefs as I did.

Perhaps due to their community-minded focus, religious organisations tend to offer a huge amount of support in non-religious areas as well. Volunteers placed together are generally very team oriented, and even those working as partners or individually often maintain close contact with other volunteers and the organisation's base through emails, blogs and newsletters. Sue Towler, the programme manager of Tearfund's volunteer programme (p208), describes the support given to a volunteer in an emergency situation:

We had a six-week Transform team in western Uganda, volunteering at a rural hospital and local school… During the trip, one girl developed suspected acute appendicitis. In close contact with Tearfund, the team immediately contacted the British High Commission and ACE Rescue (a 24-hour travel insurance company for business travellers that Tearfund uses for all Transform teams). We were in very close contact with the girl's parents throughout, as well as the doctor at the hospital the girl was volunteering at. Because she was a diabetic, her condition was too serious to be treated at the local hospital, so [we] arranged for her to be evacuated by helicopter to Kampala to receive treatment. We also arranged for her mother to fly out to Kampala to be with her. We were concerned that the incident had an impact on the team, so arranged for them all to have a full debrief on their return.

Building Bridges

Before we met, we had both spent a year volunteering in rural Africa supporting the work of the local church. So, coupled with a joint background in community development, it was no surprise to anyone that we wanted to return to Africa after we were married. Having both worked for Tearfund (an international relief and development NGO), we were not short of contacts with local organisations. However, we wanted to go through an organisation that specialised in building long-term links between different cultures and that encouraged the sharing of cross-cultural experiences in the UK (our home country).

We soon chose to volunteer with the Church Mission Society for a variety of reasons. We are both Christians and wanted to work with the church, which is generally seen as a local network ideal for bringing about long-term sustainable development. CMS has over a hundred years' experience in building links with churches around the world – but we were probably attracted more by the fact that it is an organisation not afraid of change. With a strong support base from across the UK and the world, CMS is a global community-building movement – allowing us all to learn from one another and opening up opportunities for us to question our own culture. And that struck a chord with our own reasons for volunteering.

Having left our jobs, packed and moved in with parents, we were ready to leave the UK but ended up waiting three months for visas. Even when we did arrive we were seconded to work for a different organisation in another part of the country – but that's all part of the adventure! We are supporting a national organisation in Zambia that fights poverty through empowering poor communities to stand up and speak out against the injustice of poverty, training leaders and building global partnerships. It is really important to us that we are not coming into a country and just imposing something, we are working for an organisation that is run and governed by Zambians, and which exists without a foreign organisation telling it what to do.

Through such a set-up we are able to share some of our skills and experience, as well as learn new skills from our Zambian friends and colleagues. That helps us to question our own culture. The fact that we have experience of working for donor organisations and have come through CMS with support from churches and individuals in the UK means we can help build the links between the work here and there. Hopefully this helps build and deepen relationships, which in turn builds the worldwide church community and prevents the donor–recipient imbalance that has often plagued such relationships.

It isn't always straightforward but that is the beauty of cross-cultural exchange. We have the privilege of standing with, and speaking up for, those that are suffering in the world. Being part of a wider long-term movement enables us to share that experience, both the joys and suffering, with other people from our own culture.

Matt and Polly Freer have chosen to devote three years to working with a community in Zambia, through the Church Mission Society (CMS, p206).

Matt with local co-workers

Faith Propagation

If you choose to volunteer through a religious organisation, you can feel fairly confident that the aspirations and views of the organisation will be similar to your own. It's encouraging to know that the aims underpinning a project you're volunteering on are things you believe in. This was one of the main reasons why Ele Ramsey chose to volunteer with Christian Aid in the UK and Nicaragua:

I wanted an opportunity to put my faith into action. I agreed with Christian Aid's policy of being a Christian-motivated organisation without being explicitly evangelical in its work. I had been heavily involved with the Christian Union at university and was desperate to get away from insular, theological debates and into the real world!… It was also great to act as a peer educator and inspire young people to take action in the name of their faith.

It is always important to ascertain to what extent, and under what conditions, you will be expected to propagate your faith. Does the organisation attempt to convert the local population? Many religious projects are run and managed by a local contingent of the same faith and so such issues don't arise. It's also important to be aware of how the project is perceived by the wider community in which it runs. Is it well received by the community and accepting of their culture? Find out the level of involvement of the local population and to what extent the project works and interacts with the community.

Development Placements

One of the overall aims of projects run by religious organisations is to help people in need, so it's no surprise that their programmes are almost all in the development arena. While few of these programmes require volunteers to have specific skills, most organisations welcome applicants with training or skills in relevant fields.

International Organisations

Habitat for Humanity International
UK Office: 46 West Bar Street, Banbury, Oxon, OX16 9RZ, UK
☎ +44 (0)1295 264240
fax +44 (0)1295 240230
enquiries@habitatforhumanity.org.uk
www.habitatforhumanity.org.uk
US Office: 121 Habitat Street, Americus, GA 31709-3498 USA
☎ +1 1800 422 4828
www.habitat.org
This nondenominational Christian housing charity is dedicated to eliminating poverty housing around the globe and works in around 100 countries. Volunteers are sent overseas to work in teams alongside the local community to build improved accommodation. The family for whom the house is built invests their own labour, fostering community development, dignity and pride of ownership. UK volunteers should visit the website www.habitatforhumanity .org.uk and Australian volunteers should visit www.habitat.org.au.

Status: Registered charity and company limited by guarantee.

Timing & Length of Projects: Placements are for one or two weeks, with set departure dates throughout the year.

Destinations: The organisation sends volunteers to over 40 countries over five regions: Asia and Pacific, Africa and Middle East, Europe and Central Asia, Latin America and Caribbean, and America and Canada. Recently, projects have been in Ghana, Tanzania, India, Kenya, Romania, Armenia, Chile and South Africa.

Costs: Costs vary depending on the sending and hosting country programme. However volunteers are required to raise a donation of approximately US$500 to cover the costs of building. In addition, they must be entirely self-funding.

Eligibility: Applicants must be 14 years or over, and acceptance of those over 71 is dependent on obtaining insurance cover. Every attempt is made to accommodate applicants with disabilities and acceptance is decided on a case-by-case basis. No building skills are required and all faiths are welcome.

Groups or Individuals: Volunteers travel and work in teams of approximately a dozen. You can join a team as an individual or with a friend or partner. Groups can also be accommodated, with projects designed specifically for them.

Annual no. of Volunteers: Internationally, thousands of volunteers are mobilised throughout the world.

Annual Projects: 150

Partner Programmes: The organisation works with other Habitat for Humanity groups, located in the countries where they send teams.

Selection & Interview Process: An application form is used to determine if the applicant is insurable on the building site and whether their particular needs can be accommodated. Interviews are occasionally conducted.

In-country Support: Habitat has an established network in all countries hosting volunteers, and teams are supported by a team leader through the planning process, on the ground and after the trip. The team leader remains in close contact with the hosting country staff through the planning stages and for the duration of the project.

HCJB Global
131 Grattan Rd, Bradford,
West Yorkshire BD1 2HS, UK
☎ +44 (0)1274 721810
fax +44 (0)1274 514960
vacancies@hcjbglobal.org.uk
www.hcjbglobal.org.uk

This Protestant organisation is strongly rooted in the Christian faith and has offices around the globe. Its aim is to show the love of God through its work in developing nations. Professional volunteers interested in sharing its vision can work in the media, IT, hospitals, clinics, community development, training and education.

Status: Charitable company limited by guarantee.

Timing & Length of Projects: Placements are from four weeks to a year, with departures possible year-round.

Destinations: Latin America, Europe, the Asia-Pacific and Africa.

Costs: Volunteers must be self-funding. Costs vary depending on the destination and duration of placement.

Eligibility: Volunteers must have a strong Christian commitment and be willing to complete a statement of faith. Professional skills are also required. You must apply in your country of residence (see the website for links to worldwide contact details). Applicants must be at least 18 years of age for some projects, 20 for others. Spanish is required for healthcare placements in Ecuador. Applications from those with disabilities are welcome.

Groups or Individuals: Placements are usually for individuals. Partners and friends can sometimes be placed together if an appropriate placement can be found.

Annual no. of Volunteers: 4-6

Annual Projects: 3

Partner Programmes: Depending on the project, HCJB works with many local organisations and programmes.

Selection & Interview Process: Applicants need to complete a form and supply references. They are then invited to attend an interview in Bradford.

International China Concern
UK Office: PO Box 20, Morpeth NE61 3YP, UK
☎ /fax +44 (0)1670 505622
www.chinaconcern.org

This Christian organisation works with up to 250 abandoned, disabled children in China. Its aim is to provide them with love, hope and opportunities through practical ministry. Volunteers receive an orientation in Hong Kong or Beijing and then work with children in Hunan and Henan Provinces. Placements can include various elements of the children's care, development and integration into society.

Status: Registered charity.

Timing & Length of Projects: Two-week team placements depart four times per year. Long-term placements are available for periods of three months to five years. ICC also now accepts applications from community teams – groups of individuals who wish to travel together at a time that is more flexible than the scheduled projects .

Destinations: China.

Costs: There is a £50 registration fee for all placements. In addition, two-week team placements cost £780 for food, accommodation and in-country transport. International airfares are not included. Long-term volunteers must be self-funding.

Eligibility: Applications are welcome from Christians. The minimum age is 18, but minors accompanied by an adult may be accepted. No skills are required for two-week team placements, other than a genuine desire to make a difference in the lives of the children. Long-term volunteers will preferably have experience and training in nursing, medicine or special education, or in physiotherapy or occupational, music or art therapy.

Groups or Individuals: Two-week teams and approved community teams work as a group of up to 25. Family and friends can apply together. Long-term volunteers work as part of an expatriate team.

Annual no. of Volunteers: up to 100.

Annual Projects: 3

Partner Programmes: 5

Selection & Interview Process: For a two-week placement, an application form and two references are required. For long-term placements, an application form, references, a CV and an interview are required.

In-country Support: ICC staff travel, work and live with volunteer teams during two-week placements. Long-term volunteers are based with an expat team who offer support. Many full-time staff members have medical, therapy or educational backgrounds.

International Federation of L'Arche Communities

25 rue Rosenwald, Paris 75015, France
☎ & fax +33 (0)1 5368 0800
international@larche.org
www.larche.org

L'Arche is a federation of 131 communities which provide a family-style living environment for people with intellectual disabilities. Volunteers work as assistants in a home, workshop or day programme and most often live within the community, accompanying people with disabilities in their daily routines.

Status: Not-for-profit organisation.

Timing & Length of Projects: These differ from one community to another but most volunteers stay for at least several months, if not a year.

Destinations: There are L'Arche communities in 34 countries on all continents.

Costs: This also varies. Volunteers are usually provided with accommodation and meals and sometimes pocket money. Airfares are covered by the volunteer.

Eligibility: While L'Arche communities are usually of a particular religious denomination, every community accepts people of all faiths or no faith. Age restrictions apply to volunteers in some countries. Applicants should be prepared to engage in close relationships with others – both those with and without intellectual disabilities. People with physical disabilities are invited to apply.

Groups or Individuals: Volunteers are usually accepted as individuals. It is rare that couples or friends are admitted to the same community.

Annual no. of Volunteers: L'Arche has 131 communities, each with a large number of volunteers, but is unable to provide an annual estimate. However, due to the high turnover of assistants, L'Arche communities are always in need of volunteers.

Annual Projects: There are 131 L'Arche communities worldwide.

Partner Programmes: Unable to estimate.

Selection & Interview Process: Communities usually select applicants via telephone or email. In some cases, it is the regional or national office which carries out the selection process and then dispatches volunteers to different communities.

In-country Support: Volunteers usually work under the supervision of a leader. All volunteers are mentored by an experienced member of the community, who helps to deal with difficult situations. L'Arche communities comply with the health and safety procedures of the country in which they are based.

UK Organisations

Building, Construction & Conservation

Quaker Voluntary Action
**1 Holt Lane, Holmfirth,
West Yorkshire HD9 3BW, UK**
☎ /fax +44 (0)1484 687139
mail@qva.org.uk
www.qva.org.uk

continued on p204

The Mother of Volunteering

Agnes Gonxha Bojaxhiu was born in 1910 in Macedonia, and became a Catholic missionary nun in 1928. When she died in 1997, she was known to the world as Mother Teresa and her work was synonymous with charity and volunteering and inextricably linked with the city of Calcutta (Kolkata). Mother Teresa's Missionaries of Charity work with some of the world's most needy – the ill, the starving and the dying. With more than 500 branches in over 130 countries, the order consists of around 4500 nuns whose mission is to give 'wholehearted and free service to the poorest of the poor'.

Not surprisingly, fame also brought controversy – mainly centred on Mother Teresa's insistence on a life of poverty for not only herself and her nuns, but also for those in her care. Critics question the whereabouts of the billions donated to the missions and criticise some of the missionaries' practices.

Nevertheless, each year the Missionaries of Charity's eight homes in Kolkata receive countless volunteers, both skilled and unskilled, and many find the experience rewarding, humbling and eye-opening.

Lucas' Experience

Lucas McIntyre volunteered with the mission through Seattle University's student-based Calcutta Club and speaks candidly about his placement.

My experience as a volunteer with the Missionaries of Charity in Kolkata was complex and multifaceted. Being agnostic, I was not attracted to the religious aspect of their work; however, I was attracted to their simplicity and their mission of working directly with the 'poorest of the poor'. I volunteered for three months in the men's ward at Prem Dan, the home for long-term and chronically ill patients. While I was there in 2004, Prem Dan housed 100 men and 100 women; however, when I left the centre was expanding to hold at least twice that number.

My days at Prem Dan were varied and included feeding men, dressing wounds, cleaning the facility, and simply hanging out with the patients. Most if not all of the patients at Prem Dan were brought in off the street and usually suffered from a number of afflictions ranging from starvation to wounds from street accidents to tuberculosis. Since I was a longer-term volunteer (many people only volunteer for a few days or a few weeks), and I expressed interest, I was given basic wound-care training.

During my three months at Prem Dan, which was spread out over six months between travel and volunteering with a microfinance institution, I became critical of some of the MCs' practices. While I acknowledged that they were providing better care than the patients would otherwise have received (which for most would have been none at all), this did not excuse the neglect of some easily fixed problems. For example, the MCs would wash and reuse latex gloves. This horrified me, especially since there did not seem to be a scarcity of latex gloves. They also did not segregate contagious TB patients from other patients, which caused new infections. In addition to this, while there was an Indian doctor who saw patients once a week, the day-to-day wound care of the patients was haphazard, which frustrated me.

There were positive aspects to my experience, as well. I enjoyed the direct contact with the patients and found a lot of joy in their company. I also found the eclectic group of volunteers drawn from all over the world to be a fertile source of vibrant conversation and interesting insights. Besides volunteering, Kolkata itself was an experience in its own right, with an intensity and vitality all of its own.

To share more about my experience, here are some excerpts from emails that I wrote to friends while I was volunteering:

7 March 2004

I run into my friend John, a patient who is getting better, and we share some genuinely heartfelt laughter. I can't quite articulate the intermixed swirl of suffering and joy that is Prem Dan. I can say, though, that the suffering and the joy are equally authentic.

18 March 2004

Honestly, there is little to no accountability here beyond the accountability that one holds

oneself to. No-one checks on me, and I'm not documented in regard to the work I'm doing. I become concerned when it is recommended that we perform surgery on one of the maggot-wound patients in order to remove some useless toe bone that is only causing him pain. The more experienced volunteers know how to do this, but even so, the power we have over the health of these men is astounding. And extremely frightening.

Lucas McIntyre

The Missionaries of Charity
India Kolkata ☎ +91 033 245 2277, +091 033 249; Mother House, 54A Acharya Jagadish, Chandra Bose Rd, Kolkata 700016
UK London ☎ +44 (0)20 8960 2644
USA San Francisco ☎ +1 415 563 9446, New York ☎ +1 718 292 0019
Australia ☎ +61 (0)3 9 415 1011
New Zealand ☎ +64 09 378 9061

You don't need to be a follower of the Catholic faith to volunteer with the Missionaries of Charity, although it may be easier to understand their aims and practices if you do have a Catholic (or at least Christian) background. You can simply show up at the Mother House in Kolkata (check when you arrive as to the times and days for volunteer registration and orientation), but it's a good idea to call or write ahead, particularly if you are a medical professional. For Missionaries of Charity in other locations, it is always best to get in touch before you arrive so that you can ascertain their needs and whether or not there will be room for you to volunteer. Not all of the missions accept volunteers. Below are contact details of a few of the main mission houses; write to the Mother House in Kolkata for details in other countries. Note that, in keeping with their vow of poverty and their unadorned lifestyle, none of the missionaries are contactable online.

However, the Missionaries of Charity are only one of over 200 charitable organisations working with the poor in Kolkata; many of the others may need your help just as much.

TOP One of the wards at Prem Dan
BOTTOM Lucas helping care for the 'poorest of the poor' at Prem Dan in Kolkata,

Taking a break at the market in East Timor

QVA provides practical opportunities to put the Quaker faith into action. Volunteers are placed on working retreats at Cumbria's Swarthmoor Hall, once the home of George Fox and arguably the birthplace of Quakerism. Volunteers divide their time between practical work maintaining the grounds and a guided spiritual retreat.

Status: Registered charity and limited company.

Timing & Length of Projects: Five days in May and October.

Destinations: UK.

Costs: £50 including accommodation and food. Travel is not included.

Eligibility: It is essential that volunteers are sympathetic to Quaker values and interested in exploring the faith. Overseas applicants are welcome.

Groups or Individuals: Placements are in groups of up to 10, although many practical aspects of the project are carried out in smaller groups. During the placement, volunteers shop, cook and eat together.

Annual no. of Volunteers: 20

Annual Projects: 2-3

Partner Programmes: QVA has links with many national and international organisations.

Selection & Interview Process: Following receipt of an application form, interviews are conducted by telephone.

In-country Support: A member of QVA's staff or a committee member is part of the group. Staff at Swarthmoor Hall have health and safety and emergency training.

Community Development

Assumption Volunteer Programme
23 Kensington Sq, London W8 5HH, UK
☎ +44 (0)20 7361 4752
fax +44 (0)20 7361 4757
alvpcoordinator@hotmail.co.uk
www.alvp.org.uk

An initiative of the Sisters of the Assumption, this Catholic organisation aims to give volunteers the opportunity to share their skills with people in need, in a cross-cultural context. Volunteers work alongside the Sisters and must have a 'willingness to do anything', including working in schools, orphanages, dispensaries or health centres, teaching nutrition and health or assisting with social outreach.

Status: Registered charity.

Timing & Length of Projects: Placements are for one year. Departures are in August/September or January, depending on the destination.

Destinations: The Philippines, Thailand, Rwanda, Tanzania, Mexico, the US and the UK.

Costs: Volunteers raise £750 and pay for any vaccinations.

Eligibility: The minimum age is 20. Some projects require a Catholic or other Christian commitment. While volunteers of Christian faith may feel more comfortable, volunteers with no faith are also accepted. All volunteers must be open to, and respectful of, the religious dimension and happy to work with Catholic sisters. Some placements require a degree or teaching qualifications. Whether or not applicants with disabilities can be placed depends on the ability of the overseas projects to accommodate them.

Groups or Individuals: Volunteers may be sent individually or in pairs. Applications are welcome from single people or married couples.

Annual no. of Volunteers: 5-10

Annual Projects: 2-4

Partner Programmes: 6

Selection & Interview Process: Interviews are held in person in London and training is given in London for three weekends and one full week between March and July.

In-country Support: Volunteers work with communities of Assumption Sisters overseas who offer support and in-country contact.

BMS World Mission

PO Box 49, 129 Broadway, Didcot, Oxfordshire OX11 8XA, UK
☎ +44 (0)1235 517700
fax +44 (0)1235 517601
www.bmsworldmission.org

This Christian organisation aims to improve the quality of life in impoverished communities through a large range of programmes. Placements can include working with street children, teaching basic English or helping to run church programmes. Medics and lawyers are also placed in a professional capacity. One of BMS's explicit aims is to enable the local communities to know Christ and volunteers must be committed to Jesus.

Status: Registered charity.

Timing & Length of Projects: Placements range from just a few weeks to years. Departure dates vary but are throughout the year.

Destinations: Countries throughout Africa, Asia, Europe and Latin America.

Costs: Fees vary between programmes and destinations. Two weeks as part of a medical team costs about £1300, while six weeks on a legal team is £2100 and 10 months on an unskilled project is around £3900. Fees include flights, visas, insurance, food, accommodation and training. Individual placements are entirely self-funding.

Eligibility: Applicants must be practising Christians. Age restrictions vary with projects but there are placements for those between 18 and 74.

Groups or Individuals: There are opportunities for individuals, couples and families. There are also team programmes.

Annual no. of Volunteers: 230

Annual Projects: Approximately 40 projects and partners worldwide.

Partner Programmes: Around 40.

Selection & Interview Process: BMS holds group selection events and interviews either in Didcot or Birmingham.

In-country Support: Volunteers have 24-hour emergency contacts in the country they're working in and in the UK. Volunteers are always placed alongside BMS long-term personnel or partner organisations.

Christians Abroad

CTBI Christians Abroad, 14 Millbridge Rd, Witham, Essex CM8 1HB, UK
☎ +44 (0)3000 121201
recruit@cabroad.org.uk
www.cabroad.org.uk

This organisation works with projects of all denominations and mainly with projects that have no other connection with the UK. Most placements are in schools, health centres or on community projects. Volunteers can work in a wide range of capacities, from teaching science, business or English to working in clinics or fundraising. All placements are with people and places known to CA and it tries to match the needs and religious leanings of the projects with appropriate volunteers. There is no evangelistic aspect to the placements, although some can have a religious component (for instance, teaching theology or running church programmes).

Status: Registered charity.

Timing & Length of Projects: Placements are year round with a three-month minimum. Medical electives may be shorter.

Destinations: Mainly Africa, in Cameroon, Kenya, Nigeria, Tanzania and Zambia. There are also placements in Argentina, India and Syria, depending on where there's a need.

Costs: There is a £750 deposit payable upon submission of your application. All other costs are covered by the volunteer, except for accommodation, which is generally provided.

Eligibility: The minimum age is 18, however, CA prefers volunteers to be at least 21. There are no specific denomination requirements. Specific skills may be required for some placements. People with disabilities can apply; acceptance is dependent on the circumstances of the placement.

Groups or Individuals: Usually volunteers are placed as individuals, however, couples and friends can sometimes be accommodated.

Annual no. of Volunteers: 20

Annual Projects: 15

Partner Programmes: 21

Selection & Interview Process: Christians Abroad requires a detailed application form, face-to-face interviews in London, a reference check and agreement to a code of practice. The final decision then rests with the project managers, who receive an interview report.

In-country Support: All volunteers are given UK staff emergency contacts and details of local healthcare. Day-to-day care is the responsibility of the in-country project.

Church Mission Society

Watlington Rd, Oxford, OX4 6BZ, UK
☎ +44 (0)1865 787400
fax +44 (0)1865 776375
info@cms-uk.org
www.cms-uk.org

CMS dates back to 1799 and works in over 60 countries around the globe. In 2010 it integrated with the South American Mission Society to form a new entity. Placements are in church-run projects and can include administration, nursing, work as a hostel warden or care-work in children's homes. CMS tries to match volunteers' skills to openings. One of CMS's aims is to share a love of God with all peoples.

Status: Company limited by guarantee, with charitable status.

Timing & Length of Projects: Placements are year-round, short term (four months to two years) or long term (five years plus).

Destinations: Sub-Saharan Africa, North Africa, Middle East, Central Asia, South and Southeast Asia, Latin America and Europe.

Costs: Costs depend on location and length of placement. CMS does not charge any administration fees; all money is raised and held by the individual. CMS provides 12 day residential training programme and debriefing.

Eligibility: Applicants need to be committed Christians who are actively involved in their local church, with a minimum age of 18..

Groups or Individuals: Volunteers can be single, married, and with children. CMS looks for an opportunity that suits the whole family.

Annual no. of Volunteers: 30-40

Annual Projects: CMS has long-term relationships with partner churches and is involved in on-going community work rather than a number of individual projects.

Partner Programmes: Many.

Selection & Interview Process: Applicants are given a number of interviews and are subject to medical and criminal records checks plus a weekend residential selection conference.

In-country Support: Volunteers are matched with an in-country partner church and have a nominated line manager. They also have regular contact with CMS and procedures are in place in case of emergency.

Jesuit Volunteer Community – Britain

Green Fish Resource Centre, 46-50 Oldham St, Manchester M4 1LE, UK
☎ +44 (0)161 234 2933
admin@jvcbritain.org
www.jvcbritain.org

Volunteers are welcome in this Catholic charity, which upholds and participates in values of community, simple lifestyle, social justice and spirituality. Volunteers live as small communities in Birmingham, Glasgow, Liverpool and Manchester, and are found placements in local charities, NGOs, schools and faith-based or grassroots organisations.

Status: Registered charity.

Timing & Length of Projects: The majority of placements run from September to July. There are also one-month 'taster' placements available in August.

Destinations: England and Scotland.

Costs/Pay: Volunteers are given free accommodation and a travel allowance within the UK. Each week, an allowance per volunteer is deposited into a communal account to cover living expenses like food and utility bills (the remainder is divided up for personal use). For the sake of equality, volunteers are required not to access personal funds during their placement. Flights to and from the UK are self-funding.

Eligibility: While applications are assessed without regard to gender, nationality, sexual orientation or denomination, volunteers must be willing to involve themselves in a Catholic ethos and culture. Volunteers should be 'young adults' willing to learn and participate. No specific experience is required but applicants must list skills such as language, art and cooking so that JVC can match them with appropriate placements.

Groups or Individuals: Volunteers work individually but live in communities of four or five.

Annual no. of Volunteers: 20

Annual Projects: 30

Partner Programmes: JVC works with partner Jesuit volunteer programmes throughout Europe and the US, as well as with the UK Jesuit Refugee Service.

Selection & Interview Process: Initial application is via the website. Face-to-face interviews are held for UK applicants and telephone interviews are held with international applicants. Applicants must provide three references and complete a criminal records check.

In-country Support: Inductions cover health and safety training. Each volunteer community has a coordinator available at all times for emergencies, as well as two 'community partners' to provide consistent emotional, practical and spiritual support. Volunteers are also offered individual spiritual directors.

Karuna Trust

72 Holloway Rd, London N7 8JG, UK
☎ +44 (0)20 7700 3434
fax +44 (0)20 7700 3535
info@karuna.org
www.karuna.org

This Buddhist charity is founded on the principle of 'compassionate action based on wisdom'. They work with communities disadvantaged because of their caste, gender or religion by helping to educate them about their rights, find educational opportunities and meet their basic needs. Karuna can provide volunteers with links to partner projects overseas for independent placements. There are sometimes opportunities for volunteers to work in Karuna's London office; such placements are most suitable for Buddhist applicants.

Status: Registered charity.

Timing & Length of Projects: Varies with each placement.

Destinations: UK, India and Bangladesh.

Costs: Volunteers must be entirely self-funding.

Eligibility: Skills and experience required depend on individual placements overseas.

Groups or Individuals: Usually individuals, although it is possible to arrange placements with a friend or partner.

Annual no. of Volunteers: A handful.

Annual Projects: 36

Partner Programmes: Karuna works with 36 project partners, which in total run 250 projects.

Selection & Interview Process: This depends on the requirements of the overseas project.

In-country Support: Volunteers need to be self-reliant. Partner organisations provide various levels of support.

Latin Link

87 London Street, Reading RG1 4QA, UK
☎ +44 (0)1189 577100
fax +44 (0)1189 577115
www.latinlink.org

Latin Link offers two separate volunteering programmes. 'Step' gives participants a practical introduction to mission work in Latin America, with team placements working alongside a local church community and undertaking work such as construction or running children's holiday camps. 'Stride' is for individuals, couples or families who are teamed up with a Christian-run project; placements can include project management, publishing, engineering, music, arts, teaching or urban outreach. Projects for both placements are designed to help volunteers develop their faith and explore their Christian calling.

Status: Registered charity.

Timing & Length of Projects: Step teams leave mid-March for four to six months, and in July and August for three to seven weeks. Stride placements run from six months to two years and usually start in the autumn or new year.

Destinations: Argentina, Bolivia, Brazil, Cuba, Ecuador, Honduras, Guatemala, Peru, Chile, Colombia, Costa Rica and Nicaragua.

Costs: The Spring Step projects cost £2950; Summer Step costs between £1750 and £2150 depending on the length of the placement. Prices include everything except personal spending money. Stride has an initial cost of £1950 (for one year) which covers flights, orientation, CRB checks and medical clearance, plus £450 per month for food, accommodation and supervision.

Eligibility: Applicants must have a personal faith in Jesus and be over the age of 17 for Step and 18 for Stride. Skills required depend on the placement. People with disabilities are welcome to apply.

Groups or Individuals: Step volunteers are placed in teams of eight to 12 . Ready made church, mixed age or university teams welcome to apply. Stride is for individuals, couples or families.

Annual no. of Volunteers: 150

Annual Projects: 40

Partner Programmes: Over 50.

Selection & Interview Process: Interviews are conducted in person at the Reading office or in Ireland and Scotland. References are required.

In-country Support: Each Step team receives orientation and the services of a Latin Link supervisor. Each Strider has an approved mentor, often a member of Latin Link.

Tearfund

100 Church Rd, Teddington, Middlesex TW11 8QE, UK
☎ +44 (0)845 355 8355
enquiry@tearfund.org
www.tearfund.org/en/get_involved/
go_overseas

Tearfund is a Christian-based organisation that places volunteer teams in developing countries on projects that have been initiated by local communities. These include healthcare projects, literacy classes, implementing systems for clean water and sanitation, HIV/AIDS education, and drug-rehabilitation or food-security programmes. Volunteers work through local churches and Christian agencies. Tearfund hopes that the programmes will act as catalysts for returned volunteers to continue working towards its Christian mission.

Status: Registered charity.

Timing & Length of Projects: Placements are from two weeks to four months, with set departure dates throughout the year.

Destinations: Latin America, Africa, Asia and Europe.

Costs: Two-week teams cost £1400, and summer four- to six-week teams are £1600 to £1750. Four-month teams cost £2750 to £2950.

Eligibility: The minimum age is 18 and, while specific skills aren't requested, useful training or talents are welcome. Volunteers must agree with, and sign, a basis-of-faith statement. Applicants with specific medical needs or disabilities, or who are over the age of 65, must sign additional forms and have additional insurance.

Groups or Individuals: Volunteers travel, live and work together in teams of six to 12. Tearfund prefers not to place friends together.

Annual no. of Volunteers: 450-500

Annual Projects: 40-50

Partner Programmes: Tearfund has hundreds of overseas partners.

Selection & Interview Process: Interviews are given at special information events or at the orientation which applicants attend before volunteering.

In-country Support: In-country support is provided by the local partners. Tearfund also has an emergency telephone system and a 24-hour international medical support service.

Toybox

PO Box 5967, Bletchley, Milton Keynes, MK3 6WD, UK
☎ +44 (0)845 466 0010
fax +44 (0)845 466 0015
info@toybox.org
www.toybox.org

This Christian charity works in partnership with local organisations, supporting frontline work with street children in Latin America, with the aim of making a long-term difference to these children and their communities. Volunteers help with prevention, rescue and rehabilitation programmes, providing practical help and friendship. They also work in small, specialist family-style homes, providing education and social support to families. Toybox works in partnership with Latin Link (p207).

Status: Registered charity.

Timing & Length of Projects: Placements are for three weeks.

Destinations: Guatemala.

Costs: Vary depending on the length and location of the placement.

Eligibility: Volunteers need to have a clear Christian commitment. The minimum age for placements is 17.

Groups or Individuals: Team projects are made up of eight to 12 volunteers. Families and married couples can be on the same team.

Annual no. of Volunteers: 10

Annual Projects: 1

Partner Programmes: 1

Selection & Interview Process: Applicants apply by form, supplying two references. Interviews take place in Reading or with coordinators in Scotland and Northern Ireland.

In-country Support: A local ex-pat coordinator meets volunteers in-country, sees them to their accommodation, answers queries, helps with language and is on-hand to help throughout the placement.

Kibbutzim

Big on community? Got that team spirit? Feel like you missed out on the communal living of the '70s? Then think 'kibbutz'.

The kibbutz movement began in Israel in 1910 and was organised by European-Jewish pioneers in pursuit of a communal ideal, where all members would work together, own everything in common and act as an all-inclusive assembly to make the governing rules. The first Israeli kibbutz had only 10 members – by 1940, there were 82 communities with over 26,500 inhabitants. Today there are more than 250 kibbutzim (the plural of 'kibbutz') spread across the country. They are all pluralistic and nonreligious (with the exception of the 16 HaKibbutz HaDati which are Orthodox Zionist).

Kibbutzim are an extremely popular means of combining travel with volunteering, although in recent years the movement has lost some of its lustre, amid the ongoing political and civil unrest in Israel. Nevertheless, the kibbutz movement still chugs along and welcomes volunteers from countries that have diplomatic relations with Israel. In fact, these days you may get an even warmer welcome for making the effort to bridge the growing gap between Israel and the rest of the world.

Each kibbutz is made up of approximately 600 people. As a volunteer, you will be expected to pitch in with the rest of the community, taking on tasks assigned to you and working eight hours a day, six days a week (with an extra three days of breathing space allotted per month). You might find yourself picking avocados, maintaining irrigation systems, collecting eggs or farming fish. You might also find yourself working in the kitchens, doing the laundry or helping out in the kibbutz's income-generating venture, if it has one – perhaps a guesthouse, restaurant, health spa or shop.

To volunteer, you need to be between the ages of 18 and 35, be in good mental and physical health, be able to commit to a minimum of two months and willing to leave after six, speak a reasonable amount of English and be willing to undergo an AIDS test on arrival. You'll also need to shell out US$60 for a registration fee, US$17 for a visa status alteration and US$80 for the kibbutz volunteer health insurance policy (valid for one year). These fees cover nearly everything for your stay on the kibbutz: communal meals, laundry, shared accommodation (two to three people per room), and even some monthly pocket dosh. It is possible to volunteer alongside your friends or partner but families are not welcome.

To apply, you can either show up in Tel Aviv with fingers crossed that there's an available placement (there often is), or contact the representative in your home country.

UK London (☎ +44 (0)20 8458 9235; enquiries@kibbutz.org.uk; www.kibbutzvolunteers.org.il 1A Accommodation Rd, Golders Green Rd, London NW11 8ED, UK)

USA New York (☎ +1 212 462 2764; mail@kibbutzprogramcenter.org; 114 West 26th St, Ste 1004, New York, NY 10001 USA)

Australia South Caulfield (☎ +61 (0)3 9272 5531; 306 Hawthorn Rd, South Caulfield, Vic. 3161, Australia)

New Zealand Auckland (☎ +09 309 9444; PO Box 4315, Auckland, New Zealand)

Us (United Society)
Harling House, 47-51 Great Suffolk St,
London SE1 0BS, UK
☎ +44 (0)207 921 2200
fax +44 (0)207 921 2222
enquiries@uspg.org.uk
www.uspg.org.uk
The Experience Exchange Programme is run
jointly by US and the Methodist Church and
gives volunteers the chance to share in the
life of a church and community overseas.
Placements are found to suit volunteers'
skills and can include teaching, working
on agricultural, health or building projects,
and helping in vocational and rehabilitation
institutions and or children and youth
projects.
Status: Registered charity.
Timing & Length of Projects: Placements are
for six months to a year, with departure dates
dependent on the individual. All volunteers
are required to attend a residential training
week before they go, in either July or January.
Destinations: Africa and the Indian Ocean,
Asia and Oceania, Latin America and the
Caribbean, the Middle East and Europe.
Costs: The cost depends on the placement,
destination and timing, but all placements
are entirely self-funding. US provides a
provisional budget for each placement, along
with fundraising guidance.
Eligibility: Participants must be at least 18.
Acceptance is dependent on a medical
clearance. While volunteers from all
backgrounds can apply, Christian values and
teaching are explored on weekends and
during preparation training.
Groups or Individuals: Placements are
generally for individuals as they are suited
to the volunteer's skills and preferences.
However, the programme is flexible enough
to cater for individuals, couples or friends.
Annual no. of Volunteers: 45
Annual Projects: US and the Methodist Church
partner churches around the world and
support their projects and work.
Partner Programmes: US has partner
churches in over 50 countries.
Selection & Interview Process: US offers an
Exploration Weekend in Birmingham for those
interested in volunteering. This is followed by
an Interview Day in London.
In-country Support: Volunteers are given
health advice and a medical clearance prior

to travel. Contacts of local support people are
also provided and Regional Desk Officers in
London also stay in touch.

North American Organisations

American Jewish World Service
45 West 36th St, 10th flr,
New York, NY 10018, USA
☎ +1 800 889 7146
fax +1 212 792 2930
ajws@ajws.org
www.ajws.org
The AJWS Volunteer Corps places American
Jewish professionals with grassroots
organisations effecting social change in
Africa, the Americas and Asia. Volunteers
provide organisations with technical
assistance and skills training in their areas of
professional expertise. Other group volunteer
opportunities are also available.
Status: Non-profit organisation.
Timing & Length of Projects: Three to 12
months, with shorter assignments available
for senior professionals. Departures are year-
round; there are three application deadlines
each year.
Destinations: Uganda, South Africa, Zambia,
Senegal, Ghana, Guatemala, Nicaragua,
Honduras, El Salvador, Peru, Mexico, the
Dominican Republic, Thailand and India.
Costs: A return airfare is paid for by the
organisation. Volunteers are responsible for
visas, insurance and immunisations, room
and board and local travel expenses. Partial
financial need stipends are available.
Eligibility: Applicants must be experienced
Jewish professionals of any age who are
adventurous, flexible and independent; US
citizenship is required. Programmes in the
Americas require fluency in Spanish.
Groups or Individuals: Volunteers serve
on their own, but couples can be placed
together.
Annual no. of Volunteers: 100
Annual Projects: 100
Partner Programmes: Approximately
250 NGOs.
Selection & Interview Process: US staff visit
prospective partner organisations to evaluate
their projects, personnel and capacity to
work with volunteers. Volunteers discuss
their project with the in-country organisation

prior to departure, and are assigned to programmes with a demonstrated need suited to their skills.

In-country Support: Each country has a staff representative, and a 24-hour emergency phone line enables volunteers to reach programme personnel at any time. Volunteers must contact the home office every two weeks.

Mercy Ships

PO Box 2020,
Garden Valley TX 75771-2020, USA
☎ +1 903 939 7000
fax +1 903 939 7602
info@mercyships.org
www.mercyships.org

Mercy Ships is a global charity that has operated hospital ships in developing nations since 1978. Mercy Ships brings hope and healing to the forgotten poor by mobilising people and resources worldwide, and serving all people without regard for race, gender, or religion.

Status: Registered charity.

Timing & Length of Projects: Two weeks to a year; departures year-round.

Destinations: West Africa.

Costs: Volunteers must cover airfare and visa costs, as well as varying fees for meals and lodging.

Eligibility: The minimum age is 18; no nationality restrictions apply. Many positions require specific professional qualifications, and volunteers must be in good physical condition. All applicants are required to complete a medical evaluation; some pre-existing conditions may disqualify service at certain locations.

Groups or Individuals: Volunteers live and work in groups.

Annual no. of Volunteers: 2000

Annual Projects: There are current programmes focusing on clean water and sanitation, agriculture, construction, and training of local healthcare professionals.

Partner Programmes: Local churches and educators participate in the organisation's work in each country. Mercy teams provide meaningful, customised, short-term field service opportunities for churches, schools, civic organisations and groups. Volunteers can work alongside the state-of-the-art hospital ship, the Africa Mercy, or with one of our ministry partners.

Selection & Interview Process: Volunteers' medical needs, skills and interests are considered when matching applicants to projects.

In-country Support: Professional on-board personnel supervise and direct volunteers throughout their service.

Sarvodaya USA

122 State St, Ste 510, Madison, WI 53703, USA
☎ +1 (608) 442-5945
fax +1 (608) 310-5865
info@sarvodayausa.org
www.sarvodayausa.org

Rooted in Gandhian and Buddhist principles, the Sarvodaya Shramadana Societies operate a grassroots network in 15,000 Sri Lankan villages, with the aim of development through self-governance. Thousands of projects focus on social empowerment, disaster management, IT education and development, community health, rural construction and women's issues.

Status: Non-profit organisation.

Timing & Length of Projects: Several weeks to two years; departures year-round.

Destinations: Sri Lanka and Nepal.

Costs: Volunteers bear all expenses, including travel, insurance and in-country living costs.

Eligibility: No age or nationality restrictions apply. Volunteers must be in good physical condition.

Groups or Individuals: Within every project, individual, pair and group work is available.

Annual no. of Volunteers: 140

Annual Projects: Hundreds.

Partner programs: Hundreds.

Selection & Interview Process: Volunteers are matched to projects in their field of interest.

In-country Support: Projects are conducted only in regions deemed safe by programme staffers. The organisation's headquarters is gated, with security guards on the premises at all hours.

Australasian Organisations

Interserve Australia

PO Box 231, Bayswater, Vic. 3153, Australia
☎ +61 (0)3 9729 9611; 1800 067 100
fax +61 (0)3 9729 9422
info@interserve.org.au
www.interserve.org.au

Interserve is an international mission agency offering Christians the chance to use their faith, training and skills in a unique form of service.

Status: Not-for-profit incorporated association.

Timing & Length of Projects: Six-month to one-year projects are classified as short term; two-year partner programmes are considered long term.

Destinations: Central Asia and Southeast Asia, India, Nepal and the Middle East.

Costs: Volunteers raise their own support with the assistance of Interserve. Volunteers away for one year will need around A$15,000 to A$20,000 if single, or A$22,000 to A$30,000 if a couple. Volunteers on two-year assignments will require around A$27,000 if single, or around A$48,000 if a couple with children. Keep in mind that these are approximate figures and vary depending on the destination.

Eligibility: Christians aged 18 to 70 years. Families with children can apply.

Groups or Individuals: Individuals, couples and groups.

Annual no. of Volunteers: 50 to 60 on six-month to one-year projects; eight volunteers on long-term programmes.

Annual Projects: 45

Partner Programmes: 18 partner agencies.

Selection & Interview Process: Interserve conducts face-to-face interviews in state offices (Victoria, New South Wales, Queensland, South Australia and Western Australia), along with a medical assessment and psychological testing. References must accompany applications (one reference must be from the applicant's church pastor or minister).

In-country Support: Partner agencies provide in-country support and country leaders are situated in all countries.

Options for the Under 30s

UK Organisations

Christian Aid Gap Year
35 Lower Marsh, Waterloo,
London SE1 7RL, UK
☎ +44 (0)207 620 4444
gapyear@christian-aid.org
http://www.christianaid.org.uk/getinvolved/volunteer/gapyear/gap_year.aspx
Christian Aid's gap-year placements offer volunteers the opportunity to raise awareness among UK youth about issues surrounding poverty: to lead campaigns and workshops; to help organise massive fundraising events;

An opportunity to engage with the local wildlife presents itself in East Timor and to visit summer festivals promoting the organisation's work. You'll also head overseas for two weeks to visit Christian Aid projects in the developing world. While some placements are with particularly evangelical churches, most are looking for charismatic youth leaders, regardless of faith.

Status: Company limited.

Timing & Length of Projects: The placements are for 10 months, from the end of August until the end of June. The overseas trip included in the placements takes place in October.

Destinations: The majority of the placement is spent in the United Kingdom, with a two-week trip to one of 60 countries in the developing world.

Costs: The fee is £800 for the full 10 months, including room and board, pocket money and the two-week overseas trip.

Eligibility: Applicants must be between 18 and 25 and do not have to be Christian. While no specific skills or experience are required, it is preferable if you have some related work experience (for example, youth leadership or teaching). Creativity and confidence in communicating with young people is essential. You must care about overseas development issues and be passionate about engaging young people in these issues.

Groups or Individuals: Volunteers work individually during their UK placement but train as a group and travel abroad as a group.

Annual no. of Volunteers: 15

Annual Projects: Each volunteer works in an area office in the UK and the team visits several projects while overseas.

Partner Programmes: Christian Aid has over 600 partner organisations in 60 countries.

Selection & Interview Process: The initial application is done via the website. Following this, there is an information and interview day, usually in London.

In-country Support: While in the UK, volunteers work closely with a supervisor and a mentor. They travel abroad with two Christian Aid leaders and are in constant contact with the field office. Before travelling, volunteers are given a comprehensive and thorough briefing on security and health.

Time for God

Community House, 46-50 East Parade, Harrogate, North Yorkshire HG1 5RR, UK
☎ +44 (0)142 353 6248
fax +44 (0)56 0205 3964
office@timeforgod.org
www.timeforgod.org

For over 40 years, Time for God has been placing gap-year volunteers in the UK and abroad. Its diverse projects include volunteering in outdoor activity centres and community-development or drug-rehabilitation projects. Some placements involve specifically Christian-based work, such as church youth work. While volunteers are required to demonstrate a level of devotion, the organisation is aimed at giving volunteers the space and support to explore their relationship with the Christian faith.

Status: Registered charity and limited company.

Timing & Length of Projects: UK, European and US placements start in August and January for 10 to 12 months (although January placements can be for six to seven months if requested). The timing and length of placements in Kenya and Russia are more flexible, although a three-month minimum is preferred.

Destinations: UK, Kenya, Germany, France, Sweden, USA, Hungary, Ukraine, Denmark, South Korea and Italy.

Costs/Pay: Some European placements for volunteers aged 18 to 25 are free, other placements vary with destination and length of stay. All placements include board, accommodation and a monthly stipend. Flights and insurance are not included.

Eligibility: Applicants must be between 18 and 30. For overseas placements, the minimum age is 20. No qualifications or experience are required.

Groups or Individuals: Depending on the project, volunteers work either as a team or individually.

Annual no. of Volunteers: 110

Annual Projects: 60

Partner Programmes: 14

Selection & Interview Process: Interviews are done in person, or by telephone or Skype.

In-country Support: Each volunteer is allocated a trained field officer for support and has access to 24-hour support in emergencies.

Overseas volunteers are given pre-departure training and an in-country supervisor.

North American Organisations

Passionist Volunteers International

111 South Ridge St, Ste 302,
Rye Brook, NY 10573, USA
pvimission@gmail.com
www.passionistvolunteers.org

This Roman Catholic charity recruits US and Canadian volunteers for education and community-service projects in Honduras and Jamaica. Volunteers are expected to create and conduct projects tailored to their skills and interests and local needs.

Status: Registered charity.

Timing & Length of Projects: One year, with extensions for an additional year available; annual departures in August.

Destinations: Honduras & Jamaica.

Costs/Pay: The organisation covers volunteers' airfares, insurance, room and board and in-country transportation costs; a stipend of US$100 a month is also provided. Volunteers are asked to help raise US$2000 to help defray costs.

Eligibility: The minimum age is 22; applicants must be Roman Catholic, US or Canadian citizens, and in good health. A college degree or comparable work experience is required. The Honduras programme requires a working knowledge of Spanish.

Groups or Individuals: Participants live and work with four or five other volunteers; project collaboration is strongly encouraged.

Annual no. of Volunteers: 8

Annual Projects: The number of projects at each site depends on volunteer interests and local needs.

Partner Programmes: Elms College (Chicopee, MA) sends a small group of college students to work with volunteers during spring break.

Selection & Interview Process: Candidates must demonstrate strong Catholic faith, personal initiative, flexibility, creativity and teamwork. Previous volunteer or international experience is also considered. Spanish language ability is required for placements in Honduras.

In-country Support: A three-week pre-departure session in June is followed by a two-week in-country orientation, during which logistical and cultural issues are discussed. Each site is supervised and coordinated by a 'Formation Team' of two local counterparts familiar with the programme. Volunteer housing is located in a safe area; emergency protocols are enforced.

Volunteering is a wonderful
way to really get to know
another culture and country

08 Do-It-Yourself Volunteer Placements

If you've read this far, you're probably seriously considering volunteering as part of your travels, or even as the sole purpose of an overseas trip. Previous chapters may have given you an idea of the type of work you'd like to do (see p11), and which continent or country you'd like to volunteer in. What you may be weighing up at this point, however, is the benefits and risks involved in teeing something up yourself versus paying an intermediary to arrange it all for you.

You may have arrived at this point by doing some online research and have been over-whelmed by the hundreds of agencies offering their services and charging a fee for it. But you may not feel comfortable paying a sending organisation – it may not fit with your image of what volunteering should be about. Simon Roberts, who taught English to under-privileged children with Luz del Mundo in Bolivia (p229), shared this sentiment:

A spiny forest plant from the arid southeast of Madagascar

After initial research we decided we didn't want to volunteer for an organisation where we had to pay for the experience, as we felt this was contrary to our idea of volunteering. The institution we went for was very small and had a grassroots feel to it.

How, then, do you follow in Simon's footsteps and find volunteering opportunities independently of a middle man? And what are the issues to consider when volunteering independently? For instance, would it be better to arrange the placement before you leave home, or once you arrive at your destination? And how can you ensure that you make a worthwhile contribution as a volunteer and have a good time while doing it? This chapter will give some answers to these questions.

Is Do-It-Yourself Volunteering Right for You?

In many cases the decision to do-it-yourself stems from the frustrations caused by the high costs and time restrictions associated with volunteer placement organisations. However, many prospective volunteers make a hasty decision to go it alone without properly thinking through the demands and challenges.Reflecting upfront on your strengths and weaknesses, your preferred ways of working and your skills and values will help you decided whether a do-it-yourself placement is right for you.

Kirsi Korhonen, who took on a few volunteering roles in Bolivia, including one at the animal refuge Inti Wara Yassi (p229), and a position at the boy's home Amanecer, made an informed decision to volunteer independently:

We chose to find our own opportunities, to make sure the money went where it was needed and to give ourselves more freedom. Plus, my friend and I are both very experienced in travelling and in all things travel-related.

All volunteers must possess certain core qualities if they are to make a worthwhile contribution, (see p41). However, going it alone places special demands on the volunteer. No matter how much research you've done, there'll be an element of the unknown. You will have to assume complete responsibility for yourself and your actions, as you will have no support network to fall back on. In addition, you will often be out of your comfort zone.

Elizabeth France, who performed a variety of roles with United Action for Children in Cameroon (p230), suggests that self-motivation and persistence are vital for a successful DIY experience:

From my experience, the most valuable people are those who have a 'stick-to-it' attitude, as they won't give up when the going gets tough.

Other key attributes which help in facing the kind of unpredictable situations that can crop up when you're volunteering independently include self-reliance, maturity, patience, communication and interpersonal skills, sensitivity to cross-cultural issues and a good sense of humour. In working out whether do-it-yourself volunteering is for you, you need to ask yourself honestly whether you can consistently demonstrate such qualities amid the inevitable challenges of a placement.

Pros & Cons of Going It Alone
Pros

Lower costs, and payments usually goes directly to the project

With some grassroots organisations you may not need to pay any placement fee; for others you will be expected to make a donation or fundraise. Jason Rogers, who volunteered in Baan Unrak School in Thailand and the Sunshine School in Laos (p230), paid a donation for his Thailand placement:

There was a pretty strict volunteer fee for Thailand, which included buying presents for the kids. Some of the money went directly to the centre and some went towards the Christmas presents. I think it was about US$350 total.

Elizabeth France, who volunteered in Cameroon, wanted to ensure that any fees she paid would go directly to the project:

An important factor in my decision was that the costs were to be paid directly to UAC, without a cut taken by any intermediary organisation.

Also, a large proportion of agency fees goes towards practical arrangements for volunteer placements such as board and lodging – if you're going it alone you can save money by making these arrangements yourself.

Greater ability to tailor the role to suit you

Most local charities and grassroots NGOs are small scale and do not have structured volunteer programmes, and this means you can often define your own role, matching your aptitudes and objectives to a project's needs.

The lack of structure at Luz del Mundo in Bolivia (p229) was a positive for Amanda Guest-Collins, who volunteered as an English teacher:

The set-up was very informal, so our roles and work weren't particularly structured. This meant, however, that we had the flexibility to make the roles our own.

Joan Hodkinson, a language teacher, chose to look after orphans at Loreto Day School in Calcutta, India (p229), because she was confident the pupils would benefit from her skills:

I knew that we would be teaching English as part of the work, which was something I could be successful at.

Being able to fit placements in with your plans

Choosing the agency-free route allows travellers who want the freedom of not being tied to an itinerary to arrange placements at short notice. The ability to extend your placement once you are there is another benefit, as Kristine Randall found when she volunteered on various projects with United Action for Children in Cameroon (p230):

I had originally intended to volunteer for two months. After a few weeks I decided to extend my stay for a third month, for a number of reasons, the biggest one being that I felt like I was finally settling in and didn't feel ready to leave.

You will be supporting small grassroots organisations with limited access to external resources and volunteers

Jo Shuttleworth volunteered independently in two African countries; one of her placements was as a teacher at Lila's Child Care Foundation in Ghana (p229). She comments on the rewards of working with a small-scale charity:

It is nice to find small charities that don't get much attention from the West and who genuinely appreciate your work, rather than you being yet another nameless face.

Simon Roberts, who volunteered in Bolivia, was keen to help support the work of unrecognised charities:

We wanted to volunteer in a country where the need for volunteers was greatest and where government support for small projects was in short supply.

You have direct ontact with people running local organisations or projects

Many volunteers prefer the more personal experience of dealing directly with the grass-roots organisation. In this way, they can inform themselves about the project's mission and iron out any problems in-country rather than relying on a third party – who may or may not have first-hand knowledge – to dispense information or direct matters from afar.

Deeper interaction with the local community

Volunteering independently means that you'll probably have to organise your own accommodation and entertainment, and you may be the only volunteer in a community. As a result, you'll generally be more motivated to mix with the local community – Benjamin Blakey, who helped on a construction site for Casas de la Esperanza (p228) in Nicaragua, found:

For the majority of the time I was the only foreign volunteer on the project site. This allowed me to practice my Spanish and forced me to integrate with the locals with whom I was working.

Speaking the local lingo obviously facilitates the immersion process – Kirsi Kohonen, who volunteered in Bolivia, emphasises:

In Bolivia not many people speak English, so knowing Spanish is almost a must, especially if you want to work with the locals. Otherwise you will just find yourself hanging out with the other volunteers and you won't learn anything about the country and its culture.

Cons

Hard work

There's no denying it, organising your own placement can be time-consuming. Benjamin Blakey, who volunteered in Nicaragua, spent many hours researching opportunities:

Conducting my own research and contacting organisations directly allowed me to find an NGO that did not charge a fee for volunteer placements. The difficulty was that the process required hours of internet searches, emails and dead ends before I contacted an organisation that matched my criteria and which had volunteer opportunities.

Kirsi Korhonen admits that going through an agency can be a much easier route to take:

Using an agency provides safety and support and is often hassle free compared to finding a placement independently.

No guarantees

However much advice you're given by people who have volunteered previously, to a certain extent you will be dealing with the unknown when you arrange your own placement. Local organisations or projects will not be vetted by a third party, so you may end up with something that doesn't match your expectations. As Rachel Oxberry, who volunteered in an Ecuadorian home for street children, recalls:

I was appalled at how the home was run. The bishop who ran the home beat the children and used a lot of the donations to fund his own family's education. The bishop's family ate a balanced diet, whereas the street children ate rice and beans.

Brenda Carter's placement in Ghana didn't turn out as expected either:

On my arrival, despite all the information I received that led me to believe I'd be working with a local women's group, I was taken to an expensive private school, where I was expected to teach. Not exactly the grassroots community approach I had been hoping for! To top it off, my accommodation was a room where a lady had recently died and no-one had even taken the time to remove her belongings.

If you organise a placement yourself, you'll only really find out how the local project is run, whether it is meeting genuine needs, what you'll be doing and whether you can make a valuable contribution once you are *in situ*.

Roles may not be clearly defined

Although some local charities and NGOs are used to taking on volunteers and can offer detailed job descriptions, it's more likely that you'll have to carve out your own role once you start the placement. Mary Sears' experience with Luz del Mundo in Bolivia (p229) is typical of many DIY placements:

It was up to me to make lesson plans and evaluations, to decide what I wanted to teach and how to go about it. I was the first foreign volunteer, so there was nothing in place.

There's ittle pre-departure and in-country support

Relying on a small grassroots organisation to give you significant pre-departure or in-country support, with little or no payment, is unfair and a real burden on your hosts. Nor should you expect an organisation to repay you for your help with free accommodation, food, in-country inductions, extracurricular activities etc. Jordan Jones, who volunteered at the Casa Guatemala orphanage, admits that he expected otherwise:

I hadn't done any research into it, but I assumed that volunteers would be provided with at least free accommodation, if not board.

Other key things that you will not receive support for are medical emergencies, securing visas and language tuition. Nor will you have an established safety net back home or in-country support with logistical or emotional problems.

You may feel isolated, volunteering alone

You may be working alongside other volunteers, but equally, you may be on your own, and in that case you have to deal with your experiences alone. Elizabeth France, who volunteered in Cameroon, really valued the support she received from her fellow volunteers:

For me, the greatest advantage to volunteering with another person is that you have the support of someone you trust and who can relate to you and your new experiences.

Under-supply or over-supply of volunteers can be detrimental to a project

Well-established sending agencies will carefully plan the supply of volunteers in conjunction with the local project director, to ensure that placements result in a significant and sustainable contribution. The danger of volunteers organising their own placements is that there is little continuity for the organisation, and previous work may be repeated or even undone.

Volunteers can become a burden on their host if they can't deal with uncertainty

If the going gets tough and you've paid an agency to arrange your placement, then you've usually got back-up to resolve problems. On the other hand, if you don't have a third party that you are accountable to; if the arrangement is pretty flexible; if you have paid little or no donation; and if you're the type who gives up easily, then you may simply decide to quit. But it's important to remember that you are accountable – both to the organisation that you have agreed to help and to yourself – and you do have a responsibility to honour your commitment. Should you quit, you could be disappointing the organisation, draining their resources and damaging the image of international volunteers.

The Search Begins

There are thousands of organisations around the world desperate for volunteers. Having travelled for many years and volunteered in several places, I know that it's a unique way to get to know local people and the way they live.

If this assertion from Mary Sears, who volunteered in Bolivia, is to be believed, then surely it can't be too difficult to find the right DIY volunteering opportunity? But which approach will produce the best results: arranging your placement before leaving home, while you're en route or once you reach your destination?

Arranging the Placement from Home or *In Situ*

Whether you choose to make arrangements for your placement before you leave home or *in situ* may depend upon your personal decision-making style; and specifically whether you prefer to be spontaneous or to be organised in advance. It may also depend upon the time limitations of your travel plans.

Jenny Smith chose to sort out her sea-turtle placement once she arrived in Costa Rica:

I had found out about it and contacted the organisation beforehand but it wasn't finalised until I got there.

In contrast, Jason Rogers, a volunteer in Thailand and Laos, chose to arrange all the details prior to leaving home:

Each volunteer trip was the main reason for my travels and was set up ahead of time.

Of course, there is one type of independent volunteering that doesn't involve a decision about whether to be organised in advance or not – emergency relief following a disaster. In Eoin Canny's case, volunteering post-tsunami on Koh Phi Phi with the NGO HI Phi Phi was an on-the-spot decision when he arrived on the Thai island and saw a sign requesting volunteers:

Giving help at the place of need, directly to the people that need it, regardless of the time, effort or work involved, can be an immensely satisfying experience.

The boxed text below is a first-hand account of one man's experience of impromptu emergency relief following a disaster. (See also p146, for Paul Piaia's account of working as an emergency volunteer in Pakistan following a major earthquake.)

Research Sources

Regardless of which approach to planning you adopt, matching your skills and philosophies with an appropriate organisation requires time and effort. You may be lucky and chance upon an opening when chatting to a contact at home or a local once abroad; however, a word-of-mouth lead should not be taken as a guarantee of an approriate placement.

Unexpected Volunteering

In October 2005, Guatemala was hit by Tropical Storm Stan and in a few days hundreds of people were killed in landslides and floods. I was studying Spanish in Antigua when the call went out for volunteers to help in Jocotenango, a suburb of Antigua which had been engulfed by mud when the local river burst its banks. I bought a pair of Wellington boots and took the bus to Jocotenango, which was a very sad sight, as the streets had been filled a metre deep with mud, and the people's ruined possessions were piled outside their houses. I joined the (mainly German and British) volunteers from Antigua's language schools in digging trenches to allow the dirty water to drain away. There seemed to be little organisation, but one afternoon it was decided we should build a dam to divert the water away from the houses. The dam was made of fertiliser bags filled with earth – each weighing about 30 kilos – and hundreds were needed, so it was very hard work. What was really impressive was how we organised ourselves into a team to build a substantial structure in a short space of time, and the next day I was pleased to see that our dam still stood. By then the army had arrived in force and were using machinery to clear the streets, so the volunteers helped clean out houses. On Monday it was back to school, with sore hands but with a sense of satisfaction in having done something to help.

Graham Williams

Most people who set up their placement before arriving in-country use a variety of information channels, including personal networking, websites, online directories and forums, guidebooks and volunteering fairs. Amanda Guest-Collins, who volunteered in Bolivia, browsed the internet and guidebooks for ideas:

I found the site www.volunteersouthamerica.net very useful, plus postings on Lonely Planet's ThornTree. I also looked at several entries in their *GAP Year Book* and *South America on a Shoestring* guidebook.

Clodagh Mullen, who volunteered with Safe Passage/Camino Seguro in Guatemala (p230), surfed the net and used her contacts:

After an exhaustive internet search, I met a girl at my college who had been volunteering in Guatemala for six years.

Your Personal Network

Who do you know that may be able to suggest organisations to volunteer with? What other contacts do you have that may know of opportunities? Don't just limit this to your immediate circle of friends, family and colleagues. Ask them to spread the word among their social and work networks too. Victoria Jaberi found her role in administration and translation work for Hampy in Peru (p228) through networking:

A friend of mine worked for Hope. So I contacted him and the president of Hope. Both told me they didn't have any research placements at that time, but their friends introduced me to other people who had projects as well.

It is likely that organisations in your home country working in areas that interest you will have foreign connections. If you are keen to volunteer in a school or contribute to community projects, it's worth talking to schools at home that may have links with foreign communities. This method worked for Joan Hodkinson, who volunteered in India:

I spoke to people who had worked in schools in India to get contacts and ideas.

Surfing the Web

Although the internet seems like the obvious place to look for inspiration, it is only in the last few years that independent volunteering opportunities have really become visible, thanks to the creation of several online directories dedicated to listing local charities and grassroots NGOs which accept volunteers directly (see the list of directories on p225).

The advantage of these online directories is that you can search for organisations by continent, country or type of work in just a few clicks. Some of the directories rely solely on recommendations from travellers, whereas others will check out the credentials of each listed organisation, either by visiting or by sending an in-depth questionnaire about how they work with volunteers. All directories will suggest that you use them as a starting point for your research but that you should seek other opinions, and contact organisations and past volunteers directly.

For a small fee, some directories offer a matching service, whereby you submit your interests and skills and are sent a list of appropriate DIY vacancies. Another great way to learn about opportunities is to review chat-room postings, which not only tell you about organisations and how to approach them but also discuss the benefits and pitfalls of volunteering without an intermediary organisation.

If you've already narrowed down your country preferences, national tourism websites can provide information and useful links for a good range of volunteering vacancies. Another avenue is to type 'NGOs in country x' into a search engine – this will bring up NGOs that may accept volunteers directly. For example, a search for 'NGOs in Cambodia' will bring up www.ccc-cambodia.org, an NGO member organisation which promotes information exchange and NGO coordination in Cambodia.

The Origins of www.volunteersouthamerica.net

I was keen to volunteer in South America, having visited and backpacked through the region on a couple of occasions. Although I was happy to cover my own travel, food and accommodation costs, I wanted to volunteer independently, for about six months, without paying any agency or middle-man fees. I began my research and soon discovered how difficult it was to find locally based, grassroots volunteer programmes in South America.

The problem I found was that the internet search engines were dominated by 'big ticket' volunteer placement agencies, which offer a more packaged, higher-cost volunteer experience than I was looking for.

I then began monitoring internet travel forums, particularly Lonely Planet's Thorn Tree. Over a period of time, some interesting grassroots volunteer programmes came to light – recommended by backpackers and travellers. Many of these programmes were (and are) truly inspiring, working with disadvantaged children, communities, wildlife and rainforest conservation etc. Most of these organisations didn't charge volunteers to participate and some even provided free food and accommodation to long-term volunteers.

Having found these locally run volunteer programmes, I felt a sense of injustice that the websites of these organisations were so difficult to find online. I wanted to help, so I created a website to promote these programmes and to show that free volunteering does exist in South and Central America. The site is www.volunteersouthamerica.net.

I normally update the website when I hear good or bad reports about a volunteer programme, but other than that I don't check or validate any of the organisations listed. The purpose of the site is simply to let people know that these programmes are out there. My advice is always to contact past volunteers of any programme you are interested in to get a better idea of what you may be letting yourself in for!

Steve McElhinney
www.volunteersouthamerica.net

Being proficient in the language of your chosen country will enable you to widen your search much further, as Kirsi Korhonen, who volunteered in Bolivia with the boys' home Amanecer, discovered:

I just started searching the net with all kinds of keywords and, after having decided on Bolivia, concentrated on finding opportunities there. We found Amanecer with the keyword combination *trabajo voluntario, niños de la call*e (voluntary work, street kids).

Just keep in mind that, more often than not, typing 'volunteering in country x' into a search engine will produce lists of sending agencies rather than local charities, as only a few of the latter have the resources and know-how to exploit the web effectively.

Guidebooks & Career or Travel Fairs

Elizabeth France used a variety of channels in her research, and found her university helpful:

I went to a number of career fairs and information sessions at my university and found out about different NGOs and their projects. I took information sheets from these sessions and then checked out the projects online.

With the growing popularity of international volunteering, some guidebooks also list the contact details of grassroots organisations.

Researching Opportunities In-country

Karla Gergen, who volunteered for the Child Care Foundation in Ghana, opted to find a placement once she reached her destination:

I was with some friends on a planned trip that was to include touring and volunteering for two weeks each. My plan was just to keep my ears and eyes open during the two touring weeks to find an opportunity.

Karla was able to adopt this approach in Ghana, as she spoke English, which is widely understood there. However, without a basic knowledge of your chosen country's language you may struggle to find a suitable placement. Even if you are accepted, the language barrier could limit your contribution, as Jo Shuttleworth, who volunteered in Burkina Faso, admits:

My French isn't amazing so it was limited in what I could do, but I could mark work and correct spelling.

It is useful to have at least one lead to get you started on your in-country research. Generally, in popular tourist destinations, facilities used by travellers (such as hostels, internet cafes, laundrettes, language schools and tour offices), will have noticeboards displaying ads for jobs and volunteering vacancies.

Talking to other travellers and locals connected with the travel industry, such as tour guides or hostel owners, can often point you in the right direction. Jordan Jones, who volunteered in Guatemala, tuned in to the local community to find leads:

From the day I landed and began travelling I just kept my eyes and ears open for volunteer projects. I checked bulletin boards in hostels and asked all the other travellers I met if they had heard of any projects on their travels. I would even directly ask projects and national park employees if they wanted a volunteer, even if I had no indication that they had a volunteer programme.

Another source of ideas and contacts is local newspapers – news items will cover issues affecting the local community and environment.

If you're clear about the type of volunteering activity you wish to undertake, then it makes sense to focus your search. Visit some local orphanages and schools in the area if you're passionate about working with orphans or in education (although do take school holidays into account in the latter case). Local churches or religious organisations can also be a valuable source of information for volunteering in community organisations.

Equally, if you are qualified in a particular field such as medicine or IT, then approach organisations that could most benefit from your skills: medical centres, community technical centres or local businesses, for instance.

Some Final Advice

Getting in touch with a couple of past volunteers who have worked with the organisations on your shortlist could mean the difference between a life-changing experience and total disillusionment. Of course, seeking endorsement may not be possible if you are the organisation's first volunteer or, indeed, if you are *in situ*.

Kristine Randall, who volunteered in Cameroon, emphasises the importance of seeking advice from past volunteers:

As pessimistic as it may sound, many organisations in developing countries are not managed or run to the high standards that we expect, coming from a developed country. Their answers to your queries may not always reflect the reality of the situation. I would strongly suggest contacting a previous volunteer and asking them all the same questions that you would put to the project director. You may be surprised by just how different the answers can be!

Choosing a Mutually Beneficial Placement

It's all too easy to make a snap decision when selecting a placement for yourself. You might be so keen to slot volunteering into your travel plans that you focus on practicalities such as costs and time frames and meeting your own objectives. You might not take enough time to reflect upon whether you believe in the ethos of the organisation, whether there's a clear need for you, or whether you have the necessary skills. Elizabeth France, who volunteered in Cameroon, advises:

I think it's important to remember that, although you want do to something that you'll find interesting and rewarding, you also want to do something you feel could be useful to the organisation and which will truly benefit them.

A hypothetical scenario will help illustrate this point. Imagine yourself in the situation of an orphanage with no government support, run by a single devoted individual who wants to improve the lives of people in his or her community. A foreigner turns up on your doorstep offering to lend support. You've never met an international volunteer before and you don't really know whether this stranger has the appropriate skills or attitude, but in your eyes all foreigners are wealthy and any interest and help is appreciated. Not wishing to appear ungrateful, or to refuse them hospitality, you take them in. As it turns out the volunteer ends up being a drain on your resources rather than a help. They don't speak your language, have never cared for children before and require constant supervision. They complain all the time and leave after only a few days, not having paid for their board.

Nobody wants to be a party to that kind of scenario. The last thing you want is to be a burden or a drain on an organisation's resources – it's totally at odds with the concept of ethical volunteering. So bear in mind that as an independent volunteer the onus is on you to ask the right questions and ensure that offering your skills leads to a mutually beneficial outcome. (See p26 for a comprehensive list of appropriate questions to ask an organisation to ensure this).

Further Preparation

If you're arranging the placement before you leave home, then you'll have a hundred and one things to sort out before you leave (for more on this, see Chapter 3). Even if you decide to chance it and find a placement once you arrive in the country, you will still need to sort out board and lodging and check that you have the appropriate visa.

Without a support network back home and with little, if any, support in-country, you need to be aware of the potential risks to your health and safety and general wellbeing, and put together a back-up plan for dealing with emergencies. Critical questions to consider include:

~ Is the area politically stable or unstable?

~ Are the transport links adequate if I need to get out quickly?

~ Where are the nearest medical facilities if I become sick?

~ What access do I have to telecommunications?

~ Do I have basic knowledge of the local language?

Maximising Your Contribution

Wow, that was a lot of effort fixing up an independent placement! Things should run smoothly from here on, as you've asked all the right questions. You can relax now – or can you?

Finding the placement is one thing – actually seeing it through independently requires even more effort and commitment. Here are some wise words from Kirsi Korhonen, who volunteered in Bolivia:

You need to understand that sometimes things are done differently and not get all worked up about the little things. Living abroad can be hard and you just have to take things as they come. Your attitude is the most important thing. If you think positive, things will go positively. If you let the unknown and the unexpected get you down, you're in trouble. Because the one sure thing about volunteering abroad is that there is always something unexpected, and it's not always good...

This is the advice of Karla Gergen, who volunteered in Ghana:

You need to really listen to the people you are working with, to suspend judgement and learn from them. In that process, and through the work that you do, you may be of some use. If you fall into the trap of thinking you can save the world (or this group of people or this place), you will fail. You cannot do that. In order to be of any help, you need to recognise the limits of what you can do.

The last word on independent volunteering goes to Mary Sears, who volunteered in Bolivia:

Don't listen when people tell you it's too hard. Every little bit can help in ways grander than you could ever imagine.

Directories & Useful Organisations

These websites and organisations provide the contact details of grassroots organisations and projects that accept volunteers directly.

International Organisations

Independentvolunteer.org

www.independentvolunteer.org
This web directory provides listings of projects and organisations that charge no fees other than reasonable food and accommodation costs. You can search by country or type of work, as well as read about the experiences of returned volunteers.

True Travellers Society

info@truetravellers.org
www.truetravellers.org
This Canadian-based website lists worldwide independent volunteering opportunities, which you can search as a non-member by destination or project type. If you become a free member, you can access the user's forum and a personal blog, and add your comments to any content on the site.

VolunteerSouthAmerica.net

stevem@141.com

www.volunteersouthamerica.net

This online directory lists free and low-cost volunteering opportunities in several Central and South American countries. The lists are driven by user recommendations, so it's advisable to contact returned volunteers and the project or local organisation as well.

UK Organisations

Volunteer Latin America

BM Volunteer Latin America, London WC1N3XX, UK

☎ +44 (0)20 7193 9163

info@volunteerlatinamerica.com

www.volunteerlatinamerica.com

Volunteer Latin America is an informative gateway to hundreds of low-cost and free volunteering opportunities in Central and South America in the environmental and humanitarian sectors. For a small fee you can submit your requirements and interests and get a personalised guide listing local grassroots organisations (minimum 20) and projects (30-100) that you can contact directly. The guides also offer advice on how to contact organisations and other useful tips.

World Service Enquiry

188 Ramsden Rd, London SW12 8RE, UK

wse@wse.org.uk

www.wse.org.uk

This agency offers guidance for people who want to volunteer abroad. It publishes an annual guide to volunteering opportunities (£5.75 plus postage and packing) or you can subscribe to the monthly *Opportunities Abroad* bulletin (from £6 per month). WSE also offers one-on-one guidance (priced from £50) for people thinking of a career in development work.

Worldwide Volunteering

7 North Street Workshops, Stoke sub Hamdon, Somerset TA14 6QR, UK

☎ +44(0) 1935 825588

www.worldwidevolunteering.org.uk

This organisation has a database of 1200 volunteer organisations and 350,000 volunteer opportunities throughout the UK and in 214 countries worldwide. For a fee of £10 you can conduct three detailed searches, which will provide you with a personalised list of volunteering opportunities.

North American Organisations

Action Without Borders

350 Fifth Ave, Ste 6614, New York, NY 10118, USA

☎ +1 212 843 3973

fax +1 212 564 3377

info@idealist.org

www.idealist.org

This US website has over 11,000 listings of volunteer opportunities worldwide. Volunteers of all nationalities can conduct customised searches for specific types of volunteering and you can register online to receive updates of volunteer opportunities by email.

Explorations In Travel, Inc.

www.volunteertravel.com

Initially launched to provide high-school students and teachers with international Spanish-language immersion programmes, Explorations in Travel now offers volunteer placements in conservation and wildlife, ecotourism, and education throughout Latin America and Nepal. Although group assignments are generally reserved for chaperoned high-school classes, any interested individual may apply for programmes. Some placements require specific linguistic or professional expertise, but many are unskilled. The organisation charges a fee of approximately US$800 to US$1000 to arrange work and lodging at a site and offers international travel advice; all travel, insurance and general living costs are borne by the volunteer.

Idealist

350 Fifth Ave, Ste 6614, New York, NY 10118, USA

☎ +1 212 843 3973

fax +1 212 564 3377

info@idealist.org

www.idealist.org

An online initiative of the non-profit Action Without Borders, Idealist.org is perhaps the largest and most comprehensive database of non-profit and community organisations in the world. The website lists 57,000 organisations in 165 countries, which pay to post volunteer, internship and salaried openings on the site. Individuals can search the database for domestic and international volunteer and paid opportunities by name, location and focus; receive organisation updates; create a customised search profile; and participate in online discussions – all free. The site includes a separate section devoted to international volunteering, with informational resources, links and networking tools.

International Volunteer Programs Association

PO Box 287049, New York, NY 10128, USA
☎ +1 (646) 505-8209
info@volunteerinternational.org
www.volunteerinternational.org
The International Volunteer Programs Association (IVPA) is an alliance of 34 non-profit NGOs based in the Americas, which promotes public awareness of international volunteer and internship opportunities. All member and prospective member organisations are required to adhere to specific 'principles and practices' in order to ensure programme quality. IVPA's website has a searchable catalogue of international volunteer positions with these organisations, as well as general advice on volunteering abroad and links to related sites.

Volunteer Abroad

324 East Oak St, Fort Collins,
CO 80524, USA
☎ +1 (720) 570-1702
fax +1 (720) 570-1703
info@goabroad.com
www.goabroad.com/volunteer-abroad
Originally created in 1999 as a resource for students considering international travel, GoAbroad.com contains extensive guides, online tools and directories of international study, internship and employment opportunities. The site's international volunteer section, Volunteer Abroad, allows NGOs and non-profit organisations throughout the world to upload information

and make classified listings at no charge. Browsers can search postings by region, country, type of volunteer work and project duration. A wealth of supplementary data is provided on cheap airfares and rail travel, hostel accommodation options, student discounts, and international phonecards and insurance. The site's free weekly newsletter publishes updates on paid and volunteer opportunities around the globe.

Australasian Organisations

Friends of the Earth

312 Smith St, Collingwood, Vic. 3066,
(PO Box 222, Fitzroy, Vic. 3065) Australia
☎ +61 3 9419 8700
fax + 61 3 9416 2081
foe@foe.org.au
www.foe.org.au
FoE is an international network of environmental organisations campaigning on ecological and social justice issues, including climate change, forests, energy and genetic modification. Popular with the greenie set, FoE has a reputation in Australia as a caring and practical environmental alliance. FoE doesn't have a formal volunteer programme, but encourages people to liaise with Cameron Walker at the Collingwood branch to discuss options before contacting the FoE group in the country they are interested in volunteering in. Many of the international offices are under-resourced and may not have English speakers. For a full listing of FoE member groups worldwide, refer to www.foei.org/en/who-we-are/member-directory/index.html.

Volunteering Australia Inc

Level 2, 202 City Walk, Canberra ACT 2601, Australia (PO Box 128, Civic Square, Canberra ACT 2608, Australia)
☎ +61 (0)2 6251 4060
volaus@volunteeringaustralia.org
www.volunteeringaustralia.org
This organisation exists to raise the profile of volunteering in Australia, and as such provides information on a wide variety of topics related to volunteering. The affiliated Go Volunteer website (www.govolunteer.com.au) lists around 6000 positions across Australia.

Grassroots Charities & Non-profits

These grassroots charities and non-profit organisations all accept volunteers directly.

Asociacion Widecast

San Jose, Tibas, 200 N y 25 O del Palacio Municipal, Costa Rica
☎ +506 2241 7431, +506 8818 2543
fax +506 2241 7149
www.latinamericanseaturtles.org
www.widecast.org

Volunteers help in the research on, and conservation of, the leatherback sea turtle nesting population at Gandoca beach in the Gandoca-Manzanillo National Wildlife Refuge. Volunteers can also help protect the hawksbill turtle in Cahuita.

Status: NGO.
Timing & Length of Projects: Minimum of one week, maximum of six months. Projects run from March to November.
Destinations: Gandoca-Manzanillo Wildlife Refuge and Cahuita National Park
Costs: About US$55 per day per person.
Eligibility: The minimum age is 18 years. Volunteers should be in good physical condition as there is a lot of walking, every night.
Annual no. of Volunteers: 700
Annual Projects: 4
Partner Programmes: 2
Selection & Interview Process: Volunteers must submit an application form in advance.
In-country Support: None.

Casas de la Esperanza

7 Harrison St, Somerville, MA 02143, USA/
Angelica Rivas, La Prusia, Granada, Nicaragua
☎ +1 617 625 9988
fax +1 617 496 3401
admin@casas-de-la-esperanza.org
www.casas-de-la-esperanza.org/index.html

Volunteers are required to build housing for, and teach technical skills to, families who are currently squatters, living on the outskirts of Granada, Nicaragua.

Status: Non-profit corporation registered in the USA working together with the Spanish NGO Casas de la Esperanza and with the Nicaraguan Asociacion Casas de la Esperanza.
Timing & Length of Projects: Year-round; minimum eight-week stay.

Destinations: Granada, Nicaragua.
Costs: There is no placement fee but volunteers must cover their own expenses.
Eligibility: Minimum age is 18 years. Basic Spanish is required.
Annual no. of Volunteers: Unlimited.
Selection & Interview Process: Volunteers should apply by email through the US or Nicaraguan office several months in advance.
In-country Support: Transport from the airport to the quarter can be organised ($30).

Hampy

Urb. Santa Monica, Jr. José Carlos Maritegui B-22, Cusco, Peru
☎ +51 84 9761072
www.hampy.org

This non-profit organisation based in Cusco is dedicated to providing psychological, medical and educational services to the community. Various volunteer roles are available: administration, radio broadcasting and website development at Hampy's office, assisting in the Colibri programme for street children or teaching in schools. Volunteer work for professionals in the areas of psychology, health, education, social work and legal work is also available with Hampy's partner organisations.

Status: Civil association (not-for-profit).
Timing & Length of Projects: Minimum one-month stay: projects are available all year, but primary and high schools are closed from January to March.
Destinations: Cusco and the neighbouring countryside in Peru.
Costs: Volunteers must attend a one-week volunteer workshop which costs US$300. This includes training in cultural, community and diversity awareness. Volunteers must fund their own board and lodging.
Eligibility: Volunteers must be enthusiastic and able to work under pressure.
Annual no. of Volunteers: Unlimited.
Selection & Interview Process: Volunteers should submit a CV ideally two months in advance, have intermediate Spanish, and attend a personal interview. A volunteer workshop is then held to analyse each volunteer's skills.
In-country Support: Training, mentoring, monitoring, supervision and evaluation are provided. Accommodation advice is given and extracurricular activities organised.

Inti Wara Yassi

Comunidad Inti Wara Yassi, Casilla 1600,
Cochabamba, Bolivia
☎ +591 44 136572
info@intiwarayassi.org
www.intiwarayassi.org
A wildlife refuge in Parque Machia, Villa
Tunari houses over 200 monkeys, dozens of
birds, tortoises, coatis and wild cats. All were
illegally poached and the refuge's aim is to
rehabilitate them for re-release into the wild.
Volunteers work hard during the day to clean
the cages, tend sick animals, guide visitors
and in the evenings enjoy the quiet jungle life
with friends from all over the world.
Status: Grassroots NGO.
Timing & Length of Projects: All year round;
minimum 15-day stay. Volunteers who wish
to be responsible for a specific animal need
further training and are therefore are required
to stay for a one-month minimum period.
Destinations: Villa Tunari and Parque Ambue
Ari, both in Bolivia.
Costs: US$160 to US$280 for the first 15 nights,
US$300 to US$490 for 30 nights, then US$8
to US$10 for each night thereafter. Prices
vary according to the park in which you are
volunteering.
Eligibility: Minimum age is 18 years. Families
are welcome. All volunteers must have a big
heart and be willing to work hard to save the
animals.
Annual no. of Volunteers: 1500
Annual Projects: 3
Selection & Interview Process: Volunteers do
not need to apply in advance, as permanent
staff believe that the experience of the
volunteer is as important as the work they do,
and everyone can help.
In-country Support: Support is provided at the
refuge.

Lila's Child Care Foundation

PO Box ML 53, Mallam, Accra, Ghana
☎ +233 2465 35210
lila.m.djaba@childcarefoundation.org
http://ccfghana.blogspot.com.au/2008/04/
welcome-to-child-care-foundation-in.html
Lila's Child Care Foundation was established
in 2004 to support underprivileged children.
It has been able to place about 30 children
from its school into different government and
private schools within its neighborhood.

Status: Registered charity and not-for-profit.
Timing & Length of Projects: A minimum of
four months.
Destinations: Ghana.
Costs: €400 for accommodation and food.
Eligibility: Minimum age of 18 years.
Annual no. of Volunteers: 8
Selection & Interview Process: Volunteers
must contact the foundation with an
indication of their timing and skills.
In-country Support: The foundation offers
assistance in finding safe accommodation
and recommending local trustworthy people
to show volunteers the sights.

Loreto Day School

122 A.J.C. Bose Rd, Sealdah,
Kolkata, India 700 014
☎ +91 33 2227 0229/+91 33 2246 3845
fax +91 33 2227 0228
smcyril@yahoo.com
www.loretosealdah.com
Loreto Day School has 1500 students, all
girls, of which 60% live in sprawling slums. A
sister project called the Rainbow Home needs
volunteers to assist in looking after the 150
Rainbow children who are orphans, homeless
or very deprived.
Status: Registered non-profit charitable
educational institution.
Timing & Length of Projects: Projects run year-
round; the minimum stay is 30 days.
Destinations: Kolkata, India.
Costs: There's no placement fee but
volunteers must cover their own expenses.
Eligibility: The minimum age is 21 years.
Annual no. of Volunteers: Unlimited.
Annual Projects: 2
Partner Programmes: 1
Selection & Interview Process: Volunteers
must complete an application form indicating
their timing and skills.
In-country Support: Assistance in finding
accommodation.

Luz Del Mundo

Calle 1, Plan 3000 Barrio, 12 de Diciembre,
Santa Cruz de la Sierra, Bolivia
☎ +591 3 360 8444
volunteerldm@gmail.com
www.volunteersouthamerica.net/
LuzDelMundo/ldm_index.htm
This is a grassroots childminding centre,
which local children attend to learn English

and participate in cultural activities. Volunteers are required to assist in teaching English, arts, culture, dance and theatre, as well as with fundraising and administration.

Status: Not-for-profit organisation.

Timing & Length of Projects: Projects run all year round; the minimum stay is two weeks.

Destinations: Santa Cruz, Bolivia.

Costs: There's no placement fee but volunteers must cover their own expenses.

Eligibility: There are no restrictions but volunteers need to be mature, demonstrate substantial initiative and have basic Spanish.

Annual no. of Volunteers: Unlimited.

Selection & Interview Process: Volunteers can email a few weeks prior to arrival to indicate their skills and timing.

In-country Support: There's no support, as the organisation is very grassroots.

Safe Passage/Camino Seguro

Calle Hermano Pedro 4, La Antigua, Guatemala

☎ /fax +502 7832 8428

volunteers@safepassage.org

www.safepassage.org

This organisation provides educational and medical support to children whose families work and live near the garbage dump in Guatemala City. Volunteers assist the Guatemalan teachers in the educational reinforcement and vocational programmes. Volunteers with medical qualifications are also required.

Status: Safe Passage is a registered 501(c) fundraising charity in the United States. In Guatemala, Camino Seguro is the operational part of the organisation and is a registered NGO.

Timing & Length of Projects: Projects run all year round; the minimum stay is five weeks.

Destinations: Guatemala City; Antigua for volunteers helping with administration.

Costs: Volunteers are responsible for covering the cost of their living expenses while in country. There is a limited number of long-term housing stipends available for key positions. Visit www.safepassage.org/get-involved/volunteer for more details.

Eligibility: The minimum age is 18.

Annual no. of Volunteers: 200

Selection & Interview Process: Volunteers must complete an application form and submit references.

In-country Support: The volunteer department provides help with transportation from the airport, Spanish school, accomodation with local families, orientation, placement, general support and management.

Sunshine School

PO Box 7411 Vientiane, Unit 12 Ban Phapho Sisattanak Dist. Vientiane, Laos

☎ +856 21 214522

sunshinelaos@gmail.com

http://sunshineschool.tumblr.com

Sunshine School is a Lao school with classes from nursery to junior high school. Activities include an organic farm and English classes in Somsemai and Veuntaen villages, about 50km from Vientiane. Volunteers assist in teaching English and creative activities, developing educational and PR materials, fundraising, marketing farm products and other herbal products, and with farm garden work and the development of school and farm facilities.

Status: The school is non-profit, licensed and registered with the Lao Ministry of Education as a private school.

Timing & Length of Projects: The school prefers stays of one month to one year, but will accept volunteers for shorter periods.

Destinations: Vientiane, Laos.

Costs: There's no placement fee but volunteers must cover all their expenses except lunches.

Eligibility: The minimum age is 18.

Annual no. of Volunteers: There are four to six volunteers at any given time, but the type and degree of engagement depends on their skills and experience.

Annual Projects: 2

Partner Programmes: 1

Selection & Interview Process: Volunteers are asked to submit their CV or a short description of their background in advance, listing their qualifications, experience, skills and giving their special interests.

In-country Support: The school can advise on budget accommodation.

United Action for Children

PO Box 177, Muyuka, South West Province, Cameroon

☎ +237 7772 0418/+237 9785 8394

unitedactionforc@yahoo.com

www.unitedactionforchildren.org

This organisation, which is committed to developing a caring society for children and young people, offers volunteering roles in education, vocational training, economic and agricultural development, IT, accounting, fundraising and general HIV/AIDS awareness.
Status: Registered grassroots NGO.
Timing & Length of Projects: Projects are available all year round; the minimum placement is three weeks; the maximum is six months.
Destinations: Cameroon.
Costs: Two weeks costs US$165, one month US$305, a second month is an extra US$165, and any subsequent months cost US$165.

Eligibility: The minimum age is 18 years.
Annual no. of Volunteers: 60
Annual Projects: 5
Partner Programmes: 4
Selection & Interview Process: Applicants must submit their CV in advance.
In-country Support: United Action for Children provides transport for volunteers from the airport to project sites. Food is prepared for volunteers by cooks hired by UAC. Volunteers have access to internet, computers and office space.

Useful Websites

~ **Australian Agency for International Development (AusAID;** www.ausaid.gov.au) Volunteer offers appear on this site: see the contractors' directory under 'less-experienced professionals', or check AusAID's *Focus* magazine.

~ **Australian Council for International Development (ACFID;** www.acfid.asn.au) Events and training, current volunteer positions and a member directory.

~ **Council for International Development (CID;** www.cid.org.nz) New Zealand's repository for development information, with interesting survey findings.

~ **Development Gateway** (www.developmentgateway.org) Search for volunteer positions and have learning tools and references at your fingertips.

~ **Global Focus Aotearoa** (www.globalfocus.org.nz) Articles, campaigns, events and training. A New Zealand site with a development-work database, including volunteering opportunities.

~ **Greenpeace** (www.greenpeace.org) Joining a local group enables you to help on environmental campaigns through activities like public outreach and participating in non-violent direct actions. Located in most capital cities, groups meet regularly to share information and participate in training. The Greenpeace Cyberactivist Community is an online option.

~ **International Association for Volunteer Effort** (www.iave.org) Links to national volunteer organisations.

~ **Online Volunteering Service** (www.onlinevolunteering.org) The UN site connecting development organisations and volunteers over the internet. An email newsletter is available.

~ **Relief Web** (www.reliefweb.int) A favourite of UN staff, development consultants and globetrotting volunteers.

~ **World Volunteer** (www.worldvolunteerweb.org) 'News, views and resources' from the UN, plus Millennium Development Goals (MDGs) in the spotlight.

From Mongolia to Laos on a Volunteering Adventure

I was between jobs and planned to travel, but I wanted it to be a productive time for me and I wanted to contribute to the communities that I was visiting. When I tried to locate volunteer opportunities before I left, I could only find programmes where I had to pay a considerable fee. For this reason, I located places to volunteer through word of mouth while travelling and this worked out very well for me.

I wanted to work with children, since my background is teaching and I have a Master of Education. On the train from Siberia to Mongolia I met an American living in Ulaanbaatar, and I asked him if he knew of an orphanage where I might be of help. He gave me the name of Didi Kalika, who founded and runs The Lotus Children's Centre. Before I left Mongolia, I asked her if she knew of any programmes in Laos and she told me about the Sunshine School.

At the Sunshine School I had two roles. I assisted the English teacher in the classroom. Also, as curriculum developer, I researched and added games and interactive activities to the English curriculum. I volunteered there for two months and I was able to finish the curriculum project. Even so, I was sad to leave; though it wasn't enough time to really become part of the community and to learn the language.

I felt safe when volunteering and I was able to ask for support when I needed it. Often these schools and organisations (and I speak not just of the Sunshine School, but of all the places where I volunteered) are operating on small budgets or with few staff and they need volunteers who can be independent and who don't need much hand-holding. On the other hand, I think volunteers should make sure that they communicate with the people in charge when confused or not comfortable with their tasks. This ensures that you are doing what they want and also that you have a good experience.

One piece of advice I'd give is that before you end your time volunteering, try to tie up any loose ends and leave clear notes on what you did. Many organisations get so many volunteers coming and going that improvements or suggestions can easily get lost in the shuffle.

Volunteering in a foreign country is an experience that changes you forever. You grow as a person and you meet people who are kind and generous regardless of their financial status. It was a shame that I was volunteering at each of these places for such a short time, but I see fundraising as a way of continuing to assist these people in their efforts to make these children's lives better. I think that there is a risk that, as volunteers, we drop into people's lives and have this great, rewarding experience and then we just jet back to the developed world and simply resume our lives with barely a thought for those we've left behind. For me, it is important to try to keep some contact and maintain the relationships that I made, in order to honour the kindness and generosity my hosts showed me when I was a guest in their home.

Sally Armbrecht

Sally Armbrecht took on independent volunteering roles in Laos, Mongolia and Burma during a career break.

Photo: Tirno Virtala

Driving through the moutains of
the Altai Republic, Central Asia

09 Coming Home

As the saying goes, 'All good things must come to an end.' But how will you feel once your volunteering stint is over, and what long-term impact will volunteering have on your life back home?

Leaving

When you're volunteering, you throw yourself heart and soul into a project. As Michelle Hawkins, who volunteered in Ghana and Costa Rica with Raleigh International (p108), says:

You end up putting a lot more energy into work overseas as the need is so much greater.

This often means you make strong bonds with the people you work with which can make it hard when the time comes to leave your volunteer programme. Kate Sturgeon, who volunteered in Zimbabwe with MSF (p144), remembers:

It was quite hard to leave. After 16 months I'd become very attached to all my patients, the staff and the work I'd put into the clinic. The clinic put on a wonderful send-off party where all the staff said a few words and we had a special lunch (take-away pizza, which is a real treat in the clinic!) and they gave me some leaving presents. Then a friend of mine also organised a farewell party at the MSF house where we were living and a surprise band, which was fantastic. They had to drag me to the airport the next day, I really didn't want to leave.

Jacqueline Hill volunteered for a year with VSO (p94) in Bangladesh and felt the same way:

There is a strong tradition of celebration at Dipshikha. I not only had more than one 'leaving do' with speeches and gifts, but they also put on a party with cake, balloons and a photographer for my 40th birthday. Leaving was quite an emotional time, as I realised that I might never see these people who I had spent one of the most significant years of my life with again.

If you have volunteered with children, become part of their lives and started to care about them, leaving can be heartbreaking. Poonam Sattee who worked with street kids in Guatemala, recalls:

I was incredibly upset leaving. I felt like I was abandoning the children – particularly as they equated 'needing to leave' with 'wanting to leave' and they couldn't understand the difference. Before I left, I organised a thank-you party for the children to say thanks for everything they shared with me: the fun times, their patience with me and for accepting me like a friend. I was given lots of handmade cards with messages that were incredibly beautiful and meant a lot – my emotions were really running high that day.

And it is not that much easier if you have volunteered as a team member on an environmental rather than development project. Robin Glegg, who has volunteered on three separate expeditions in the Altai, Namibia and Oman with Biosphere Expeditions (p174), says:

On all three expeditions there was a sense of deflation and disappointment that they were coming to an end. Everybody bonds, enjoys the work and the time just goes too quickly.

Reverse Culture Shock

It is hard to know which is greater: the cultural unease that you can feel when you start your placement, or the shock of life back in your home country when you return. Reverse culture shock is a perfectly natural thing to experience on coming home.

Poonam Sattee found it very hard to adjust after one year in Guatemala:

I hated being home! I think the biggest culture shock was when I was sent into the SavaCentre by my mum to buy some tinned tomatoes. I was used to buying plain fresh tomatoes from the market! I went into the aisle for tinned veg and saw tinned tomatoes, chopped tomatoes, tomatoes with peppers, tomatoes in juice, brined tomatoes, tomatoes in salsa etc, and I pretty much had a breakdown in the aisle (tears and everything). I couldn't understand the consumer society we live in where we sell about 25 different varieties of tomatoes. It was ridiculous.

After 12 months in Bangladesh, it was mayonnaise that did it to Jacqueline Hill:

I felt quite numb for a few months. I put off seeing people for the first couple of weeks because it was enough just to absorb being with family and in a modern, Western house again. I went to the supermarket one day and was paralysed by the choices available. 'Mayonnaise' said the list. There were two rows of different types. How to decide? In Bangladesh there was only ever one of anything, if it was available at all! I regret having everything available all the time. I loved the seasonality of food in Bangladesh. I miss the excitement of the run-up to the very short lychee season and the gloriously long mango season. My first trip on the London Underground felt like I was in some kind of night-mare, futuristic movie. No-one smiled and they were all wearing black and grey.

It's not just the abundance and waste of commodities that returned volunteers find hard to accept, but the values and attitudes of people back home. Kate Sturgeon remembers:

I found everyone incredibly superficial and preoccupied with how they looked and what people thought about them and all those neuroses everyone has. Compared to how I'd been living, it all seemed grossly out of proportion. I found it very hard working back at the hospital, as I was overwhelmed with the amount of drugs, resources and equipment; I was so sad and angry thinking about how little we had in Zimbabwe where the real need is. I also hated the way patients expect so much here and are forever complaining. They just don't realise what they have. Everything's taken for granted.

Elaine Massie and Richard Lawson, who have volunteered on some 15 wildlife projects, agree wholeheartedly:

It has made us realise how lucky we are and how much we as a society take for granted. In Mexico very little is thrown away, even old nails are taken out of wood to be reused, yet we live in a throwaway society where just about everything is disposable.

These experiences certainly make you stop and think which society is 'developing' one. But what about friends and family; do they help you get back into the swing of things back home? It's hard to generalise, but Poonam Sattee says:

Talking to friends and family was hard as my life there, the culture, my living conditions etc were so different. They just couldn't comprehend why I found it so difficult to adjust.

However, coming home is a much more positive experience for some volunteers. Ann Noon, who volunteered in Peru for 10 months, recalls:

At first it was almost as if I hadn't been away. I'd expected to have trouble settling back in, but really I just slipped right into my old ways – probably because it was just so great to see people again and be back in my flat. It was probably three months down the line when I realised that I was restless and missing the beauty of the Sacred Valley around Cusco.

And, even for Jacqueline Hill, who had trouble readjusting after a year in Bangladesh, there were compensations for being home in the UK. As well as creature comforts, there was the reassuring thought that she'd left certain creatures behind:

I had to get used to not reacting to flying insects which were unlikely to bite me and creepy crawlies which were likely to be nothing more alarming than small spiders. I could also leave a glass of juice on the table without finding it full of ants! I found sleeping without a mosquito net quite unnerving at first, but gloried in being able to leave the washing-up knowing that it would survive without becoming overrun by cockroaches!

Settling Back In

Resuming your life back home after a placement requires practical planning. For many people, it also means establishing links that will help them to integrate their volunteering experience into their life in a meaningful and rewarding way for the long term.

Debriefing

Many organisations have a formal process of following-up with returned volunteers. For medium- and long-term volunteers who have worked in development, a face-to-face debrief interview is often arranged. Kate Sturgeon explains:

I had one debriefing session in Barcelona with MSF Spain, who I had gone out to Zimbabwe with, and I had another session in the MSF UK office, talking to different people: human resources; communications; managers etc. I felt like I had a lot of support. Some people asked to see a counsellor if they'd seen a lot of trauma, but I felt OK just talking to MSF and friends and family.

A debrief is an excellent opportunity to talk about what you did, what it was like and how you feel at the end of it. It is also a chance to offer constructive feedback on the organisation's procedures and systems and suggest improvements. Poonam Sattee, who worked with street children for one year, says:

I went to the Casa Alianza office and talked the experience through, which really helped put perspective on the year. I gave recommendations on how certain things could be improved or changed. Debriefing helped me begin to build positively on the experience and go forward, as opposed to just missing being there.

Some organisations make a whole day or weekend out of the debriefing experience. Kerry Davies, who volunteered in Cambodia for two and a half years, remembers:

At first I buried my head in the sand, but then I attended a VSO Returned Volunteer Weekend and realised I was feeling the same as everyone else. I felt much better afterwards.

Sometimes a debrief may simply take the form of a questionnaire sent out to all returned volunteers, possibly followed up by a telephone call. Other organisations email out debrief information, as Martyn Roberts, who has volunteered on six environmental expeditions, explains:

Biosphere Expeditions has an email debrief package that every volunteer is sent immediately after each 'slot'. The page includes information on when the expedition report will be out, details of their website where photos can be shared, and information on the alumni network and the Friends of Biosphere organisation.

Of course, if you choose to find a volunteer placement yourself, you will forgo any support when you return to your home country. Also, post-placement 'after care' is not a feature of all sending agencies; so if you think this service will be important to you, ask about follow-up procedures.

Medical Checks

As well as debriefing, it is wise to arrange a thorough medical examination once you arrive home. Try to have this done with a specialist organisation that knows what to look for in returned volunteers. In the UK your best option is **InterHealth** (☎ +44 (0)20 7902 9000; fax +44 (0)207 902 9091; info@interhealth.org.uk; www.interhealth.org.uk; 63-67 Newington Causeway, London, SE1 6BD), a charity that specialises in healthcare for international NGOs, aid and development agencies. The **International Society of Travel Medicine** (☎ +1 404 373 8282; fax +1 404 373 8283; istm@istm. org; www.istm.org; 315 W Ponce de Leon Ave, Suite 245, Decatur GA 30030, USA) offers an extensive online directory of travel medicine practitioners specialising in immunisations and post-trip consultations throughout the world. In Australia, the **Travel Doctor** (www.tmvc.com.au) offers medical reviews for returned volunteers who may have been ill while away or who may be symptomatic upon return.

Returned Volunteer Networks

If you volunteer for a short while only, it is likely you'll pick up your life where you left off. Even so, your experience might set you apart from those closest to you, which is hard when you want to talk in-depth about what happened, how you feel, and what you want to do with your experience. As Jacqueline Hill says:

I developed a very short response to the question 'How was it?' as most people had very short attention spans.

If you volunteer medium- or long-term, the sense of 'otherness' at having done something that most people don't fully comprehend is 10 times greater. Your debrief will help process these feelings, but often you'll crave some longer-term mechanism for continued support and involvement with volunteering.

Many sending agencies recognise this and actively encourage you to stay in touch, not only with themselves, but with other returned volunteers as well. Many have a magazine or email newsletter that you can sign up to and/or write for. Others may have a more formal network for returned volunteers. Martyn Roberts, who has volunteered in Namibia, the Azores, Slovakia, Sri Lanka and Brazil, explains:

I have stayed in touch with Biosphere Expeditions ever since my first volunteering expedition with them. They have an alumni network comprised of people who have been on two or more expeditions, and who offer to be points of contact for potential volunteers and to stay in email contact with other returned volunteers. They also provide journalists and others with information on what it is like to be on an expedition. The organisation also encourages you to join Friends of Biosphere Expeditions, which is a support network of people who want to become or stay actively involved.

Once you come home, you'll realise that there are hundreds of different ways you can still be part of the world you left behind. For Oliver Walker, who volunteered in Sri Lanka, it worked this way:

MondoChallenge asked me to interview potential volunteers in the light of my experiences.

And, Kate Sturgeon explains:

I often go to MSF meetings, scientific days or nights out and I've done interviews for them and talks at universities. They keep in touch with me via email or phone.

Many North American international volunteer organisations have strong alumni networks to support returned volunteers. Perhaps the largest is the **National Peace Corps Association** (www.rpcv.org), which has affiliate branches throughout the US. Several other organisations featured in this book also foster similarly active alumni communities, such as the American Jewish World Service (p210) and IESC Geekcorps (p140). Even if your organisation doesn't formally sponsor a returned volunteer network, alumni frequently run Yahoo! Groups and local social chapters on their own.

Most organised volunteer programmes in Australia and New Zealand offer some form of debriefing or networking. Programmes like Australian Youth Ambassador for Development (AYAD, p112) and Volunteer Service Abroad (VSA, p123) have excellent post-volunteering options. AYAD has four formal debriefs a year, publishes a newsletter, *Exchange*, profiling returned volunteers (known as RAYADs) and encourages career progression with

Photo: David Palazon/Raleigh International

Raleigh International volunteers roll up their sleeves on a construction project in Ghana optional 20-day development internships (funded to the tune of A$1200 from the programme). Alumni are encouraged to continue to participate in the AYAD selection process, state representative programmes, promotional events and mentoring outgoing AYADs.

If you did not volunteer through an organisation in your home country, you may miss not being part of any formal returned volunteer network in your part of the world. If this is the case, contact an umbrella organisation that represents the views of international aid and development agencies in your country. There is a list of these with contact details on p241.

Money

If you are a short-term volunteer, chances are you didn't give up your job or accommodation before going overseas. However, if you volunteered for longer and didn't manage to negotiate extended time out from your employer, settling back in at home may involve a degree of financial planning.

Some of the larger sending agencies that dispatch skilled volunteers overseas long term offer a resettlement grant to returned volunteers. If you don't volunteer with one of these, you might have to budget (see p50) for your return home. Depending on your personal and professional circumstances, money is often required to untie all those 'loose ends' covered in Chapter 4, like finding a job or somewhere to live.

Sian Davies, who volunteered in Tanzania for two years with Médecins du Monde (p142), makes this point succinctly:

If you are away for a length of time, you have no credit rating so you have to pay upfront for rent etc. Make sure you have a few thousand saved up for when you get back.

Job-hunting

If you are returning home from a longish volunteering stint, one of your primary considerations is likely to be finding yourself a job. The good news is that in most cases international volunteering is an asset on your CV and should be highlighted as opposed to buried. Many volunteers choose to list it as one of their achievements, showing fully what skills they learnt and developed while away. It is also a subject that often comes up in job interviews – employers can be genuinely interested in what you did, what it was like and how you think it was of benefit.

John Lees, career coach and best-selling author of *Take Control of your Career* and *How To Get a Job You'll Love,* says:

International volunteering is great for your CV because it shows resourcefulness and imagination (choosing and planning to do it), and also gives you a broader perspective on the world. The danger is that the experience says little to a recruiter. Communicate why you did it, what you learned and achieved, and how this experience makes you a smarter/ sharper/wiser employee!

If possible, you should also try to obtain a reference from a key person on your volunteer programme. If you have difficulties arranging this, a reference from the sending agency or charity you volunteered with will be just as good.

Changing Careers

Karen Hedges is very clear about what nine months of volunteering did for her life, career (and hair):

Volunteering literally changed my life. It enabled me to change careers and I am now doing something I truly love (working in the press office of an international development charity). It also taught me that I CAN live without a hairdryer (if I have to).

When you volunteer overseas you step out of your usual environment and step back from your current life and your profession. This gives you an unusual degree of objectivity, which can lead to reassessing your career and life choices.

Virtual Volunteering

Writer Isaac Asimov said 'I do not fear computers – I fear the lack of them,' and certainly in this age of technology haves and have-nots, access to information is at the cutting edge of raising living standards worldwide. It is predicted that the entire human race will be online by 2016, changing the face of sustainable development in the process. It's no surprise then that a new space for 'virtual volunteering' has emerged on the information superhighway. Virtual volunteering refers to volunteer tasks completed, in whole or in part, via the internet. It's for people searching for volunteer opportunities they can complete via computer because of time constraints, personal preference, a disability or a home-based obligation that prevents them from volunteering on-site. Virtual volunteering allows anyone to contribute time and expertise to organisations that utilise volunteer services, without leaving home.

But how do you get involved in virtual volunteering? The United Nations has set up a website promoting an online volunteer service (www.onlinevolunteering.org) to bring development organisations together with people who can contribute their skills and expertise online, from administrative staff to translators to web designers. You can register on the website and then browse through a database of projects. Another useful organisation is InterConnection (www.interconnection.org), which recruits volunteers to provide free or low-cost websites and virtual training for charities and NGOs. You can search for virtual volunteering opportunities world-wide on the Volunteermatch website (www.volunteermatch.org/search).

And you can always keep an eye out for your own virtual volunteering opportunities. Spotted a small-scale weaving operation on your South East Asian travels that could benefit from having a website designed for it, for instance? Travelling is a great way to spot grassroots organisations that could do with an extra set of hands.

A significant percentage of international volunteers come home and decide to change their career paths, go freelance or start their own businesses. For example, Jacqueline Hill returned to consultancy work when she came back to England from Bangladesh, but only for four days a week. On the fifth day she volunteered for the charity **WaterAid** (☎ +44 (0)20 7793 4500; fax +44 (0)20 7793 4545; wateraid@wateraid.org; www.wateraid.org; 2nd Flr, 47-49 Durham St, London SE11 5JD, UK) and **Hope and Homes for Children** (☎ +44 (0)1722 790111; fax +44 (0)1722 790024; info@hopeandhomes.org; www.hopeandhomes.org; East Clyffe, Salisbury, Wiltshire SP3 4LZ, UK). Six months later she set up as a sole trader offering management consultancy services to the charity sector at substantially reduced rates. Similarly, Katherine Tubb worked in tourism, but after she volunteered on VSO's Youth for Development Programme in Nepal (p95) she returned home and set up her own not-for-profit sending organisation called 2Way Development (p182).

Interestingly, some returned volunteers end up working for the sending agency they volunteered with. After doing a masters degree in marine biology, Jan-Willem van Bochove worked as a postman before volunteering with Coral Cay Conservation (p134):

I was a Project Scientist and Expedition Leader on two Coral Cay projects in Southern Leyte in the Philippines and Marsa Alam in Egypt. I was working voluntarily to oversee the science programme, give scientific training to volunteers, set up Marine Protected Areas and do community work to increase awareness of the issue and help local people to develop their coral reefs in a sustainable manner. When I was in Egypt, the founder and Managing Director of Coral Cay Conservation called me and asked if I would be interested in a paid position as the Chief Technical Adviser on the Southern Leyte project. I said 'yes' immediately and am now responsible for writing up the final reports, analysing the data and overseeing the scientific work.

And, after five months volunteering with Trekforce (p115) in Belize and Guatemala, Robert Driver now works in their marketing office:

I can proudly say that I am now working for them! I tried working at a few big companies and found I was not inspired by anything they did. I really wanted something to challenge me, but also I wanted to believe in what the organisation did. A position opened up at Trekforce so I jumped at the opportunity and am now loving every minute of it.

Of course, not only can volunteering enhance your CV, it can also give you valuable work experience so you can change your career in a more strategic way when you come home. This is what Michelle Hawkins, who volunteered in Costa Rica and Ghana, did:

I consciously chose to use my career break as a springboard into the charity and aid sector. Job ads frequently state that you need experience in the sector. How can you get the experience unless you already have a job in that sector? It's a catch-22. My solution was to pay to be a volunteer staff member on two Raleigh International expeditions. This made my transition into the competitive charity sector easier. I also got the Raleigh International Expedition leaders to write me two references that I attached to my CV when applying for jobs. It took me a year of applying, but I did it! I now work for the international aid organisation Médecins du Monde as the communications and fundraising officer.

Next Steps

Depending on what you did and how long you were away for, it can take between six and 12 months for you to settle back in properly, sometimes longer. In many cases, a volunteer experience is not something you can, or want to, forget. Often you will wish to integrate it into your life in some way. Some returned volunteers do this by changing careers, others by becoming more involved with their charity or sending agency in their own country. Others do it by volunteering locally or even internationally again.

Longer-term Links

It is often possible to maintain ongoing links with volunteer sending agencies once you return home. After two and a half years of volunteering in Cambodia, Kerry Davies says:

I am now on the VSO steering committee. I am also an email and telephone contact person for prospective volunteers either in the health sector or in Cambodia.

Poonam Sattee has gone one step further:

I stay in contact with the kids. I regularly send them cards, some are in email contact with me and at Christmas I send out presents. I am also a newly appointed trustee for Casa Alianza UK and that has helped me to still feel part of the organisation and to still be part of the lives of the kids in an indirect way. I also fundraise for them.

And, Karen Hedges, who went to Madagascar with Azafady (p132), has also become involved with the charity at this higher level. She explains:

When I came home I was keen to stay involved. After spending nine months living and working in Madagascar I felt I could not just come home and forget about the projects and the people. The managing director saw that I was keen to stay involved and approached me about becoming a trustee. We have four or five trustee meetings per year, which usually happen on a Sunday and take up most of the day. We discuss how the charity is run by analysing income and expenditure, fundraising ideas, web content, strategic planning and the volunteer scheme. What I like about being a trustee is that you get involved in all aspects of the charity. All trustees have different backgrounds so that helps us to bring different expertise to the charity.

Sarah Turton volunteered as an art, photography and English teacher in Ghana with the Junior Art Club (p182) after she'd finished her Postgraduate Certificate in Education (PGCE). When she came home she started her first proper teaching job in her home country. Ten months later she explains:

I am developing the link between the school in Ghana and the one I am now teaching in. A Year 7 group has done the same photography project and next month we are exhibiting both sets of work and raising money through sales and donations for both the school and the organisation. In the longer term, we are hoping to take a team of teachers out on a research trip with a view to getting an exchange programme up and running, plus enhancing all areas of both curricula.

You might also establish longer-term links on a more personal level. When Jacqueline Hill left Bangladesh she thought she might never see the people she worked with again, but as she says:

As it turned out, I went back to visit in 2005 and hope to host a visit by two of my former colleagues to the UK this year.

Volunteer Locally

As the old saying goes, 'Charity starts at home.' If you've travelled to the ends of the earth to volunteer and are now hooked, there are plenty of volunteering opportunities in your home country.

In the UK one of the best places to start researching the options is at your local volunteer centre. Otherwise, there are a number of useful websites that have comprehensive databases of volunteering opportunities in your area:

UK Websites

~ **Community Service Volunteers (CSV;** www.csv.org.uk) The UK's largest volunteering and training organisation.

~ **Do-it.org.uk** (www.do-it.org.uk) Lists over 650,000 volunteering opportunities in the UK. It is free to register.

~ **Retired and Senior Volunteer Programme** (www.csv-rsvp.org.uk) Part of CSV, this site encourages those aged 50 plus to volunteer in England, Scotland and Wales.

~ **Timebank** (www.timebank.org.uk) Register your details and receive a list of organisations in your area that need volunteers.

~ **vinspired** (http://vinspired.com) Aimed at 16- to 24-year-olds, this site encourages young people to devote a period of time to volunteering. Certificates are awarded for 50 and 150 hours volunteering.

~ **Volunteer Development Agency** (www.volunteering-ni.org) Support, training and information on volunteering in Northern Ireland.

~ **Volunteer Development Scotland** (www.vds.org.uk) Ditto for Scotland.

~ **Volunteering England** (www.volunteering.org.uk) National volunteer development organisation for England.

~ **Wales Council for Voluntary Action** (www.wcva.org.uk) The voice of the voluntary sector in Wales.

North American Websites

~ **AmeriCorps** (www.americorps.gov) Often dubbed 'the domestic Peace Corps,' AmeriCorps offers community service opportunities lasting 10 months to a year throughout the USA.

~ **CoolWorks** (www.coolworks.com/volunteer) This database lists volunteer jobs in great places in the US, many in national parks.

~ **Mercy Volunteer Corps** (www.mercyvolunteers.org) Volunteer programmes in health, education and poverty relief in rural and urban America; administered by the Catholic Sisters of Mercy.

~ **Serve.gov** (www.serve.gov) Established by President Bush in 2002, USA Freedom Corps links individuals to local service opportunities.

~ **Teach for America** (www.teachforamerica.org) A vehicle for recent college grads to teach in underprivileged schools across the US.

~ **Volunteer Canada** (www.volunteer.ca) With Volunteer Centres offering local service positions throughout Canada, Volunteer Canada is one of the nation's most prominent forums on volunteering.

~ **VolunteerMatch** (www.volunteermatch.org) Over 40,000 American non-profit organisations recruit through this site.

Australasian Websites

~ **Volunteering Australia** (www.volunteeringaustralia.org) This group spearheads International Volunteer Day (5 December) and is the peak body promoting volunteering in Australia.

~ **Volunteering New Zealand** (www.volunteeringnz.org.nz) Promotes and supports volunteering in that country.

Volunteer Internationally...Again

For some, volunteering abroad just once is not enough. Whether you want or are able to commit to another placement depends very much on your personal circumstances.

Deborah Jordan and David Spinney, who volunteered in Ethiopia with VSO (p94), are both retired, so they have a little more time:

We are in contact with other returned volunteers and VSO in London, and have friends in many parts of the world. We have recently been to a meeting to discuss strategies for recruiting more 'mature' volunteers. And, yes, we have just re-volunteered ourselves and are looking forward to discussing options with our placement officer!

Catherine Baroun, who has volunteered on a number of wildlife programmes with Earthwatch (p171), says:

I can't stop myself now. This year I am heading to Kenya with Earthwatch to do a Forest Monkey Survey. Next year I am hoping to find a longer volunteering project to celebrate my 40th birthday.

And as she explains, her volunteering doesn't interfere with her full-time job:

Projects I have participated in have ranged from five to 13 days, so I have just booked the time off work.

Martyn Roberts, who works full time but spends his holidays volunteering, is in a similar boat:

Having done one I knew as soon as I got back home that it was something I would do again. I think I've become something of a volunteering addict. Since my first expedition in November 2002, I have always had the next one planned.

However, a short-term conservation or wildlife programme that you can easily fit into a busy professional life is very different to a long-term development placement. Kate Sturgeon admits:

Yes, I'd definitely like to do another volunteer placement but I needed to have a substantial rest when I came back. I felt quite exhausted by the whole process, however positive it was, and I really felt I needed to recharge my batteries before going again. I also have commitments in my current job and have to give two months' notice before leaving, so I think I will go again but not until next year.

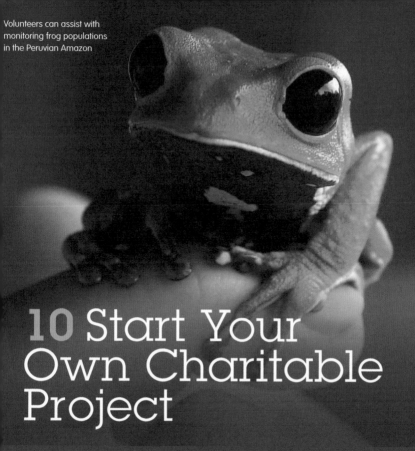

Volunteers can assist with monitoring frog populations in the Peruvian Amazon

10 Start Your Own Charitable Project

You may not fancy yourself as a budding Mother Teresa or Princess Di – but chances are that if you're reading this chapter, you've been overseas, have seen a need and want to do something substantial to alleviate it. Perhaps you identified this need as an international volunteer; maybe it presented itself to you while you were travelling, or perhaps you've spent years doing business in a region and feel that it's time to give something back. Whatever your motivations are, starting up your own aid organisation can be fulfilling and exciting. It can also be hard work and a lifelong commitment.

What you aim to do could take many forms. The organisation you set up might turn out to be a volunteer-sending agency, a fundraising charity, or it might simply involve you raising money at home and returning to a particular place to make tangible improvements. While these all sound like noble aims, it is important to remember that even the most well-intentioned efforts can create more problems than they solve by inappropriately injecting funds, volunteers or projects into an area on the basis of a presumed 'need'. To avoid such a negative outcome, it's crucial that your project is based on local participation and that it aims for sustainability. You need to be sure that the local community is fundamentally supportive of what you're proposing and that you're in it for the long haul. With these things in mind, the rest of this chapter will give some starting points from which to embark upon the adventure of a lifetime.

The Idea

This may seem obvious, but first and foremost you need to have an idea. In many cases, this is sparked by something you've experienced and a desire to 'do something' about it. Alex Tarrant, co-founder of Personal Overseas Development (PoD, p168), describes the dawning of the idea that gave rise to his organisation:

It all started in the summer of 2001 when Mike, Rach and I (old friends and now business partners) spent time in Tanzania, volunteering our time to help set up a small British charity. It was an amazing trip that turned out to be career changing for all of us. One of the ideas that came out of the work was to recruit volunteers from the UK to go and work with the charity in Tanzania, and this led to us starting PoD.

The fact is, you may have hundreds of ideas, but trimming them down to the core aims of an organisation is essential. To arrive at this point, some of the searching questions you might need to ask yourself are: What is it that I want to achieve? How do I plan to go about it? Has it been done before? Is there a genuine community need for the services I envisage? Whose experiences can I learn from? A good way to kick off the process is to get out there and talk to as many people as possible, to find out how others got started, the obstacles they encountered on the way, and soak up any advice they're willing to dole out. Details of NGOs worth approaching can be found on the websites listed in the Getting Help section on p252.

Aim for a Participatory Project

The crux of a successful project is that it's participatory. This means more than simply talking to the local people where you plan to initiate your project. It means that the idea for the project should essentially come from them. It also means including them at every step: discussing the project with them; taking their views and ideas on board; and giving them as much hands-on involvement as possible – including involving them in the day-to-day running of the project. In essence, it means working *with* the local community towards a common goal.

It is important to stay in regular contact with the local community to ensure that the community remains supportive of the project and that it's continuing to meet their needs. It also helps if your project has the capacity to evolve along with the community's needs. Key ways to ensure that a project remains participatory and well connected to the community include employing locals as project managers and staff and basing the organisation in the overseas community, rather than as a satellite in your own country. Katherine Tubb, founder and director of the volunteer-sending agency 2Way Development (p182), points out some ways in which her organisation remains participatory:

We only work with existing organisations that have been in operation for one year or more when we place volunteers. At all times, the organisation directs the nature of the voluntary placements we organise, as we are looking to address specific skill shortages they have identified. We do not run any of our own projects, but support locally driven activities... Overseas, we have about three or four volunteer researchers who are based in areas where we place volunteers. Their role is to monitor charities that we work with and source new information...

Alex Tarrant talks about using similar means in implementing PoD projects (note the strong presence of the word 'local' in his description):

Most of our projects are 'local' projects, driven and managed by the local community. In other cases, the local community is always involved and all our projects are evaluated on their benefit to the local community... We either respond to local requests to provide volunteers or we approach local projects and ask if they would like volunteers. We feel [spending time in the overseas communities] is important, and that is why we either have our own staff in each country, or we work with an organisation or charity that is based

More Harm Than Good

The Teach Ghana Trust (www.teachghanatrust.org.uk; enquiries@teachghanatrust.org.uk) is a UK-based charity, established in 2003 to advance the education of children in Ghana. The founders' motivation for setting up the Trust was a frustration with many volunteer-sending agencies who didn't appear to be prioritising the needs of the overseas communities in which they were operating. In reaction to this, the Trust aimed to arrange volunteer teaching placements in schools in Ghana with the needs of the children being the absolute priority. However, as the trustees developed their programme and began to interview for volunteer placements, they began to seriously question the consequences of their volunteer placements and whether or not they had chosen an appropriate means of achieving their initial goals. In early 2006, the Trust reviewed its policies and voted not to pursue any further volunteer placements.

While this may seem like an odd move, it is well worth considering the motives behind this decision. The Trust's experience highlights the necessity of *really* considering the impact of a project on a community, the importance of placing the needs of the community ahead of your own aims and agendas, and the realisation that the best way to help isn't always the most obvious. Here are some of the reasons that prompted the Trust to end its volunteering programme:

We knew that, as an organisation, we were in a good position to arrange placements in schools in Ghana. However, we wanted to make sure that any volunteering scheme we implemented was offering real, long-term and sustainable solutions to the issues we were seeking to resolve.

We did not want to make schools in Ghana reliant on volunteers. There was a danger that a reliance on volunteers would lead to schools not recruiting Ghanaians to teach, which would not be good for employment levels and the domestic economy.

Equally, the Teach Ghana Trust had no guarantee that it would be able to send out volunteers consistently – in fact numbers would fluctuate throughout the year. As such, we would not be able to guarantee a consistent service to schools, making it difficult for them to plan effectively.

The majority of our applicants were unqualified. We were anxious that we could not be sure that we were arranging a placement for somebody who would make an able teacher and who would be of real benefit to the children they taught.

There are already a number of organisations which offer excellent volunteering schemes. We did not want to duplicate their work, or increase competition for volunteers and funding that are so badly needed elsewhere.

Ultimately, the goal for the Teach Ghana Trust would be for schools in Ghana to no longer require volunteers, but to be able to teach pupils with a staff of trained, salaried Ghanaian teachers. We believe that a better way to ensure this would be to act as a charity which endeavours to ensure a greater number of able, locally trained teachers rather than alternatives to such teachers.

there. It is very important to keep in touch with the local communities and we feel it is also essential to have strong local support for volunteers. From the UK, we make visits each year to our overseas projects.

Penelope Worsley founded the successful Karen Hilltribes Trust (p169). She describes how she maintains local participation in the Trust's projects:

We depend on the overseas communities to tell us what they need. We insist that they complete reports, surveys and are monitored before we fund the projects. We work together… [The overseas communities] are not only the beneficiaries but also the managers of the projects, so they are fully involved in the projects. It is extremely important that we visit the projects and see where the money is spent and discuss plans for the future. I visit three times a year for 10 days at a time.

Anthony Lunch founded the MondoChallenge Foundation on the back of MondoChallenge (p167), a volunteer-sending agency he'd previously initiated. When asked how much the local communities participate in the charity's projects, he provides great examples of the extent to which an organisation's work can be driven by the community:

In every conceivable way! They often provide the on-site work, with materials funded by the Foundation. Sometimes they are teachers at the school we support with desks, books and sports equipment. When we fund the 'seeds projects', whereby kids are encouraged to learn about growing plants they can then eat to supplement their diet, the teachers are the local organisers and we merely provide the small grants needed to set the project up. Our HIV Small Grants Programme in Tanzania and Gambia is totally run by local volunteers, backed up by MondoChallenge. We only work with organisations who have demonstrated their commitment over a period of time.

I travel [to the overseas community] three times a year on average. Usually my trips last two weeks, but occasionally I go for longer periods when I need to put new operations in place in a particular country, such as Tanzania. Our UK-based country managers also make occasional visits to their countries. These visits are absolutely vital. Emails are great but nothing can beat face-to-face contact. The visits are usually partly to monitor ongoing programmes, meet the volunteers and renew contacts with our partners. They also serve as training opportunities for our local managers and, perhaps even more importantly, as a source of new ideas for our UK team!

While participation may seem like an obvious component of any aid initiative, in reality constant vigilance and an ongoing commitment are required to ensure that it endures for the life of the project.

Aim for Sustainability

Working towards sustainability is one of the biggest challenges faced by volunteering organisations. Organisations and their projects (or programmes) should aim for a long lifespan, and come to an end only when the original goal is achieved or the instigating needs are alleviated. What they should not be about is the knee-jerk dumping of resources, money or volunteers into a community on projects that will rapidly peter out. To build the trust of a community and to see the effects of your work, you will need to be both committed and patient. The aims of most aid projects are ongoing – things like counteracting environmental degradation or decreasing poverty are obviously not issues that are solved overnight. One of the fundamental aspects of programmes based on sustainable action is that they're underpinned by empowerment rather than charity. They're about helping people to help themselves and to achieve their own goals, rather than simply ladling out aid.

When Katherine Tubb describes her organisation, the notion of sustainability is deeply embedded in her description:

We are passionately concerned about the communities in which volunteers work, and ensure that at all times the work of volunteers leads to long-term, sustainable, local development. We also make sure that volunteers are appropriately experienced for whatever role they hold. We achieve these goals by interviewing all our volunteers and working closely with them in organising placements. We also have 150 partner organisations worldwide that we place volunteers within, and we evaluate all of these according to their needs, the benefits of their work to development and their ability to host volunteers.

Examples of ways projects can be sustainable include:

~ Training members of the local community in a needed occupation such as teaching, medicine, IT or anything else identified by the community.

~ Providing practical knowledge in things like nutrition or first aid.

~ Helping to establish local, income-generating enterprises.

~ Assisting in improving people's living conditions as a means of improving health and increasing confidence.

~ Helping to set up ecotourism projects.

Even a project that initially appears sustainable can play out differently in reality; for an example of this, see the box More Harm Than Good (p245). It's therefore crucial to constantly re-evaluate the work of your organisation to ensure it's continuing to foster sustainable outcomes.

Communicating Across Cultures

You think you've got your idea all sorted out. You've discussed it at length with the local community, they've given their consent and you've shaken on it. But can you be sure that nodding actually means 'yes' in the local body language? It might just mean 'maybe'. Or it could even mean a flat 'no'. And do handshakes mean anything at all in the local culture?

Open and mutually understood communication is essential to establishing a participatory and sustainable project. And while you may be adept at communicating at home, throw a foreign culture into the mix and you might just be left wondering which way is up – or worse, believing that you've got a deal sewn up when the local community is actually completely opposed to your proposal.

Cross-cultural misunderstandings can stem from issues with spoken language, body language and etiquette. In some cultures, for instance, there are 20 ways of saying 'yes' but half of these actually mean 'no'. In other cultures, women are unable to speak openly or express their views in the presence of men. Some cultures equate being direct with being

continued on p250

Getting Funding

Good news. There are thousands of charitable foundations, many of which exist for the sole purpose of giving grants. However, the size and form these foundations can take varies enormously. Some give nationally and others internationally, while others only give to organisations in a particular region. Some give to a variety of causes, others to organisations pursuing specific goals such as work with children or healthcare. Some give millions every year, others give only a few hundred here and there. But the bottom line is: they all give.

Foundations tend to fund projects that offer aid to disadvantaged groups. Of the £2 billion given by foundations annually in the UK, for example, by far the largest chunk goes towards health and social-welfare initiatives. A decent-sized portion of the pie goes towards arts and recreation and a smaller slice goes to faith-based projects. As foundations' funds come from private endowments and the like, their funding is not geared towards what's trendy in mainstream society or a particular government; instead they give to whatever takes their fancy.

Some foundations are very well known for their generous giving – for instance the Wellcome Trust, the Joseph Rowntree Foundation and the Diana, Princess of Wales Memorial Trust. Nevertheless, if you're looking to apply for funds, don't just go for the big fish. Filling out funding applications is a mammoth task, taking up lots of time and energy, and so the first, fundamental step is to wade through the various options and select those most likely to look favourably upon your cause. The next step is filling out the application itself, making sure it's tailored to the foundation's criteria, and that it's clear about what you hope to achieve and gives specifics as to how you will spend the funds.

See the Association of Charitable Foundations (p252), Foundation Center (p253) or Philanthropy Australia (p256) for help and useful publications and resources. UK residents should also check out **The Directory of Social Change** (www.dsc.org.uk) for guides to UK trusts.

Go For It!

Katherine Tubb is the founder and Director of 2Way Development (p182), a non-profit organisation that links appropriately skilled volunteers with grassroots projects in the developing world. Here she speaks about how she came to establish the organisation, the participatory means she uses to achieve her aims, and the role that her own experience as an international volunteer played in motivating her.

I've always wanted to work in international development, and during my degree I spent the best part of a year organising an overseas voluntary placement in Nepal for myself. I worked on developing a visitor and community centre in a major national park, which tackled the issues of tourism in developing communities and fragile environments.

Volunteering overseas focused my goals, was the starting point of my career and was fundamental to the choices I subsequently made. While overseas I gained an understanding of international development issues and met some fantastic people. Both these things were invaluable in setting up my own organisation. Now, in my work placing volunteers overseas, I

Top: A local participant in a
2Way Development partner
programme in Bolivia

Bottom: Katherine
with colleagues in Nepal

can adequately prepare them for their roles and support them once they assume them, as I have been through it all myself.

I set up 2Way Development with the aim of contributing something new to the path of international development. The organisation provides a flexible way to address the need for human resources and expertise in local not-for-profit organisations in the developing world. It also gives volunteers a personal service, enabling them to direct their placements according to their skills, time frames and preferences.

Attending a conference on ecotourism in Cairns, Australia, in 2003, I met with the Director of the Tibetan Tourism and Development Board. He asked me how he should go about training a local Tibetan community in the skills needed to receive tourists. Their traditional industries had died and tourism was a way of securing the livelihood of the community. We hadn't placed any volunteers at this stage. My answer to his question led me to recommend a volunteer that could help implement a training manual and tourism development programme to kick-start a community-wide development strategy aimed at fostering tourism in the area. Such grassroots initiatives are where the benefits of volunteering and the work we do in organising placements can be seen at their best.

In fact, a lot of problems faced by local development organisations in the developing world are due to a lack of expertise and human resources. Without volunteers, many smaller organisations would not survive. By working closely with host organisations we can ensure that volunteers are channelled into appropriate areas of need. In assisting with project development, training or research, a volunteer can empower organisations to engage in projects that offer long-term, sustainable solutions to development issues. While working overseas as a volunteer, I noticed a growing need for human resources expertise in the local not-for-profit organisations I was working with. I often saw genuinely skilled volunteers carrying out work that was a complete mismatch between their skills and abilities and those actually required by the organisation. These volunteering experiences gave me the inspiration to establish 2Way Development.

Katherine Tubb

Going into Business

With thousands of charities in existence, it is a sound idea to ask whether it's worthwhile establishing yet another one, as the need you're proposing to address may already be met by an existing organisation. A better alternative may be to plunge in solo with some hands-on action or an environmentally sustainable business.

Former Australian Youth Ambassador for Development (AYAD, see p112) Amber Rowe worked as a research development officer with the Centre for Environmental Awareness and Education (CEAE) in the Philippines, where she spent 12 months researching and writing an environmental education module with a local counterpart. The work she began greatly influenced her work practices and future direction. Amber created an environmental education portal with the assistance of the RAYAD Development Internship. She also established the fair-trade business Trash Bags, offering an attractive range of environmentally friendly and ethical products made from recycled materials by livelihood and community organisations in the Asia-Pacific region. Amber says:

Our collection of bags and homewares are made by community-managed and operated organisations who, by the creation and selling of these wonderful products, are securing a better future for their communities and our shared environment.

Amber currently also works for the Australian Human Rights Centre and volunteers at the FTAANZ (Fair Trade Australia and New Zealand) New South Wales branch.

rude and pushy. In other cultures, spitting is not considered bad mannered but blowing your nose into a hanky and stuffing it into your pocket is truly rude. Even seemingly trivial things such as the colour of the ink that you choose to write in can cause offence. Showing the soles of your feet can be taken as an insult, and touching (or not touching) the person you're speaking to can be taken amiss. You must also be aware that within any one country subcultures exist based on factors such as gender, ethnicity and social status and that differing communication strategies might be required within these.

Kalene Caffarella is an Intercultural Consultant with **Caffarella Cross Cultural** (kcaffarella@gmail.com) in Australia and offers some great starting points for successful exchanges:

Showing respect for the local community in which you are volunteering is the first step in avoiding cross-cultural miscommunication. It is crucial not only to see things from the local point of view, but to be able to respect that point of view as valid and logical. Ask yourself how a local person would go about accomplishing the task that you want to accomplish. Would they communicate in a direct manner, or would they use indirect communication to get their message across? Would people need to build trust with others before they begin working together, or would they focus on the task alone?

For example, you may want to go into a meeting with local community members to brainstorm new ideas or give feedback on how a project is going. If locals see the purpose of a meeting as simply getting information from the local head, then chances are you may not get any input. Think, instead, of how locals would gather suggestions. Be aware of the strategies local people use and adapt to doing things their way.

While communicating across cultures is likely to lead to at least a few misunderstandings, there are ways to minimise them. Many adult educational institutions offer cross-cultural introductory courses and, depending on where you are planning to work, you may find that a cultural centre exists in your home country where you can discuss possible barriers or differences. Also check out chapters on culture and etiquette in guidebooks, and visit the country's official tourism website. Arm yourself with as much knowledge and awareness as possible and remember to keep an open mind.

Getting It Rolling

Committing Your Time & Money

How long it takes to set up an aid organisation, the amount of money you'll need, and the number of hours you'll need to commit depends greatly on the size and breadth of the project you're setting up and whether or not there's already an infrastructure in place upon which to build. For example, when Catheryn Goodyer (see the case study on p254) established a small organisation, she had an appropriate business on which to base it and a facility in place overseas where the project was needed, wanted and ready to be played out. She therefore only had to commit a small amount of money, which was easily fundraised, and she worked on the project for only around five hours per month. Katherine Tubb, on the other hand, spent a year researching, developing and planning and had this to say about her experience of setting up a larger organisation:

The actual registration of the organisation and starting trading was really easy – it was building the foundations that took time… People used to say to me that it would be a slow process setting up an organisation and that it would take time to build. I never believed them and thought I would be up to speed in a few months. The reality is that it has taken two to three years to get to a stage where I feel we are placing a good number of volunteers and that the organisation is running in a way that I am happy with. I see it like a wine maturing: it takes time and actually, the slower you take things, the better they often are in the end.

These days, Katherine works 40 to 50 hours per week and makes enough to fund the organisation's immediate overheads. Such long hours are common among people running aid organisations. Anthony Lunch works 'never less than 50 hours' per week and describes his biggest challenge as, 'The time it takes to do things the way they need to be done, when staffing is minimal and the activities are full on!' Despite the hours he commits, he assures us that it's a labour of love rather than a road to wealth:

I do not make a living from the charity. In fact nobody does, as there are no employees! However, I do earn my living from the MondoChallenge volunteer organisation (a not-for-profit company)… But the expression 'earn one's living' is somewhat of an exaggeration! Everybody employed at MondoChallenge is earning substantially less than the market rate and thereby making their own personal contribution to the work we do…

Consider at the outset how much time you have and how much you're willing to devote to your organisation. If you're planning to dedicate your 'free time' to it and work it in around your present job, think seriously about what you'll have to give up and whether you'd be willing to do this for an extended period of time. If you are placing volunteers overseas, it is not at all unusual for it become a seven-day-a-week job. As Alex Tarrant explains:

When we are in England, it's usually about 40 to 50 hours a week, but there is a need to be flexible as we have volunteers overseas at all times of the year and need to be available at any time to provide assistance if required.

The amount of money you'll initially need varies immensely; the type of equipment you'll require, whether you'll need to pay rent or have administrative overheads all play a role. Initial set-up costs are almost always one of the biggest hurdles you'll have, with marketing and running costs quickly adding up. You might consider fundraising to cover the initial set-up cost, getting a bank loan or applying for a grant. See Getting Help (p252) and Getting Funding (p247) for more on this. You may also want to pay an accountant to crunch your budget: a good accountant can set you up with a bank that is sympathetic to the needs of a fledgling non-profit organisation. Keep in mind that the not-for-profit scene is just as competitive as any industry, so being realistic about fundraising potential is crucial.

Penelope Worsley reflects on how she overcame the financial hurdles involved in setting up her organisation and gives some invaluable advice:

The only tip I would give is to suggest that you look around to see where support can be found… We get major sponsorship. Most people hear about our work and approach me. Occasionally I will search out groups of people (expat groups in Bangkok or community groups in the UK, for instance) and talk about the Trust's work. All kinds of support came from talking to the wider community about the work… Be very focused about what you need money for and make sure you know how the money will be spent. Tell the story! If the story is right, the money will come.

If you think telling stories isn't going to get you far, pay attention to this account from Anthony Lunch:

The amazingly powerful testimony from one of our volunteers on site in Sri Lanka was our launch vehicle and we raised £30,000 in one month for Sri Lankan causes. From then on, the momentum continued and we gathered support for our causes in other countries. In the first year we raised £70,000.

He goes on to say, 'You must have 100 per cent belief in what you are doing and 100 per cent enthusiasm in getting it off the ground. The rest will follow.'

Getting Help

Aid organisations are all about cooperative work. This cooperative approach needn't be restricted to the work you do overseas but can, in fact, play a major role in the initial set-up of your organisation. There is lots of help available out there – and there are organisations established for the very purpose of supporting, assisting and funding aid organisations and new businesses. Here are just a few options listed by region:

UK Organisations

~ **Association of Charitable Foundations** (☎ +44 (0)20 7255 4499; www.acf.org.uk; Central House, 14 Upper Woburn Pl, London WC1H 0AE, UK) This UK-based organisation posts a huge list on its website of its 300-plus members – trusts and foundations that fund various projects. It also has a guide to applying and writing applications for funding. Well worth a visit.

~ **Bond** (☎ +44 (0)20 7837 8344; www.bond.org.uk; Regent's Wharf, 8 All Saints St, London N1 9RL, UK) British Overseas NGOs for Development is a network of voluntary organisations that promotes the exchange of experience, ideas and information among its members both in the UK and internationally. BOND also offers its members training, advocacy and information.

~ **Business West** (☎ +44 (0)1275 373373; www.businesswest.co.uk; Leigh Court Business Centre, Abbots Leigh, Bristol BS8 3RA, UK) Offers advice and support with all aspects of setting up, such as writing a business plan, recruiting staff, management and website design. It also hosts networking events and hooks you up with marketing opportunities.

~ **Charity Commission** (☎ +44 (0)845 300 0218; www.charity-commission.gov.uk; PO Box 1227, Liverpool L69 3UG, UK) The regulator and registrar for charities in England and Wales, this body also supports and supervises charities and offers sound advice to those starting up new organisations. Look to it for guidance on applying for charitable status and for accountancy help.

~ **Companies House** (☎ +44 (0)303 1234 500; www.companieshouse.gov.uk; Crown Way, Mainday, Cardiff CF14 3UZ, UK) The UK's regulator for registered companies, this organisation has a good selection of online booklets on company formation, regulations, administration, management and legislation. It also organises seminars to fill you in on your obligations for filing taxes.

~ **Friends of the Earth England, Wales & Northern Ireland** (☎ + 44 207 490 1555; www.foe.co.uk; 26-28 Underwood St, London N1 7JQ, UK) A grassroots environmental network which unites over 70 diverse national member groups and 5000 local activist groups around the world to campaign jointly on environmental and social issues. With patrons like Margaret Atwood and Bruce Cockburn, joining a group like this can add legitimacy to your organisation and give you some much-needed support.

~ **Princes Trust** (☎ +44 (0)20 7543 1234; www.princes-trust.org.uk; 18 Park Square East, London NW1 4LH, UK) This respected and very well-established trust offers business loans, guides to starting up a business, a legal helpline and can set you up with a business mentor. Its work is aimed at British 'youth' (ie the under 30s).

North American Organisations

~ **Canada Revenue Agency** (www.cra-arc.gc.ca/chrts-gvng/menu-eng.html) This is the tax information site for charities in Canada.

~ **Charity Village** (https://charityvillage.com) In Canada, check out this site for tips and links to relevant government authorities, helpful outfits and discussion forums.

~ **Friends of the Earth USA** (☎ +1 202 783 7400; www.foe.org; 1100 15th St NW, 11th floor, Washington DC 20005, USA). The American branch of this worldwide network of organisations can offer plenty of advice. There's also a Canadian group (see www.foecanada.org).

~ **Foundation Center** (http://foundationcenter.org) Information on grant-seeking and a directory of foundations, as well as useful statistical information, publications and training courses.

continued on p256

The Gift of Giving

You have the incentive to start your own charity but haven't the time or energy to commit to it. Or maybe you've discovered that there's already somebody out there putting your idea into action, so starting up your own organisation would only increase competition for scarce funds and volunteers, and ultimately reduce the benefits to those most in need. In such situations, it's still possible to direct your energies in a positive and fulfilling way. Supporting an established charity or organisation with your time or money can be a practical and productive means of both giving and receiving. The organisation will benefit immensely from your support and you'll feel… well, good. This is exactly what Lennox McNeely has done in sponsoring Casa Guatemala (p160), a community for orphaned and needy children in Central America. He tells of his satisfying experience and how his sponsorship evolved:

I travelled throughout South America in a van in 1970 – one of the original travellers on what later became the Gringo Trail. We drove from Whistler, British Columbia, to Chile to ski and then on to Buenos Aires and up to Rio. We had been warned the most about Colombia and Guatemala, however we found our reception in these two countries the best of all.

About 26 years later, I took my two daughters down to Galápagos and Machu Picchu and they were very disturbed by the poverty they saw there. In my career as an international investor I had made many trips to South America and Asia, and felt it was time to give something back. Shortly thereafter, I read an article in one of the Vancouver newspapers on Casa Guatemala. Oddly enough, we had received assistance only six miles from where the orphanage is located on the Rio Dulce back in 1970. So, I simply phoned up the man… who was organising Vancouver fundraising and told him I would help out.

The help became more than I initially anticipated as the orphanage has borne the brunt of four natural disasters: two floods; a lightning strike and a devastating earthquake in July 1999. The earthquake destroyed about 75 per cent of the Casa's structures.

The experience has been rewarding and fun, particularly being Santa on four occasions, getting to know some of the volunteers and making friends. I would encourage anyone who may have profited from travelling or investing in developing countries to roll up their sleeves and contribute to a community project in these less-fortunate lands. Whatever you give, you will be rewarded for it many times over through both the gratitude you receive and your personal sense of satisfaction.

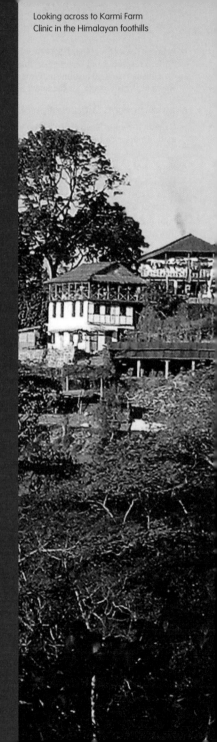

A Healthy Dose

Catheryn and Paul Goodyer established the not-for-profit Karmi Farm Clinic in the foothills of the Himalayas. The secret of their successful endeavour has been at least one part experience and know-how, one part contacts, and a very strong dose of commitment. Here, Catheryn shares a little bit about the beginnings of the project and the highs and the lows.

What first compelled you to start a charity?

We were recommended Karmi Farm as a place to stay by a friend of the guesthouse owner. Andrew, who runs the guesthouse, had only just set it up when we first visited in 2000. The house was originally owned by his grandmother who fled the area during the uprisings. His grandmother used to run a small clinic to treat the local subsistence farmers. When Andrew reopened the guesthouse some years later, the local farmers started turning up again with their health problems, which Andrew found himself having to deal with as best he could. He was the only one in the area with any kind of transport as well. I should point out that the nearest hospital is a three- to four-hour walk away and is not a pleasant place to be. On top of this, even though the hospital is meant to be free, most people are charged and quite often given placebos instead of medicines. As the local farmers don't earn money – apart from what they can raise from surplus crops – they simply cannot afford to go to the hospital.

As [we are] the owners of a pharmacy which produces high-grade medical travel kits, Andrew asked if we could leave our medical kit to help him out. We are also owners of travel vaccination clinics, so have a lot of contact with medical staff. We suggested to Andrew that if he could allocate a room to use as a clinic, we could find volunteer medical staff to come and work at the clinic. Andrew was very supportive of this idea and the clinic was launched in August 2001.

How long did it take to establish the organisation?

No time at all. We held a fundraising evening in August 2001 which made £1500 and found the first nurse, who funded her own airfare, very quickly. She arrived in September 2001 and stayed for six months to set the clinic up. As the clinic is just a front line to deal with small first-aid problems and simple conditions such as diarrhoea, scabies etc, we had no need to invest in expensive high-tech equipment. The original funding raised was sufficient to run the clinic and cover the nurse's board and lodging for nearly the whole of the first year. Now, as more and more guests visit Karmi Farm from the UK, we have established many loyal supporters to its cause. In fact, we now have enough money to pay for the local farmers to be treated at the much better private hospital in Darjeeling, which give us special rates.

Are you able to make a living through running your charity?

Our aim has never been to make a living from it. We intend to keep it as small and tight as possible. In this way, we are able to avoid running costs yet at the same time maintain a good service.

What has been the most rewarding experience?

Seeing the improvement in health standards of the local farmers. For example, we are currently having a big anti-scabies drive and have invested money in burning bedding and clothing and replacing it with new items. In addition, we have set up washing facilities for the farmers who have difficulty in getting water. This has reduced the scabies rate dramatically.

Also, one of the local boys who spoke some English started to help the nurses with translation. He is now employed full-time by the clinic and has just spent four months in the UK receiving training.

What was the biggest hurdle or difficulty?

Giving it the time it needed when we were both working full time with a family.

What advice would you give to someone thinking of starting up a charity?

Don't be overly ambitious. Running a charity is like anything; when you first have an idea and start making it happen, you are full of enthusiasm and energy and this is infectious. To sustain your efforts over time, however, you'll have to accept that you'll soon be focusing on day-to-day realities with the occasional high point. You need real commitment to sustain these efforts and you have to be realistic from the start about the time commitment you can make over the life of the project.

Catheryn & Paul Goodyer

~ **Internal Revenue Service** (www.irs.gov/charities) The IRS has all the details of tax exemptions for US non-profits online.

~ **National Council of Nonprofit Associations** (www.councilofnonprofits.org) This group offers a wide range of assistance to up-and-coming organisations.

~ **Starting a Nonprofit Organization** (http://managementhelp.org/startingorganizations/start-non profit.htm) Browse Carter McNamara's excellent online guide to starting a charity in the US for many useful resources.

Australasian Organisations

~ **Australian Agency for International Development (AusAID;** www.ausaid.gov.au) The latest information about Australia's international development inputs and an 'NGO Package of Information'.

~ **Australian Council for International Development (ACFID;** www.acfid.asn.au) Some practical information under 'Facts and Figures' on how to start your own NGO, including accreditation procedures and the ACFID Code of Conduct.

~ **Australian Taxation Office (ATO;** www.ato.gov.au/nonprofit) The tax office's non-profit area is the place to learn more about charity tax concessions in Australia. You'll also find a guide for volunteers and not-for-profit organisations called *Volunteers and Tax*, which looks at the treatment of certain payments and whether they are taxed or not.

~ **Friends of the Earth Australia** (☎ +61 (0)3 9419 8700; www.foe.org.au; 312 Smith St, Collingwood, Victoria 3066, (Box 222, Fitzroy, Victoria 3065) Australia) A useful resource, FoE supports various environmental and social campaigns. There is also an FoE New Zealand (☎ +64 9 360 9149; foenz@kcbbs.gen.nz; PO Box 5599, Wellesley St, Auckland, New Zealand).

~ **Inland Revenue New Zealand** (http://www.ird.govt.nz/notforprofits) Tax information for New Zealanders.

~ **Pathways Australia** (www.pathwaysaustralia.com.au) This group offers information, management and marketing services to not-for-profit organisations.

~ **Philanthropy Australia** (www.philanthropy.org.au) The information hub for all things giving-related Down Under including the annual *Giving Australia* report.

Status

Should you go for registered charity status, limited company status, or not-for-profit status? How about registering as a Non-Government Organisation (NGO)? Deciding which form your organisation is going to take can be difficult. To legally register, and refer to yourself, as any particular breed of organisation you'll need to closely consider the requirements of each. There can be benefits to some; for instance, registering as a charity can give you favourable tax treatment and allow you to apply for funds not available to non-charities. Depending on tax laws in your country and/or state, having charitable status can also mean that donors can deduct their donations from their tax liabilities, and this can make a massive difference to the amount of money people are willing to give.

It's a good idea to seek professional advice on which status to apply for. Often, the best route is not the most obvious one. Catheryn Goodyer who established the Karmi Farm Clinic (see the case study A Healthy Dose on p254) explains her company's reasoning for not registering as a charity:

We have not applied for charitable status. We enquired right at the beginning with the Charities Commission. Reading between the lines, we discovered that if your application is turned down, you, as an individual, are not allowed to apply again. The Charity Office also recommended that we run the clinic for at least a couple of years so that we had

East Timorese kids pose for the camera of an Australian Aid International volunteer

Photo: Paul Plaia

accounts to show. In addition, they recommended that we take on a charity lawyer to reduce the risk of having our application turned down, which is quite an expensive thing to
do. The only reasons we could see for registering were for fundraising and tax purposes.
As we have had no problems raising funds unregistered and most of our purchasing is
carried out in India (where costs are very low and no VAT applies) and the clinic only
needs a small amount of funding, we decided it wasn't worth spending the money on a
lawyer at this point.

Catheryn isn't alone in putting off applying for charitable status. In fact, for the reasons
she's described, it's often worth waiting until you're established. In the interim, many
organisations choose to set up as a limited company. Alex Tarrant describes why they've
chosen this status for PoD:

When we first set up we looked at the various options and decided that becoming a private limited company would give us the most flexibility, allow us to get up and running
immediately, and suited our business model the best. At the time we were working with
a single overseas project which was already registered as a charity in the UK, so we didn't
see the need to duplicate.

However, one reason for wanting to register as a charity is for the credibility that comes
with it. For instance, a sending agency may be concerned that potential volunteers would
prefer to sign up with a charity, as they're less likely to fear that profit motives might come
before the desire to help overseas. If charitable status isn't quite on your horizon yet, an
alternative is to become a company limited by guarantee, also known as a not-for-profit
organisation. This means that the organisation's earnings must be directed towards defined, non-profit aims.

For some guided assistance in making your way through the status minefield, check out
some of the organisations under Getting Help on p252. If necessary, consider enlisting
the help of a lawyer familiar with non-profit law to assist with incorporation and tax
matters.

Rewards

You may well ask yourself, 'What makes it all worthwhile?' The answer lies in that 'feel-good' factor. Alex Tarrant describes his most rewarding experiences in running a volunteering organisation:

It's definitely two things: dealing with people who have chosen to volunteer their time; and working with small overseas projects and charities. Seeing the contribution that volunteers make, and the enjoyment and personal development they gain in the process, is fantastic. It's also wonderful to see how we have helped small projects and charities to grow and become stronger and, as a result, have enabled them to provide greater help to the communities they work in.

In the Maasai village of Longido in northern Tanzania, volunteers are helping teach in the local primary school and in an adult-education centre through MondoChallenge

ACKNOWLEDGEMENTS

This book was commissioned and managed in Lonely Planet's Melbourne office by Bridget Blair and Will Gourlay. It was edited by Alison Ridgway, Elisa Arduca, Francesca Coles, Elizabeth Jones, Lorna Parkes and Luna Soo. The book was designed by Travis Drever and laid out by Jacqui Saunders, Mik Ruff, Nicholas Colicchia and Frank Deim. The cover was designed by Mark Adams.

Thanks From the Authors

From Charlotte

I would like to thank my commissioning editor, Bridget Blair, for being so collaborative about the nature of this book and for being so lovely to work with. I'd also like to thank: all the returned volunteers whose words I have poured over endlessly (I even feel I know the ones I haven't met); our Special Advisors who gave up their time to meet me, help with the brief and who I'd call day or night with some thorny volunteering question that needed answering straight away; Jez Sweetland who offered invaluable advice about the charitable sector; David Orkin who checked the travel information in Chapter Three; John Masterson of Trailfinders who checked the visa section; and my husband, Simon, who took the girls to school as frequently as he could so I could get on and write.

From Nate

I'd like to dedicate my work to my love Florence Chien, and thank her for bottomless reserves of patience, a ruthless eye for unnecessary verbiage, and the ability to bring me back to normal after a long day of being cooped up in my office. I'd also have been completely awash without the help of co-authors Korina Miller and Charlotte Hindle and commissioning editor Bridget Blair. For the advice I'd like to thank John Ruiz, Matt Cavalieri and Matt Meuller. For the support, I'd like to thank Rob Harvilla, Garrett Kamps, Tommy Craggs, Matt Palmquist, Joe Hayes, Vanessa Kong, Cory Mescon, Ben Baumer and last but hardly least, Danny Palmerlee, who inspired me to work for Lonely Planet with his excellent Baja guide and kind advice.

From Rachel

My big thank you goes to all the independent volunteers who have shared their stories with me and to the grassroots charities and online directories for answering my questions. I am delighted that the book has received such a positive response. I am also very grateful to Charlotte Hindle for her support and advice.

From Korina

A big thank-you to Bridget Blair for including me in this challenging but very rewarding project. Also thanks to my co-authors and the publishing and production crews at LP. Special thanks to the countless organisations and volunteers who gave me their time, shared their insight and answered my unending questions; extra thanks to Anna Demant, Katherine Tubb, Alex Tarrant, Penelope Worsley, Catheryn Goodyer, Lennox McNeely, Kalene Caffarella, Anthony Lunch, the Teach Ghana Trust, Seattle University's Calcutta Club (particularly Lucas McIntyre), Matt & Polly Freer, Peggy Fussell, Katie Yewdall, Eileen Bennicke and Clare Wearden.

From Mike

Thanks go to my long-time friends for their encouragement, my Peace Corps colleagues for their inspiring example, and my parents and family for their constant support. You know who you are.

From Sarah

A heartfelt thank you to commissioning editor and fellow yogi, Bridget Blair, and coordinating author, Charlotte Hindle, for being such a pleasure to work with. I am also grateful to the following people who aided my research: Andrew Criss (AYAD); Andrew Jack (i-to-i Australia); Belinda Williams (ASF); Brad Atwal (World Expeditions); Cam Walker (Friends of the Earth); Christine Crosby (AVI); Colin Salisbury (Global Volunteer Network); Danny McDowell (Interserve Australia); Erin Cassidy (Global Volunteer Network); Erin Green (VIDA); Irene Bukhshtaber (Volunteering Australia); James Nichols (MSF); John Webber (Live Animal Imports – AQIS); Marita Lofts (Travel Doctor Clinic); Rhodri Wynn-Pope (RedR); Shona Jennings (VSA); Steve Bradbury (TEAR Australia); Tim Burns (Volunteering NZ); Tim Prohasky (Engineers Without Borders); Terry Hoey (World Youth International) and Veronica Culjak (ATO). Peter Hodge's *Volunteer Work Overseas for Australians and New Zealanders* (Global Exchange; 2004) was a helpful resource. Thanks to fellow RAYADs, Amanda Allen-Toland, Jacqui Pringle and Amber Rowe for sharing their thoughts, and a salute to the Intake 14 volunteers – a cool crew. Cheers to my extraordinary friends (what *sànùk* we did have) in Bangkok. And special thanks to Mum and Dad for letting me work from the holiday house (an oxymoron indeed) and making my transition from volunteering overseas that little bit smoother. As the late Audrey Hepburn wrote, we have two hands: one is for helping ourselves and the other is for helping others. Volunteers around the world are living proof of this.

Thanks From Lonely Planet

Special thanks to the following volunteers and organisation staff members who gave their time and enthusiasm to contributing to this book.

Amanda Allen-Tolland, Ryan Andersen, Sally Armbrecht, Pat Barker, Catherine Baroun, Sharon Baxter, Peter Bennett, Eileen Bennicke, Michael Best, Benjamin Blakey, Richard Boden, Liz Bodner, Jackie Bowles, Kalene Caffarella, Emma Campbell, Eoin Canny, Brenda Carter, Catherine Chimes, Vikki Cole, Tabitha Cook, Hannah Crewe, David Daniels, Kerry Davies, Sian Davies, Sue Davies, Robin Dawson, Ben Donaldson, Robert Driver, Louise Ellerton, Samantha Elson, Ian Flood, Karen Foerstel, Elizabeth France, Matt Freer, Polly Freer, Claire Fulton, Laurence Gale, Karla Gergen, Robin Glegg, Catheryn Goodyer, John Gordon, Gerrard Graf, Heather Graham, David Grassham, Edwin Griffiths, Amanda Guest-Collins, Rachel Guise, Michelle Hawkins, Karen Hedges, Jacqueline Hill, Katie Hill, Joan Hodkinson, Samantha Holland, Alice Hughes, Dale Hurd, Victoria Jaberi, Jordan Jones, Julie Jones, Deborah Jordan, Ben Keedwell, Kirsi Korhonen, Mike Laird, Richard Lawson, Claire Loseby, Ben Martin, Elaine Massie, Steve McElhinney, Kerri McGuinness, Lucas McIntyre, Lennox McNeely, Peggy Melmoth, Oliver Middlemiss, Michele Moody, Jo Morgan, Clodagh Mullen, Gemma Niebieszczanski, Ann Noon, Clodagh O'Brien, Rachel Oxberry, Paul Piaia, Jacqui Pringle, Patrick Pringle, Ele Ramsey, Kristine Randall, Martyn Roberts, Simon Roberts, Jason Rogers, Amber Rowe, Colin Salisbury, Andrew Sansom, Poonam Sattee, Mary Sears, Ness Sellers, Jo Shuttleworth, Sandra Sinclair, Jenny Smith, Dave Spinney, Judith Stephen, Antonia Stokes, Kate Sturgeon, Phil Sydor, Matthew Sykes, Alex Tarrant, Alice Tedd, Heather Thompson, Sue Towler, Michael Tuckwell, Diane Turner, Sarah Turton, Jan-Willem van Bochove, Nick Van Buskirk, Mian Vich, Oliver Walker, Linda Walsh, Clare Wearden, Maggie Wild, Tom Wilmot, Nayna Wood, Penelope Worsley, Katie Yewdall

Thanks also to the readers of the first edition who wrote in to us with helpful suggestions: Natalie Kirkhope, Claire Neden, Chinarut Ruangchotvit, Anis Salvesen. Send us your feedback at lonelyplanet.com/contact.

NOTES

INDEX

INDEX

DESTINATIONS INDEX

DESTINATIONS INDEX

ORGANISATIONS INDEX

ORGANISATIONS INDEX

VOLUNTEER

A TRAVELLER'S GUIDE TO MAKING A
DIFFERENCE AROUND THE WORLD

August 2013

Published by
Lonely Planet Publications Pty Ltd
ABN 36 005 607 983

Lonely Planet Offices
Australia Locked Bag 1, Footscray, Victoria 3011
USA 150 Linden St, Oakland, CA 94607
UK Media Centre, 201 Wood Lane, London W12 7TQ

ISBN 978 1 74321 689 7

Printed in China
10 9 8 7 6 5 4 3 2 1